ARIADNE AUF NAXOS

UNIVERSITY OF NORTH CAROLINA
STUDIES IN THE GERMANIC LANGUAGES
AND LITERATURES

Initiated by RICHARD JENTE (1949-1952), *established by* F. E. COENEN (1952-1968)

Publication Committee

SIEGFRIED MEWS, EDITOR   JOHN G. KUNSTMANN   GEORGE S. LANE

HERBERT W. REICHERT   CHRISTOPH E. SCHWEITZER   SIDNEY R. SMITH

65. Wolfgang W. Moelleken. LIEBE UND EHE. LEHRGEDICHTE VON DEM STRICKER. 1970. Pp. xxxviii, 72. Cloth $6.50.
66. Alan P. Cottrell. WILHELM MÜLLER'S LYRICAL SONG-CYCLES. Interpretation and Texts. 1970. Pp. x, 172. Cloth $7.00.
67. Siegfried Mews, ed. STUDIES IN GERMAN LITERATURE OF THE NINE-TEENTH AND TWENTIETH CENTURIES. FESTSCHRIFT FOR FREDERIC E. COENEN. Foreword by Werner P. Friederich. 1970. 2nd ed. 1972. Pp. xx, 251. Cloth $9.75.
68. John Neubauer. BIFOCAL VISION. NOVALIS' PHILOSOPHY OF NATURE AND DISEASE. 1971. Pp. x, 196. Cloth $7.75.
69. Victor Anthony Rudowski. LESSING'S *AESTHETICA IN NUCE*. An Analysis of the May 26, 1769, Letter to Nicolai. 1971. Pp. xii, 146. Cloth $6.70.
70. Donald F. Nelson. PORTRAIT OF THE ARTIST AS HERMES. A Study of Myth and Psychology in Thomas Mann's *Felix Krull*. 1971. Pp. xvi, 150. $6.75.
71. Murray A. and Marian L. Cowie, eds. THE WORKS OF PETER SCHOTT (1460-1490). Vol. II: Commentary. 1971. Pp. xxix, 534. Cloth $14.50; Paper $13.00.
72. Christine Oertel Sjögren. THE MARBLE STATUE AS IDEA. COLLECTED ESSAYS ON ADALBERT STIFTER'S *DER NACHSOMMER*. 1972. Pp. xiv, 121. Cloth $7.00.
73. Donald G. Daviau and Jorun B. Johns, eds. THE CORRESPONDENCE OF ARTHUR SCHNITZLER AND RAOUL AUERNHEIMER WITH RAOUL AUERNHEIMER'S APHORISMS. 1972. Pp. xii, 161. Cloth $7.50.
74. A. Margaret Arent Madelung. THE LAXDOELA SAGA: ITS STRUCTURAL PATTERNS. 1972. Pp. xiv, 261. Cloth $9.25.
75. Jeffrey L. Sammons. SIX ESSAYS ON THE YOUNG GERMAN NOVEL. 1972. Pp. xiv, 187. Cloth $7.75.
76. Donald H. Crosby and George C. Schoolfield, eds. STUDIES IN THE GERMAN DRAMA. A *FESTSCHRIFT* IN HONOR OF WALTER SILZ. 1974. Pp. xxvi, 255. Cloth $10.75.
77. J. W. Thomas. TANNHÄUSER: POET AND LEGEND. With Texts and Translations of His Works. 1974. Pp. x, 202. Cloth $10.75.
78. Olga Marx and Ernst Morwitz, trans. THE WORKS OF STEFAN GEORGE. 1974. 2nd, rev. and enl. ed. Pp. xxviii, 431. Cloth $12.90.
79. Siegfried Mews and Herbert Knust, eds. ESSAYS ON BRECHT: THEATER AND POLITICS. 1974. Pp. xiv, 241. Cloth $11.95.
80. Donald G. Daviau and George J. Buelow. THE *ARIADNE AUF NAXOS* OF HUGO VON HOFMANNSTHAL AND RICHARD STRAUSS. 1975. Pp. x, 272. Cloth $12.95.

For other volumes in the "Studies" see pages 270 ff.

Send orders to: (U.S. and Canada)

The University of North Carolina Press, P.O. Box 2288
Chapel Hill, N.C. 27514

(All other countries) Feffer and Simons, Inc., 31 Union Square, New York, N.Y. 10003

NUMBER EIGHTY

UNIVERSITY OF NORTH CAROLINA STUDIES IN THE GERMANIC LANGUAGES AND LITERATURES

The *ARIADNE AUF NAXOS* of

Hugo von Hofmannsthal and Richard Strauss

by

Donald G. Daviau

and

George J. Buelow

Chapel Hill
The University of North Carolina Press
1975

© University of North Carolina

Studies in the Germanic Languages

and Literatures 1975

Library of Congress Cataloging in Publication Data

Daviau, Donald G.
  The Ariadne auf Naxos of Hugo von Hofmannsthal and Richard Strauss.

  (University of North Carolina studies in the Germanic languages and literatures, no. 80)
  Bibliography: pp. 254-269.
  1. Strauss, Richard, 1864-1949. Ariadne auf Naxos.
  2. Hofmannsthal, Hugo Hofmann, Edler von, 1874-1929.
Ariadne auf Naxos. I. Buelow, George J., joint author.
II. Title. III. Series: North Carolina. University. Studies in the Germanic languages and literatures, no. 80.
ML410.S93D35   782.1'092'4 [B]   74-14835
ISBN O-8078-8080-9

Preface

The impetus for this book came from an interdisciplinary seminar taught by the authors at the University of California, Riverside, in 1967. The purpose of that seminar was to introduce students from the fields of German literature and music to the complexities and artistic merits of the opera collaborations of Richard Strauss and Hugo von Hofmannsthal. Although the seminar permitted us to examine in some detail all six operas that were produced, it soon became evident that a book covering all six operas would be beyond the scope of any single publication. Since one of the striking conclusions of the seminar was the importance, indeed, the uniqueness of *Ariadne auf Naxos* in the history of the collaboration, it was this opera that became the focal point of interest. Much of the information relating to *Ariadne* is equally applicable to their other joint works, and an understanding of *Ariadne* will contribute to greater appreciation of all of the Strauss-Hofmannsthal operas.

Originally, we hoped to make our book a comprehensive examination of every facet of the *Ariadne* collaboration, but this plan was revised when the result became an unwieldy manuscript of excessive length. It was necessary, therefore, to eliminate two chapters examining Hofmannsthal's final adaptation of *Der Bürger als Edelmann* as a drama and also Strauss's arrangement into a suite for orchestra of the music used in that final dramatic version. Two additional chapters that were intended to show the place of *Ariadne* in the framework of both artists' overall creative output were also omitted.

In its final form the book attempts to present in detail the extraordinary development of the *Ariadne* idea from its conception to the final operatic version. Uppermost in our minds was the intention to represent fully the viewpoint of both the composer and librettist, so as to enable the reader to comprehend the enormous personal and artistic complications which were overcome to produce this opera. Accordingly, the workshop correspondence is quoted extensively; for here the reader who might otherwise be unfamiliar with these fascinatingly informative letters has the opportunity to sense the give-and-take struggle that animated this collaboration.

In one sense it has been difficult to write a study that will appeal to the musicologist, the literary specialist, and also to the general reader. In some instances one group of readers may possibly feel the material to be superfluous. However, such background information as is found in the early chapters, for example, we felt was necessary for the general reader. Also, clearly, the literary specialist may not know any more about Richard Strauss than the musicologist may know about Hugo von Hofmannsthal. The book is intended to be self-contained, and for this reason, too, reviews of the premiere performance have been quoted in detail, simply because they are not readily available, and because they contribute importantly to an understanding of the initially hostile critical reception which led to the subsequent decision to revise the work.

Throughout the main part of the text we have employed English for the convenience of readers who might not know German. Since the documentation in the footnotes will be of interest primarily to the specialist, we have cited this material in the original language. However, in the four chapters discussing the literary and musical interpretations of the opera, both the original German and an English translation are included on the page to facilitate reading, for locating the passages in the score, and for making the meaning of the text immediately unambiguous. Unless otherwise indicated, all translations are the authors'; in the case of the text from *Ariadne,* it should especially be noted that the English is meant to be fairly literal, not poetic.

Although there are a number of studies and books on *Elektra, Der Rosenkavalier, Die Frau ohne Schatten, Arabella,* and *Die Ägyptische Helena,* this is the first major study in any language of *Ariadne auf Naxos,* and the first full-length work in English on any of the Strauss-Hofmannsthal operas. It is also, as far as the authors are aware, the first attempt to discuss an opera jointly by both a literary and a music critic. Finally, this is one of the few books to appear to date in English on Hofmannsthal, and we hope it will serve to increase the awareness of English-speaking readers to one of the world's great writers.

The authors wish to express their gratitude to the University of California at Riverside and to Rutgers, the State University of New Jersey and its Research Council for supporting the preparation of this study generously from its inception to its publication. Many colleagues and students have contributed freely of their time in reading the manuscript and making invaluable suggestions, and to them we extend our sincere thanks. A special debt of gratitude is owed to Dr. Ada Schmidt, whose sensitive reading and helpful ideas benefited the manuscript greatly, and to Dr. Jorun Johns, who, in addition to numerous textual suggestions, carefully proofread the manuscript. Finally, the authors wish to thank Collins Publishers for permission to quote extensively from *The Correspondence between Richard Strauss and Hugo von Hofmannsthal,* edited by Franz and Alice Strauss and translated by Hanns Hammelmann and Ewald Osers (London, 1961), and the publishers of *Ariadne auf Naxos* by Richard Strauss: Copyright 1912, 1913, 1916, 1922, 1924 by Adolph Fürstner and Fürstner, Ltd. Copyright Renewed 1940, 1941, 1944, 1949, 1951. Copyright and Renewal assigned to Boosey and Hawks, Ltd. Reprinted by permission.

Riverside, California

New Brunswick, New Jersey

Donald G. Daviau

George J. Buelow

Contents

Every living thing and every landscape reveals itself once and completely: but only to a deeply moved heart. (Hofmannsthal, *Prosa* III, 26).

Thus, I believe I will always be able to give you something, only what I can give you will, of course, always depend upon what you contain within yourself. (Hofmannsthal to Franckenstein, *Briefe* II, 38).

Introduction

Ariadne auf Naxos, with libretto by Hugo von Hofmannsthal and music by Richard Strauss, the third in a series of six operatic collaborations of two of the greatest creative personalities of central Europe at the turn of the twentieth century, has never been adequately interpreted as an opera; that is, as a complex theatrical unity combining effectively words, music, dance, gesture, mime, staging, and lighting. Nor has the pivotal position of this work within the overall production of the two men ever been fully investigated.

The failure of previous studies to do justice to *Ariadne auf Naxos*—and incidentally, to the other operas of Hofmannsthal and Strauss as well—results from their unilateral scholarly approach. Musicologists concentrate almost exclusively upon musical problems, while literary critics, who generally lack musical training, have of necessity omitted any consideration of the music from their judgment of the libretto. Hence, the purely musical analyses fail to appreciate the subtleties and complexities that give Hofmannsthal's text its exceptional poetic depth and significance. The exclusively literary interpretations violate the basic premise of the operatic form by disregarding the important fact that *Ariadne auf Naxos* is not a self-contained drama but a libretto.

To approach *Ariadne* other than as a totality of musical and poetic forces is to destroy the very unity that Hofmannsthal and Strauss struggled so arduously to achieve and to misunderstand the ambition to create a new genre which originally brought the two artists together. Hofmannsthal felt after 1900 that he had reached the limits of his expressive powers with words alone. He turned to the writing of librettos against the well-meant advice of his friends, specifically in order to expand his means of artistic expression through the addition of music.

Just as Hofmannsthal had wearied of writing lyric dramas and was experimenting with new artistic forms, Strauss had tired of writing symphonic poems. When he approached Hofmannsthal concerning *Elektra* in 1906, he had already written three operas, including the internationally successful *Salome*. He recognized that opera was his destiny. He also knew that his future career would succeed only if he could obtain opera librettos of high poetic quality that he required to stimulate his musical genius.

1

The goal of their collaboration is perhaps best expressed by Hofmannsthal in his "Unwritten Postscript to Rosenkavalier": "A work is a unified whole, and the work of two men can also be a unified whole. Much is common to contemporaries, also of one's own. Threads run back and forth, related elements run together. Whoever separates, will do wrong. Whoever picks out one thing, forgets that, unnoticed, the unity always suffers. The music ought not to be torn from the text nor the word from the animated scene. This work is made for the stage, not for the book or for the individual at his piano" (*Prosa* III, 43).

Although these words were written as a postscript to their second opera, *Der Rosenkavalier,* they are more relevant to their next work, *Ariadne,* which was the first opera that the two men wrote together from the beginning. Therefore, to ignore any of the concomitant artistic aspects of *Ariadne auf Naxos* is to overlook the carefully unified form of the opera expressly intended by its creators.

Accordingly, the present authors have proceeded from four basic assumptions: (1) that *Ariadne* can only be understood as a totality; (2) that the collaboration of two artists such as Hofmannsthal and Strauss, each preeminent in his own discipline, is unique in operatic history; (3) that *Ariadne* commands a significant position not only among the six operas of Strauss and Hofmannsthal but in the framework of their overall production; (4) that this work is epochal in the history of early twentieth-century German opera.

The reasons underlying the first assumption have been suggested already. Concerning the second assumption, the history of opera, while recording a number of productive collaborations between famous men, reveals few instances in which both author and musician were equally gifted masters of their respective arts. Among the most famous were Mozart and Da Ponte, Verdi and Boito, Puccini and Giacosa and Illica, Gilbert and Sullivan, and more recently, Stravinsky and Auden, and Brecht and Weill. Except for Gilbert and Sullivan, none of these partnerships endured over as long a period, none achieved the consistently high quality of text and music, and none experimented as vigorously as did Hofmannsthal and Strauss in their endeavor to expand and enrich the form of opera.

By collaborating with the composer through every phase of his work, Hofmannsthal struggled to transcend the limitations of the older concept of opera as simply drama with music. Instead, he envisioned a tantalizing goal: a totally unified creation of all of the contributing art forms, harmoniously and inseparably blended into a superior vehicle of expression. Reaching back through the Austro-Bavarian baroque tradition to the Greek roots of drama as festival, he sought to create an artistic form that would permit a greater depth of insight into the unseen forces and unity of the world than any art form could achieve independently. He aspired to nothing less than to develop opera into a leading art form if not actually into the predominant genre of the twentieth century.

2

Hofmannsthal's idealism was matched only by his audacity, considering the lack on his part of any technical knowledge of music. In fact, in the beginning, he lacked even a realistic understanding of the artistic problems that would confront him in writing librettos. Although he may have failed ultimately in his quest for a new genre, this does not diminish the value of his experiment. Works like *Ariadne auf Naxos* and *Die Frau ohne Schatten,* the two operas coming closest to Hofmannsthal's ideal, stand on their own merits. Moreover, the possible influence of this experimentation on such later collaborations as Brecht and Weill and more recently Dürrenmatt and Burckhardt remains to be investigated.

The uniqueness of the collaboration is further underscored by the published record of their workshop correspondence, making available the rarest form of insight into their ideas, creative working methods, goals, disagreements, satisfactions, and disappointments. Since Strauss lived and worked primarily in his Alpine retreat in the Bavarian resort of Garmisch-Partenkirchen, while Hofmannsthal remained relatively secluded in his modest rococo villa at Rodaun in the suburbs of Vienna, they met only infrequently and communicated largely by letters. These documents present the genesis and evolution of their combined work with a richness of detail previously unknown in the history of music.

The third basic assumption of this book is that among the six operas produced by Strauss and Hofmannsthal—*Elektra, Der Rosenkavalier, Ariadne auf Naxos, Die Frau ohne Schatten, Die Ägyptische Helena* and *Arabella*—*Ariadne* most nearly realizes Hofmannsthal's ambition for a genuine synthesis of various art forms. *Ariadne auf Naxos* was the first of their combined works conceived from the beginning as a libretto and worked out jointly in every aspect from start to finish. Hofmannsthal had written *Elektra* as an independent drama before he had joined forces with Strauss, and it was performed as a play before Strauss set it to music.

Although the libretto to *Der Rosenkavalier* benefited from many suggestions by Strauss, particularly with regard to the character of Baron Ochs von Lerchenau, it was still written mainly as an independent play. The descriptive designation applied to the work by Hofmannsthal—*Komödie für Musik*—shows the relationship of the text to the music. Like *Elektra, Der Rosenkavalier,* too, has been staged as a spoken drama, a fact which demonstrates the independent nature of the libretto. As the letters reveal, Hofmannsthal had still not fully mastered the technique of writing a text for music. Despite its immediate success and popularity, Hofmannsthal acknowledged to Strauss that *Der Rosenkavalier* did not satisfy him in every respect; that is, he had failed to achieve the homogeneous blend of forms he had envisioned. By contrast, *Ariadne auf Naxos,* imagined and executed throughout in terms of the perfect fusion of text and music, became Hofmannsthal's favorite creation and the one that he never ceased to defend and cherish.

From the standpoint of technique, *Ariadne auf Naxos* presented the greatest challenge to its creators (and to the critics and public), for it was a bold attempt to give somewhat faded and outmoded traditional forms a new life and meaning. In a then daring blend of baroque and classical styles and structure, the opera is thoroughly modern. Judged by present-day standards of art, in which unity of style and form have been virtually obliterated through various formal experiments with the grotesque and bizarre, *Ariadne auf Naxos* seems conservative. Yet, at its premiere in 1912, the seemingly abnormal combination of forms and styles aroused the antagonism of critics, who attacked this fragile experimental work as an eccentric, aberrational example of avant-garde art.

This brings us to our final basic assumption: the significant position of this opera in the modern period. The distinctly neo-classical elements of Strauss's opera, the employment of a minimum number of instrumentalists that spelled the abandonment of the huge symphonic forces of late nineteenth-century German music, and the return to baroque and classical models of vocal style, all combine to make *Ariadne auf Naxos* the first neo-classical opera of the twentieth century. Completed in 1912, the opera antedates all of the major neo-classical works of Hindemith and Stravinsky, even though the latter are usually cited as having first employed the neo-classical in music. It would not be an exaggeration to trace the influence of Strauss's innovations in *Ariadne* as far as 1951 when Stravinsky completed his neo-classical opera, *The Rake's Progress.*

The departure from traditional operatic form produced most of the early misunderstandings that have clung to *Ariadne* through the years and has been one of the major drawbacks to its general acceptance. No other independent or combined work of Hofmannsthal and Strauss, including the much more obscure symbolic work, *Die Frau ohne Schatten*, which is a direct outgrowth of *Ariadne*, has been enmeshed in such confusing controversy. No other work was plagued with so many difficulties in its creation, performance, and critical reception.

Although *Ariadne* was originally meant to be a mere interlude between important works, Hofmannsthal, as he became increasingly aware of the significance of the theme to his overall development, turned aggressively protective toward his creation and adamantly stubborn in its defense. The more Strauss expressed indifference toward the work and proposed various compromises, the more emphatically Hofmannsthal insisted on its integrity and quality. Despite his early deferential attitude toward Strauss, partly because of his unsure beginnings as a librettist in *Elektra* and *Der Rosenkavalier,* Hofmannsthal asserted his intellectual superiority in the course of protecting *Ariadne* and became the dominant partner during this collaboration.

Ariadne auf Naxos was the sixth of fifteen operas that Strauss composed during the remarkably extended creative period between 1893, the year in which he completed *Guntram,* and 1941, when *Capriccio* was finished. *Ariadne* is the strategic work, containing the key to the future artistic development of Strauss. Just as *Ariadne* represents the creative midpoint for Strauss, the opera stands chronologically almost at the exact center of Hofmannsthal's career which extends from 1891 to 1929. Thematically as well as formally, *Ariadne auf Naxos* represents the culmination of his early development as an artist and contains the seeds of almost all of his later works.

The first version of *Ariadne auf Naxos*, which was intended as a chamber opera to climax Hofmannsthal's adaptation of Molière's famous comedy *Le Bourgeois gentilhomme,* met with only limited success, for reasons we shall detail. Despite Strauss's strong protests, Hofmannsthal finally won him over to revising the whole work. The new version of 1916 eliminated Molière's play and substituted a new *Vorspiel* to be sung preceding the actual opera. Since only this revised version is performed today, our analyses of both text and music will concentrate on the final rather than the original version.

The textual analysis aims to show the significance of the libretto in terms of Hofmannsthal's overall production as well as in terms of its own importance. The same general plan has been followed in the interpretation of Strauss's music. Finally, our aim has been to interpret this work as an opera; that is, as a synthesis of major art forms, in an attempt to determine how far Hofmannsthal and Strauss actually succeeded in creating a new art form.

Chapter I

Hofmannsthal and Strauss

The miracle of the collaboration between Hugo von Hofmannsthal and Richard Strauss is not that these two artists should have produced six works of such consistently high quality, but that they could work together at all. Two individuals of differing nature and temperament, both as men and artists, could scarcely be imagined. Paradoxically, their dissimilarity proved to be the great strength of their relationship, for each man complemented the personality and professional genius of the other.

Strauss was one of the most gifted orchestral conductors of all time and had years of experience conducting in most of the European opera houses. He had grown up musically in the opera house, acquiring a practical understanding of the total range of opera production and a sensitivity to the elements of dramatic action that were essential to effective musical theater.

Hofmannsthal, who readily admitted that Strauss possessed the stronger dramatic instinct, had only limited experience with the practical side of the theater. While he knew a number of directors and actors and was interested in the problems of staging, he never attempted to direct or produce a play independently. His major efforts in this area were an unsuccessful attempt in 1904 to collaborate with Gordon Craig in designing the stage setting for a production of Hofmannsthal's drama, *Das gerettete Venedig,* and his assisting of Max Reinhardt in creating a production of another of his dramas, *Der Tor und der Tod,* in Berlin in 1908.[1] As a dramatist, Hofmannsthal only rarely overcame the lyrical orientation of his early works to produce a theatrically compelling work such as *Elektra.* Although Hofmannsthal was by no means the decadent aesthete critics often considered (and still consider) him to be, it is true that throughout his career he remained essentially a symbolic writer of extremely refined taste and high artistic standards. Rather than compromise his artistic integrity to achieve popular success, he was willing,

[1] Hofmannsthal regarded this episode in his life as an important phase in his development as a dramatist. To his father he wrote in May 1908: "Es scheint mir sehr möglich, daß man einmal von diesem oder von dem vorigen Sommer die Zeit meiner eigentlichen Theaterschriftstellerei wird datieren können." Hugo von Hofmannsthal, *Briefe* II (Vienna, 1937), 324. Unless otherwise indicated, all works cited are by Hofmannsthal.

if necessary, to leave his works to the judgment of posterity. Strauss, conversely, was much more interested in texts that were theatrically effective, since he knew this ingredient was essential to his success as an opera composer.

The impact of each personality on the other occurred at a critical juncture in the life of both artists. Hofmannsthal, after a brilliant decade as a lyric poet and lyric dramatist was searching for a new artistic direction to follow. His experiments over several years in a wide variety of artistic forms, including classical tragedy, ballet, pantomime, and dance, attracted him increasingly to the rich possibilities of expression inherent in music. Strauss, who had grown bored with his own extensive exploration of symphonic forms in general and the tone poem in particular, needed a librettist who could provide him with appropriate texts to inspire his essentially word-oriented musical genius. Throughout the composer's career, he wrote his best music when led to tone through verbal concepts, whether they were words by Lenau to *Don Juan,* the humor and pathos of Cervantes's *Don Quixote,* or the sensuousness and depravity of Wilde's *Salome.* Strauss tried his own hand at writing a libretto for his first opera, *Guntram,* but quickly realized that he lacked literary talent.

Hofmannsthal originally approached Strauss in 1900 with a ballet scenario he had just completed, entitled *Der Triumph der Zeit.* The composer graciously declined the opportunity to set it to music on the grounds that he was currently working on a ballet of his own composition (which he never finished) and doubted he would wish to undertake a second ballet at that time. Contact between the two men was not renewed until 1906 when Strauss, who had just completed the opera *Salome,* took the initiative and asked Hofmannsthal for permission to use his drama *Elektra* as the basis for an opera. From this beginning the collaboration between these two men, who felt they had "been brought together by something higher, perhaps, than mere accident,"[2] continued in an unbroken line until Hofmannsthal's sudden and untimely death in 1929. The final item of correspondence in the published volume of their letters is a telegram from Strauss to Hofmannsthal dated 14 July 1929, conveying Strauss's thanks for the completed text to the first act of *Arabella.* Hofmannsthal died before the message reached him.

To have been approached by Strauss about one of his works must have impressed Hofmannsthal as an event of considerable magnitude. The years from 1899 to 1906, while productive in terms of quantity of ideas, drafts, and sketches, had been relatively lean in the number of completed and published works. Many of the projects attempted during

[2] *The Correspondence between Richard Strauss and Hugo von Hofmannsthal,* ed. Franz and Alice Strauss, trans. Hanns Hammelmann and Ewald Osers, arranged by Willi Schuh (London, 1961), p. 106. Hereafter cited in the text as *C.* followed by page number.

8

this period remained fragments.[3] Hofmannsthal himself later attributed the difficulties of this critical phase in his literary career, when his talent for lyric poetry had atrophied,[4] and when he had wearied of writing lyric dramas,[5] to the process of maturing.[6]

As a writer Hofmannsthal had reached the point where he wished to concern himself more actively with life in its broader social forms rather than remaining an introspective onlooker. He now realized that to comment on life in beautiful, melancholic lyric verse was neither a sufficient compensation nor an adequate substitute for living which, in his view, demanded social participation of the individual through commitment to others.[7] The contemplative, introverted existence, he discovered, was debilitating, and even a life devoted to beauty could be stifling. As he wrote in 1896 to his good friend Leopold von Andrian, another writer who was experiencing the same problem: "The beautiful

[3] A good case in point is Hofmannsthal's attempt in 1901 to adapt Robert Browning's epic, *The Ring and the Book,* into a Renaissance tragedy, entitled *Die Gräfin Pompilia.* Although he worked on this project for over two years (1901-1903), the manuscript was never completed and has never been published. For a detailed discussion, see Hanna B. Lewis, "Hofmannsthal and Browning," *Comparative Literature,* 19 (1967), 142-59.

[4] In a letter to the German poet Richard Dehmel on 1 December 1901, Hofmannsthal stated: "Sonderbar ist es mir selber, daß in vielen Monaten, und Monaten von glücklicher Konzentration, nicht mehr ein einziges Gedicht entstehen will. Das tut mir innerlich recht leid." *Briefe* II, 61. Only a few poems were written after 1900, and these are generally not ranked with Hofmannsthal's best efforts.

[5] In a letter written in early 1899 to Hermann Bahr, Hofmannsthal commented: ". . . jetzt wird's immer ernsthafter, ich bin schon gar nicht mehr so jung, ich verlange mir die Bühne doch viel stärker als früher, . . ." *Briefe* I, 276-77. For additional comments by Hofmannsthal in the same vein see his letter to Otto Brahm in *Briefe* I, 324, and his letter to Schnitzler in *Briefe* II, 53.

[6] A most revealing letter to his close friend R. A. Schröder, dated 14 February 1902 shows Hofmannsthal's understanding of his problem and his optimism for the future: "Es war mein 28ter Geburtstag, und ich glaube die beängstigende nun seit fast zwei Jahren—mit gewissen trügerischen Unterbrechungen—anhaltende Erstarrung meiner produktiven Kräfte auch so auffassen zu sollen: als den mühsamen Übergang von der Produktion des Jünglingsalters zu der männlichen; als einen tiefen, nach außen nur durch Schmerz und Dumpfheit fühlbaren Prozeß der inneren Umwandlung." *Briefe* II, 67.

[7] Hofmannsthal confessed to his confidant Bodenhausen that the majority of his poems were written during the loneliest period of his life. "Meine Gedichte sind fast alle aus *einer* Zeit meines Lebens, aus der allereinsamsten: der zwischen meinem achtzehnten und einundzwanzigsten Jahr. Mitten aus dieser Einsamkeit heraus, die merkwürdig stark war und immer wie außen war, sind diese Gedichte entstanden—sie rufen ihre Liebe an das Dasein über diesen Gürtel von Einsamkeit hinüber—jetzt aber ist diese Zone von Einsamkeit nicht mehr da, es ist überall die Liebe verteilt, wenn auch noch in sehr unzulänglicher Weise, aber doch verteilt—und ich bin um vieles, unvergleichlich, glücklicher als damals. Aus dieser Verfassung heraus könnten vielleicht wieder Gedichte entstehen, ebenso reine und starke, aber ganz anders als die damaligen, und solche werden vielleicht auch noch entstehen, aber wahrscheinlich bin ich für diese noch nicht reif." Hugo von Hofmannsthal—Eberhard von Bodenhausen: *Briefe der Freundschaft,* ed. Dora Freifrau von Bodenhausen (Düsseldorf, 1953), p. 128. Actually, Hofmannsthal never regained his gift for lyric poetry per se, although all of his later works continue to be suffused with lyricism.

life impoverishes one. If one could always live as one desired, one would lose all his strength."[8] Hofmannsthal's acceptance of his own awareness that life demanded the involvement of deeds, not just words, led him to the theater and particularly to the comedy as his major form. Drama enabled him to show people engaged in social interaction and provided the means of presenting his life ethic in plastic, visual terms.

Thus, although he remained a writer, Hofmannsthal's works underwent a change of focus from the I to the Thou, a shift of emphasis that was as much for his own benefit and guidance as for that of the public. His view was most concisely stated in the autobiographical comments contained in *Ad me Ipsum:* "The way to the social as the way to the higher self: the non-mystical way: a) through the deed, b) through the [literary] work, c) through the child."[9] His personal way of attaining human contact in life or what he called "das Soziale" was through his comedies.[10] The change of artistic direction was also partly motivated by his desire to achieve genuine popular success instead of merely the *succès d'éstime* of his early lyrical writings. Hofmannsthal was eager to reach the people and not only a small circle of connoisseurs. In Austria, perhaps the most theater-going nation in the world, drama represented the most direct route to the general public, to recognition, and, not an unimportant consideration, to financial success. Despite his reputation, Hofmannsthal was never financially secure.

The transition was not easy. But the severity of the experience proved ultimately beneficial, for it made Hofmannsthal receptive to new forms and led him eventually into the promising fields of comedy and opera. His experiments during this period with pantomime[11] and ballet benefited his later dramas and operas which involve greater reliance on gesture, dance, and mimicry. Because these forms represent the basic ingredients of drama, such experimentation demonstrates Hofmannsthal's willingness to return to the beginnings of dramatic tradition in order to attain the technical proficiency necessary to create successful theater. Following these experiments, and to sharpen his understanding of dramatic form, Hofmannsthal began a series of adaptations of famous dramas, including Otway's *Venice Preserved* and Sophocles's *Elektra,* the tragedy that attracted Strauss's attention in 1906.

Richard Strauss was by this time internationally famous both as conductor and composer. More than any other composer writing in the final years of the nineteenth century, Strauss dominated the long and

---

[8] *Hugo von Hofmannsthal—Leopold von Andrian: Briefwechsel,* ed. Walter Perl (Frankfurt am Main, 1968), p. 64. All translations in the text were made by the authors unless otherwise indicated.

[9] *Aufzeichnungen* (Frankfurt am Main, 1959), p. 217.

[10] "*Das erreichte Soziale, die Komödien,*" ibid., p. 226.

[11] For a discussion of Hofmannsthal's work in pantomime as well as an analysis of one example, see Donald G. Daviau, "Hugo von Hofmannsthal's Pantomime: *Der Schüler,*" *Modern Austrian Literature,* 1/1 (1968), 4-30.

inevitable decline of Romantic music. With this domination he shared the tragic fate of German Romantic art in its ultimate destruction during the forties of our century. Strauss, who was born in Munich on 11 June 1864, came upon the world when the musical events of the nineteenth century had produced an outpouring of genius rare in the history of the art. Richard Wagner, Johannes Brahms, Anton Bruckner, Giuseppe Verdi, Gustav Mahler, Claude Debussy, were but a few of the many great musical personalities of the period.

Strauss was born into a family of outspokenly conservative musicians. His father, Franz Strauss, was first hornist in the Royal Bavarian Court Opera orchestra and, in addition, taught at the Royal Conservatory in Munich. He protected his son with a fierce passion from what he thought were the perverted scores of Wagner. In his opinion Mozart and Beethoven were the only true geniuses of music, and with strict musical discipline he permitted his son to discover few lesser gods than von Weber, Schubert, Mendelssohn, and Spohr. Only later, when he became more independent and followed his own judgment and inclination, did Strauss's musical world become saturated with Wagner's music.

Strauss's mother, Josephine Pschorr Strauss, daughter of the wealthy Munich brewery family, gave her son his first piano instruction. He also quickly learned violin and the rudiments of music theory. Although he never formally attended a conservatory of music, he had mastered harmony, counterpoint, the study of form, and instrumentation by the age of sixteen.

His early career as a composer was largely overshadowed by a singular determination to be a conductor, and he had the good fortune to become the protégé of Hans von Bülow, one of the most influential musicians of the later nineteenth century. Bülow, a superb concert pianist, teacher, and conductor, was a prime force in the early recognition of the music of Wagner and Brahms, and it was his interest in Strauss that led to the latter's employment as Bülow's assistant at the court orchestra of Meiningen in 1885-1886. This initial position, Strauss's first success as a professional musician, led to a lifetime of conducting activity that often dominated his career as a composer. After a series of engagements at the opera houses in Weimar and Munich, Strauss obtained the most coveted of all conducting posts, the directorship of the Berlin Philharmonic, which he retained from 1898 to 1910. During these years, Strauss not only conducted in Berlin but led an incredibly active life as guest conductor of nearly every major symphony orchestra and opera company in Europe, amassing a total number of engagements in excess of seven hundred performances.

Even before gaining the high honor of the Berlin position, Strauss, at the age of twenty-four, achieved international fame with the publication of his remarkably vital and original symphonic poem, *Don Juan*. In rapid succession, he found time between conducting engagements to compose a series of major symphonic works that gave him a meteoric career. As both conductor and composer Strauss piled one success upon another. Following *Don Juan* (1888), he wrote *Tod und Verklärung* (1889), *Till Eulenspiegels lustige Streiche* (1894-1895), *Also Sprach Zarathustra* (1895-1896), *Don Quixote, Phantastische Variationen über ein Thema ritterlichen Charakters* (1897), *Ein Heldenleben* (1898), and *Sinfonia domestica* (1903).

Interspersed between this series of massive orchestral works were Strauss's first two attempts in the field of opera, *Guntram* (written to his own libretto), completed in 1894, and *Feuersnot* (text by Ernst von Wolzogen), in 1901. Although both are works of powerful and splendid music, neither achieved any real success. Strauss had reached an impasse in his career, and he seemed destined to rest on the laurels of his orchestral works written before he was forty years old.

Then in 1902 he saw Hedwig Lachmann's translation of Oscar Wilde's *Salome* in the Berlin staging by Max Reinhardt. The impact of this performance led to his second career, as one of the most successful opera composers of the early twentieth century. The notoriety of his operatic setting for *Salome* spread quickly following its premiere in 1905. The score was exceedingly complex and dissonant for the time, and audiences were both shocked and overwhelmed by the musical portrayal of the psycho-sexuality of Princess Salome. Strauss himself related that the setting of Wilde's tale, the oriental background, "inspired me with truly exotic harmonies, which sparkled like taffeta particularly in the strange cadences. The wish to characterize the *dramatis personae* as clearly as possible led me to bitonality, since the purely rhythmic characterization Mozart uses so ingeniously did not appear to me sufficient to express the antithesis between Herod and the Nazarene."[12]

The combination of masterful orchestral virtuosity, a libretto of shock-value for the staid bourgeois audiences of a disintegrating Victorian society, and tonal magnificence, unheard before in quite such an exotic context, brought Strauss the ultimate measure of fame and, not least important to him, considerable wealth in royalties. Therefore, at this fateful moment when Strauss and Hofmannsthal were about to draw together in their artistic collaboration, Richard Strauss seemed again to have reached the zenith of his career. Yet, he was eager to continue writing operas, provided he could find a poet who could produce librettos of a quality and style to stimulate his creative imagination.

From his very first experience with *Elektra,* which he saw performed in Reinhardt's theater in Berlin, Strauss recognized the potential quality of Hofmannsthal as a librettist. This is evident from his letter of 11 March 1906: "In any case, I would ask you urgently to give me first refusal with anything composable that you write. Your manner has so much in common with mine; we were born for one another and are certain to do fine things together if you remain faithful to me" (*C.,* 3). Just

---

[12] Richard Strauss, *Recollections* (London, 1953), p. 150.

how prophetic this statement would turn out to be, Strauss himself could not even have dreamed at this time.

The correspondence dramatizes the opposite personalities of the two men. Hofmannsthal's letters are generally lengthy and written in a formal, broadly flowing style. Strauss's letters are inclined to be short and to the point, more informal, colloquial, and conversational in tone. Hofmannsthal feels compelled to philosophize in broad generalities about the moral and aesthetic significance of their work. He also likes to dwell on their obligation as leading artists to the world and to their art. Strauss displays no such concern in his letters, not because he was actually less interested in general artistic questions, but simply because he was more inclined to accept these things as self-evident. Hofmannsthal, by nature introspective, methodical, logical, and uncompromising, never took anything to do with art for granted.

Not surprisingly for a Viennese contemporary of Sigmund Freud, Hofmannsthal was deeply interested in psychology and was constantly analyzing himself and the world about him. He was rarely as self-assured and self-possessed as Strauss. One reason for his long letters was the opportunity they provided him to work out ideas for himself as well as for Strauss. While Strauss's letters are frequently charged with his ebullient sense of humor, most of Hofmannsthal's letters are serious. Although Hofmannsthal possessed a keen sense of humor and considerable self-irony, these were facets of his personality seldom surfacing in this correspondence, which suggests that the poet never really felt relaxed with Strauss.

Hugo von Hofmannsthal was born in Vienna on 1 February 1874. The patent of nobility had been bestowed upon his great-grandfather, Isaak Löw, in 1830 by Emperor Ferdinand in recognition of the high esteem in which he was held by his community and his country. Löw, who was a well-known Talmudic scholar as well as a successful businessman, had thirteen children. One of his five sons, August Emil, the grandfather of the poet, managed a branch office of the family firm in Lombardy, where he was baptized and married an Italian girl, Petronilla Cecilia Ordoni, daughter of an old, aristocratic family. Hofmannsthal held this grandmother in high esteem because of her vital and practical nature and commemorated her in his play, *Der weiße Fächer* (1897).

When the Austrian rule of Upper Italy collapsed, so did the firm in Italy and most of the family fortune. Hofmannsthal's grandparents moved to Krems in Austria where they lived in modest circumstances. Their son, Hugo, the father of the poet, became a lawyer and served as director of the legal bureau of the Central Bank. He married Anna Maria Fohleutner in 1873, the year of a major stock market crash in Austria. Although the family no longer possessed its former wealth, Hofmannsthal's father earned a good salary and supported his family in more than ample circumstances.

Through the combined heritage of the various bloodlines—Bohemian, Swabian, Italian, Austrian, and Jewish—contributing to his personality, Hofmannsthal was as cosmopolitan as the city of Vienna in which he was raised; although he was one of the most universal writers of his generation, he remained, nevertheless, unmistakably Viennese. With few exceptions his works, regardless of setting, betray their author's Viennese heritage in atmosphere, tone, and outlook.

After being tutored at home, Hofmannsthal attended the famous Akademisches Gymnasium in Vienna from 1884 until 1892, where he received a thorough background in humanistic studies. He was an extremely precocious child and by the age of twelve his mind was already as developed and receptive as that of a normal twenty-year-old. Although he enjoyed sports such as bicycling, sailing, tennis, and hiking, he also read avidly, a habit that remained with him throughout his life. It was his contention, shared by other writers of his generation, that no man could become a truly great author without reading. Hofmannsthal was reputed to be able to write in five languages and could read in eight.

The genius of Hofmannsthal mirrors the potential of Vienna at this time. The Austrian capital during the last decade of the nineteenth century enjoyed a true renaissance in all of the arts and became a Mecca for creative talent. In addition to the older, established writers such as Ferdinand von Saar, Peter Rosegger, Richard Kralik, and Marie von Ebner-Eschenbach, a new generation of writers, artists, and musicians had appeared. Hermann Bahr described the situation in retrospect:

> [It was] the time when Hugo Wolf was still alive; when Burckhardt was rejuvenating the Burgtheater and Mahler the Opera; when Hofmannsthal and Schnitzler were young; Klimt maturing: when the secessionist art movement was beginning; when Otto Wagner founded his school; Roller, the 'malerische Theater'; when Olbrich, Hoffmann, and Moser created the Austrian school of Applied Art; when Adolf Loos and Arnold Schönberg appeared; Reinhardt dreamed, unknown, among the quiet byways of the future; when Kainz returned; Weininger went out in flames; Ernst Mach held his popular scientific readings; Joseph Popper wrote his *Phantasies of a Realist;* and Chamberlain fleeing from the distractions of the world, came to our kindly city and here wrote his *Foundations of the Nineteenth Century.* . . . Those must have been wonderful days in Vienna![13]

Hofmannsthal quickly distinguished himself among his peers on the basis of his first verses, and in true admiration was readily acknowledged as a genius. At sixteen he was accepted as a regular member at the Café Griensteidl, one of the most prominent gathering places for writers in Vienna. His early works, published under the pseudonyms Theophil Morren or more commonly Loris, earned Hofmannsthal a European reputation by the age of nineteen, making him one of the most remarkable writers in German and Austrian literary history.

[13] Hermann Bahr, *Expressionism* (London, 1925), pp. 55-56.

At the University of Vienna, Hofmannsthal studied law in conformity with his father's wishes. This profession, however, attracted him so little that after taking his first state examination and after spending a required year of military service in the Dragoons (1894-1895), he returned to the University to study romance languages. Hofmannsthal completed his dissertation entitled "Über den Sprachgebrauch bei den Dichtern der Plejade" in 1898 and received the degree Doctor of Philosophy the following year.

Still uncertain as to his future career, Hofmannsthal decided to apply for a position teaching French literature at the University of Vienna. In order to qualify for this post, he completed the so-called Habilitations-schrift or *venia legendi,* on the subject of Victor Hugo.[14] For reasons that are still not clear—possibly he feared rejection or experienced a change of heart—Hofmannsthal withdrew his candidacy pleading personal reasons.[15]

The period 1900-1903 marked a major turning point in Hofmannsthal's life. The difficulties he experienced in attempting to change from lyric poet to dramatist, the failure to attain a teaching post at the University, and the general uncertainty of his financial condition and future earning capacity, caused him considerable nervous strain, which was reflected in his inability to complete many works. Although this was perhaps the longest and severest "crisis"[16] which Hofmannsthal ex-

---

[14] This essay was later published under the appropriately academic-sounding title "Studie über die Entwicklung des Dichters Victor Hugo." Now included in *Prosa* I (Berlin, 1950), 367-463.

[15] In a letter to Dean Theodor Gomperz, Hofmannsthal stated: "In der Angelegenheit meiner Habilitation Schritte zu tun, verbieten mir innere Gründe von zwingender Eindringlichkeit: diese Gründe haben mich veranlaßt, in einem respektvollen Schreiben an das Professorenkollegium mein Gesuch um Zulassung zur Dozentur zurückzuziehen." *Briefe* I, 338. However, in a later letter to Gomperz, Hofmannsthal admitted his disappointment at the time, although he felt then that things had worked out for the best. *Briefe* II, 73.

[16] Karl J. Naef, whose book *Hugo von Hofmannsthals Wesen und Werk* (Zürich, 1938) is still the most comprehensive work on Hofmannsthal to date, entitles the chapter containing the discussion of the Chandos letter (see below) as "Die Krisis," pp. 70 ff. Most critics tend to attribute the "crisis" of these years to a purported loss of faith in words by Hofmannsthal, citing the now famous *Ein Brief* (1902), an imaginary letter by Lord Chandos to Francis Bacon, as evidence. See Richard Brinkmann, "Hofmannsthal und die Sprache," *Deutsche Vierteljahrsschrift,* 35 (1961), 59-65. Also Paul Requadt, "Sprachverleugnung und Mantelsymbolik im Werke Hofmannsthals," *Deutsche Vierteljahrsschrift,* 29 (1955), 255-83.
There is unquestionably a personal basis to this work, for in a letter to Andrian, Hofmannsthal describes how he had used his own experience as a basis for *Ein Brief* (*Briefe* II, 99-100). However, it is an error to judge this work as a literal biographical document. *Ein Brief* is a symbolic portrayal of Hofmannsthal's own experiences carried to a theoretical extreme. It is also possible that Hofmannsthal is portraying the fate of Andrian, who wrote one book in 1895, *Der Garten der Erkenntnis,* and then lost his talent. See Donald G. Daviau, "Hugo von Hofmannsthal and the Chandos Letter," *Modern Austrian Literature,* 4/2 (1971), 28-44.

perienced, it was not an isolated occurrence. Periods of despondency and extreme nervousness afflicted Hofmannsthal all through his life from 1892 on. In 1907, for example, he experienced a loss of his ability to write, stating that even his notes made no sense to him.[17] A similar crisis occurred in 1908-1909 because of nervous anxiety.[18] Even with his dispostion to hypochondria he hardly had reason to be downcast in 1901, for his financial problems were resolved,[19] he married Gertrud Schlesinger, leased an attractive rococo mansion in Rodaun, a village located about fifteen miles from Vienna, and settled down in comfort and moderate security to a career as a writer.

During these years Hofmannsthal experimented with wordless forms such as pantomime and dance, not because he had lost faith in language, but because he had recognized the limitations of what could be expressed by words alone. He decided to break away from the relatively exclusive forms of lyric poetry and drama with appeal only to a limited audience, in order to work in more immediate art forms that would reach a wider public on a more direct, intuitive level.[20]

Hofmannsthal's progression to musical reinforcement of his texts was a natural development, for music was implicit in his writing from the

[17] In a letter to Bodenhausen he stated: "Ich war diese Wochen in einer sonderbaren Lage—und dafür hätte ich mir die Fahrt nach Degenershausen zu Euch nicht versagen brauchen: durch volle 5 Wochen ging ich herum, in einer solchen absoluten Senkung des dichterischen Vermögens—wie sie mir kaum je begegnet ist: ich verstand (mitten in der Arbeit, nach vollendetem ersten Aufzug) meine eigenen Notizen nicht. . . ." *Briefe* II, 292.

[18] To Schröder he wrote in January 1909: "Über meine Gesundheit, diese ganze, fast bizarre Erregbarkeit meiner Nerven, mach' Dir keine Gedanken. Es ging mir abscheulich, es geht mir wieder recht gut, es wird mir gelegentlich wieder abscheulich gehen, aber ich habe unendlich viel Gutes und mein Dasein ist übermäßig begünstigt unter menschlichen Existenzen." *Briefe* II, 349.—To his father he wrote in the same year: "Bei mir natürlich vollständige Stockung. Ich verstehe meine Notizen nicht einmal! Gottlob, kenn' ich das Werkel so vollständig, habe das so oft erlebt, daß es mich nicht mehr als nötig ärgert. Es gehört einmal zu meinem Metier und meiner Natur. D.h. das Metier paßt nicht zu der Natur, die Natur nicht zum Klima. Trotzdem bin ich ja aber im ganzen ganz vergnügt und schreibe schließlich eben so viel als ein anderer." *Briefe* II, 372-73.

[19] Hofmannsthal had signed a contract with the Insel publishing company which guaranteed him 1,500 Marks a year. He also had received other royalties from his published and performed works. See *Briefe* II, 32.

[20] As the critic Hanns Hammelmann aptly comments in his perceptive study of Hofmannsthal: "It was the attempt to express himself in a medium more direct, more fluent and more telling than words which led Hofmannsthal to pantomime and ballet, to drama and to the opera. The stage, which in mime and gesture reveals the unspoken and deeply hidden, and music, which makes directly felt that which is 'too vast, too true to be encompassed in words'—these were the means he wished to invoke to touch the imagination, the receptive and creative instincts of his fellow men." *Hugo von Hofmannsthal* (London, 1957), pp. 24-25.

beginning, as he himself later acknowledged in a letter to Strauss, written in 1924:

> For it strikes me as something great and at the same time necessary in my life that, eighteen years ago, you approached me with your wishes and needs. There pre-existed within me something which enabled me to fulfil—within the limits of my gifts—these wishes and made this fulfilment in turn satisfy a most profound need of my own. Much of what I had produced in all the loneliness of youth, entirely for myself, hardly thinking of readers, were phantastic little operas and Singspiele—without music. Your wishes, subsequently, supplied a purpose without restricting my freedom. (*C.* 384-85)

Thus Hofmannsthal's decision to write opera texts represented not so much a shift in direction as a logical development and expansion of tendencies inherent in his unique artistic talent. The union of his poetic texts with music can be regarded as the inevitable fulfilment of a creative gift which had always been primarily lyrical in nature. The inner necessity that impelled this final step to music is evident in the following self-assessment by Hofmannsthal:

> One speaks of the poet and the musician who come together for mutual endeavor. Corneille with Lully, Calzabigi with Gluck, da Ponte and Schikaneder with Mozart. But aside from the fact that this exists—one can scarcely imagine how necessarily *I* came to this form. I find this statement in the section of Nadler's literary history dealing with me: my very first dramas had already betrayed an unconscious desire for music, a condition indicated only imprecisely by the word "lyrical." He is absolutely correct; but the word, for my feeling, is sufficiently precise. The French call an opera a lyric drama, and perhaps in doing so, they were always instinctively closer to classical antiquity than we; they never forgot completely that classical tragedy was sung.[21]

Clearly, Hofmannsthal recognized and accepted as fact the essential lyric unity of his work. Equally revealing and important are the last lines of the quotation, which indicate that by adding music to his words he was also consciously (and conscientiously) striving to return to the classical origins of drama, the same purpose that had motivated his interest in pantomime and dance. Moreover, this turning to the past also represented the natural and consistent final goal of Hofmannsthal's tendency toward traditionalism in his writings, one important phase of which found expression in his emphasis on the Austro-Bavarian baroque tradition. There will be more to say about this later in connection with his participation in founding the Salzburg Festival.

In order to keep Hofmannsthal's work as a librettist for Richard Strauss in proper perspective, it must be remembered that his opera librettos represent but one aspect of his career as a writer. It should also

[21] *Prosa* IV, 441-42.

17

be noted that his decision was motivated by practical as well as artistic reasons, for actually he regarded comedy as the particular form he wished to master. The earnings from his librettos for Strauss helped to alleviate his constant financial needs so that he could find the freedom and peace of mind to create his comedies.[22]

Viewed as a totality, Hofmannsthal's writings reveal an overall stylistic and thematic unity. Only his focus shifted from the negative stance in his early works to a positive approach after 1900; that is, his condemnation of the decadent, aesthetic philosophy of the nineties evolved naturally into the attitude of responsible social commitment found in his mature works. Hofmannsthal's dedicated concern for improving society led him to an interest in politics, in pedagogy, and above all in the use of literature in general and the theater in particular as a means of moral and educational guidance. His many essays written for newspapers and journals, and his series of great Austrian books collected under the title *Österreichische Bibliothek,* assembled to remind Austrians of their literary heritage, are examples of his sincere desire to speak to as wide an audience as possible. Throughout his later works tradition is emphasized as an important unifying factor in Austrian life. Hofmannsthal's major role in establishing the Salzburg Festival, together with Strauss and Max Reinhardt, is further evidence of his genuine commitment to the idea of serving and uniting his countrymen.

As will be seen, Hofmannsthal considered the fragmented nature of existence in Austria, the isolation of the individual, to be one of the major problems of his day. He knew this problem from personal experience, for he too had felt isolated in his youth. His enormous correspondence was one means he adopted to combat loneliness. By his own admission, he had been a difficult person to get along with.[23] Initially, writing had been a substitute for life, a tendency that he later recognized and overcame. The lyric beginnings of his poetry are a reflection of his early introversion. The basic hurdle in his life was the shift from the subjective, almost narcissistic orientation of his youth to the social, outward direction of his life and works after 1900. This change of outlook that motivated the shift from lyricism to drama and opera took years of development. As early as 1893 Hofmannsthal indicated his desire to change: "I am very tired of everything fine, subtle,

---

[22] In a letter to his father he stated in 1909: "Ich bin jetzt doch überzeugt, daß ich das eigentliche Metier (speziell der Komödie) ganz gewiß und sicherlich erlernen und schließlich Komödien schreiben werde, die ebensosehr mich befriedigen als auch auf dem Theater wirken werden. Neue Stoffe strömen mir immerfort zu, ich weiß nicht einmal, welchen ich als den nächsten anpacken werde. Daß ich mit diesen Dingen durch die äußerst glückliche Kombination mit Strauss für absehbare Zeit auf den materiellen, augenblicklichen Erfolg nicht angewiesen bin, ist ein großes Glück und eine große Entlastung und erleichtert mir diese Phase meiner Produktion sehr." *Briefe* II, 376-77.

[23] "Ich kann kaum begreifen, daß Sie [i.e., Richard Beer-Hofmann] mich in früheren Jahren haben vertragen können: denn ich habe doch eine schwer erträgliche Art gehabt, und auch eine gewisse Schlechtigkeit, kommt mir vor." *Briefe* I, 304.

closely analyzed, impressionistic, and psychological and am waiting for the naive joys of life to fall upon me from the trees crudely and fragrantly like pine cones. Unfortunately the tree of life is enormously headstrong and cannot be shaken."[24]

Hofmannsthal died in 1929 at the early age of fifty-five. The cause of his death was a stroke, possibly induced by grief over the suicide of his twenty-six-year-old eldest son Franz. Hofmannsthal was a deeply religious Catholic (though never a Catholic writer in the strict sense of the term) and, in accordance with his wish, he was buried in the habit of a Franciscan monk.[25]

To adequately describe Hofmannsthal the man is a difficult if not an impossible task because of his enormous complexity. Erika Brecht, one of his greatest admirers and an early biographer, has left perhaps the warmest account of the poet as a compassionate human being, while stressing the complications involved in portraying him: "It is only an attempt, that will perhaps remain fruitless, for to capture his essence was as good as impossible even during the years of our friendship; his friends called him 'Ariel' or compared him to a butterfly that perched for a moment on a friendly hand but, unearthly and shy, immediately flew away again."[26]

Hofmannsthal preferred to live a withdrawn life devoted to his work, and his more even-tempered, capable wife Gerty devoted herself to sheltering him as much as possible from the ordinary annoyances of life and unwanted intrusions. Extremely sensitive, with his moods frequently dependent upon the season and the weather,[27] Hofmannsthal did not encourage uninvited guests to come to his home in Rodaun, not even his closest friends. He preferred to deal with Strauss by letter rather than in personal meetings. He did not accept Strauss's frequent invitations, nor did he invite the musician to visit him. On one occasion Strauss and his wife dropped in unexpectedly while passing through Vienna on their

[24] *Briefe* I, 84-85.
[25] Leopold von Andrian, however, disputes the widely held notion that Hofmannsthal died a Catholic and was buried in a habit. See "Erinnerungen an meinen Freund," Helmut A. Fiechtner, ed., *Hugo von Hofmannsthal* (Vienna, 1949), pp. 62 f.
[26] Erika Brecht, *Erinnerungen an Hugo von Hofmannsthal* (Innsbruck, 1946), p. 5.
[27] See *Hugo von Hofmannsthal—Eberhard von Bodenhausen: Briefe der Freundschaft,* p. 153. One of Hofmannsthal's eccentricities was his belief that he could only write when the sun was shining. Rainy and dull weather depressed him. Jakob Wassermann, a close personal friend and great admirer of Hofmannsthal reported in *Hofmannsthal der Freund* (Berlin, 1920), p. 29: "Durch seine Abhängigkeit von Klima und Bewölkung, von Feuchtigkeit und Luftdruck, Einflüssen, die gewöhnlichen Sinnen kaum zugänglich waren, erschien er so kreatürlich und so wehrlos leidend, daß man innig wünschte, er möchte nicht bloß mehr Gewalt über seinen eigenen preisgegebenen Körper haben, sondern auch über die Gestirne und Elemente, deren Feindseligkeit ihn zu bitteren Klagen hinriß und von paradiesischen Ländern träumen ließ, wo Atmen, Denken, Bilden selbstverständliche Lust war, nicht dem Zufall der günstigen Stunde abgetrotzt werden mußte. Er hatte bei heißem Wind, der über das Südgebirge kam, Tage der Niedergeschlagenheit, in denen kein Zuspruch ihn aufmunterte, alles Tun wurde wertlos."

way to Italy. Although Hofmannsthal made the best of the situation, he later wrote.to Strauss, begging him never to impose in that fashion again. The two men did, of course, meet periodically to discuss their work with the lamentable result of gaps in the correspondence. The loss is all the more regrettable, for these meetings were generally held when the artists were at an impasse over particularly complex problems.

The two men, so dissimilar in tastes, background and outlook, had little in common on the personal level. Hofmannsthal's wife once mentioned to her husband that Strauss had complained to her about never seeing his collaborator. To this well-meant form of flattery, Hofmannsthal replied in his next letter to Strauss: "Besides, between two men like us there is nothing but our joint work and, properly speaking, no other common topic."[28] This statement seems almost ironic considering that it is Hofmannsthal who throughout the correspondence engages in self-revelations, self-analysis, and self-justification, while Strauss only occasionally introduces a personal element.

In another letter to his confidant, Eberhard von Bodenhausen, a close personal friend who administered Hofmannsthal's estate for him and one of the few people to whom he entrusted his innermost thoughts, Hofmannsthal reported: "My personal relationship with Strauss, as always, casual but charming. In his dealings with me he is a fine, really delightful fellow."[29] At the same time he made it clear that his judgment of Strauss, the man, did not influence his opinion of Strauss, the musician. He states that his hair stood on end when Bodenhausen in his letter compared Strauss to Beethoven.[30] Later, Hofmannsthal wrote several letters to Strauss attesting to the genuine friendship that had developed between them. It is notable that Strauss, who initially referred to his partner as "My Dear Herr von Hofmannsthal," began in 1916 to call him "My Dear Friend and Poet," and thereafter most often simply "Dear Friend." Hofmannsthal, however, with few exceptions,

---

[28] *C.*, 361. In an earlier letter Hofmannsthal had explained to Strauss himself why a closer personal relationship between them was impossible: "I am always, and each time anew, pleased to see you. But we are spoilt; we have shared the best men can share; being united in creative production. Every hour we have spent together was connected with our joint work; the transition to an ordinary social relationship would now be almost impossible. And I *wish* to remain united with the creative artist in you, in a serving, participating capacity, always. If the collaboration with Kerr were to materialize, I might dovetail myself into it in an assistant, advisory capacity (unnamed, even without Kerr's knowledge); nothing I would like more. Take me as I am: you have no better friend." *C.*, 342-43.

[29] *Hugo von Hofmannsthal—Eberhard von Bodenhausen: Briefe der Freundschaft*, p. 161.

[30] Ibid. Hofmannsthal revealed his candid opinion of Strauss also in a letter (June 1909) to his good friend Harry Kessler: "Wenn ich einen raffinierten künstlerischen Componisten hätte. Alles was er sagt, was er sich wünscht, wonach er tendiert, degoutiert mich ziemlich stark." *Hofmannsthal—Kessler Briefwechsel 1884-1929* (Frankfurt am Main, 1968) p. 244.

continued to address the composer as "Dear Dr. Strauss" throughout the entire period of their friendship.

The correspondence affords a vivid insight into the character of the two men. For example, depending on his mood, Hofmannsthal exhibits a wide range of characteristics from warm friendship to almost hysterical excitability and petulance to outspoken hostility and aggressiveness. Strauss, who enjoyed enormous self-confidence as well as great patience and forebearance, displays a much narrower emotional range and provides the stabilizing influence for the partnership. Despite his prominence as a writer, Hofmannsthal was often unsure of himself, resulting in temperamental outbursts and severe attacks of despondency. The slightest upset to his routine could put him into a nervous state that would virtually incapacitate him for weeks. He required constant encouragement, and whenever Strauss was not sufficiently prompt with the appropriate praise for texts received from Hofmannsthal, showing that he understood and appreciated them, the latter, with equal measures of annoyance and patient resignation, called attention to his oversight with lengthy, explanatory letters, lecturing Strauss on the quality of his work. The often quoted *Ariadne* letter (see pp. 124-25) in which the poet analyzed his own libretto for the benefit of the musician represents one such outburst. Strauss's casual, almost indifferent acknowledgement of the completed manuscript of *Ariadne* provoked Hofmannsthal into a detailed account of the merits of his work and the reasons why he deserved a considerably more enthusiastic response from the musician.

Hofmannsthal possessed a formal, dignified, rather unbending nature, and there is little in the personal information about him as an adult that indicates spontaneity or casualness. The writer Jakob Wassermann considered him the most aristocratic person he had ever met, and this quality was reflected in the punctilious and meticulous correctness of his social behavior. Yet, he also displayed great warmth, compassion, and even a good sense of humor in his letters to such close friends as Arthur Schnitzler, Eberhard von Bodenhausen, and Edgar Karg von Bebenburg. No doubt his early introduction into the adult world because of his genius influenced his outlook. He grew up under fairly protective circumstances, and, although he had a number of friends his own age, he associated for the most part with talented men considerably older than himself. His closest friends in the circle of writers known as Young Vienna—for instance, Schnitzler, Beer-Hofmann and Bahr— were all a dozen years his senior. Although a brilliant conversationalist, according to every account of him,[31] Hofmannsthal was virtually incapable of small talk. He lived almost exclusively for his work, and judging from his letters to Strauss, he seems to have measured his happiness primarily in terms of his literary accomplishments.

[31] See. R. A. Schröder, "Hofmannsthal im Gespräch," pp. 343 ff. and E. Buschbeck, "Bahr und Hofmannsthal im Gespräch," pp. 222 ff. Both in Fiechtner, *Hugo von Hofmannsthal*.

The main quality of Hofmannsthal's writing, refined thought rendered in polished, controlled imagistic language, is a further reflection of his personal character. Although he could be practical and even tough-minded if necessary, he was basically anti-materialistic in life and anti-naturalistic in art. Not only in his writings but even in conversation, he avoided terms like *reality*. His work and his interests approached life as a multi-dimensional unity[32] in which the invisible aspects were as real as the visible and tangible. As a writer his aim was not to imitate the recognized forms of existence, but rather to use phenomena as symbols to express the intangible connections between all forms of life. By this means he attempted to mediate between this world and the trans-cendental world, to make comprehensible the unseen unity and harmony of existence.[33] The very nature of his artistic ambition eventually led him to music as the best means of achieving these goals.

Like many major artists, Hofmannsthal inclined toward myth and allegory as the best means of capturing what he termed "the world behind the world." His usual technique was to cast over his poetic world an aura of unreality as a means of disguising, or at least muting, surface reality so that its deeper meaning could be perceived. He once

[32] In a jesting note to Schnitzler, Hofmannsthal indicated not only his belief in the unity of the world but pointed out the unity of his own writings: "Wenn ich an der Bretterwand hinflieg' und mir das Genick brech' (unwahrscheinlich, aber möglich), sollt Ihr meine vielen Notizen auf Zetteln herausgeben, in Gedankengruppen geordnet, mit einem sehr einfachen, die Assoziationen aufdeckenden Kommentar. Denn meine Gedanken gehören alle zusammen, weil ich von der Einheit der Welt sehr stark durchdrungen bin. Ich glaub' sogar, ein Dichter ist eben ein Mensch, dem in guten Stunden die Gedanken 'ausgehen,' wie man beim Patiencelegen sagt." *Briefe* I, 165. In another letter to his father, he shows that his sense of the unity of nature led him to become a writer rather than a philosopher: "Wenn mir, was Du Philosophie nennst, so sehr am Herzen läge, das abstrake Erkennen des Daseins, wär' ich wohl Theolog geworden, und mit der Zeit vielleicht Schismatiker. So aber steh' ich ja ganz auf dem Goetheschen: Natur hat weder Kern noch Schale—alles ist sie mit einem Male." Ibid., 168.

[33] For Hofmannsthal's clearest statement concerning the role of the poet, see "Der Dichter und diese Zeit," *Prosa* II (Berlin, 1951), 264-98. Here he states: "Er [der Dichter] ist es, der in sich die Elemente der Zeit verknüpft. In ihm oder nirgends ist Gegenwart" (p. 282). He also defines the poet's mission, stating that poets exist ". . . die Unendlichkeit der Erscheinungen leidend zu genießen und aus leidendem Genießen heraus die Vision zu schaffen; zu schaffen in jeder Sekunde, mit jedem Pulsschlag, unter einem Druck, als liege der Ozean über ihnen, zu schaffen, von keinem Licht angeleuchtet, auch von keinem Grubenlämpchen, zu schaffen, umtost von höhnenden, verwirrenden Stimmen; zu schaffen aus keinem anderen Antrieb heraus als aus dem Grundtrieb ihres Wesens, zu schaffen den Zusammenhang des Erlebten, den erträglichen Einklang der Erscheinungen, zu schaffen wie die Ameisen, wieder verstört, wieder schaffend, zu schaffen wie die Spinne, aus dem eigenen Leib den Faden hervorspinnend, der über den Abgrund des Daseins sie trägt." Ibid., pp. 290-91. In *Jupiter und Semele,* he wrote: "Des Dichters eigentliches Gebiet: das Verhältnis von Geist zu Körper, von Idee zum Ausdruck, Mensch zum Tier . . ." *Dramen* II, 504.

reported that his works generally took form in his mind first as an atmosphere.[34] At the same time he established distance in his works (long before Brecht conceived of his technique of estrangement) by setting them in the past, so that people could come to the essential meaning that lay behind the surface details. For this reason, he felt that opera was his form, stating: "It is quite certainly so—that in opera, that is, of course, particularly in my opera, I can have the 'significant,' that which matters, the essential, emerge not from a custom, but from the purely felt deeper condition of things—it always becomes a matter of purity—this drama, as I intend it, can also bring the tragic inherent in things to appearance without a break."[35]

Hofmannsthal, working in terms of this principle of "precise vision," tried to create a timeless, mythical atmosphere, occasionally even devising, as in *Der Rosenkavalier*, his own artificial language that is simultaneously synthetic and analytic.[36] He often invoked an oriental atmosphere, for he loved the fairy tale aura and mystery of the East. Both *Ariadne auf Naxos*, although based on a classical legend, and *Die Frau ohne Schatten* possess poetic elements of orientalism.

Despite his preference for symbolism over realism, for poetry over prose, and for the visionary realm of the imagination to the world of

[34] In answer to a questionnaire, inquiring how his works took shape, Hofmannsthal replied as follows: "Ich glaube: mich reizt vag eine gewisse Vorstellung, Vorstellungsgruppe, vorgestellte Atmosphäre, die in ihrer Vagheit unendlich inhaltreich und auch gegen andere Vorstellungsgruppen ganz scharf abgegrenzt ist—aber sie selbst ist begrifflich gar nicht faßbar: sie selbst ist z.B. heroische Atmosphäre, patriarchalische Atmosphäre, bürgerlich-eingeschränkt-idyllische Atmosphäre—alle diese Bezeichnungen sind aber viel zu begriffsmäßig, zugleich zu eng und zu weit. Denn die Atmosphäre ist viel nebelhafter, ist nicht etwa Landschaft, nicht etwa Vision menschlicher Zustände, nicht etwa zeitlich-historisch gefärbt—sie enthält ein schwebendes Durcheinander aller dieser Elemente. Andererseits ist sie viel bestimmter als alle diese Worte, ist ganz einheitlich von einem bestimmten Duft durchsetzt, von einem bestimmten Lebensrhythmus beherrscht, sie ist eine Möglichkeit ganz bestimmter Gestaltungen, die miteinander ganz bestimmte Rhythmen bilden können und keine andern—dann tritt, oft nach Tagen oder Wochen, aus dieser Atmosphäre ein Einzelnes heraus, wie die Fichte am Bergeshang, wenn der Morgennebel sich klärt: dieses Einzelne ist dann eine Gestalt mit bestimmter Gebärde, ein Ton (Ton eines Monologs, Ton einer Unterredung, einer Massenszene) oder eine ganz kleine Anekdote, mit deutlich scharfgesehenen Details.

Diese präzise Vision läßt sich dann verstehen. Sie ist immer Symbol, wie alles im Leben, wenn man es in einem günstigen Augenblick tief genug erblickt. Dann verzweigt sich das Begriffliche, formt den Stoff in seinen Teilen, und aus jener vagen schwelenden Atmosphäre, in die der Gedanke immer wieder taucht, holt er sich seine ihn völlig umhüllende Metaphorik, worunter ich Gestalten, Hintergründe, Rede und Gegenrede und alles verstehe." *Briefe* I, 336-37.

[35] Fiechtner, *Hugo von Hofmannsthal*, p. 339.

[36] In discussing *Der Rosenkavalier*, the writer Walther Brecht commented on the musicality of the language, to which Hofmannsthal replied: "Es liegt vor allem in der Sprache. In der Sprache liegt überhaupt alles. So wie der ganze 'Rosenkavalier' in dieser fiktiven Halbmundart liegt, die nie so gesprochen worden ist. Was darin vorkommt, ist ja ganz gleichgültig, die Geschichte, die Fabel." Fiechtner, *Hugo von Hofmannsthal*, p. 340.

everyday life, Hofmannsthal was no ivory tower aesthete. Rather, he was a man of practical sense and humor, totally dedicated to improving the world in which he lived. His life displays a spirit of *noblesse oblige* thoroughly in keeping with his aristocratic nature. The record of his commitment to men and causes expands in ever broadening circles from his efforts on behalf of individual friends to his efforts to promote European unity.

Strauss was almost the exact opposite of Hofmannsthal's type, although, as in Hofmannsthal's case, a detailed portrait of the man is difficult to formulate and remains still to be written.[37] His personality was rooted in two contradictory heritages: the rough, simple coarseness of the upper Bavarian peasant lineage of his father, and the suave, aristocratic self-confidence and refinement of the wealthy city merchant, the Pschorr family of his mother. Physically Strauss was thin and very tall, and he made an imposing figure on the podium, quite in contrast to almost all the famous musicians of his time. His personality affected those who knew him in various ways. The French author, Romain Rolland, though a devoted friend of Strauss, found reflected in him much that he disliked in Germans as a race. Rolland met the composer in 1899 and recorded the following impressions in his diary:

> Very young face: dark hair receding, very little hair on the forehead, which is rounded, full and rather handsome: very pale eyes: the moustache so fair as to be almost white. Speaks French with difficulty, but sufficiently. Tall, but holds himself with extreme lassitude. Childish and involuntary shyness in his smile and gestures: but one feels underneath a pride which is cold, self-willed, indifferent or contemptuous of the majority of things and people, and which must blame itself, when alone, for not having asserted itself more, for having given in yet once more in conversation to social conventions.[38]

Several years later, Rolland returned to his diary to record another description of Strauss:

> Just now, looking at the big portrait of Strauss which I have at home and which Strauss gave me, I was thinking: it's very idealized; they've created him with a character which he does not possess. Strauss, in real life, hasn't that vigour of expression; the impression he gives is pale, uncertain, eternally youngish, a little inconsistent. —But when seeing him close to, at the concert, conducting his or-

---

[37] In the large Strauss literature, few authors have attempted to give more than a superficial examination to Strauss the man, despite the ample insight into his character available from his enormous correspondence. The best biographical portrait, which we shall refer to, is by Otto Erhardt, *Richard Strauss, Leben, Wirken, Schaffen* (Freiburg im Breisgau, 1953).

[38] The diary, which was not published in Rolland's lifetime, is included in *Richard Strauss & Romain Rolland: Correspondence, Diary, & Essays,* ed. Rollo Myers (Berkeley, 1968), p. 112.

chestra, I was struck by the *other* Strauss: his face is aging, hardening, shrinking; it is acquiring and retaining an intense seriousness, which not the slightest gleam of gaiety illumines for an instant. In profile, with his thick crown of hair, set very high up, and framing a monk's tonsure, with his enormous bulging forehead, his nose which appears small and short, and his sulky mouth, he looks like a barbarian from Asia, one of those Huns who founded a family in Germany. —But there is one thing which his portraits do not convey at all: that is the pale blondness of hair and complexion.[39]

Another Frenchman, composer Claude Debussy, in observing Strauss on the podium commented: "He has . . . the head of a musician; but his eyes and gestures are those of a Superman, to quote Nietzsche, from whose teaching he must have imbibed his energy. From Nietzsche too he must have learned his lofty scorn of feeble sentimentalities and his desire that music should not go on forever providing a more or less satisfactory illumination for our nights, but that it should shine like the sun. I can assure you that there is sunshine in the music of Strauss. . . . I say again that it is not possible to withstand his irresistible domination."[40]

Just as Strauss was the opposite physical type to Hofmannsthal, he also reflected a totally opposite viewpoint in his relation to the world around him. Unlike Hofmannsthal, he remained for most of his career almost oblivious of everyday politics.[41] His early life developed in a world of monarchy, and Strauss never seemed to have changed his outlook that all governments were autocratic and were to be cultivated to serve his art. He neither understood the menace of Nazism nor paid heed, until it was too late, to ample warnings of the impending tragedy that would result from its rise to power. As an old man he witnessed the collapse of his whole cultural world, found his own family in dire threat of a concentration camp (his daughter-in-law, Alice Strauss, was Jewish), and found Stefan Zweig, his only satisfactory substitute for Hofmannsthal, officially blacklisted because of his Jewish heritage.[42]

[39] Ibid., p. 141.

[40] Claude Debussy, *Monsieur Croche, the Dilettante Hater,* trans. B. N. Langdon Davies (New York, 1948), pp. 123-24.

[41] Because Strauss did not repudiate the Nazi Government, he has been accused by George Marek in his book *Richard Strauss: The Life of a Non-Hero* (New York, 1967) of ruthless opportunism. That Strauss exercised bad judgment is true, but Marek's charge is biased and unfounded. Strauss was politically naive. His error, not to be overlooked or minimized, was lack of concern. However, he considered only his work to be important, feeling that good art is an enduring value, while governments come and go.

[42] What Zweig as well as Hofmannsthal meant to the composer and how Strauss tried to protect his new librettist is shown in the following letter from Strauss to Zweig: "Denn glauben Sie mir, den Dichter, der mir ein brauchbares Opernbuch schreiben kann, gibt es nicht, auch wenn Sie ihm großmütig und uneigennützig 'helfen' wollen. Seien Sie herzlich bedankt für Ihren hochherzigen Vorschlag! Ich habe sowohl Minister Goebbels wie Göring, wiederholt erklärt, daß ich seit 50 Jahren nach einem Librettisten suche, viele Dutzende von Operntexten wurden mir zugeschickt, mit allen deutschen Dichtern

Finally, Strauss himself became *persona non grata* to the Nazi regime. The party headquarters sent the following telegram to all members on 24 January 1944: "RE: Richard Strauss. The personal association of our leading men with Dr. Richard Strauss is to cease. However, as the Führer specified to Dr. Goebbels, no difficulties are to be placed in the way of performance of his works. Bormann."[43]

Strauss lived almost entirely in an isolated world of music. He had no apparent interest in religion of any kind and always remained disinterested in the type of philosophical theorizing and analyses of self, life, and the world that fascinated Hofmannsthal. Strauss possessed few personal weaknesses or eccentricities and was not often subject to temperamental behavior. Yet Strauss was certainly not a simple man. The characteristic of his inner personality, as Erhardt aptly summarizes,

> . . . is its ambiguity, which, parallel to the contrasting themes of his music, allows the extreme contrasts of the man to exist organically along side one another.
>
> His bearing: rather unpathetic and that of a "Grandseigneur." His dress: casual and meticulously groomed. His character: naive and refined, altruistic and egotistical, generous and miserly. His intellect: intuitive and rationally controlled. His appearance: determined and modest.
>
> He is simple and complicated, receptive to feelings and thinker, dreamer and formalist, outdoorsman and man of the world, gourmand and gourmet—but he has always remained the type, about which Schopenhauer said: "Whoever does not to a certain extent, remain a big child throughout his life, but becomes a serious, prosaic, thoroughly settled man, can be a very useful and virtuous citizen of his world, only never a genius."[44]

Throughout his life Strauss cultivated a fine sense of self-irony, and not infrequently he chose to disparage his own work. Humor was an important primary force in his life and in his work. His two great obsessions were his work and playing the card game Skat. The outdoors and nature also meant a great deal to him as his magnificent country home in the rugged Bavarian Alps attests. His gregarious, extroverted,

---

(Gerhart Hauptmann, Bahr, Wolzogen, etc.) habe ich verhandelt. Ein Glücksfall war der Salome-Fund, die 'Elektra' leitete mein Beziehungen zu dem einzigen Hofmannsthal ein, nach seinem Tode glaubte ich endgültig verzichten zu müssen, ein Zufall (kann man es so nennen?) führte mich zu Ihnen. Ich gebe Sie auch nicht auf, auch nicht, weil wir jetzt gerade eine antisemitische Regierung haben." *Die Welt um Richard Strauss in Briefen*, ed. Franz Grasberger (Tutzing, 1967), p. 363.

[43] See Walter Panofsky, *Richard Strauss—Partitur eines Lebens* (Munich, 1965), pp. 326-36, for an excellent account of Strauss's relationship to and his difficulties with the Nazis during the war years. Also see pp. 281-99 for Panofsky's perceptive review of Strauss's confrontation with the Nazis in regard to the premiere performance of *Die schweigsame Frau* with libretto by Stefan Zweig.

[44] Erhardt, *Richard Strauss*, p. 64.

26

spontaneous , and impulsive behavior was foreign to Hofmannsthal who considered Strauss to be without nerves. Strauss suffered from none of the extreme artistic sensitivity that ruled Hofmannsthal's personality, and he cared little for the poet's rarified approach to art. In a word, Strauss epitomized the bourgeois man of culture in pre-World War I Germany.[45]

Strauss readily made compromises to achieve his goals, while Hofmannsthal both as artist and man was incapable of compromise. He made the highest demands on himself and on everyone around him. He had unimpeachable integrity, and if at times this made him seem cold or callous, there was no acceptable alternative for him. To make concessions out of convenience or even out of friendship was unthinkable to him. When, for example, Strauss was willing to have *Ariadne* performed without Reinhardt as director, because of scheduling difficulties, Hofmannsthal exploded with anger, threatening to withdraw the work rather than to see it jeopardized for the sake of expediency. Since he was writing for posterity, Hofmannsthal was not concerned primarily with the immediate public success of his works, a viewpoint that he frequently tried to impress upon Strauss.

Strangely enough, however, in another of the many paradoxes existing in this collaboration, Strauss, who is renowned for his love of money, never mentions the subject, while Hofmannsthal brings up the topic repeatedly. This reflects the difference in financial status between the two men as well as the fact that Strauss acted generally as the business agent, handling the contracts and the financial arrangements for their works. Hofmannsthal always received less money than Strauss for all of their joint works.

The difference in the two artists' outlook is emphasized in another letter to Bodenhausen during the writing of *Die Frau ohne Schatten:*

> I have finished writing the third act of the opera in the past few days—I think it is very nice, and if I had a composer who was less famous but closer to my heart, to my way of thinking, I would feel much better. In the "fairy tale," in which I now want to bury myself with all my strength, I am alone—must master the beautiful, truly limitless subject completely and in all its depth—naturally I will not succeed in representing its content completely—but something beautiful perhaps at any rate—of course even then not directly, but through the mysterious study of character and through analogy . . .[46]

The contrasting personalities and conflicting outlooks of the two men led naturally to misunderstandings about the aim of their works. Hof-

[45] See Barbara Tuchmann, *The Proud Tower* (New York, 1966) in which she chooses Richard Strauss as the most characteristic artistic personality in Germany during the period leading to World War I.
[46] *Hugo von Hofmannsthal—Eberhard von Bodenhausen,* p. 167.

mannsthal, especially in connection with the works *Ariadne auf Naxos* and *Die Frau ohne Schatten,* was distressed by Strauss's apparent inability to understand the meaning of his texts. Strauss's insistence that the libretto for *Ariadne* was too subtle and not clear enough for comprehension by opera audiences touched Hofmannsthal where he was most vulnerable, and defensively he was quick to inform the composer of his disagreement. Finally, the normally patient Strauss snapped back in annoyance: "Why do you always get so bitterly angry if for once we don't understand each other straight away?" (*C.,* 243). At other times Strauss put Hofmannsthal in his place, telling him not to be concerned with a musical problem, but to depend on the musician to solve it to the best advantage. Obviously, to blend their ideas together into a meaningful, cohesive union, it was necessary for these two artists to question and to criticize each other freely and candidly. Only because each man was receptive to the ideas of the other and yet refused to yield beyond a given point could they come to any final mutual understanding on the consistently high level that they achieved in six operas.

Hofmannsthal readily recognized that he was not a born librettist. His feeling for music was derived purely from intuition and an instinctive artistic comprehension of the form. He did attempt to learn something about musical styles and forms, and whenever Strauss mentioned a specific type of aria he intended to use, Hofmannsthal would study the models suggested by Strauss to illustrate the idea. Subsequently, in writing *Die Frau ohne Schatten* and *Arabella,* Hofmannsthal's confidence in his musical knowledge grew to such an extent that he began blocking out the text in terms of set numbers. He knew very clearly his value to Strauss as a librettist as well as the path he was following in his librettos, as this letter to Strauss concerning *Ariadne* shows:

> It is certainly not chance which made two men like us meet at the same period in history. And I would ask you not to ascribe to a mere freak of creative fancy any single step along the road which we have to travel together, nor any one step which I have taken and which you have had to take with me. What, between ourselves, I would wish you to appreciate above all as a high merit of mine, and one earned with loving care, is not my libretti as such, but that which is implied in them. After *Salome* and *Elektra* had made it obvious to me that certain things, once done, were not to be repeated—for in art everything can only be done once—I set out in another direction with *Rosenkavalier,* which on the one hand required an unprecedented degree of pithiness and animation in the conversational style, while it re-admitted on the other, through the back-door, so to speak, a seemingly remote stylistic method, the method of set numbers. Now I have felt compelled to probe to their very limits these set numbers and the formal and intellectual possibilities which they offer. Hence the choice of a subject of almost contrapuntal severity; hence the stylizing of emotion and—to make this possible, palatable and, in a higher sense,

true—the idea of this archaistic setting; all of them rather intricate, by no means obvious propositions. I know where I now am, yet I had rather not demonstrate it in words, but by deeds—that is through a work of art which possesses complete and pure operatic form. I hope this work, when compared with da Ponte's, Goethe's, Wagner's output, will prove itself true and genuine, not excogitated and entirely uncontrived. (*C.*, 154-55)

Although Hofmannsthal at the beginning of the collaboration felt that he could work alongside of Strauss as an equal and independent partner, he gradually understood and willingly accepted his secondary position in the relationship. He came to recognize that the music was the most important aspect of an operatic work, and he always deferred to Strauss's judgment in matters of musical technique and craftmanship. However, he regarded himself as the keeper of style for both men and protector against lapses of taste to which he felt Strauss was prone. Such concerns led to his temporarily assuming the dominant role in their relationship during the work on *Ariadne*.

In judging the impact and influence of each man upon the other, it is evident that each benefited as much as he gave. Strauss's insistence on clarity and theatrical effectiveness enabled Hofmannsthal to produce librettos of literary quality that at the same time possess wide audience appeal. Similarly, through Hofmannsthal's guidance, Strauss was forced to change the direction of his musical style and to achieve greater artistic success than he had ever attained before.[47] These exhortations, combined with imaginative texts of superior poetic quality, provided the stimulation that brought out the finest in Strauss's artistry in both *Ariadne* and *Die Frau ohne Schatten*.

---

[47] In a letter to Strauss in 1912, Hofmannsthal wrote: "It does me good to think that I, who hardly consider myself as standing even at the extreme periphery of your art, should have found—with that instinct which is the common bond between all creative artists, over the heads, so to speak, of the rest of the crowd—the right thing to do in producing this particular work which literally forced upon you a definite style, only to give you back your freedom more fully on a higher plane." *C.*, 132-33. Later, in 1916, Strauss, in one of his most revealing letters to Hofmannsthal, stated: ". . . thanks to our highly beneficial conversation, I have become so uncertain that I no longer know what's successful and what's bad. And that's a good thing, for at my age one gets all too easily into the rut of mere routine and that is the death of true art. Your *cri-de-coeur* against Wagnerian 'note-spinning' has deeply touched my heart and has thrust open a door to an entirely new landscape where, guided by *Ariadne* and in particular the new Vorspiel, I hope to move forward wholly into the realm of un-Wagnerian emotional and human comic opera. I now see my way clearly before me and am grateful to you for opening my eyes—but now you go ahead and make me the necessary libretti à la *Domino Noir*, *Maurer und Schlosser*, *Wildschütz*, *Zar und Zimmermann*, *La Part du Diable* à la Offenbach—but peopled by human beings à la Hofmannsthal instead of puppets. An amusing, interesting plot, with dialogue, arias, duets, ensembles, or what you will, woven by real composable human beings à la Marschallin, Ochs, Barak. In any form you like! I promise you that I have now definitely stripped off the Wagnerian musical armor." *C.*, 262.

Despite their accomplishments and the success of their works, Hofmannsthal, who never permitted himself any illusions and who always strove for perfection almost impossible to attain, continued to look ahead to the potential fulfillment of their work together in the perfect fusion of forms that he envisioned.

The uniqueness of Hofmannsthal's contribution can be shown by Strauss's works after the poet's death. Despite the collaboration with Stefan Zweig, Clemens Krauss, and Joseph Gregor, Strauss never again found another writer with whom he could work as closely and as successfully. His letter of condolence to Hofmannsthal's widow appropriately summarizes his true opinion and his appreciation of his friend and collaborator:

> This genius, this great poet, this sensitive collaborator, this kind friend, this unique talent! No musician ever found such a helper and supporter.—No one will ever replace him for me or the world of music! Posterity will set up to him a monument that is worthy of him and which he has always possessed in my heart—ineffaceable gratitude in the heart of his truest friend will be the feeling that I shall preserve for him in admiration to the end of my days. (*C.*, 537)

There could be no more fitting conclusion to this chapter, describing these two gifted men, their foibles and aspirations, than the following letter, in which Hofmannsthal expresses the full meaning of this collaboration to him and his hopes for the works that resulted:

> Imbued with the idea, which growing insight has but served to confirm, that the individual can produce nothing of lasting value unless it be linked to tradition, I have learnt far more from what I was able to gather from the features of older, still living works of similar literature than from any "demands of our time" which might seem to be in the air. As a result nothing of what I have done for you possessed at first sight any great appeal to our contemporaries and their spokesmen; what I had created was dismissed as nothing out of the ordinary, my humor was set aside as not humorous, my sentiment as not moving, my imaginations as not imaginative. Everything was precisely not what, in the judgment of these oracles of wisdom and good taste, it should have tried to be. Invariably the essence has been missed, never did the marksman hit the mark—invariably it is the libretto which bears the full brunt of the scorn of all those who are forever longing for beauty, but will die rather than see it. The only person who always recognized whatever there was, who received it with real joy, received it productively and translated it into higher reality, was you.
>
> This is how you have rewarded me, as richly as any artist can reward another—the rest our works did for themselves and I believe that they, not all of them, but nearly all of them with their inseparable fusion of poetry and music, will continue to live for some considerable time and will give pleasure to several generations. (*C.*, 385)

Chapter II

The Genesis of the Opera

The history of *Ariadne auf Naxos* begins without ceremony; indeed, the casual manner with which both author and composer approached the work, an opera to become centrally significant in the overall production of each man, is but the first of many paradoxical elements in its genesis. Strauss and Hofmannsthal met in Dresden in January 1911 to attend the premiere of *Der Rosenkavalier*. In a letter to his father Hofmannsthal mentions their next plan to adapt Molière's *Comtesse d'Escarbagnas* into a small opera which Reinhardt could perform as an interlude in one of his productions. This "little interim work" was intended to express the gratitude of the two artists to Reinhardt for his help with *Der Rosenkavalier*.[1] The poet must have also mentioned, either then or a little later, his idea for an opera tentatively entitled *Das steinerne Herz,* the work that later became *Die Frau ohne Schatten,* for the first mention of these works in the correspondence substantiates Strauss's familiarity with Hofmannsthal's plans: "I am most anxious to hear what you have to tell me about *Steinernes Herz* and the little Molière piece. Don't forget: I've still no work for the summer. Writing symphonies doesn't amuse me at all any longer" (*C.,* 75). This letter, dated 17 March 1911, initiates the protracted labors on what was to become the most arduous collaboration to face the two artists.

Intended specifically as an interim work between major operas, *Ariadne,* for Hofmannsthal, was a practical experiment in solving various problems he had encountered in learning to write a libretto. Despite the impressive success he and Strauss had achieved in *Der*

---

[1] "Ich fühle mich richtig wohl in dieser Luft des Lebens und der Möglichkeiten, die mich hier umgibt und besonders Reinhardts Person und Gegenwart wirkt auf mich immer und unter allen Umständen unendlich angenehm und belebend. Auch Strauss ist wirklich fabelhaft nett gegen mich, und geht auf alles ein, was mir durch den Kopf geht, und da er auch sehr unter dem Charme Reinhardts ist und riesig dankbar für dessen Hilfe in Dresden, so wollen wir zusammen eine ganz kleine Oper nur für Kammermusik machen, die bei Reinhardt als Einlage in ein Schauspiel gespielt werden kann, und zwar werde ich zu diesem Zweck eine Adaptation der charmanten comtesse d' Escarbagnas von Molière machen, eine kleine Zwischenarbeit, die aber sehr wohl dem Reinhardt über eine ganze Saison weghelfen kann. Dies alles bespricht man hier so zufällig beim Essen, ebenso wie die wichtigsten geschäftlichen Dinge, . . . " Quoted in Leonhard M. Fiedler, *Max Reinhardt und Molière* (Salzburg, 1972), pp. 9-10.

Rosenkavalier, Hofmannsthal clearly understood that his text was far from perfect as a libretto. He recognized that as a dramatist his major deficiency was his penchant for symbolism and subtly ambiguous psychological characterizations which acted to the detriment of a clearly outlined, dramatic plot action. It was Strauss who had rescued the libretto of *Der Rosenkavalier* by urging upon Hofmannsthal a more dramatic climax to Act II (*C.,* 36-39). At this stage in their collaboration Hofmannsthal still had not learned how much Strauss the composer could be relied upon to supply dramatic musical climaxes where none apparently occurred in the text.

Just how a poet fashioned words to serve the needs of opera, this hybrid among art forms, remained for the moment an elusive solution for Hofmannsthal, who hoped he could improve his technique by additional practice on a smaller scale. Even though Hofmannsthal eventually came to concede the primacy of music, Strauss himself was always plagued by the question of which was more important in opera, the words or the music. As any opera-goer anticipates, music usually predominates in opera. At will, the composer can obscure the intelligibility of words by permitting the orchestra to cover over the singer's voice. If the words are to be heard, it is the determined effort of the composer that will make this possible, for he must carefully marshall the forces of the orchestra by dynamic control, by reducing the number of instruments, or by scoring with transparent instrumental textures. The whole history of opera can be viewed as a series of fluctuations between word-oriented and music-dominated concepts of the form.

A good librettist must relate a plot with the utmost conciseness of expression, simplicity of action, and economy in both words and dramatic developments. The drama of opera is the province largely of the music, not of the dialogue, although, of course, without an appropriately chosen text the basis of musical drama becomes ineffective. To write an effective libretto, as Hofmannsthal learned, was a totally contrasted task to the writing of a drama, and by his own admission more difficult. Hofmannsthal tried initially to retain his literary autonomy, expecting to create poetic works independently, then to turn them over to the composer for the musical setting. This was the usual procedure composers had followed in writing operas in the past.

Early in their joint relationship, Hofmannsthal stated with a self-assurance based on almost total ignorance of the problems facing him: "Rest assured, my dear Dr. Strauss, that over the whole text I shall rely upon myself alone and not at all on the music; this is indeed the only way in which we can and must collaborate. But your music will then add something most beautiful, something far exceeding, of course, what the actors and the stage-designer can ever give me" (*C.,* 13-14). On another occasion he restated his need to work independently: ". . . never could I attempt to formulate the text from the outset in this lyrical manner which leaves most of the characterization to the composer. To do this would make me lose all certainty of touch and so produce something that falls between two stools. On the other hand, once the comedy is done and has succeeded on the stage, and once each character has gained, so to speak, something of an independent existence, then it is possible to summon up the necessary effrontery to treat it all, if need be, very much *en raccourci*" (*C.*, 15).

That this more or less traditional approach to opera was inadequate despite the sanction of past practice, Hofmannsthal discovered increasingly in their succeeding joint works. Their second opera, *Der Rosenkavalier,* already represented a departure from the premise of working independently. However, *Ariadne auf Naxos* became the first work in which, as Hofmannsthal stated, each man played into the hands of the other. Here they attempted to achieve a unified work of art from beginning to end.

Because of his particular talents as a dramatist, learning to write a libretto was inordinately difficult for Hofmannsthal. The major defects of his early dramas from the standpoint of theater presentation were their predominantly lyrical, symbolic qualities with the stress on psychological or emotional conflicts within the characters. Hofmannsthal wanted to probe the obscure aspects and resources of human existence, including the influence of demonic and metaphysical forces. None of his early dramas has a strong central plot or any appreciable external action; all transpire in an atmosphere of bitter-sweet sadness, the very emotion enabling Richard Strauss to compose his most memorable lyrical passages. Mood was exceedingly important to Hofmannsthal, and as mentioned, his creative process often started with an atmosphere rather than with an idea.

For Hofmannsthal to become a successful librettist demanded a considerable shift in his normal working technique, for the skeletonized plot of a libretto provides little opportunity for detailed psychological characterization. The purpose of the text is to provide a central fable and visual surface action to which the music adds the dimension of depth. The moods and emotions of the characters are primarily expressed by the music, reinforced by gestures rather than by words.

Hofmannsthal greatly feared being misunderstood, and since he saw complexity in life where most others beheld only simplicity, he struggled to state his ideas with ever greater refinement. Here, Strauss, with his more practical, basically unphilosophical nature and surer dramatic instinct, was often able to act as a buffer and to guide Hofmannsthal by concrete suggestions whenever he felt that the poet was becoming too abstract. In particular, Strauss stressed the need in the comedies for more genuine, laugh-provoking humor. However, he never succeeded in bringing Hofmannsthal very far in this direction, for boisterous humor was not Hofmannsthal's strong point. His comedies usually evoke smiles, not laughter. Amusement stems less from overt humor than from wit in which the basic ingredient is irony. Left to himself, it is doubtful that Hofmannsthal could ever have created the robust, vulgar character of Ochs von Lerchenau in *Der Rosenkavalier*.[2]

In the development of Hofmannsthal as a librettist, *Ariadne auf Naxos* commands the position of highest importance. Not until *Ariadne* did the collaboration begin to achieve the harmony of ideas and blend of art forms that Hofmannsthal deemed necessary to take opera into new directions and to achieve new goals.[3]

Ariadne was not, however, a subject that immediately excited Strauss. The plot lacked a strong erotic element to fire his imagination. Nor did nature, another of his favorite subjects for musical setting, play any important role. He was much more eager for Hofmannsthal to begin writing the libretto for the fairytale-fantasy *Die Frau ohne Schatten*, a large work of Romantic coloring as well as considerable dramatic pretensions, that struck Strauss as the ideal text to follow the comic opera *Der Rosenkavalier*. He found the dramatic structure of *Ariadne* "rather thin," although his musical curiosity had already been stimulated by the possibility of writing some "pleasant salon music" for the incidental dances in the Molière play (*C.*, 81).

However, the idea of *Ariadne* and the potentialities of the form had by this time fully captivated Hofmannsthal, who then became unshakable in defense of "this slight interim work." On 15 May 1911 he wrote excitedly to Strauss how the idea of using an adaptation of Molière's *Le Bourgeois gentilhomme* and substituting a new opera for the original's concluding Turkish ceremonial ballet by Jean Baptiste Lully had come to him while he was in Paris. Initially he had been thinking vaguely of using a minor drama by Molière, but seeing this masterpiece again made him realize that it was ideally suited to their purpose. Because the play has no specific climax but ends in a ceremonial ballet, they could easily substitute their own original work without marring the drama.

---

[2] Another important factor in the dramatic effectiveness of *Der Rosenkavalier* is the often overlooked collaboration of Harry Kessler, one of Hofmannsthal's closest friends, who felt that he should have been designated as a co-author of the work. See *Hugo von Hofmannsthal—Harry Graf Kessler: Briefwechsel 1898-1929*, ed. Hilde Burger (Frankfurt am Main, 1968), pp. 296-300.

[3] "This slight interim work will perhaps make it still clearer to me how to construct a dramatic piece as a whole so that the *set numbers* regain more and more their paramount importance, and help me to find the right treatment for that which lies between the numbers, where one cannot fall back upon *secco* recitative and prose. (Or perhaps one can, after all. But how? and how far?) After all, one thing is quite clear: if possibly we are to collaborate further, and again, everything must follow a definite line of development in the matter of style. (Of course I do not mean this as dry theory, but as something one feels, an instinct, an inner compulsion.)" *C.*, 77. For a detailed account of these changes in both libretto and music effected by the mutual suggestions of the two artists in their first four operas, see Jakob Knaus, *Hofmannsthals Weg zur Oper "Die Frau ohne Schatten,"* (Berlin and New York, 1971).

34

Thus, Hofmannsthal's preference for Molière led Richard Strauss to a momentous point in his creative life; for the very nature of the work he agreed to pursue with his librettist demanded a radical alteration in his own musical style. *Ariadne auf Naxos,* as an opera in a baroque setting, could neither be conceived of in musical terms reminiscent of the Viennese waltzes at the heart of *Der Rosenkavalier* nor in the technique of the starkly dissonant and somber score for *Elektra.* The implications of this drastic stylistic metamorphosis could not have been predicted by the composer at this time. Yet, in effect, everything Strauss would write in the future would be the fruit of the new direction embarked upon in *Ariadne.* In one sense, then, the history of German opera in the early twentieth century was profoundly affected by the decision of Hofmannsthal to recreate in an eighteenth-century French baroque setting one of the great classical myths.

The question might appropriately be asked, why Molière?[4] Since Molière was a popular author in Austria and was recognized by Viennese writers as a model comedy writer, the choice of a text by the classic French dramatist was not surprising for Hofmannsthal, who had earned his doctorate in French literature. In 1909 Hofmannsthal's attention was drawn to Molière when Max Reinhardt asked him to translate Molière's one-act play, *Le Mariage forcé,* which he produced under the title *Die Heirat wider Willen* in the Berlin Kammerspiele in October 1911.[5]

The translation of *Le Mariage forcé* in 1909, while not in itself particularly significant, does document Hofmannsthal's continuing involvement with Molière. Doubtless during that period Hofmannsthal read a number of other works by Molière. Molière's play *Monsieur de Pourseaugnac* furnished the basic plot and many precise details of *Der Rosenkavalier,* and the character of Baron Ochs and Molière's Mon-

---

[4] The article by Helmut Wocke, "Hofmannsthal und Molière," *Neuphilologische Zeitschrift,* 2 (1950), 127-37, furnishes details about Hofmannsthal's knowledge of the French language and literature as well as showing in general terms the importance of Molière to Hofmannsthal. Other articles dealing specifically with the Hofmannsthal-Molière relationship are: Victor A. Oswald, Jr., "Hofmannsthal's Collaboration with Molière," *The Germanic Review,* 29 (1954), 18-30; Hilde Burger, "Hofmannsthal's Debt to Molière," *Modern Languages,* 39 (1958), 56-61; Wolfram Mauser, "Hofmannsthal und Molière," *Innsbrucker Beiträge zur Kulturwissenschaft,* Sonderheft 20 (Innsbruck, 1964), 1-16.

[5] Hofmannsthal, for his own reasons, refused to allow his name to be used in connection with this work. The translation was not published independently during his lifetime but is now contained in volume III of *Lustspiele* in the collected works. There are other instances of works appearing anonymously, usually signifying Hofmannsthal's dissatisfaction with the finished product. His free adaptation of Molière's *Les Fâcheux* in 1916 was performed by Reinhardt the same year with no mention of Hofmannsthal as author, although the poet did publish this work in the *Rodauner Nachträge* (1918) under the title *Die Lästigen.* The final adaptation of *Le Bourgeois gentilhomme* as a drama entitled *Der Bürger als Edelmann* was published and performed in 1918 without Hofmannsthal's name but is included in *Lustspiele* III, 67-161. For the most detailed discussion of Hofmannsthal's Molière adaptations for Reinhardt, see Leonhard M. Fiedler, *Max Reinhardt and Molière* (Salzburg, 1972).

sieur de Pourseaugnac display considerable similarity. Moreover, the delineating of Faninal as the socially-ambitious *nouveau riche* bourgeois with more money than intelligence is too similar to be anything but a derivation from Monsieur Jourdain of *Le Bourgeois gentilhomme*.

When Hofmannsthal told Strauss that the idea for *Ariadne auf Naxos* was "distilled from the two theatrical elements of Molière's age: from the mythological opera and from the *maschere,* the dancing and singing comedians" (*C.*, 101), he was perhaps still thinking of Molière's *Comtesse d'Escarbagnas* as the foundation for the new work. As has been mentioned, only in Paris did Hofmannsthal conceive the idea of linking the opera *Ariadne* to *Le Bourgeois gentilhomme* by inserting the opera in place of the *Turkish Ballet.*[6] The opera would become the *divertissement* ostensibly staged by Jourdain for the entertainment of Dorimène, whose favor he was trying to win. With a degree of enthusiasm generally reserved for the solution of difficult artistic problems, Hofmannsthal exclaimed that the style of *Ariadne* was so genuinely of the period in question that "Lully might have set it to music, Callot might have drawn it. At first sight indeed one would hardly be surprised to find this whole *divertissement* printed as part of the text—the original text of our comédie-ballet *Bürger als Edelmann*" (*C.*, 101).

The more Hofmannsthal worked with his adaptation of *Le Bourgeois gentilhomme,*[7] the more optimistic he became about the decision to use

[6] Rudolf Hirsch mentions that such a combination had already been made previously: "Zwar übertrug Hofmannsthal damals die Gräfin von Escarbagnas, kam aber von der Verknüpfung mit dem Divertissement 'Ariadne' ab, suchte nach einem Rahmen eigener Erfindung und entschied sich dann für den 'Bürger als Edelmann,' eine Kombination, die es schon einmal gab, 1772 in Weimar, als die Seylersche Truppe dasselbe Stück von Molière mit einer Ariadne-Oper Anton Schweitzers als Einlage zur Aufführung brachte." "Auf dem Weg zu *Ariadne*," *Neue Zürcher Zeitung* (15 November 1970), p. 49. Hirsch gives no indication that Hofmannsthal was aware of this precedent, and no other evidence has been found to support this idea.

[7] Oswald in "Hofmannsthal's Collaboration with Molière," *The Germanic Review,* 29 (1954), 22-23, has succinctly described the manner in which Hofmannsthal shaped Molière's play to suit his own requirements: "He adapted *Le Bourgeois gentilhomme* to Ariadne almost exclusively by wielding a ruthless pair of shears. Working with Bierling's translation of 1750, he cut the play to the bare bone. His version ends with the banquet scene, with which Act IV of the Molière play begins. Out goes the hilarious Turkish Ceremony; out with the love intrigue; out with Jourdain's daughter, Lucille; out with Cleonte and Covielle, his Figaro. Of the principal figures in the original version, there are left only Jourdain and Mme. Jourdain, Dorante as the elegant trickster, and Dorimène as the unsuspecting goal of Jourdain's attentions. The result is, in effect, a *Caractère* rather than a play. Hofmannsthal added only one song, some additional dialogue and a ballet for the banquet scene, a few passages *en passant* that refer to *Ariadne* as the piece to follow, and a final scene that is, in effect, a spoken prologue to the opera." Wocke further demonstrates how closely Hofmannsthal emulated the Bierling text in style and tone, documenting the fact that he used the actual wording of his model in a number of places. "Hofmannsthal and Molière," *Neuphilologische Zeitschrift,* 2 (1950), 131.

that play as the pedestal for their original opera *Ariadne*. To Strauss's argument that the plot of the drama was weak, Hofmannsthal replied that this apparent weakness actually worked to their advantage: "The play, as you quite rightly say, possesses no real point and this is exactly what serves our purpose—the insertion of our *divertissement*—so well. One could hardly tack an opera onto a play which culminates in an effective and pointed curtain" (*C.*, 81). Hofmannsthal's confidence in his plan stems partly from the support he received from Reinhardt. Before writing to Strauss, he had discussed the project in detail with Reinhardt, who felt that he could fill out the action excellently in performance with amusing ceremonial and other stage business.

Thus, Reinhardt, who kindled Hofmannsthal's interest in Molière at this crucial junction in his career, became in the poet's mind an indispensable participant in the project. Hofmannsthal never abandoned his initial prerequisite that Reinhardt must stage the premiere, even though this insistence led to one of his severest disputes with Strauss. The project in its finished form was dedicated to Reinhardt as a testament of the "respect and gratitude" of Hofmannsthal and Strauss for his excellent work with *Der Rosenkavalier*.

Hofmannsthal reported to Strauss that the opera was to be a "spirited paraphrase of the old heroic style, interspersed with buffo ingredients." He adds the significant suggestion that in this work there will be "ample opportunity . . . for set numbers: duets, trios, quintets, sextets. It would be good if you were to indicate to me points where you mean to place definite *numbers,* and where you intend merely to suggest them as you did repeatedly in *Der Rosenkavalier*. This slight scaffolding for your music will have served its purpose if it gives you an opportunity of expressing yourself on a deliberately reduced scale, half playfully and yet *from the heart*" (*C.*, 80).

This commentary of Hofmannsthal underscores his growing awareness of the role of a librettist as well as the development of his musical understanding. Strauss had urged Hofmannsthal more than once in *Der Rosenkavalier* to give him greater opportunities for lyrical moments in set operatic forms. The composer had gradually outgrown his earlier operatic adventures with "continuous melody" which was largely Wagnerian in spirit and had reached the point where his essentially lyrical genius demanded more occasions for song. It was this particular hurdle for the poet—how to create poetry for set musical pieces within a dramatic framework—that had led to the experimentation of *Ariadne* in the first place. The very nature of the work with its attempt to imitate an historical style made the whole problem considerably simpler, since *Ariadne* would be, on the surface at least, a typically baroque opera consisting mainly of recitatives, arias, and ensembles. Yet, Hofmannsthal could not leave his little opera at that routine level, nor for that matter could Strauss write baroque music. The finished product filled the baroque format with a complexity and richness of poetic and musical ideas beyond anything that either partner could have anticipated in the spring of 1911.

To guide Hofmannsthal in the construction of the text, Strauss on 22 May 1911 outlined the following set musical numbers:

(a) Recitative and aria of Ariadne.
(b) Harlekin's Song.
(c) Great coloratura aria and *andante,* then rondo, theme with variations and all coloratura tricks (if possible with flute *obbligato*) for Zerbinetta, when she speaks of her unfaithful lover (*andante*) and then tries to console Ariadne: rondo with variations (two or three). *A pièce de résistance.*
(d) Male quartet (Harlekin): "Komm mit mir" going over into quintet with Zerbinetta.
(e) Male trio (buffo), after Harlekin and Zerbinetta have disappeared.
(f) Finale (unbroken and continuous), beginning with the Najad's warning. (A hymn-like march theme, add the duet of Ariadne and Zerbinetta, rising towards a climax and concluding with Bacchus's entry.)
Love duet.
Final ensemble. (*C.,* 82)

From the very beginning Strauss had organized the little opera into a succession of set forms linked together by recitative-like passages. Further, he had already decided upon the kind of singers he would need:

Ariadne ....contralto (later to become a soprano)
Bacchus ....lyric tenor
Naiad, Dryad ....ordinary sopranos
Zerbinetta (star role) ....high coloratura soprano (Kurz, Hempel, Tetrazzini)
Harlekin ....light baritone
the other three ....buffo tenor and two basses

For the orchestra, which he felt should approximate the historically-correct size and sound of the baroque atmosphere, he decided upon: "2 violins, viola, cello, double-bass, 1 flute, oboe, clarinet, bassoon, 1 or 2 horns, harpsichord, harp, celeste, harmonium (perhaps also a trumpet and some percussion instruments; 15 to 20 players)" (*C.,* 83). Strauss later increased this original estimate to thirty-six performers of soloistic capabilities and replaced the harpsichord with a piano.

Hofmannsthal was delighted with Strauss's letters showing that *Ariadne* had apparently at last gripped the composer's imagination as intensely as it had his own. As a result he felt they had entered upon a period of much closer collaboration than had been achieved in their earlier efforts. Strauss, on the other hand, while gradually warming to the prospect of composing music for *Ariadne,* had not yet completely overcome his reservations about the theatrical potential of the plot: "*Ariadne* may turn out very pretty. However, as the dramatic framework is rather thin everything will depend on the poetic execution" (*C.*, 81).

Hofmannsthal's answer illustrates clearly the totally disparate dramatic views of the partners. He is quite unconcerned about the apparent lack of dramatic conflict *per se*. Patiently and somewhat pedantically he points out the qualities of his text which in his mind substitute for direct, overt action:

> You call the scenario a little thin—that is quite true. Perhaps a still better way of putting it would be: a little rectilinear, possibly a little too rectilinear. There is no turning, no proper dramatic twist. When I think of heroic opera, whose spirit we mean to invoke, when I think of Gluck, of *Titus* or *Idomeneo*, this kind of thin, rectilinear quality, does not seem to me a fault. The intermingling with the other, the buffo element, possesses moreover great attractions and disposes of monotony. I am flattered that you should promise yourself so much from my poetic diction, but we must not expect too much from the diction *alone*. "There is nothing in the skin but what was bred in the bone," Goethe says somewhere. A framework which *failed to satisfy* your imagination, *if* it were to fail in that, could never be made to appeal to you, and to inspire you, by diction only. Let us never forget this. Even in a dramatic trifle like this it is the peculiar poetic quality of the text which must inspire you to composition, its relative emotional wealth, the contrasts, the structure—and not just the diction, which is to be compared to a nice complexion that only becomes pleasing in a woman with a good figure. Besides, my verse is not really rousing or glowing. Its true quality, which can hardly be questioned, is something else: it is meaningful, concise, rhythmically flexible; never flat, sugary or vague—works as diverse as *Elektra* and *Rosenkavalier* have sufficiently proved that to you. (*C.*, 84)

Although he was not convinced by this argument Strauss postponed any further objections. In truth, the character of the opera that most appealed to him was Zerbinetta. He found it difficult at first to become enthusiastic about the stylized and relatively austere figure of Ariadne, who seemed to be more of an abstraction than a real womanm But he understood and admired the colorful coquette Zerbinetta with her gaiety and zest for life. Under these circumstances, and in the mistaken belief that as before his was the controlling opinion in their joint enterprises, Strauss began to plan a starring role for Zerbinetta. She was to be given the most elaborate and musically-exciting materials of the opera. As he envisioned it, this part with its great artistic demands upon the artist would require one of the great coloratura sopranos of the day for its execution (see Chapter VIII).

Although Strauss's independent plans for Zerbinetta came unexpectedly to Hofmannsthal, after consideration he hesitantly agreed to the idea:

That you intend to place Zerbinetta so distinctly in the musical limelight surprised me at first, but finally quite convinced me. I shall make myself acquainted with the formal requirements of coloratura. . . . Altogether I am somewhat perplexed to find you putting down the names of Kurz, Hempel, Tetrazzini. For even apart from the fact that they are financially out of the question . . . the prospect of working with women who cut such appalling figures on the stage, with prima donnas devoid of all talent as actresses, would literally paralyse my imagination, especially when it comes to a part like Zerbinetta's. If I am to write this with relish, I must think of it as something most subtly contrived both in style and production (this is surely also your idea), something thoroughly à la Reinhardt, and nothing in the slightest way reminiscent of court opera. Preferably an exotic cast, a charming American girl, a Dane or Italian with an exquisite (not an unduly big) voice, a Farrar, Mary Garden, or a young Bellincioni—this is surely your idea too, is it not? (*C.*, 83-84)

The differences of opinion over the character and importance of Zerbinetta remained a problem that was never fully resolved. Their varying interpretations offer another clear example of the opposing artistic personalities of the two men. As for Hofmannsthal's objection to requiring a star singer for the character of Zerbinetta, Strauss replied bluntly on 28 May 1911 without attempting to hide his true opinion about the work as a whole:

Of course a Farrar or young Bellincioni would be best: indeed for Reinhardt's production we shall have to find some such 'budding specialty.' But where? And if, after Reinhardt, the Court Theatres with associated playhouses (such as the Munich Residenztheater) are to take up the piece with any success or profit there must be some star singing parts in it, for the plot as such holds no interest and interesting costumes won't turn the scale either. Personally, I am not particularly interested in the whole thing myself: that was why I asked you to spur your Pegasus a bit, so that the ring of the verses should stimulate me a little. You probably know my predilection for hymns in Schiller's manner and flourishes à la Rückert. Things like that excite me to formal orgies, and these must do the trick where the action itself leaves me cold. Soaring oratory can drug me sufficiently to keep on writing music through a passage of no interest. The interplay of forms: the formal garden must come into its own here. Otherwise we are *d'accord!* (*C.*, 85)

Hofmannsthal was severely offended by Strauss's unenthusiastic attitude toward their newest artistic venture (*C.*, 85-86). This project had thoroughly taken possession of his imagination, and he tried hard to make Strauss see its value by expounding at considerable length the aspects and qualities of the work which he felt were of paramount importance:

During the past few days (before your letter arrived, the effect of which would have been to put me off rather than to encourage me) I have got through the hardest and most attractive part of the work; namely, to settle the psychological motives of the action, to establish, in my own mind, the relations between the various characters and between the different parts of the whole thing—in short, to sketch a detailed outline of the underlying motives which the poet must have before him (rather as you must have to picture your symphony) if he is to be attracted, roused and held by the work. The essence lies in this tracery of ideas, and all the rest (what you so strikingly call the formal garden) is mere trimming, just as in *Rosenkavalier* the period flavour, the ceremonial, dialect, and so on lie merely at the fringe of the essential meaning. Now, this essence of the relationship between Ariadne and Bacchus stands before my mind's eye so finely graded, so delicately animated, psychologically so convincing and at the same time so lyrical, that my execution would have to be wretched indeed if in the end it failed to arouse your interest as much as the lyrics of your songs, or the scenes between the Marschallin and Octavian. An ordinary composer could not have made anything of these, and yet you created something entirely original and wholly enchanting which does full justice to the words. (*C.,* 86)

Unwilling to compromise his newest creation, Hofmannsthal suggested that if Strauss still felt no attraction for *Ariadne* even after this explanation of its qualities, then he should by all means leave it alone. Hofmannsthal would harbor no ill feelings. However, if they were to continue the project, it would have to be done his way. Confronted by Hofmannsthal's emotional defense of his play, which amounted virtually to an ultimatum, Strauss tactfully ceased to object and returned to work. Hofmannsthal accepted Strauss's apologies, and the difference of opinion was laid aside for the moment.

Hofmannsthal's regard for *Ariadne* had changed radically. The work could no longer be regarded as a "trifle" but rather had assumed the position of a major dramatic creation. Not only did he recognize the distinction of *Ariadne* as an experiment in form, but gradually he began to realize the significance of the theme to his evolving poetic development. Strauss, by contrast, although spurring his poet on to complete the libretto, still maintained strong reservations about the work. When the completed manuscript finally reached Garmisch, the composer greeted it in a letter dated 14 July 1911 in terms that make no attempt to conceal his disappointment:

The whole of *Ariadne* is now safely in my hands and I like it well enough: I think there'll be some good use for everything. Only I should have preferred the dialogue between Ariadne and Bacchus to be rather more significant, with livelier emotional *crescendo*. This bit must soar higher, like the end of *Elektra,* sunnier, more Dionysian: harness your Pegasus for a little longer, I can give you another four weeks at least before I've caught up on you with the music. . . . Zerbinetta's rondo is partly sketched out: you see, I'm not idle; but for the conclusion I need something more soaring: "Freude schöner Götterfunken." (*C.*, 92)

Strauss's allusion to Schiller's *Ode to Joy* used by Beethoven in his Ninth Symphony indicates precisely the kind of poetic material he wanted as the basis for his musical climax at the conclusion of *Ariadne*. Such a reference heaped injury upon abuse in Hofmannsthal's mind, believing as he did that the manuscript was equally as good, original, and novel as *Der Rosenkavalier*. To persuade the composer of its quality once and for all, he proceeded to an elaborate interpretation of his text in what is now generally referred to as the *Ariadne* letter (see pp. 124-25).

Strauss apologized politely but without contrition for his disappointing response, rejoicing instead that his indifference had coaxed such a marvelous letter out of Hofmannsthal. He readily admitted that he had not understood the meaning of the text, but the fault, he insisted, was not his alone. He urged Hofmannsthal to compare his letter of interpretation with the text to see if some of the points in his letter could not be put into the libretto itself to make the symbolism clearer.

Hofmannsthal refused even to consider the possibility that his libretto needed clarification. To avoid the issue he delivered a pedantic lecture to Strauss about receptiveness to poetry in general, maintaining that the external conditions of Strauss's life at the time had caused his lack of responsiveness and not the libretto's alleged obscurity:

> To your kind letter, let me first of all reply this: there exists a certain productivity not only of creation, but also of reception. One day I may take up my Goethe or Shakespeare and find that they produce in my imagination a heightened response; another day the essence may be missing, the contact between mind and mind, that luminous, scintillating medium through which alone the image takes full shape in the imagination. Now in so delicate a matter as the production of a poetic text intended for music I must be able to count on this kind of productive receptivity on your part. During the past few weeks you have lacked it. Being alone at home without your wife; a chronic and irritating, though slight, nervous depression which has resulted from your giving up cigarette smoking—each one of these causes would be quite enough by itself to make this negative condition understandable; how much more, then, the two coming together. I knew of it, or felt it, when I sent you the *Ariadne* sheets. I felt we were not in contact when you failed to inform me, of your own accord, that you had returned to your home and were impatient to have the text. Two years ago, when I sent you the first fragments of *Rosenkavalier*, your frame of mind was just the opposite; at that time the welcome you gave to what I had done exceeded my expectation and I was well aware how much of this delight was due to your own receptive productivity.

That this time I was obliged to "rub in" the merits of a really successful achievement is for me a matter of momentary disappointment; but it cannot seriously depress me, just as I did not at-
tach undue and exaggerated importance to your enthusiasm on the
former occasion. (*C.*, 97)

Richard Strauss surely had sufficient provocation in these comments
for a healthy explosion. Yet one of the unique aspects of the
collaboration of Strauss and Hofmannsthal was how fully the composer
understood the poet and was willing to make allowances for his temperament. Even though Strauss could easily have clarified his grounds
for disappointment in the *Ariadne* libretto, he valued too highly the artistry of Hofmannsthal, whose particular genius created some of the
most superb poetic imagery any composer has ever had an opportunity
to set to music. Despite his own feelings to the contrary Strauss decided
to defer to Hofmannsthal's confidence in the theatrical effectiveness of
his text. At this point in their collaboration Hofmannsthal took over the
leading role which he was not to relinquish again until after *Die Frau
ohne Schatten*.

Hofmannsthal, for his part, was reconciled to misunderstanding by the
public and critics from the beginning, for as he commented:

Let me now say something about the point which agitates you at the
moment, about the question of understanding and not-understand-
ing, about your own original non-understanding, about the probable
incomprehension of the public, the certain incomprehension of the
critics. The pure poetic content of a work of art, the real meaning it
contains is never understood at first. What is understood is only
that which needs no understanding, the obvious, plain anecdote:
Tosca, Madame Butterfly and such like. Anything more subtle,
anything that really matters, remains unrecognized, *invariably.* May
I remind you of the book Wagner wrote in 1851 [*Oper und Drama*]
where he describes (what is almost inconceivable to us today) how
works so simple, and constructed with such unfailing stage sense, as
Lohengrin and *Tannhäuser* failed to be understood—not the music,
but the poetic texts. His audience lacked the slightest inkling of the
broad and simple symbolism, based though it is on popular fairy
tales, and they actually ask themselves: "What is all this about?";
they thought the action of the characters absurd and incomprehensible. And what about my own straightforward libretto
for *Rosenkavalier:* is that understood—or rather, is it understood
by the critics? Everyone who does understand it has discovered its
charm, yet the critics have never seen any charm in it. And is it not
true that, bogged down in irrelevancies—the frequent occurrence of
the word "blood" and the violent, vehement diction—less than one
tenth of the critics recognize or apprehend even today the true basic
theme of the "famous Elektra"? No, my dear friend, the essence of
poetic meaning comes to be understood only gradually, very
gradually; this understanding emanates from a very few people who

are in close touch with the world of poetry, and it takes decades to spread.

But it is equally true that the poet's text must possess yet another attraction, through which it can effectively reach even the non-comprehending majority, and such attraction lies in the fact that it exhibits something which is neither insubstantial nor commonplace. This is what made *Elektra* and *Rosenkavalier* effective. In the case of *Ariadne* the attractive style of this supporting opera, the bizarre mixture of the heroic with buffo elements, the gracefully rhymed verses, the set numbers, the playful, puppet-show look of the whole piece, all this gives the audience for the time being something to grab and suck like a child. I have, what is more, been at pains to treat the main action in such manner that it is something thoroughly familiar to the average spectator: Ariadne, deserted by Theseus, consoled by Bacchus, *Ariadne auf Naxos* is in fact, like *Amor and Psyche,* something everybody can picture to himself, even if it be only as a plaster of Paris ornament on the mantelpiece. As for the symbolic aspect, the juxtaposition of the woman who loves only once and the woman who gives herself to many, this is placed so very much in the centre of the action, and is treated as so simple and so clear-cut an antithesis, which may be heightened still further by an equally clear-cut musical contrast, that we may hope at least to avoid utter incomprehension by the audience (and it is on them, and not on the critics, that our success depends). (*C.,* 98-99)

Although the tone of this letter exudes confidence, in reality Hofmannsthal's self-assurance had been somewhat weakened by Strauss's arguments. He decided to follow his partner's suggestions at least partially, as is revealed in his changed conception of the transitional scene connecting the play to the opera. Before their discussion Hofmannsthal had considered this scene as follows:

The transition to the actual opera takes place on the open stage; I shall lead up to it by a short scene in prose in which Dancing Master and Composer—who are responsible for arranging this opera performance at Jourdain's house—talk about the public, critics, etc. During this conversation the stage is being set for the opera in the big hall; Harlekin and Ariadne are making up, others are bustling to and fro half dressed for the performance. The lights are being lit, the musicians are tuning their instruments, Zerbinetta tries a few roulades, Jourdain and his guests appear and take their seats in the fauteuils—and at this point, I must say, a little overture seems to me stylistically indispensable; a little symphony of the old kind which brings together the main themes from the opera would, I feel, be charming. (*C.,* 90)

The change in outlook is shown when, a month later, to insure that the audience would understand the libretto, the poet planned to make the transitional scene into a short prose interlude that would serve to introduce the opera and underscore for the audience the central idea:

44

I have, furthermore, another vehicle to bring home to people this central idea; I mean the prose scene which is to precede the opera. In this scene the stage is being set, the singers are about to make up, the orchestra tunes its instruments. Composer and Dancing Master are on the stage. The Composer, we are told, is to conduct a short heroic opera: *Ariadne auf Naxos;* Ariadne is to bewail her lot and to long for death until Bacchus appears and carries her off. After the opera, a light-hearted afterpiece is planned for the Italian comedians (Zerbinetta and her companions) who are to dance and sing under the direction of the Dancing Master. That is how the programme reads. And now Jourdain suddenly sends his footman with the message that he wishes the two pieces to be performed *simultaneously,* that he has no desire to see Ariadne on a deserted island; the island is on the contrary to be peopled by the Italian players who are to entertain Ariadne with their capers. In short Jourdain asks them to arrange one show out of the two operas. Consternation. The Composer is furious, the Dancing Master tries to soothe him. Finally they summon the clever soubrette (Zerbinetta); they tell her the plot of the heroic opera, explain to her the character of Ariadne, and set her the task of working herself and her companions as best she may into this opera as an intermezzo, without causing undue disturbance. Zerbinetta at once grasps the salient point: to her way of thinking a character like Ariadne must be either a hypocrite or a fool, and she promises to intervene in the action to the best of her ability, but with discretion. This offers us the opportunity of stating quite plainly, under cover of a joke, the symbolic meaning of the antithesis between the two women. Does this appeal to you? (*C.,* 99)

For the first time Strauss became genuinely interested in the project. Relishing the idea of a prose scene preceding the opera, he contributed a number of suggestions for material to be included. By the end of his letter his enthusiasm had grown to such an extent that he urged the poet to make the transitional scene the core of the piece:

In your letter you moot the brilliant idea of preparing the ground for *Ariadne* by a big scene which would explain and motivate the whole action. That's excellent. The best thing would be if your last letter to me could be read out. The Composer and the Dancing Master are anyway two Molière figures which could be enormously expanded. They are well conceived, but only you can make them topical.

Give your sense of humour its head, drop in a few malicious remarks about the "composer"—that sort of thing always amuses the audience and every piece of self-persiflage takes the wind out the critics' sails. Molière's piece is a little silly, but it can become a hit provided you develop the two parts of Composer and Dancing Master in such a way that everything is said that can be said today about the relationship of public, critics and artist. It could become a companion piece to *Meistersinger:* fifty years after. Pack into it everything that's on your chest, you'll never get a better opportunity! Is there enough malice in you? If not, take a collaborator; such things are usually best done by two people. . . .

The only purpose of this letter is to confirm you definitely in your intention: the scene preceding the opera must become the core of the piece. Zerbinetta might have an affair with the Composer, so long as he is not too close a portrait of me. (*C.,* 100-101)

When Strauss inquired about a possible date for the *Ariadne* premiere a new crisis arose, again threatening the continuation of the collaboration. He learned that Reinhardt, because of overwork, felt unable to direct *Ariadne* during the 1911 season. However Hofmannsthal clung adamantly to his view that no one else would be permitted to stage the premiere, even if it meant a delay of a year. Settling this difference led to some of the sharpest exchanges of the entire correspondence, with Hofmannsthal fighting for the integrity of their work and Strauss anxious to set the opera before audiences. To Hofmannsthal the idea of a premiere of the work without Reinhardt was simply unthinkable: "About the *Ariadne*-Reinhardt question, I would like to say only this today: you know I am not obstreperous, but wild horses will not get me to carry out this adaptation of Molière and the introductory scene, unless Reinhardt is to produce it; I say this not for sentimental reasons, but because the whole bizarre piece of work can only exist in the special atmosphere of Reinhardt's theatre for which it is designed" (*C.,* 105).

Hofmannsthal's alarm at the mere thought of performing *Ariadne* without Reinhardt compelled him to send a second letter, emphasizing that a split on this issue could jeopardize their entire future collaboration. He appealed to Strauss's better nature, invoking the higher powers which had brought them together: ". . . remember how much is at stake between the two of us who have been brought together by something higher, perhaps, than mere accident; between the two of us who are meant to derive joy from each other and who must do all in our power not to be deflected from this purpose—a danger which seems to threaten us at this critical juncture" (*C.,* 106).

Hofmannsthal contended that since honoring Reinhardt had been one of the original reasons for undertaking the work, the director would be justifiably offended if they took *Ariadne* away from him. He did not leave Strauss in doubt about what such a step could mean to Hofmannsthal himself:

. . . I must tell you that you would be doing a grave injustice to the work *and to me* if, without absolute and compelling necessity (such as cannot emerge for several months), you were to take away the original première, which is decisive for the impact of this work, from the one theatre for which, and for the special qualities of which, I have devised and executed it in every detail. This "opera," with its subtle stylistic make-up, with its profound meaning hidden beneath the playful action, framed as it is by the Molière piece, a

46

fact itself symbolic in intention (for Jourdain stands for the public), is a conception of the most fragile, the most incommensurable kind. It is one of my most personal works and one I cherish most highly. It is conceived as a whole composed of several parts, and can only exist, or come into being, where a theatrical genius of a superior order knows how to weld the parts together; were it to fall into the hands of some colourless routine producer, then even the man in charge of the production himself would not feel, or even suspect, the unity of the piece as a whole—so how could there be the remotest chance of projecting it into the minds of the audience? . . . Here I must dig my heels in, or show myself as an amateurish bungler and worse. (C., 106-107)

Apparently Strauss had entertained the possibility of the world premiere of *Ariadne* at the Königliches Opernhaus, where *Der Rosenkavalier* received its Berlin premiere (14 November 1911), possibly in the expectation of capitalizing on the success and publicity of the latter work. However Hofmannsthal, who had attended the Berlin performance of *Der Rosenkavalier,* was convinced that *Ariadne* would be destroyed in the hands of the Schauspielhaus personnel who would be responsible for the Molière play:

> . . . I have spoken kindly to you and to other people about that which is praiseworthy in the *Rosenkavalier* production; but if I stop to think, and tell myself quite soberly how this production is pervaded with the most thick-skulled barrack-room spirit, how drill-sergeant thoroughness and vast expense of money literally trample out all subtle charm, blur all contrasts and flatten all emphasis to drab monotony—if I add to this the insult of the crude blue curtain on to which a painter, practised in lavatory decoration, has daubed figures *from the work itself*—this, translated into your sphere, is like a player-piano strumming the principal passages of your music in the theatre bar or in the cloak-room while people are taking off their coats and hats—if on top of all this I tell myself that, whereas the Berlin Opera at least enjoys an occasional gust of cosmopolitan air, the Schauspielhaus is the embodiment of the dreariest mediocrity and provincialism, then I must inform you that I am incapable of stooping so low as to entrust to such hands a work of extreme delicacy and subtlety like this; that I would therefore *in no circumstances* give my consent to a première with Hülsen [the director of the Schauspielhaus]. (C., 107)

Hofmannsthal continues this peroration with some of his most embittered words, showing that in his mind this was a fundamental issue which, unless resolved to his satisfaction—that is, according to his ideas—would affect their entire possible future collaboration. Despite his recognition of the musician as the more important partner in their collaboration, Hofmannsthal was fully aware of his value to Strauss as a librettist. He had great self-respect and was completely conscious of his personal dignity as a poet of rank who had agreed to write librettos:

47

I know—and I say this with all humility towards the imperishable masterpieces of our literature—I know the worth of my work; I know that for many generations past no distinguished poet of the rank with which I may credit myself amongst the living, has dedicated himself willingly and devotedly to the task of working for a musician. So long as the value of this collaboration is recognized by almost everyone whose judgment matters to me, and while it is so singularly welcomed by the public at large, I can afford to treat with contempt a few hundred pen-pushers up in arms against me for some reason or other; their shafts cannot touch me, or touch me only where I am proof to them.

But that in this case *you* should find it possible to disregard everything that matters to me, to disregard all that the realization of this work of my imagination means to me, to force me into a theatre where I could not appear without a sense of debasement, this *does* touch me; the mere idea that you on your part should entertain such a possibility does hurt me, and hurts me more than just momentarily. Here I find myself misunderstood and injured by you at the most vulnerable point in our relationship as artists. How, if you have so little regard for the unusual nature of this work beyond your own share in it—I mean for the poetry-cum-music aspect, which you must after all bring to fusion if our collaboration is to produce anything of value—how in such circumstances am I to devote myself with joy to the task of working out another project of a similar kind? How am I to write a single line of *Die Frau ohne Schatten* if, over this affair, you not only upset my own relations with Max Reinhardt—and who, in the feverish world of the theatre, would ever get over a disappointment like that?—but face me with the certain prospect of having to abandon altogether every hope of Reinhardt's assistance in the preparation of this future work, subtle and allergic to all routine as it is bound to be, and so of having to do without the very help I need above all else? (*C.*, 108)

His emotional defense of artistic principle carried him to the point of threatening to give up writing librettos. He mentions that the operas have not brought him either any particularly great financial gain or artistic prestige. While these arguments are at least relevant to the point at issue, he also dredges up from the past the old hurt over Strauss's failure to wax enthusiastic over the *Ariadne* libretto, which denied him the kind of personal pleasure he so fully enjoyed during the *Rosenkavalier* collaboration. Although he had interrupted his own drama *Jedermann* in order to complete *Ariadne* for Strauss, who had requested a text to work on, his cooperation was not appreciated.

His main point remains the same as always, his conviction that only Reinhardt could bring about the requisite perfect initial performance of *Ariadne*. Hofmannsthal regarded Reinhardt, a fellow Austrian, as a kindred spirit who, like himself but through his own media, strove to convey the mysterious and miraculous elements of life. Hofmannsthal's respectful attitude toward Reinhardt bordered on hero worship, and he unquestionably held him in a degree of esteem that he accorded few other men.[8]

Hofmannsthal's sense of urgency for the fullest perfection in all areas of the production reflected his awareness of the complexity as well as the fragility of *Ariadne*. Since the opera lacks a strong plot to carry the meaning, everything depended on a proper execution to create the mood and atmosphere of the miracle of transformation. It would not be sufficient merely to have the characters state what has happened, as they do of course, but, as will be shown in the interpretation later, the audience must actually feel the change in Ariadne. To achieve this goal, every means of stagecraft must contribute. Hofmannsthal had taken on the responsibility for everything connected with the stage sets, including style and design as well as the dances, indicating how important this facet of the production was to him. With his stress on the visual aspects of the production in addition to the previous dimensions of libretto and music, Hofmannsthal emphasized its conception as *Gesamtkunstwerk*. To accomplish this overall unity Reinhardt, the master of baroque presentations, was indispensable in Hofmannsthal's view (*C.,* 112).

Under this barrage of relevant and irrelevant arguments, Strauss capitulated and agreed to postpone the premiere for a year. The intimate court theater at Dresden was to be the place and Reinhardt the director. Hofmannsthal relied on Reinhardt to create a performance which would serve as a model and set the standard for subsequent productions by other directors. Such idealistic hopes for the premiere failed to impress the more practical Strauss. While he grudgingly agreed to all of Hofmannsthal's conditions for the sake of harmony, he was not for a moment convinced that the Molière play as directed by Reinhardt would determine the outcome of the premiere: ". . . believe me, it's the end that will determine its success, i.e., the opera by Hofmannsthal-Strauss and not the Molière-Reinhardt" (*C.,* 113).

Further complications arose and had to be settled before the location of the premiere of *Ariadne* was finally arranged. Strauss learned that the little theater in Dresden would be unavailable, and on 2 January 1912 he adamantly opposed the use of the large opera house, fearing that an inferior group of performers would be forced upon them by the director. On his own initiative he inquired whether the management of the newly-constructed Court Theater of Stuttgart would be interested in the world premiere, provided they agreed to a cast chosen by Hofmannsthal, Reinhardt, and himself. Hofmannsthal was again discouraged by

[8] Hofmannsthal's great personal regard for Reinhardt, an important chapter in his life that remains to be fully investigated, goes beyond the scope of the present study. The poet's respect and admiration for the director can be seen in the several essays dedicated to Reinhardt: "Das Reinhardtsche Theater" (1918) in *Prosa* III, 429-35; the *Vorrede* to the book *Reinhardt und seine Bühne,* ed. Ernst Stern and Heinz Herald (Berlin, 1920); "Reinhardt as an International Force," *Max Reinhardt,* ed. O. M. Sayler (New York, 1924).

this newest change in plans and gloomily predicted that Reinhardt would not come. He was especially downcast at the thought that all of their work would have been undertaken for two performances in a theater with only eight hundred seats (*C.,* 115-16).

Contrary to Hofmannsthal's fears, however, Reinhardt declared himself amenable to the idea of Stuttgart and agreed to direct the premiere there with his own cast to be brought in from Berlin. The enterprising Strauss managed to line up, tentatively, a brilliant cast of singers, including Frieda Hempel and Emmy Destinn. He assured Hofmannsthal: "This is going to be something that, Bayreuth apart, has never been seen before, and certainly not at a Court theatre." After the Stuttgart performances in mid-October, he felt that Dresden could follow suit in November "with an ordinary performance by its 'own efforts.'" Both men were now satisfied that *Ariadne auf Naxos* would be given the ideal premiere, and the issue was closed.

At this point Hofmannsthal suddenly began to waver in his earlier conviction that the meaning of *Ariadne* was self-evident. He suggested to Strauss the desirability of publishing *Ariadne* prior to the premiere either in the leading Viennese newspaper, the *Neue Freie Presse,* or in the literary journal, *Neue Rundschau,* feeling that such pre-publication would be of the greatest benefit to the audience's understanding of the opera. He hoped to gain a personal advantage as well, for advance acquaintance with his text would improve his chances for comprehension by the reviewers, especially since the performance would be judged exclusively by music critics. Whereas Hofmannsthal had rejected Strauss's earlier suggestion that he have some of his literary friends write on *Ariadne,* he now considered asking the writer and scholar Oscar Bie to publish an explanatory article on *Ariadne* prior to the performance.

Strauss, happy to see his temperamental partner come around at last to his way of thinking, endorsed the idea wholeheartedly. The complete text of *Ariadne* with a brief introduction by Hofmannsthal was published in the *Neue Freie Presse* on 26 May 1912. Although neither Bie nor any of his other friends wrote on *Ariadne* at this time, Hofmannsthal himself published an additional essay entitled *Ariadne und Molière* in the Stuttgart *Neues Tageblatt* (12 October 1912).

Once the details surrounding the premiere, the pre-publication of the text, and the explanatory essay had been worked out satisfactorily, the two men worked at readying the play and opera for presentation. Hofmannsthal was plagued mostly by the attempt to expand the transition scene between the Molière play and the opera proper. The scene was planned without music. While the actors make up for the opera, they converse about Jourdain's order to combine *opera seria* and *opera buffa* and also about the meaning of the opera. Catching the proper tone and style for this interlude was not an easy task, as Hofmannsthal reported, for it ". . . ought to be concise and colourful, discreet and at the same time gay, must not jar with the Molière and must yet contain the whole key to Ariadne: a hellish chess-problem. Still I think it has turned out well" (*C.*, 125). Strauss hoped that Hofmannsthal would exploit this opportunity to inject some much-needed humor into the piece: ". . . do, please, let off rockets of malice and satire and every kind of self-persiflage" (*C.*, 123). Within limits, Hofmannsthal did try to follow this advice.

With Reinhardt signed to direct the work and Hofmannsthal pacified, Strauss suddenly raised his own doubts about the director as well as about Ernst Stern, the stage designer to whom Hofmannsthal wished to entrust the premiere. The reason Strauss had originally attempted to divert the first performances away from Reinhardt's influence can easily be understood from Strauss's inquiry to his collaborator:

> Are you going to be in Stuttgart with Reinhardt and Stern about the middle of May, so that you can discuss the last and most important points on the spot? For God's sake see to it that Stern doesn't produce any trashy effects. The last Reinhardt productions of *Turandot* and *Dandin* are to me inspired trash: inspired, but nevertheless trash. I'm still in favour of Roller who is a much more solid and thorough worker. With Stern everything looks *dashed off quickly for cheapness.* Please keep at him. I'm holding you responsible for seeing that it turns out *very* beautiful. Go on prodding Stern and make sure that everything is ready before July so we don't have the usual Reinhardt rush at the last moment. I absolutely detest this business of putting the final touches on a theatrical production at the dress rehearsal. (*C.*, 123-24)

Suddenly the roles of the two men seem to have been reversed. The composer now appears the protector of artistic standards he fears will be lost in the production. Clearly Strauss did not share his colleague's high opinion of Reinhardt, and he seriously doubted whether this director, despite his reputation, possessed the genius necessary to solve the production problems of *Ariadne auf Naxos.* True to form, Hofmannsthal defended his choices, rationalizing to excuse Stern's previous artistic failures:

> If a highly gifted man is being driven and pressed, day in, day out, to improvise, and to produce cheap work, the result is bound to be trash of a sort. He longs to work for us with care, solidity and splendour. . . . I perfectly understand your dislike of work done, à la Reinhardt, only just in time for the première—but the reverse, not giving people enough time from the outset, is equally mad. Stern is faced here with an infinitely subtle and complicated task. His designs and colours must, in a spirited, half-historical, half-anachronistic manner, balance against each other two different conceptions of the world—a task which is quite beyond the solid, but altogether unimaginative Roller. (*C.*, 126)

The first rehearsals in Stuttgart in May were successful although, curiously, Hofmannsthal found it impossible to attend them personally, unexpectedly deciding that he needed a vacation in Italy at that very moment. Strauss, however, who was present, found them enjoyable and predicted: "I believe the score is going to signpost a new road for comic opera, for those who are capable. For with this chamber music style the white sheep will quite clearly be divided from the black." And with typical Straussian élan: "My score is a real masterpiece of a score: you won't find another one like it in a hurry" (*C.*, 132).

Despite Hofmannsthal's earlier insistence that he assume full responsibility for the staging, Strauss continued to stress his concern over various phases of the presentation. He was especially worried that if the play led into the opera without a curtain, the transition scene and possibly the opera itself would have to be played too far back on the stage.

More serious and at the heart of the composer's anxiety about *Ariadne's* chance of success was the lingering fear that the public and critics would not understand Hofmannsthal's ambiguous symbolism. In his opinion the short introduction to the published version in the *Neue Freie Presse* did not by any means clarify the play sufficiently. He particularly missed in it Hofmannsthal's detailed explanation of the *Ariadne* problem which the poet "had supplied so beautifully" in his celebrated Ariadne letter. He pleaded with Hofmannsthal to correct the omission by writing an essay for the *Almanach für die musikalische Welt*. The latter reacted rather testily to the suggestion:

> I talked today on the telephone to Dr. Leopold Schmidt and promised him something of the kind for his *Almanach*—just as I made a similar promise some months ago to M. Ecorcheville for his *Revue Musicale S. I. M.* to pacify the French musical world. You see I am glad to do what I can. But that introduction in the *Neue Freie Presse* was never intended to do more than enable me to speak authentically about the ticklish question of the link with Molière; what could have given you the idea that I ought there to have commented, and given explanations, about *Ariadne*? Everything I was obliged to tell you in that letter of mine is now, in the transition scene, being driven into the heads of the audience with a sledgehammer, point for point. Nor can anyone fail to understand it except conceivably those who, like the Frenchman whose twaddle you have sent me, distort everything out of obvious malice, and make it appear as if we meant merely to raise a laugh. Anyway, as I have said, I shall comment upon myself once again, as a work of supererogation, in the *Almanach;* only let us make sure that the daily papers reprint as much of it as possible, so that it gets known. (*C.*, 135)

Despite Hofmannsthal's belief that the transitional prose scene explained the opera completely, Strauss single-mindedly persisted in his own view:

You are mistaken if you believe that everything's already been said adequately in that scene you've added. Only for the very subtle! But as for the general public, and particularly those gentry of the press, you just can't pile it on too thick or stick it too close under their noses. But it must be done in advance; before those first stupid slogans gain ground from which a man might suffer for the next fifty years. Anticipate all criticism and instruct them in detail just what they've got to think and to feel, and how they've got to take the whole thing. I consider this preliminary job every bit as important as the work itself. And you write so splendidly: so please do make the effort and use the letter you wrote me at the time. It was quite excellent. (*C.*, 136-37)

Hofmannsthal finally complied with Strauss's wishes, and his original *Ariadne* letter of 28 July 1911 was published in a slightly abridged version in the Berlin journal, *Almanach für die musikalische Welt,* in August 1912. For the benefit of French audiences and to anticipate some of the criticism bound to result from abridging Molière, a sacrosanct French national treasure, the essay "Ce que nous avons voulu en écrivant *Ariadne à Naxos*" was written for the Parisian *Revue Musical S. I. M.* in 1912.

Strauss announced that *Ariadne* was finished on 21 August 1912. The only detail remaining, aside from a number of small changes, was the arrangement for the celebration banquet following the performance. Even this routine procedure ran aground with Hofmannsthal who, revealing the snobbish side of his character, balked at rubbing shoulders with the philistines. He protested angrily to Strauss because of a newspaper story stating that he would attend the banquet

> . . . at which anyone [sic!] can participate on payment of ten marks. This is really beyond any joke! I hope you can dispose of it by an energetic protest in Stuttgart, and would be much obliged. For my part I refuse from the outset to spend an evening, which I hope to hold precious in my memory, rubbing elbows with newspaper-hacks and Stuttgart philistines who will slap you and me on the back over a glass of champagne. The seating order, I shouldn't be surprised, to be drawn up by one of the clerks of the theatre management, and my wife to sit between Mr. D. and a theatre director from Zwickau! No, thank you! I am a very liberal-minded person, but I do draw the line when it come to social intercourse. So I beg of you to redeem the situation by word of mouth. (*C.*, 145)

Strauss obligingly redeemed himself by arranging for separate tables for Hofmannsthal and his friends. He continued to write enthusiastically about the successful rehearsals and found the pieces "tremendously effective" and the Molière "unspeakably funny." Although unintended, Hofmannsthal's reply strikes a note of self-satisfaction bordering on condescension: "I am immensely pleased to hear that the enormously poetical and dramatic qualities of the Molière have now been brought home to you, and with them also the real significance of this combination of a work not mine with my own" (*C.*, 146).

Chapter III

The Premiere in Stuttgart

The world premiere of *Ariadne auf Naxos,* which together with Hofmannsthal's German adaptation of Molière's *Le Bourgeois gentilhomme* comprised one of the most unusual and hybrid productions in opera history, took place in the Stuttgart Hoftheater, Kleines Haus, on 25 October 1912, as the climax to an entire week of Strauss opera performances.[1] The majority of the critics were confused by the juxtaposition of styles and art forms, beginning with a sharply cut version of Molière's most famous play, interlarded with Strauss's incidental music, followed by a short transitional prose scene, and finally concluding with an opera containing a remarkable amalgamation of musical elements—which to that first-night audience must have seemed far removed from the previous style of Richard Strauss. Not surprisingly, the critics, confronted by such an unexpected novelty when anticipating perhaps another opera like *Der Rosenkavalier,* ranged in their reviews from lukewarm praise to outright condemnation. Although frustration born of incomprehension no doubt accounted for some of the more extreme denunciations, a prominent anti-Strauss and anti-Hofmannsthal press, which had been waiting for just such an opportunity to attack the composer and the poet, also played a role.

Hofmannsthal, speaking from personal experience, had early voiced his fears to Strauss about the long-term adverse effects of bad first-press notices, and events unfortunately proved him right. Despite the publication prior to the premiere of the text as well as of his explanatory letter to Strauss,[2] the work was not understood. The depreciatory evaluations of *Ariadne* contained in the majority of the first reviews set the critical tone for years to come. As late as 1921, Paul Bekker repeated what remained the typical view of *Ariadne;* namely, that it was too aesthetic in nature and not theatrical enough.[3] This line of interpretation followed what was until recently a major miscon-

---

[1] See K. Grunsky, "Von der Stuttgarter Strausswoche," *Blätter für Haus- und Kirchenmusik,* 17 (1912), 45-46.

[2] According to a letter from Bodenhausen to Hofmannsthal, the letter to Strauss was not understood: "Dein Brief an Strauss wird vielfach mißverstanden. Aber das ist das Los und Schicksal alles Lebendigen." *Briefe der Freundschaft* (Berlin, 1953), p. 142.

[3] Paul Bekker, *Kritische Zeitbilder* (Berlin, 1921), p. 95.

ception about Hofmannsthal as an aesthete, a pejorative label erroneously affixed to him early in his writing career.

The mixed but mainly negative critical reception cannot be attributed solely to the work itself, however, for despite Hofmannsthal's careful planning and his hope for a model production under Reinhardt's direction, the ideal first performance did not materialize. Hampered from its very inception by misunderstandings, the bad luck that seemed to pursue *Ariadne* perpetuated itself, upsetting rehearsals through a combination of apparently malicious forces. Strauss, who helped supervise the arrangements as well as begin to rehearse the orchestra in Stuttgart in June, expressed initial satisfaction with the way matters were progressing in a letter to his wife dated 6 June 1912.[4] But his early optimism was not fully justified, and he later recorded in good-humored fashion some of the numerous difficulties surrounding the dress rehearsal.[5]

Reinhardt's Berlin ensemble was responsible for the performance of Molière's play, while Strauss selected the thirty-six soloists for the orchestra as well as the singers for the operatic cast. Reinhardt had agreed to bring his troupe to Stuttgart only for the premiere performances on 25, 26, and 27 October 1912, which were to serve as models of staging and interpretation for all other directors and performers to emulate. The play was then to be turned over to the regular dramatic and operatic casts of Stuttgart. This arrangement aroused resentment and jealousy among the Stuttgart repertory players who, although they were responsible for all of the preliminary rehearsals before the arrival of the guest artists, were only to participate after the first performances as a second cast. In what seems to be an incongruous state of affairs, Reinhardt, on whom so much was staked, apparently had sent his group ahead with Ernst Stern, the stage and costume designer, in charge. When

---

[4] Richard Strauss, *Eine Welt in Briefen* (Tutzing, 1967), pp. 198-99: "Regie, Chöre tadellos und sehr schöne Solokräfte. Der Tenor Erb hat nicht den letzten Reiz an stimmlichem Glanz in der Höhe, aber die Stimme ist hoch und sehr angenehm, und er ist ein ausgezeichneter Darsteller und in der Erscheinung wie angegossen dem jugendlichen Bacchus. Ich werde ihn also nehmen. Im Orchester, das sehr tüchtig, werde ich mir wahrscheinlich die ersten Berliner Bläser ausbitten, trotzdem die hiesigen auch genügen würden. Aber es soll das alles prima sein. Die gestrigen ersten Orchesterproben von *Ariadne* abends von 7-9 Uhr waren mir die große Genugtuung. Es klingt prachtvoll, schöner als alles, was ich bisher gemacht habe. Ein ganz neuer Stil und neue Klangwolken. Also alles sehr erfreulich. Alle kommen einem hier, besonders Schillings und Gerhäuser, mit so großem Verständnis für die neuen Aufgaben entgegen, daß ich mich jeder Stunde freue, daß ich mich nicht wieder in dem dämlichen, altmodischen Dresden herumzuärgern habe. Hier gilt mein Wille als Befehl: da muß ich nicht immer katzebuckeln, wenn ich meine einfachsten künstlerischen Forderungen verwirklichen will. Welch ein Unterschied hier in der gestrigen *Feuersnotprobe* gegen die vor 3 Jahren in Dresden, wo der dortige Regisseur keine Ahnung hatte und Schuch jedes Tempo besser wußte als der Komponist. Nun, hier wird's famos . . . Jedenfalls bin ich selig, daß mir *Ariadne* so gut gelungen ist. Es klingt über meine kühnsten Erwartungen."

[5] Richard Strauss, *Recollections and Reflections* (London, 1953), pp. 161-64.

he arrived to assume the direction personally is unknown.[6] However, apparently no great number of rehearsals were held with Reinhardt present in Stuttgart. Since Reinhardt's rehearsals normally were chaotic affairs right up to opening night, he was presumably not daunted by the last-moment confusion. But Strauss, who liked orderly arrangements, grew nervous, and he admitted that he apparently offended the producer Berhäuser when he answered one of the latter's questions with Hofmannsthal's stock reply: "Reinhardt will settle all that."[7]

Strauss attributed the complications at the dress rehearsal to "forces of destiny." Whatever the causes, all witnesses present at the occasion agreed that it did not come off well. Strauss himself remarked that everything was turned upside down: "The painter, Stern, acted as stage manager, although he had no idea of stage managing—singers made their entrances either too late or at the wrong time, the sets were all wrong. In short, it was a mess."[8]

Stern gives a brief but informative account of his participation in the premiere of *Ariadne* in his autobiography, *My Life, My Stage*. He had entered the picture in a roundabout way. Hofmannsthal demanded Reinhardt, Reinhardt wanted his own scenic artist and costume designer Stern, and since Strauss's instructions were law for the Stuttgart Opera management, everyone got his wish. Stern later reflected: "At the time I had no idea what difficulties had to be ironed out and what obstinate resistance had first to be overcome before an official letter arrived from Stuttgart confirming my engagement, or I might have declined with thanks, scenting the difficulties still to come."[9]

Stern was instructed by the music publishers to complete a portfolio of designs for both sets and costumes. The plan was to reproduce these drawings so that they would serve as the definitive designs for all theaters. After studying French costumes from the volume *La Mode au XVII siècle* and from valuable architectural and theatrical material in Hofmannsthal's personal collection, Stern decided to base his designs for the costumes on French society of 1700.[10] Reinhardt and Hof-

---

[6] It has proved impossible to locate any precise information on Reinhardt's participation at Stuttgart. Books on Reinhardt generally fail to mention these performances at all. Alfred Brooks, Director of The Max Reinhardt Archives at the State University of New York at Binghamton, has been unable to furnish any precise documentation for this episode in Reinhardt's career. However, Reinhardt's published *Regiebuch*, containing diagrams indicating the placement of the stage settings and the movements of the actors on stage, makes it evident that he organized this production.

[7] Strauss, *Recollections,* p. 162.

[8] Ibid., pp. 162-63.

[9] Ernst Stern, *My Life, My Stage* (London, 1951), p. 126.

[10] Ibid., p. 127. In a prefatory statement to the English translation of the libretto, Hofmannsthal emphasizes that the opera is a genuine period piece and not a parody: "The opera of Ariadne is in scenery (and costume) not to be treated in the manner of parody, but seriously in the operatic style of the older period (Louis XIV or Louis XV)." *Ariadne on Naxos* (London, 1943), p. 4.

mannsthal agreed and in five weeks, including periodic visits to Strauss to be inspired by the *Ariadne* music, Stern had completed everything. The costumes were delivered to Stuttgart three weeks before opening night.

The stage sets involved greater complications. While Stern was at the opera house examining the scenery that had been assembled, he received an official letter summoning him to an interview with the Director of the Royal Opera House the next day. At the interview Stern was subjected to a criticism of his sets and costumes that sounds as if Jourdain himself were sitting in judgment:

> For example, he wanted to know why the walls of Monsieur Jourdain's living-room were cream coloured and why his dining-room was decorated only with a few pilasters; why the furniture was not more delicate, and so on. When I pointed out that it was a question of the period in which the piece played, he merely shook his head doubtfully, and when I said that the walls had been kept just cream coloured in order to show off the costumes to better advantage, he exclaimed: "The costumes! Oh, they are quite a chapter on their own. But let us keep to the scenery for the moment." And he indicated the palms for the Isle of Naxos scene: "I have been in the tropics myself," he informed me, "and I know what palms look like. Why have you given them such strangely contorted shapes and garlanded them with flowers? And some of the leaves have been painted pink. Didn't you consider that we should have to use the palms for other plays as well?"
>
> No, I certainly hadn't considered that, and I pointed out that they had been designed specially for "Ariadne" and with nothing else in mind. . . .
>
> Even the fact that I had designed the costumes in the fashion of Molière's day was regarded as an entirely superfluous experiment. Why hadn't I designed the costumes in the rococo period as usual? Louis Quatorze costumes were really an expensive luxury for a theatre with a regularly changing programme.
>
> And so it went on. Like master, like man. Encouraged by the disapproval of the All Highest, his subordinates began a general campaign of complaints and grumbles; nothing was right. The wood from which the Berlin manufacturers had made the stage furniture was allegedly of inferior quality; the upholstery was poor, the tables and chairs were much too heavy, and so on. And the costume department was worst of all; they grumbled at the quality of the materials used; they grumbled at the cutting; they even grumbled at the way the buttons were sewn on. But at last they went too far and I had them on the hip.[11]

---

[11] Ibid., pp. 128-29. Stern's last comment refers to the incident of the embroidered flower pattern in Jourdain's coat. He was summoned once again to account for the fact that the flowers had been sewn on upside down. Stern was able to prove that they had to be this way because of the text. Ibid., p. 130.

Since Stern did not possess Strauss's or Hofmannsthal's reputation, he became the target for all of the petty hostilities at Stuttgart: "None of them dared to approach Strauss himself, or Hofmannsthal, for Hofmannsthal was an aristocrat, but failing that they could vent their spleen on the unwanted guest from Berlin, and, in fact, as he was not used to opera, he certainly made minor mistakes here and there, and that was the longed-for opportunity for a certain Herr M. N., the permanent operatic producer attached to the Opera House. Forth he would then rush, spouting musical technicalities, in order to give the interloper from Berlin, the man who knew it all better, an unkind lesson."[12]

The sabotaging of the production showed no sign of abating, according to Stern, and he was happy to depart from Stuttgart and forget *Ariadne* as soon as the premiere ended. The most curious aspect of Stern's exceedingly informative account is his failure to mention when Reinhardt arrived to take charge or what Reinhardt contributed to the performance. Stern also omits any verdict on the outcome of the performance.

In Strauss's opinion, the premiere was successful. He attributed the lack of critical acclaim to unforeseen factors that were not sufficiently taken into account: first, the audience eagerly looked forward to the Strauss opera so much that it did not show sufficient interest in the Molière, although it was performed admirably by Reinhardt's actors; second, during an intermission following the Molière play the King of Württemberg held a reception lasting three quarters of an hour. This delay meant that *Ariadne,* which lasts an hour and a half, began about two and one half hours after the beginning of the play, so that the regular audience, not sharing in the royal festivities, grew somewhat impatient. Nevertheless, Strauss reports that the result was still good, although the evening on the whole was too long.[13]

One factor that might have negatively influenced the audience's appreciation, according to Strauss, was the elimination of the transitional prose scene in order to shorten the program.[14] Since this interim scene

---

[12] Ibid., pp. 130-31.

[13] Strauss, *Recollections,* p. 163.

[14] Walter Panofsky also mentions this fact. Since Panofsky gives no source for his information about dropping the prose scene, it must be pointed out that Reinhardt's *Regiebuch* contains the scene, although in a slightly modified form from the printed first edition of the libretto. Since the scene in Reinhardt's version is not designated as the *Vorspiel* but appears as a continuation of the Molière play, there is always the possibility that Panofsky might be mistaken. According to Panofsky, who considers the premiere a failure, this decision was made by Reinhardt: "Aber *Ariadne* wird erst im Juni 1912 'fertig': Hunderte von Details wurden noch ausgefeilt. Doch alle Mühe war umsonst. Max Reinhardt, dem das Werk vom Komponisten wie vom Dichter gewidmet ist, erkannte auf den ersten Proben die Hypertrophie des Ganzen. Er strich das Vorspiel der Oper, aber die Molière-Komödie dauerte allein schon fast zwei Stunden. Und zu allem Malheur fiel es dem König von Württemberg, Wilhelm II., ein, in der Pause vor *Ariadne* ausgedehnt Cercle zu halten. Ermüdet, als hätte es den ersten Akt der *Götterdämmerung* zweimal hintereinander erlebt, ließ das Publikum nach dem *Bürger als*

presents the most important ideas of the opera, it was indispensable for audience comprehension, and its absence could easily have affected the outcome. How Reinhardt could have sacrificed this scene and, even more bewildering, how Hofmannsthal, who knew its importance for understanding his work, could have permitted it, remains one of the perplexing aspects of the premiere. Most likely, this is another instance of the poet's deference to what he considered to be Reinhardt's superior judgment. As for the feeling of Reinhardt and Panofsky that the performance was too long, this, too, seems curious, since even with the lengthy intermission the premiere barely ran over four hours. *Der Rosenkavalier* lasts almost as long and *Die Frau ohne Schatten* even longer without anyone objecting to their length.

Strauss himself exonerated the premiere performance of *Ariadne* and placed the burden of blame on the lack of sophistication of the audience:

> The first idea was fascinating: beginning in the most sober of comic prose and proceeding via ballet and *commedia dell'arte* to the heights of the purest symphonic music, it failed at last owing to a certain lack of culture on the part of the audience. The play-going public did not get its money's worth, the opera public did not know what to make of Molière. The producer had to put on dramatic and operatic casts simultaneously and instead of two box-office successes he had one doubtful one. . . . The charming idea . . . had proved a practical failure; to express it plainly, because the play-going public has no wish to listen to opera and vice versa. The proper cultural soil for this pretty hybrid was lacking.[15]

Yet, the limited audience of about eight hundred (the capacity of the intimate court theater) was highly selective. Increased prices caused some complaints but helped maintain the selectivity. Representatives from every major country, largely music critics from various journals and newspapers, converged on the Stuttgart Hoftheater. A Strauss-Hofmannsthal premiere was not an everyday musical event, and this one, particularly considering the director and the cast involved, certainly marked the high point of the 1912 opera season. Maria Jeritza sang Ariadne, Hermann Jadlowker, Bacchus, and Margaret Siems, Zerbinetta. The appearance of the King of Württemberg underscores the special importance of this premiere in Stuttgart, a city not frequently so honored, although as seen from Strauss's comments, the King's good will actually interfered with the proper performance of the work.[16]

Edelmann nun auch noch die Oper *Ariadne* über sich ergehen. Da halfen alle Regiekünste Reinhardts nichts, da konnte der dirigierende Komponist alle Schönheiten seiner Musik enthüllen: am Premierenabend schon ist klar, daß die Schlacht verloren wurde." Walter Panofsky, *Richard Strauss: Partitur eines Lebens* (Munich, 1965), pp. 182-83.
[15] Strauss, *Recollections,* pp. 161, 163.
[16] According to Max Marschalk, the King, probably in recognition of the special cultural significance attaching to this premiere in Stuttgart awarded "die große goldene Medaille

The premiere was extensively reviewed, and while there was wide variation of opinion in the reviews, a consensus emerged that may be summarized as follows: the work was an ambitious experiment but a failure, an unprecedented and hence unsatisfactory blend of forms, because Molière's comedy was unrelated to the Hofmannsthal opera and vice versa. Much of the criticism attacked Hofmannsthal's adaptation of Molière; the verdicts ranged from the outrage of French critics at the desecration of a national masterpiece to the charge that the Molière comedy as modified by Hofmannsthal lacked humor. Nevertheless, many critics agreed that they would be reluctant to forego the comedy, not for its own sake, but because of Strauss's beautiful musical interludes. The more hostile critics concentrated all of their antagonism on the libretto by Hofmannsthal. Some demanded, some urged, and others pleaded, but most agreed that Strauss should find a new librettist who could provide him with more suitable operatic material. They looked to Strauss to create a great German comic opera masterwork to succeed Wagner's *Die Meistersinger,* but they felt that even with all his musical talent he could never accomplish this goal as long as he remained tied to Hofmannsthal.

The critics' bafflement over the novel and certainly unexpected combination of a play with an opera is understandable to a certain extent because of the deletion of the transitional scene, which made more difficult a comprehension of the opera's meaning. Nevertheless, it is remarkable that—deceived perhaps by the lightness and the playful air of much of *Ariadne*—so few of the critics, who were predominantly music critics, assumed that Hofmannsthal and Strauss must have had a reason for this seemingly incomprehensible mixture of forms. Instead, not having had the meaning pointed out to them via the omitted scene, an error of judgment on the part of Reinhardt, few critics searched for the artistic purpose of joining drama and opera, comic and serious elements in the same work. Even those perceptive enough to sense that there was a purpose in this contrast treated it as a purely stylistic problem, ignoring the fact that form must of necessity be directly related to the content and the meaning.

Bekker typifies the excessively vehement tone found in much of the critical opinion when he states: "One could say, to put it crudely, that in the inclination to copy old opera the authors succeeded beyond their intention. *Ariadne* shares the fate of most operas by having a bad text and good music."[17] Hofmannsthal's fear of critical incomprehension proved to be well-founded, as is shown by the following sample of opinions. Max Marschalk in the Berlin *Vossische Zeitung* called the work an

für Kunst und Wissenschaft" to Strauss and Hofmannsthal. *Vossische Zeitung,* No. 547 (26 October 1912), Erste Beilage, p. 3. The certificate bestowed on Strauss by the King is found today in the Strauss Archive at Garmisch-Partenkirchen.

[17] Bekker, *Kritische Zeitbilder,* pp. 94-95.

aesthetic experiment that did not add up to an effectively unified work of art.[18] In a further commentary in the evening edition of the *Vossische Zeitung* for the same day, Marschalk continued: "Like the entire play, the opera *Ariadne auf Naxos* is also an unsuccessful, aesthetic playful experiment."[19] The work achieved no satisfying totality, in his opinion, and even beautiful musical passages could not overcome the deficiencies of the inadequate text.[20]

As if the value of art could be measured by the price of a ticket, Edgar Istel in *The Monthly Musical Record* (London) 2 December 1912 reported his annoyance over the exorbitant price of admission (£2.10) that led him and the rest of the audience to conclude that they would witness something special. Instead, what he received for his money was ". . . an inartistic medley of Molière, Hofmannsthal, Strauss's most modern freaks, and small pseudo-antique *intermezzi*. . . ." The performance, too, was unsatisfying: "Then the performance—apart from the wonderful orchestral rendering under Strauss—was somewhat provincial, and even Reinhardt's management and Stern's mounting could only slightly help matters, so it resulted in the noisy applause of a minority. The great number of theatre folk and critics, however, ominously shook their heads. In short, a badly disguised fiasco, for which the blame lay with Hofmannsthal rather than Strauss."

Istel found Hofmannsthal's rendering of Molière's comedy coarse, and considered barbaric the poet's compression of the original work into two acts in order that it might merely serve as a prelude to an opera. Finally, Istel attacks the mixture of styles: "But Jourdain, the Bourgeois gentilhomme, is not only satisfied to perform with it a serious opera, *Ariadne auf Naxos,* but allows a comic opera in the style of the *Commedia dell'Arte* to be given simultaneously [!], so that there arises a mad medley of two styles which are quite unsuitable to each other." For Istel the work was "an interesting artistic experiment, but not an art-work which will enjoy lasting stage life."[21]

From the French critic Emil Vuillermoz, in the Parisian *Revue Musicale S.I.M.,* came one of the most violent reactions against Hofmannsthal's allegedly cavalier treatment of the Molière play. Apparently he had not read Hofmannsthal's essay, *Ce que nous avons voulu en écrivant Ariadne à Naxos,* published earlier in the same journal, for there the poet had defended himself in advance against just this kind of attack on grounds of nationalistic pride. Vuillermoz declares on the one hand that one must close one's eyes to this sacrilege, this

---

[18] Max Marschalk, *Vossische Zeitung,* morning ed. (26 October 1912), first supplement, No. 547, p. 3.

[19] *Vossische Zeitung,* evening ed. (26 October 1912), second supplement, No. 548, pp. 1-2.

[20] Ibid.

[21] Edgar Istel, *Monthly Musical Record* (2 December 1912), p. 315.

mutilation of Molière, and look at the opera itself. He then dismisses the opera as "une lamentable chose" and with the finely honed knife of French satirical prose proceeds to cut it to ribbons.[22]

The Leipzig *Illustrierte Zeitung* printed a number of pictures of the settings and costumes along with a commentary by O. Sonne who, while aware that the authors were attempting a new form, also regarded the work as a bold experiment that would not endure on the stage. The purpose or meaning of the experiment, he did not see at all.[23] Although he had nothing good to say about Hofmannsthal's text, Strauss's music was another matter calling for his purplest of prose.[24]

---

[22] Emil Vuillermoz, *S.I.M. Revue musicale* (8 November 1912), pp. 52-53: "Cet interminable monologue d'Ariane gémissante coupé par des entrées injustifiables de personnages allégoriques de la comédie italienne (ah! les minauderies wurtembergeoises d'Arlequin, de Scaramouche, de Zerbinette et de Truffaldin jouant avec des battes taillées en massues!) ces lamentations kilométriques qu'interrompent çà et là les plaisanteries musicales des bouffons, plus lourdes, plus indigestes, plus navrantes que les récriminations de la veuve inconsolable, cette inénarrable romance à vocalises où l'infortunée Zerbinette, le visage contracté, le cou tordu et l'oeil hors de l'orbite, doit lancer durant vingt-quatre pages un nombre paradoxal de contre-ut, de contre-ré, de contre-mi et de contre-fa dièze, douloureuse demi-heure qui vous laisse pantelant, les nerfs brisés et les dents grinçantes, ces sauts alternatifs, éternellement symétriques d'une scène de larmes à une scène de ricanements sur un texte d'une banalité inconcevable, tout concourt à vous irriter contre la vanité et l'inutilité d'un tel effort. On sent la partie perdue et l'insistance indiscrète des auteurs devient exaspérante. Impossible de deviner une possible ironie réconfortante dans ce fatras héroi-comique; tel effet grotesque sent sa parodie d'une lieue, mais la gravité admirative de l'auditoire vous prouve que les auteurs n'ont pas eu l'intention de plaisanter! Et c'est fini de rire! Rien ne saurait donner une idée de la consternation et de l'accablement dans lesquels peut vous plonger cet effroyable spectacle dont la durée excède les forces humaines!"

[23] O. Sonne, *Illustrierte Zeitung* (Leipzig, 31 October 1912), No. 3618, p. 803. Sonne felt that the combination of the opera with the play "bestätigt vollauf die Annahme, daß es den Autoren diesmal um ein vollkommen neuartiges Genre zu tun war, um ein Produkt, das weder als Oper oder als Musikdrama noch als Lustspiel mit musikalischen Einlagen klassifiziert werden kann. Da auch Tanz und melodramatische Szenen nicht fehlen, so erscheint das Opus auf den ersten Blick als eine neue kühne Etappe in der Entwicklungsgeschichte des dramatischen Kunstwerks. Aber nur bei flüchtigem Hinsehen, denn bei näherer Bekanntschaft löst es sich zunächst in zwei nur locker und ganz äußerlich miteinander verknüpfte Organismen auf, deren zweiter Teil wiederum das Experiment darstellt, zwei nach jeder Richtung hin gänzlich heterogene dramatische Materien zu einer Einheit zu verschmelzen, ein Experiment, das, wie vorweg festgestellt sei, nicht in dem Maße gelungen ist, um an seine dauernde Lebensfähigkeit ernstlich glauben zu können."

[24] "Hier nun tritt Richard Strauss als Sieger und Retter auf den Plan. Die Musik, die er zu dem Vexierspiel schrieb, ist zum größten Teil von ganz wundersamer Klangpracht und einer Innigkeit der Empfindung, die die Erinnerung an die warmherzigen Liebeslieder seiner Jugendzeit hervorzaubert. Von staunenswertem Ausdrucks- und Farbenreichtum ist seine Orchestersprache, die, im kompliziertesten Kammermusikstil gehalten, auf Schritt und Tritt dem souverän mit allen erdenklichen Farben und Kombinationen alten und neuen Stils spielenden Meister bekundet, wobei im Gegensatz zu seinen vorhergehenden Werken auch in üppiger Blüte prangende, weiche und vornehme Sinnlichkeit das Ohr bestrickt." Ibid., p. 804.

Sonne was one of the few critics to comment on the staging, and he enthusiastically endorsed Reinhardt's production: "The performance of the enormously complicated work in the Stuttgart Court Theater was a rare artistic feat of the first rank, for the accomplishment of which a select group of artists was assembled from Berlin, Vienna and Stuttgart."[25]

August Spanuth, from Berlin, joined those who attributed the failure of *Ariadne* primarily to Hofmannsthal. Yet, in his opinion, Strauss, who had hopelessly succumbed to the aestheticism of Hofmannsthal, must also share the blame; for how could he, who normally saw so clearly, devote his best energies to such unimportant, merely aesthetic creations as Ariadne and Bacchus unfortunately had become through Hofmannsthal's distillation. Although willing to concede that the central problem of the opera was important, Spanuth still managed to twist this positive attribute into a negative judgment by stating that the subject was not suitable for musical treatment: "Concerning the problem of having to forget and not wanting to forget, clever treatises can be written, but this philosophical prize question cannot be set to music, at least not with emotion."[26]

A perceptive and contrasting critical viewpoint is found in Paul Stefan's review in the Berlin journal *Die Schaubühne*. He found the singers excellent and Strauss's direction, after the strain of rehearsals and the performances during the Strauss week, an admirable feat. He also correctly realized that the music was more mature and displayed more virtuosity than anything Strauss had previously written. Although he had some reservations about the overall form, he expressed his gratitude for the production.[27]

Another enthusiastic reviewer, Oskar Schröter, similarly felt that he had witnessed something special and predicted that when the history of the Stuttgart Theater was written, this day would claim a special chapter. Nevertheless, he thought that the work was not without flaws. Like the other commentators, he found Strauss's musical interlude for Molière's play the most charming aspect of Hofmannsthal's adaptation. Concerning the opera, he stressed the dangers inherent in the attempt of modern artists to employ an older setting in which they are not at home. Although he recognized that *Ariadne* contained a modern outlook and technique in the guise of the seventeenth century, Schröter unfortunately

---

[25] Ibid.

[26] August Spanuth, *Signale für die musikalische Welt* (30 October 1912), No. 44, pp. 1437-42.

[27] "Daß das Ganze vielleicht nur für Künstler ist. Daß es dem Publikum doch nicht entgehen dürfte. Daß dieser Tag in Stuttgart wieder etwas Leuchtendes war, eine der Freuden, die man nicht missen möchte. Daß man vielleicht eine andre, knappere Form des Werkes ersinnen kann, daß sich aber zuerst und vor allem eines ziemt: Dank. So danke ich Richard Strauss, danke Hofmannsthal, danke Reinhardt und allen, die mitwirkten. Und danke dem Stuttgarter Theater." Paul Stefan, *Die Schaubühne*, 18 (1912), 450.

considered this an artistic flaw rather than to search for a purpose behind the juxtaposition. He apparently felt that the aim was or should have been to create a costume drama and judged the work on how accurately the authors had recreated the period in which the opera was set. Schröter never considered the possibility that Hofmannsthal's intention was to revive the past in terms of the present, and thus he missed one of the main points of the work.

Schröter did, however, discern the hazard involved in trying to weld this curiously constructed opera to the original play by returning to the frame action of the Molière drama after the opera to have the conclusion spoken by Jourdain. He considered this particular feature of the work a failure,[28] and the correctness of Schröter's insight into a potentially troublesome feature was substantiated by Hofmannsthal's later recognition and rectification of the problem. Hofmannsthal became aware that any attempt to recall the play by means of a postlude, highlighting Jourdain and his problems, undercut and endangered the climactic effect of the opera; for it transferred the minds of the audience back to the bourgeois world of Jourdain rather than allowing them to be carried with Ariadne and Bacchus into the transcendent realm of the spirit. Accordingly, Hofmannsthal dropped the realistic conclusion in the second version and ended the work with the opera.

In an ambitious effort to place *Ariadne auf Naxos* into a historical perspective, Will Fred (pseudonym for Wilhelm Schmidt-Gentner) in *Westermanns Monatshefte* attempted to explain the achievement of *Ariadne* in terms of form by comparing the experiment of Hofmannsthal and Strauss to Wagner's search for the *Gesamtkunstwerk*. Fred was one of very few critics who discussed Reinhardt's achievement. In his view, Hofmannsthal and Strauss, by dedicating the work to the director, had attempted to show the world that Reinhardt was the master "through whose hand alone these experiments even became possible." The director, as Fred pointed out, contributes meaningfully and creatively to the performance of a work by means of his techniques, just as the poet does through the word, the composer through music, and the actor through gesture.

What he praised as particularly excellent in both *Der Rosenkavalier* and *Ariadne* was the cooperative effort of Hofmannsthal and Strauss from beginning to completion in an attempt to create works that were completely unified and harmonious throughout. In contrast to the majority of critics, Fred found the play and opera unified in style, motivated by one thought and one life philosophy. He emphasized par-

[28] "Nach dem Schluß zu, in dem klanglich üppig mystisch gefärbten Zwiegesang von Ariadne und Bacchus verflüchtigt sich der vorher breit angeschlagene Komödienton des Ganzen immer mehr, und der Versuch des Musikers und Dichters, ihn mit einem kurzen Wirbel der Komödiantentruppe und einer zur Oper selbst nur in loser Verbindung stehenden Bemerkung Jourdains wieder zu fassen, mißglückt." Oskar Schröter, *Die Musik*, 12 (1912), 228.

ticularly that the characters were not figurines as had been the case in theater for decades, but "the spirit that animated the entire work was not only put into words by Hofmannsthal and into music by Strauss but also was expressed by the painter and the regisseur in gestures and the rhythm of the stage."[29] In attempting a new form of opera that was neither tragic nor comic but both at the same time, the two artists had created an extremely ingenious work of art.

Yet, while Fred believed that in *Ariadne* the authors had realized their artistic aims, the work, in his opinion, amounted to nothing more or less than a divertissement in a higher sense, a pleasant piece for entertainment: "a means of pleasure, of the most refined pleasure, to be sure, but nothing more than that." Such a concluding comment shows that for all his perceptive ideas on the performance, Fred failed to penetrate the deeper meaning behind the work.

Another reviewer for *Westermanns Monatshefte,* the musicologist Georg Schünemann, wrote a brief critique which still was one of the most perceptive early critiques. He was one of the few reviewers to realize that a contrast was intended by juxtaposing Zerbinetta and her dance troupe with Ariadne and Bacchus. However, since he did not understand the full implications of this contrast, he felt that the idea was not completely developed. Like most critics of the time, Schünemann underestimated the significance of Hofmannsthal's text, although he did recognize and stress the genuine importance of Strauss's music.[30]

Not surprisingly, later critics, working from the vantage point of greater perspective, have come a long way toward recognizing the true worth and significance of *Ariadne auf Naxos.* The turning point toward a positive approach to *Ariadne* can possibly be dated from the appearance of two books, Richard Specht's two-volume *Richard Strauss und sein Werk* (Leipzig and Vienna, 1921), and Karl Joachim Krüger's *Hugo von Hofmannsthal und Richard Strauss* (Berlin, 1935). Krüger's book was one of the most comprehensive and objective accounts up to that time and still is one of the most detailed and successful treatments of this collaboration. Among more recent critics, the distinguished music historian, Alfred Einstein, called *Ariadne auf Naxos* the masterpiece of Strauss and Hofmannsthal without, however, providing any explicit evidence to support his conclusion.[31]

[29] Will Fred, *Westermanns Monatshefte,* 57 (1912), 729-38.

[30] "Der Wert und die Bedeutung des Stückes liegen allein in der Musik, die in die Opernliteratur etwas ganz Neues bringt: *die moderne Verwertung und Umbildung älterer Kunstformen und Klangmittel.*" Georg Schünemann, *Westermanns Monatshefte,* 57 (1913), 640. Another critic, August Richard echoes the sentiments of Schünemann and in addition predicted that "this curiously bizarre and yet so unbelievably interesting work" would claim a place in the history of modern opera. August Richard, *Schweizerische Musikzeitung und Sängerblatt,* Jg. 52, No. 28 (2 November 1912), pp. 400-401.

[31] "This interlude in their labours is their masterpiece. What is the reason? Why do we find in it the perfect encounter between the poet and the composer? It is a question which can only be answered with difficulty. The reason is that the poet, lagging behind and heavy

The German literary critic Hans Mayer, writing in 1962, observed that Strauss and Hofmannsthal probably never achieved a greater unity of musical and poetic substance in their collaboration than in *Ariadne*.[32] Again, however, the claim is basically undocumented. In a recent book on Strauss's operas William Mann acknowledged, if reluctantly, the central position of *Ariadne auf Naxos* in the collaboration of the two men: "It is an opera of considerable charm, and makes a significant contribution to the 20th-century development of chamber opera. But in the tale of Strauss's fifteen operas it makes a less progressive step, and if I have called it the crucial work in Strauss's collaboration with Hofmannsthal, this is because with the completion of the prologue Strauss declared himself won over to the cause, so inimical to his fruitful development, which Hofmannsthal had been urging upon him."[33]

Since Mann viewed this work solely with reference to Strauss, he saw its importance as the moment in Strauss's career when he becomes determined to shed his Wagnerian armor and become receptive to new developments. This judgment in itself is inaccurate and misleading. Mann does not indicate that he recognized the many other reasons for the central position of this work within their collaboration. He disregarded the issue entirely with respect to Hofmannsthal, who increasingly came to recognize *Ariadne* as the focal point of his production.

Most recently, Norman Del Mar in his vast three-volume survey of Strauss's music, gives a lengthy and wholly sympathetic treatment to the complex history of *Ariadne auf Naxos*. Del Mar concludes with the comment that "for all the tribulations of its engendering *Ariadne* is a masterpiece, and Hofmannsthal could justly claim the credit for the vision behind its creation."[34] Thus, for the first time in music literature, *Ariadne auf Naxos* receives a fully positive and favorable treatment. A new era in the work's history has begun.

As this survey of reviews and commentaries shows, all of Hofmannsthal's careful planning and pre-publication of the text availed him nothing. Following the premiere of *Ariadne* he was, for the most part, reviled as a poet more vehemently than ever before. Since Strauss and Hofmannsthal were together at the premiere, there are no letters to reveal their immediate reactions to the reception of their troublesome infant. Judging from later letters, however, it does not take great imagination to deduce Hofmannsthal's frame of mind.

laden, represents everything in the mirror with the baroque frame, in the frame of an almost inconceivable mixture of styles, which makes it possible to say with impunity what is most serious, most profound, and most exquisite; and also that the piece called forth the best in the composer—his superabundant technique, his most delicate sensuousness, his delight in parody." Alfred Einstein, *Essays on Music* (New York, 1956), p. 256.

[32] Hans Mayer, *Ansichten zur Literatur der Zeit* (Hamburg, 1962), p. 21.

[33] William Mann, *Richard Strauss: A Critical Study of the Operas* (London, 1964), p. 116.

[34] Norman Del Mar, *Richard Strauss,* II (London, 1969), 103.

Even before the premiere took place, *Ariadne* had been booked for other performances and appeared in succession at Brunswick, Hamburg, Munich, Coburg, Dresden, Karlsruhe, Mainz, Freiburg im Breisgau, Cologne, Zürich, Basel, Bremen, Prague, Stettin, and Dessau. Some of these performances must have been miserable. For example, Arthur Seidl, in a lengthy article entitled "Das *Ariadne*-Problem" condemned the entire conception of the work on the basis of a production in Dessau.[35] Yet, Hofmannsthal heard the opera in Dresden and reported to Strauss that he was "once again profoundly moved by the delicacy and beauty of this work" (*C.*, 147).

Since Hofmannsthal felt that *Ariadne* was suitable only for small theaters, he was agitated at the news that it was being presented in the large opera house in Munich:

> The Molière in the big house strikes me as absurd. The performance was very poorly attended, and there is something saddening in the comedy being acted in a vast half-empty hall; we must do everything to avoid a repetition of this in Munich. Looking at the whole thing—as it is now performed (not without serious loss) in a manner, and in theatres, different from those for which it was intended—I still draw lasting pleasure from the thought that I forced upon you so unusual and important a work. But at the same time I cannot help realizing that the subtlety and refinement of the whole piece, although they are gains to its musical purity, have made it hard for this work to hold its own in the face of a refractory public, which (even in opera) is prejudiced in favour of verism, and a press which, so far from popularizing the ideas behind this work or even entering into their spirit as it ought, invariably pitches into it like an axe into a tree. That *Ariadne* is a decidedly well-rounded figure, in the music and in the poetry, far better fashioned and rounded than many thousand Miss Müllers or Mrs. Meiers we get on the stage whose addresses and incomes we are told in detail, no less "round" than *Elektra* or *Salome,* this is something which these louts cannot comprehend; any more, so it seems, than they can look upon a genius as lucid and radiant as Molière with anything but inveterate, indeed professional, antagonism. (*C.*, 147)

By the time of the Berlin premiere (27 February 1913), which he did not attend, Hofmannsthal had fairly well given up all hope of maintaining the work in its original form. He told Strauss he would have joined him had he thought his presence could have been of any use;

> . . . But the piece being what it is, there is no improvising one can do apart from the appropriate cuts in the Molière, and the scope of these we have settled. That the success of the Molière depends utterly upon the availability of comic actors, of real actors, this is plain beyond doubt—the mistake, for which I must take the blame,

[35] Arthur Seidl, "Das *Ariadne*-Problem," *Deutsche Musikbücherei,* 8 (1913), 192-226.

was that I overrated the capacity of German theatres. "Yawning" is every second word I see whenever I come across the silly twaddle retailed by these miserable journalists; "yawns" during the Molière, notwithstanding the "excellent" Herr Wohlmut or whatever his name may be. Who yawned at Stuttgart, I should like to know! It really mortifies and depresses one, for the moment at least, to hear that a great classic has been hissed in Munich; to discover that people consider they are getting *too little* when, in addition to an opera of the dimensions of *Elektra,* they may listen for an hour to a melodrama with enchanting music, and words by Molière; and that, over the opera *Ariadne,* not one man Jack among these pen-pushers gives the writer of the libretto credit for this singular experiment, for the incomparable purity of the music and for making such singular delicacy and grace possible through the deliberate subordination of the words and through the specific construction and purpose of the whole as a work of art—yes, this does mortify, this can depress one, at least for the moment.

But in the end what remains is the knowledge that something so very beautiful has come into being, which moves one even in recollection, that this work of beauty will last, and that at least the nonsense about your "extrovert" music, about the "heaping of resources" etc., etc., has now collapsed at one fell swoop. Strange to remember that two years ago, when I wrote *Ariadne,* I would have much preferred to give her a framework of my own devising: a little comedy which takes place at a castle in Bohemia, a young heiress with three suitors, who, to please her, bring an opera company and a troup of harlequins to the castle. I suppressed this idea deliberately so as not to endanger your work by combining it with the première of a Hofmannsthal comedy. As it happened, our dear German public could not very easily have given me a worse and more sullen reception than they have given to the greatest comic dramatist of modern times—everything, in fact, would presumably have gone better. But then I thought of Reinhardt; with him I was sure the Molière would vanquish and live—and this is what did happen in Stuttgart. The rest, alas, I did not foresee. (*C.*, 155-56)

The continuing attack on his work by journalist critics caused Hofmannsthal to wonder about "the almost unbelievable degree of antagonism this light and poetic work of art has aroused among the scribbling race, which really puzzles me. Is it that these people sense in it what they apparently hate more than anything else; this turning away from merely ephemeral effects, from the mere *semblance* of reality, this search for transcendental meaning? Is that what arouses their hatred and antagonism? If so, the future of this kind of work should indeed be pretty safe" (*C.*, 158-59). Although willing to accept the blame for the failure, Hofmannsthal was also puzzled by the small sale of piano music from the piece. For there the fault could not be attributed to his libretto and to the Molière play, and "all the world is agreed that the music is among the most beautiful you have ever written!" (*C.*, 159).

For a time the disappointed authors continued to try to protect their newest creation as best they could, first permitting performances in large theaters for the benefit of the opera and later insisting upon having the work returned to small theaters to the advantage of the comedy. Nothing they tried produced any satisfactory results, and Hofmannsthal eventually confessed his feelings that the Molière play was a lost cause, adding: "my belief in the future of *Ariadne* is, to tell the truth, greater than in her present fate" (*C.,* 162). Thus matters were left for the time being, while the idea of severing the Molière play from the opera grew in Hofmannsthal's mind as the only practical solution to the dilemma.

Chapter IV

"A Curse on All Revision"

Even though Strauss was deeply involved in performances of *Ariadne* in mid-summer of 1913, the librettist had for more than six months given thought to revising the whole work. During one of their infrequent meetings, in Berlin in December 1912, Strauss apparently suggested eliminating the Molière play and revising the prose scene preceding the opera into a *Vorspiel* which was to be sung. Hofmannsthal wrote just prior to that important meeting, in a letter dated 9 December: "I was very glad of our talk the other day, and about your happy idea concerning the *secco* recitatives (in view of this I shall recast that brief scene and cut out all allusions which refer back to the Molière)" (*C.*, 148). Hofmannsthal began work immediately during the Christmas holiday of that year and reported to Strauss: "Between 28.12. and 5.1. I am at Neubeuern am Inn. . . . At Neubeuern I mean to take up the *Ariadne* Vorspiel and go through it to cut out all allusions which refer back (to *Bourgeois*) so as to make the whole thing as suitable as possible for treatment with *secco* recitatives as an enduring pedestal for *Ariadne*" (*C.*, 152).

On 9 January 1913 the poet again mentioned the *Vorspiel:*

> Your idea about *secco* recitatives for the *Ariadne* Vorspiel strikes me as very promising, and on hearing *Figaro* in Munich recently its possibilities began to gain substance in my mind. I am thinking of rewriting this introductory scene; it will give me quite a lot of work (which I shall not mind), but ought to be a very real gain, perhaps even a solid foundation for the whole future of the piece.
>
> This Vorspiel, then, with the established characters (Composer, Dancing master, singer, tenor, Zerbinetta, and others) is to take place not *on* the *Ariadne* stage, but behind it, in a hall where the dressing rooms have been improvised. The scene of the action to be described as: the big country-house of a rich gentleman and patron of the arts. The Maecenas (Jourdain) himself remains un-named, allegorical, in the background, represented only by his footmen who transmit his bizarre commands. More strongly even than before the focal point will be the musician's destiny, exemplified by the young Composer. The action will remain by and large as it is, but I shall make it still more lively and more of a comedy (the Composer as a man in love, fooled, as guest, child, victor and vanquished in this

world); it ends with the steward giving the sign to begin. This whole Vorspiel, designed for *secco* recitative, will run to twenty-five or thirty minutes; a not too long entr'acte follows, then *Ariadne* without any cuts—the whole thing to fill a normal evening's bill, for performances abroad to start with, but eventually also here. If you like this little scheme, I feel I could carry it out with success. When would you want it? Please let me have a line. (*C.*, 152-53)

After some delay in answering, for which he apologized, Strauss replied that there was no hurry about revamping the work. He felt that they should not announce their plans to revise the work to anyone so as not to interfere with the current production which he hoped would be accepted for America.[1]

Following the premiere in Hamburg, where the prose scene was restored to its original form, Strauss attended the Berlin opening on 27 February 1913. He was pleased by this performance,[2] and now clearly opposed any attempt to begin anew on *Ariadne,* even though apparently he had suggested originally altering the work. Unfortunately, the extent of Strauss's opposition will always remain unknown, for a two-month lapse exists in the correspondence at this critical juncture in the history of the opera, while Strauss and Hofmannsthal motored together in Italy. The purpose of this first extended personal visit on the part of the two artists was to discuss plans for their next opera, *Die Frau ohne Schatten;* however, *Ariadne* must have figured prominently in a number of their conversations.

On 1 June 1913, Strauss wrote enthusiastically about a performance of *Ariadne* that he had conducted at Coburg and again counseled Hofmannsthal against trying to make any further changes in the drama. Hofmannsthal, however, had grown thoroughly discouraged over constant reports of poor Molière performances and had already decided upon the drastic step of separating the play from the opera:

> What is the use of tinkering, of cutting this scene or that, or patching it up; why should I care whether the philosopher's scene is being done by clods or not done at all, whether they rattle off my dressing-room scene or leave it out altogether? I cannot even think

[1] "In short, full justice should be done one of these days to the grand job that we have jointly made of *Ariadne,* a valuable job which I won't have anybody belittle. For this reason also I am against any re-arrangement or separation of the opera from the comedy, and negotiations are now taking place with America to have the piece performed there next winter, in English, in a small theatre, in the way we've written it." *C.,* 180-81.

[2] "*Ariadne* was staged in a really wonderful production the day before yesterday. The comedy without Reinhardt's genius, but neatly and finely acted. Vollmer as Jourdain still a great comic actor—the rendering of the opera accomplished beyond all words, décor very charming, cast not to be bettered. . . . Whether the success here will spread to the broad masses remains to be seen. The performance, accomplished as it was (the acoustics in the Schauspielhaus were ideal), was a cultural achievement in itself. And a thing like that always bears fruit." Ibid., p. 157.

71

of the whole business, wrecked and ruined as it is, without profound despondency, and this might easily upset me now while this happy productive mood is upon me. . . . I cannot imagine anything in the world I detest more than wasting my energy on a lost cause.

What is the use of all these lame attempts to patch the thing up? The only real remedy has been on my desk for the past week. . . . I have rewritten the Vorspiel, the dressing-room scene, with great zest and vigour; the Composer now occupies the very centre of the scene; he is, symbolically, a figure half tragic, half comic; the whole antithesis of the action (Ariadne, Zerbinetta, Harlekin's world) is now firmly focused on him; everything has been extended and enriched; there are slight, witty occasions for arias, so that it need not be all in *secco;* the genesis of the tune ("Du Venussohn") runs through the whole scene; there is even a hint of a little duet (Zerbinetta-Composer).

Get down to it at once, it is all neat and round, gay and serious; set it in *secco* recitative, put in a few highlights and have it performed from the manuscript in Munich in August after three rehearsals—it will be an enchanting surprise for everybody. It will take a real load off my mind, and, believe me, off yours too, once that unnatural connection between the dead and the living has been severed (I thought the stage would enable me to galvanize the defunct, but the instrument failed me!). Please believe what I say! Imagine how crystalline and complete, how harmonious our beautiful *Ariadne* will emerge once she is placed on this pedestal. Believe me, please. (*C.*, 168-69)

Because he had conducted *Ariadne* frequently during the 1912/1913 opera season, Strauss could not rekindle the proper mood to consider writing additional music for the revised *Vorspiel*. Upon receiving Hofmannsthal's rewritten text, Strauss reacted with an evident lack of enthusiasm. He found much of the new version distasteful and concluded by objecting to the entire idea of changing from their original conception:

. . . to be quite frank, I have so far not found it to my liking at all. Indeed, it contains certain things that are downright distasteful to me—the Composer, for instance: to set him actually to music will be rather tedious. I ought to tell you that I have an innate antipathy to all artists treated in plays and novels, and especially composers, poets and painters. Besides, I now cling so obstinately to our original work, and still regard it as so successful in structure and conception, that this new version will always look to me like a torso. And to produce such a thing, for which I have no inner urge, I would have to be driven by pressure of circumstances—which, at the moment, is not the case. . . .

Moreover, I am so oversated with *Ariadne* after the many performances last winter that I must first regain some more distance from the piece before I can feel any inclination again to work on it.

> In any case I can't accept as justified your wish to have this second version regarded as the only valid and definitive one. To me, its first version is still the right one and the second no more than a makeshift. (*C.*, 171-72)

At this point both men had completely reversed their original positions and still remained at odds about the final version of the work. Strauss, who was as annoyed as Hofmannsthal over the hostile reception accorded *Ariadne,* was further angered by the journalistic acclaim given to the opera composed by Wolf-Ferrari based on Batka's adapatation of Molière's play *Le Médecin malgré lui.* With considerable indignation Strauss reported to Hofmannsthal that critics were hailing this work as the long-awaited musical comedy of the day, "the correct 'rebirth of Molière' from the spirit of the music. In fact, the very thing that I have failed to achieve with *Ariadne* because of your 'clumsiness'" (*C.*, 179).

Strauss urged Hofmannsthal to encourage some of his friends like Bahr or Schnitzler to counterattack in print, defending the poetic conception of *Ariadne.* In his remarks Strauss became almost lyrical and revealed the depth and sensitivity of his appreciation of Hofmannsthal's comedy and its relationship to the opera.[3] Although pleased by Strauss's impassioned defense of *Ariadne* as he had conceived it, Hofmannsthal vetoed the idea of enlisting his friends to promote their work. In a tone of resignation that bespeaks one accustomed to misunderstanding, he replied that as long as Strauss and a few other people who mattered understood him he could put up with the misconceptions of the mob. He was content with the pleasure and satisfaction his work gave him and remained confident that eventually its quality would assert itself (*C.*, 181).

---

[3] ". . . must I go on waiting patiently until people realize for themselves how stylistically delicate your own work has been in *Ariadne* and how of the Molière only those elements have been preserved which, in this as in all other plays, are immortal—such as the type of Jourdain? How subtly your comedy has distilled from Molière all that which is musical, and how it all leads gradually to the very spirit of music and finally scales heights of which even the reborn Molière could have had no inkling? Doesn't it make you sick to read how the audience of the charming Wolf-Ferrari-Batka musical comedy was kept deliciously amused throughout the whole evening, whereas during our short Molière, in which you have really retained only what is amusing and typical, they were bored to tears and could scarcely wait for the opera to begin? Must one really take all this lying down? Have you no one among your friends—Schnitzler or Bahr or whoever it is—who could at long last utter a little word, forthright and clearly audible, that would explode the myth of the boring *Bourgeois?* A myth which has persuasively spread throughout the world and which was born of the trivial circumstance that, at the world première in Stuttgart with its two entr'actes of fifty minutes each, for which the Royal party was to blame, the audience was kept waiting three hours for the eagerly expected opera by the operatic composer Strauss and interpreted this impatience as boredom with the Molière-Hofmannsthal comedy. That by way of a little example! Yet none of these louts has had the guts to correct this Stuttgart-born tag of the unending, boring Molière, which in Stuttgart, including the entr'actes, ran for three hours but which now runs for just one hour at all performances. *Ibid.*, pp. 179-80.

At this juncture the question of revision was forgotten while the two worked on *Die Frau ohne Schatten*. This opera engaged their full attention for the next two years. Also Hofmannsthal was called into active military service prior to the outbreak of war in August 1914. The hapless *Ariadne* lay dormant with all of the problems regarding its future form still awaiting final resolution.

Despite the war, Hofmannsthal and Strauss managed to continue their collaboration. Strauss was too old for military service, and Hofmannsthal, although called to active duty because of his commission as a Lieutenant of Reserves in a light cavalry regiment, was considered by the high command too much of a national asset to risk being stationed near any fighting. Through the intervention of his close personal friend, the politician Josef Redlich, Hofmannsthal was transferred from field duty to service at the war ministry.[4] However, even this light assignment was a torture for him, and in April 1915, again with the help of Redlich, Hofmannsthal was placed on indefinite furlough pending special assignments.[5]

Although his military obligations interfered with his writing as did his concern over the illness of his father to whom he was very attached, Hofmannsthal nevertheless managed to continue work on *Die Frau ohne Schatten*. Once this opera was nearly completed, he and Strauss returned to their ill-fated *Ariadne*. In February 1916, Strauss, Reinhardt, and Hofmannsthal attended a performance of *Ariadne* in Berlin and at this time re-examined its future. Hofmannsthal admitted now for the first time the validity of Strauss's criticism that the work was not clear enough. Once having recognized this fault as the chief reason for the opera's failure and having accepted the responsibility, Hofmannsthal suddenly became optimistic about the prospects of improving *Ariadne:* "I am now full of hope that this hapless child will be rehabilitated. The incomprehension of the public for anything with a deeper meaning is another matter. But here, after all, quite a lot was wrong with the work itself; between vision and realization, between the libretto, the music, and the possibilities of the theatre there was a hiatus" (*C.*, 238).

Yet, in a subsequent letter to Strauss's wife, Hofmannsthal maintained, somewhat surprisingly in view both of the letters quoted above and his earlier correspondence with Strauss, that if it had been up to him alone to decide the question of *Ariadne,* he would have proceeded differently and in a way more beneficial to the work: "I should certainly have withdrawn the work from the stage after the unsuccessful performance in Stuttgart, to bring it out again, perhaps years later, as

---

[4] Hugo von Hofmannsthal—Eberhard von Bodenhausen, *Briefe der Freundschaft* (Berlin, 1953), pp. 170-71.

[5] Günter Erken, "Hofmannsthal-Chronik," *Literaturwissenschaftliches Jahrbuch,* 3 (Berlin, 1962), 285. The special assignments consisted of giving lectures in Germany, Scandinavia, Belgium and Switzerland as well as writing essays on topical and patriotic subjects.

something untarnished and fresh" (*C.*, 240). However, previously, when Strauss had suggested withdrawing the work rather than to see it mutilated, Hofmannsthal had pleaded with him to keep it in the repertoire. Indeed, this was the first occasion upon which Hofmannsthal openly admitted that the Stuttgart performance, Reinhardt notwithstanding, was not the success he had anticipated.

The decision to revise *Ariadne* led immediately to a number of problems in composing the *Vorspiel*. Since Strauss disliked tenors, he readily accepted a suggestion of Leo Blech, composer and Generalmusikdirektor of the Berlin opera, that the role of the Composer be sung by a woman. In the Berlin production the role would be intended for Mlle. Lola Artôt de Padilla, a star at the theater on Unter den Linden. In order to attract a prima donna to the part, Strauss felt that some expansion was necessary to make it a starring role. This practical approach to art agonized Hofmannsthal and reopened the chasm of opposing views toward this work that had existed throughout its composition. Witness Hofmannsthal's bitter words:

> I fear your opportunism in theatrical matters has in this case thoroughly led you up the garden path. In the first place the idea of giving the part of the young composer to a female performer goes altogether against the grain. To prettify this particular character, which is to have an aura of "spirituality" and "greatness" about it, and so to turn him into a travesty of himself which inevitably smacks a little of operetta, this strikes me as, forgive my plain speaking, odious. I can unfortunately only imagine that our conception of this character differs once again profoundly, as it did over Zerbinetta! Oh Lord, if only I were able to bring home to you completely the essence, the spiritual meaning of these characters. I am not, on the other hand, quite so opinionated as not to understand what you want to avoid: the frightful tenor! Yes, I can understand that. None the less; in Berlin they happen to have Mlle. Artôt, but who is to sing the part elsewhere? In Vienna, for instance? And what is more: if you do adopt this irrational idea of giving the part to a woman, you must not, for heaven's sake, cut the part *to fit the performer.* An outstanding woman like Artôt will have to get right into the character of this earnest young man, otherwise you'll have let go of the bird in hand for the sake of the ten in the bush. (*C.*, 241-42)

Hofmannsthal felt that with all its high spots, moods, and shadings, the role of the Composer was already a star part. Nevertheless, despite his protests, he eventually relented in the face of Strauss's determination, and he even suggested places where the lyrics were suitable for musical expansion.

The ending of the opera also caused considerable difficulty and controversy before the poet and musician once again reached complete agreement. Strauss suggested that the close of the opera should be followed by a return to the context of the *Vorspiel,* adding that this would be one means of expanding the part of the Composer to suit Mlle. Artôt: ". . . perhaps you could write an additional pretty little solo scene for the Composer at the end (after *Ariadne!*): wistfully poetical—possibly by making him burst out in despair after *Ariadne:* 'What have you done to my work', and then the Major-domo could appear and pay the poor devil his salary, or the Count might appear and pay him some compliments, announce the acceptance of the opera by the Imperial Opera House in its present form (with the Zerbinetta scenes), or any other amusing idea that comes to your mind—and then a wistfully-poetical final contemplation" (*C.*, 241). This proposal repulsed Hofmannsthal, who replied acrimoniously:

> And finally, whether man or woman—this idea for the end is truly appalling; if you will forgive me, my dear Dr. Strauss, this letter was not written in one of your happiest moments. Consider the lofty atmosphere which we have striven so hard to reach, rising ever higher from the beginning of the Vorspiel to the glorious opera, then the entrance of Bacchus, reaching in the duet almost mystical heights. And now, where the essential coda ought to be over in a trice (as with Jourdain's famous last words), now some rubbish of this kind is to spread itself once more (the emphasis is on *spread*): the major-domo, the fee, the Count and God knows what else! And all this merely to make the part an inch longer! To say nothing of the stylistic absurdity of this demand for something "lyrical" in the framework, which, after the opera has just reached its greatest lyrical climax, would destroy the distinctive nature of this framework. In fact, of course, the only thing to do is to return from this lyrical climax to characterization, first the comedians, and then a characteristic brief speech, given now, if you insist, to the Composer, though 'twas better coming from Jourdain. Please send me a few words by express, telling me that you understand me; I feel quite faint in mind and body to see us quite so far apart for once! (*C.*, 242)

Strauss heatedly replied that Hofmannsthal need not become so angry when they did not understand each other instantly. He readily acceded to Hofmannsthal's objections about his proposed ending, admitting that his comments were only unconsidered suggestions which the poet should have thrown into the wastepaper basket without another thought. However, for solid artistic reasons, Strauss remained absolutely intractable concerning the choice of Artôt for the part of the Composer. He could not consider a tenor for the part, since even for the role of Bacchus a *primo tenore* could not be engaged by the opera management because his fee would be too high. Moreover, the role was too small to attract such a star. A leading baritone would not sing the Composer; thus Strauss felt the only genre of singer not yet represented in *Ariadne* was his Rofrano (Octavian in *Der Rosenkavalier*), for whom an intelligent female singer would be available anywhere.

Hofmannsthal would not budge from his viewpoint that the Composer must not return after the opera, for he feared that this step would make nonsense of the whole text. The problem confronting the men at this point resulted from their adherence to the original conception of the opera as play within a play, even though the Molière had been sacrificed:

> It is quite extraordinarily difficult for me to put into the mouth of the Composer the final words which belong to the very fringe of the framework. Coming from Jourdain, the man of prose, that *Monsieur tout-le-monde* who hasn't an idea of what he has been up to and what he has set afoot, the words were organic. But coming from the Composer! For him to complain where the opera has after all succeeded in forging harmony out of the two components, that would be absurd; for him to rejoice would be more absurd still. There is a risk that this will make nonsense of the whole thing. A curse on all revision! I shall try my best to find a possible solution. What if the Major-domo were to speak these final words with an air of smug satisfaction, to the Composer? In prose, like Jourdain? (*C.*, 245)

This question resolved itself temporarily when the staging for the ending was decided. The action would conclude with the opera and would not return to the framework of the play. Hofmannsthal agreed with Strauss's suggestion that the cave should disappear. Ariadne and Bacchus would remain visible walking down toward the sea where Bacchus's flower-decorated ship had appeared mysteriously.

The two men met in Munich in the middle of August to work out final details of the revision. The producer Erich von Wymetal had written to Joseph Gregor (a mutual friend of himself and Strauss who later produced three librettos for the composer) that he felt some consternation about the ending after talking to Hofmannsthal. The latter's prickly reply when apprised of the situation reveals that in the interim he had devised a new idea for the ending: "Should like to know what grounds there could be for 'consternation'! W[ymetal] is the type who perpetually raises futile objections, . . . they are all out to make trouble for others, to push themselves forward and so on. Please stick to it firmly that some stage device which envelops (isolates) the two main characters at the end of the trio is indispensable, and that is that!" (*C.*, 261).

Eventually the device chosen was a baldachin that descends mysteriously from above and envelops the lovers during the final scene. Why Hofmannsthal did not follow his original idea of having the lovers enter Ariadne's cave rather than introducing the artificial contrivance of a canopy is unclear. After all, the bed which Ariadne calls "ein seliges Lager/ Einen heiligen Altar!" is in the cave which now they never enter, for the new version concludes with the lovers under the canopy. This is one of the discrepancies left in the text, although Hofmannsthal was aware of it. As he wrote to Strauss: "I would leave the references to the cave as they are; better a slight incongruity like this than verses tacked on as an after-thought. You must mark the exact moment for the change of scene, for the chandeliers to disappear, for the cave to vanish, and so on" (*C.*, 250).

The ending, one of the most troublesome features of the entire work that had not been satisfactorily solved at Stuttgart, went through four versions. In the original libretto the lovers were to enter the cave and sing their love duet, while outside Zerbinetta and her dancers celebrated the apparent triumph of their point of view. The couple then emerged from the cave and strolled off together, followed by the dancers. In Reinhardt's *Regiebuch* the lovers stand at the entrance to the cave bathed in a mystical light, while above thousands of stars shimmer in the sky. Ariadne clings to Bacchus in complete surrender and happiness, while Zerbinetta accompanied by her dancers has the last word, singing in mocking triumph most of her earlier rondo. The action then reverts to Jourdain for the conclusion. The third version resembles the original scenario, except that the lovers walk to the ship which is visible on stage. This idea for the ending, while often used by later directors,[6] was, as has been shown, expressly rejected by Hofmannsthal. The final version, with Ariadne and Bacchus enveloped in a baldachin, actually makes the least sense of any of the endings. The sheer erotic quality of their relationship, so clearly evident in the text, is not emphasized as strongly by having them concealed within a canopy as it was by their entering the cave. At the same time the canopy adds an unnecessary, inexplicable ingredient (where does it come from?) and negates the soaring quality that is suggested by having the lovers slowly ascend the hill over the cave, seemingly headed for the heavens and eternal life. Yet, this static ending was the one Hofmannsthal preferred.

Whatever opinion one may hold with respect to the canopy solution to the ending, Hofmannsthal was right in his opposition to the ship on stage. For the presence of the ship, by intruding an aspect of reality, destroys the poetic ambiguity of the ending as well as the infinite, spiritual quality that is imperative for a successful climax to the opera. The question of whether Ariadne actually dies, that is, dies as one person to be reborn transformed, on a different, presumably higher level of existence, is lost or at least rendered more difficult to conceive with the

---

[6] Clemens Krauss, for example, discussed its use as follows: "Die Ariadne-Insel muß größer werden, so daß eine Spielmöglichkeit für das Duett gegeben ist. Die Ankunft des Bacchus auf dem Schiff muß poetischer gelöst werden. Ich hätte am liebsten, wenn sich das Paar am Schluß auf dem Schiff umarmen würde und nach dieser Umarmung das Schiff langsam auf das Meer hinausgleiten würde. Die Insel müßte zu diesem Zweck vorher teilweise verschwinden. Also Schlußbild: Sternenhimmel, Meer, Ariadne und Bacchus in Umarmung auf dem weggleitenden Schiff. Ob das auszuführen sein wird? La Roche hätte es gekonnt." Oscar von Pander, *Clemens Krauss in München* (Munich, 1955), pp. 120-21.

physical presence of the ship. Instead of implying the ultimate transcendental journey of the lovers into eternity, the ship tends to keep the opera on a mundane, realistic level. There is in such staging more justification for Zerbinetta's view that exactly the events she had predicted were coming to pass, and that Ariadne was no different than any other woman. She had remained faithful to one man only until the next one came along.

The appearance of Zerbinetta at the end of the opera, which occurs in the final version, created more friction between Hofmannsthal and Strauss than almost any other problem. In fact, the character of Zerbinetta ultimately proved such a barrier to complete harmony of conception between the two men that the opera is technically flawed. It retains an inner ambiguity because of the differences of opinion about Zerbinetta that were never resolved. Strauss insisted to Hofmannsthal that two opinions were possible about Zerbinetta, and he clung to his own conception of her in the music.

After her major scene, Strauss wanted Zerbinetta simply to disappear. It does seem a defensible point of view that if any reference to the *Vorspiel* can be avoided at the end of the opera, figures such as Zerbinetta, who represented the real world of the *Vorspiel* in the opera, could disappear also. However, Hofmannsthal insisted that Zerbinetta must return near the end and present her mocking presence:

> . . . it would be a shameless betrayal of the work and its future for me to concede—out of pusillanimity—that the human counterpart (Zerbinetta) should be deprived of some last word!
>
> That would be, allow me to say so, deliberately and openly sacrificing the fundamental idea, the spiritual meaning of the whole work for the sake of an effective curtain; we might possibly get away with it on this occasion, but I doubt it, for the critics have the first version of the libretto at hand. They have had the symbolic meaning of the whole work dinned into them so often in the past that they will not be such fools as to miss the opportunity of attacking us with glee for sacrificing so capriciously the point of the whole piece on which the spectacle was avowedly based from the outset (that contrast between the heroic ideal and its denial, or whatever you may wish to call it), for sacrificing it just for the sake of the "curtain."
>
> Even if we now succeed in getting it past with tolerable success, the time will come when an aging work of art, like an aging face, is left only with its spirit—and then the fact that for a moment we were pusillanimous and irresponsible will be taken out on our *Ariadne*.
>
> Where then is the compromise between your legitimate proposal and my: "Thus far and no further!" I believe it is here: I will only insist that the counter-voice, represented by the sole figure of Zerbinetta, should be heard at the end for a second. Something like this: while to the rear of the stage the couple step down towards the sea, and before the orchestra opens the epilogue, Zerbinetta appears

in front, right, in the wings, but visible, waves her fan mockingly over her shoulder towards the back and proceeds to sing her couplet:

> Kommt der neue Gott gegangen, hingegeben sind wir stumm,
> Und er küßt uns Stirn und Wangen, etc. . . . gefangen . . .
> Hingegeben sind wir stumm!

If need be let her only begin to sing, sing the first line—then let the orchestra drown her, so that the rest is to be found only in the libretto; I am satisfied with her symbolic, mocking presence and exit. I am even inclined to believe that such spicing of the sentimental with its opposite is quite in your spirit, like that charming touch of irony in the sentimental little duet at the end of *Rosenkavalier;* in short I can only hint at a solution, but something of this kind is indispensable. (*C.,* 246-47)

Strauss agreed to Hofmannsthal's wishes, and Zerbinetta reappears to sing two lines of her former aria. However, although Hofmannsthal intended her presence to be mocking, Strauss followed his own interpretation and subdues her song to a hushed, awe-struck hymn. The composer through his music (as Chapter VIII will show) had the last word. For Zerbinetta witnesses the miraculous event with sympathy and appreciation, despite her lack of comprehension and her former cynical attitude.

Through his interpretation, Strauss enriched Zerbinetta's character by suggesting that she possesses the capacity for human warmth and compassion. In Strauss's view, Zerbinetta differs from Ariadne only in her inability to find the right man who could awaken her to genuine love and constancy as Bacchus has awakened Ariadne. Hofmannsthal, on the other hand, because he intended Zerbinetta as the absolute contrast to Ariadne, insisted that she retain a superficial and one-dimensional character, incapable of feeling anything more than sensual attraction.

The dispute over Zerbinetta's final appearance continued even while Ariadne was in rehearsal for the Vienna premiere. Hofmannsthal, who apparently had been attending the rehearsals, finally was compelled to ask Strauss to intervene:

I know you willingly trust me in matters of art, so please do in the present instance: my own feeling grows from rehearsal to rehearsal, and is wholly confirmed by the judgement of people of taste, that scant justice is being done, either by the music or on the stage, to the gay figures at the end—they are being dropped—so that one has, unfortunately, a sense of being left in mid-air. The music cannot be changed, but the production on the stage can, and you must settle it by a word with W(ymetal), as your (and my) express wish, that *Zer-binetta* (coming up the staircase,) *must be accompanied by her com-*

panions and they must all stand there for a moment, receiving the spot light. Please oblige me over this; it looks unimportant, but is not. (*C.*, 263-64)[7]

But Strauss did not insist, for the published text gives no indication that Zerbinetta's companions should reappear; they have been omitted completely.[8] Since the poet had sole control over the published version of his libretto, the absence of the dancers at the end indicates that he must have finally capitulated to Strauss's view.

The first performance of the second version took place in Vienna on 4 October 1916. The two artists were in Vienna at the time, and there are no letters concerning the premiere. However, in a letter to Bodenhausen, Hofmannsthal expresses his satisfaction with the way the work turned out: "*Ariadne* was on the whole a completely charming affair, one of the almost completely successful theater works that I know."[9] While the work did not receive the outstanding popular acclaim previously accorded *Elektra* and *Der Rosenkavalier,* it was enthusiastically received by the audience. The fears of the authors about Vienna being an unfavorable place for a premiere proved to be unfounded in this instance. Considering the general political conditions, the premiere of such a work was an act of boldness; for by 1916 Vienna suffered the effects of the Allied blockade with shortages of food, clothing, and even coal for heat in the theaters. It seemed hardly a propitious time to expect an audience to surrender itself in appreciation

[7] In a letter to Bodenhausen discussing the forthcoming Berlin performance, Hofmannsthal wrote: "Das große scenische, auch in Stuttgart *nicht* gelöste Problem liegt in der Schluß-Grotte. Er möchte die Verwandlung sinnenfällig machen, durch langsame Nebelentführung, was ich stark ihm auszureden versuchte. Es sollte durch Verdunkelungen ohne Bewegung der beiden zu erreichen sein. Aber er meint, das gehe nicht." *Briefe der Freundschaft,* p. 142. As late as 1926, he still defended the canopy ending: "In *Ariadne* I tried to avoid this advancing backwards and kept the black ship off the stage, so that the couple are enveloped by the canopy where they stand (and this I still consider the most beautiful solution for the specific problem in *Ariadne*). *C.*, 423.

[8] Hofmannsthal was correct in his fear that critics would miss the irony at the end as seen in the following letter from Rolland to Strauss: "Je regrette aussi que, dans la version définitive d'*Arianne,* les bouffes aient été éliminés de la fin. De deux choses l'une, où il aurait fallu terminer par la frénésie dionysiaque d'un Cortège de Bacchus (choeurs et grand orchestre) ou,—conservant l'ironie de la donnée première, mêler à la fin la tragédie pompeuse et la comédie bouffe,—écrire un septuor des cinq bouffes, de Bacchus et d'Arianne: cela, c'eut été le *ne plus ultra.*—J'ai le sentiment que Hofmannsthal commence chacun de ses 'pastiches' d'un temps passé, avec un dessein ironique, mais que son admirable virtuosité les réussit avec tant de succès qu'il finit toujours par les prendre au sérieux. Et c'est dommage: un sujet-pastiche, comme *Arianne,* n'a toute sa valeur que par l'ironie; et cette ironie doit surtout s'épanouir à la fin." Strauss—Rolland, "Correspondence," *Fragments du Journal Cahiers Romain Rolland,* III, ed. G. Samazeuilh (Paris, 1951), p. 109. Unfortunately, there is no reply by Strauss, who had been mainly responsible for this omission of the irony at the end of *Ariadne.* Rolland made mention of this defect in *Ariadne* also in his notebook. Ibid., pp. 172-73.

[9] *Briefe der Freundschaft,* p. 222.

to a pseudo-Baroque opera, a work of subtle comic whimsy and Hof-mannsthalian excursions into the philosophy of existence.

Despite these handicaps the opera was relatively successful, mainly because of the singers and the production even without Reinhardt who, with the dropping of the Molière play, ceased to be an issue as director. Yet, although the opera had been revised, the reviews tended to repeat previous judgments. The music critic of the influential *Neue Freie Presse,* Julius Korngold, retraced at length the history of *Ariadne* from the first version to the new one. He also included a lengthy digression on past versions of the Ariadne theme in opera to demonstrate that Hof-mannsthal's idea for blending "commedia dell'arte" and classical tragedy was not new. Essentially, his viewpoint follows the consensus opinion of the first version; namely, that the opera consisted of a poor text and a beautiful score.[10]

Ferdinand Scherber, in a review entitled "Die Wiedererweckung der *Ariadne*," returns to the same negativism he had adopted toward the Stuttgart premiere. He liked the staging and some of the music but in general considered the opera little improved. He not only failed to un-derstand the relationship of the *Vorspiel* to the opera[11] but, in contrast to Korngold, Scherber found even the music of the *Vorspiel* displeasing except for the love duet between Zerbinetta and the Composer.

Both reviewers agreed on one point: the debut of Lotte Lehmann in the part of the Composer was outstanding. This young singer had just come to Vienna from Hamburg and had not yet been given the op-portunity to prove herself. She held little expectation from her newest assignment, for she was only the understudy for the star, Marie Gutheil-Schroder. When the latter, because of a cold, could not attend the last rehearsals, Lehmann was summoned, and after auditioning her, Strauss assigned her the part. According to her own account, this role made her

---

[10] *Neue Freie Presse,* 5 October 1916, p. 5. Korngold's lack of comprehension is revealed in this comment: "Nur begreiflich daher, daß der moderne Textdichter für die unaktive, starr-pathetische Ariadne eine heiter sinnliche, bewegliche Zerbinetta zur Gesellschaft suchte. Aber auch Zerbinetta und das graziöse Tanzspiel, das sie mitbringt, belebt nur die Szene, nicht die Handlung selbst." Ibid., p. 3.

[11] "Die Vorgänge folgen einander, wie man sieht, weder reichlich noch spannend. Im Vor-spiel wird die magere, schmächtige Handlung noch auf das Prokrustesbett eines längeren Aktes gestreckt, der zweite ist erfüllt mit den beiden langen Konzertarien und einem Konzertduette, die nicht deshalb dramatisch wirken, weil Künstler im Kostüme auf der Bühne sie singen. Man kann wirklich sagen, die Oper will weder anfangen noch aufhören. Ein bißchen für Abwechslung sorgen nur die lustigen Personen, so daß die dumme Idee des gräflichen Hausherrn schließlich gar nicht so dumm ist, als uns der Dichter weis machen will. Der Ariadne-Akt ist mit dem Vorspiel nur logisch aber nicht dramatisch verbunden und, da mit dem Ende des Ariadne-Spieles die ganze Oper schließt, so hängt der Akt als selbstständiges Gebilde in der Luft." Ferdinand Scherber, "Die Wiedererweckung der Ariadne," *Signale für die musikalische Welt* (11 October 1916), 688.

famous overnight and was decisive in leading to her brilliant career.[12]

The Berlin premiere of the new *Ariadne* took place on 11 November 1916 and failed to achieve even the moderate success of Vienna. The critic Joachim Beck vehemently attacked the text of the new version, particularly the *Vorspiel,* which he recommended deleting entirely.[13] Paul Schwers was more positive in his judgment. He was impressed with the new version, although his praise was qualified. He attributed some of the fault of the premiere to an inadequate cast but felt in addition that the problems of the work had not been entirely resolved, although Strauss surmounted most of the difficulties by his music.[14]

Ariadne in its new form was performed in a number of theaters with varying degrees of success. In Mannheim, which staged a Strauss week, *Ariadne* was presented, as Strauss reported: "very prettily and wittily by Dr. Hagemann, the Vorspiel botched completely at the most heavy-footed pace by F[urtwängler], otherwise a very gifted conductor, and eventually put right by me for Switzerland, in three rehearsals: it's odd how difficult it is even for the most gifted people to get into a new style" (*C.,* 265).

Strauss later wrote to Hofmannsthal that the new *Ariadne* was a "triumphal success" in Switzerland, Jeritza as Ariadne and Oestvig as

---

[12] Lotte Lehmann, *Five Operas and Richard Strauss,* trans. Ernst Pawel (New York, 1964), pp. 3 ff.

[13] "Was Hofmannsthal diesmal im Vorspiel bietet, ist: ein direkter, doktrinärer und umständlicher Kommentar als *captatio benevolentiae* für das Stilgemisch der Hauptoper; mehr verwirrend als entwirrend, weil ohne einheitliches Grundmuster; voll vielfältiger, vieldeutiger, unklarer Beziehungen, Beziehungen höchstpersönlicher Art; Spitzen fürs Publikum und die Rechtfertigung der eignen zu Kompromissen bereiten Politik; eine unter Wehen abgedruckste, spindeldürre Komik; Blicke hinter Kulissen und in verängstigte Künstlerseelen—als Auftakt zu langatmig, zu gewichtlos, um gleichberechtigt neben der Volloper zu stehen, das Opus eines trocken spekulativen Kopfes." Joachim Beck, "Die neue Ariadne," *Die Schaubühne,* 12 (1916), 436.

[14] "Der seltsame, vom Dichter Hofmannsthal geschaffene und vom Komponisten in genialer Manier charakterisierte stilistische Zwiespalt dieser Bühnenschöpfung konnte freilich auch durch diese Verbesserungen nicht aus der Welt geschafft werden. Es gehört schon ein erhebliches Maß ästhetischer Freizügigkeit und Anpassungsfähigkeit dazu, um dem oftmals krassen Nebeneinander der Stimmungen und Stile gegenüber einen Standpunkt zu gewinnen, der dieses artistisch-literarische Gaukelspiel natürlich erscheinen läßt und der damit zum vollen Genießen der unerschöpflichen musikalischen Schönheiten führt. Diese Freude am artistischen Problem ist so ganz Straussens Sache, die Lösung solcher Aufgaben seine Stärke. Niemals ist mir sein Können—dieses im höchsten Sinne des Wortes—in so absolut überzeugender Weise zu Bewußtsein gekommen wie hier, angesichts der Ariadne-Partitur, die für den Hörer zu einem Born ununterbrochener musikalischer Schönheiten wird. Seine starke Schöpfernatur schreitet über alle hier sich bietenden Schwierigkeiten mit beinahe selbstverständlicher Mühelosigkeit hinweg." Paul Schwers, "Ariadne auf Naxos in Berlin," *Allgemeine Musikzeitung* (November 1916), p. 1.

Bacchus were "positively ideal." He commented also on the Zerbinetta of Mlle. Eden in Mannheim, as very "charming and piquant," adding: "A pity one can't tour the whole of Germany with such performances, or at least all the smaller towns. How much misunderstanding could be cleared up!" (*C.*, 265). Despite such optimism the criticism did not relent.[15]

Following these comments upon *Ariadne,* there was a lapse of discussion about the work while the two men turned their full attention to the revised version of the Molière play. No step of the collaboration on any phase of their original work was to be easy, and completing *Der Bürger als Edelmann* with Strauss's incidental music, the final chapter in the collaboration on *Ariadne,* was no exception.

Hofmannsthal found the opportunity in May 1918 to praise Strauss for *Ariadne* and to assert, as he often had in the past, that they must continue their collaboration along the direction of the *Vorspiel.* He repeats this thought, as well as commenting on the significance of *Ariadne* in their relationship, in a letter written in a particularly warm and open frame of mind, a state induced by the death of Bodenhausen,

> . . . the best, most faithful and most noble of friends. . . . I am glad you look back on your stay in Vienna as a happy one. From my point of view, too, these days meant a great deal and the *Ariadne* performance, which rounded them off, gave rise to important ideas which I shall try and elucidate to myself and to you at an early occasion. Of all our joint works this is the one I never cease to love best, every time I hear it. Here alone you have gone wholly with me and—what is more mysterious—wholly even with yourself. Here for once you freed yourself entirely from all thought of effect; even what is most tender and most personal did not appear too simple, too humble for you here. You have lent your ear to the most intimate inspiration and have given great beauty; of all these works, this is the one which, believe me, *possesses the strongest guarantee that it will endure.* From this point the road leads on, even for me, when I think of you; not one road but several. (*C.*, 299)

[15] In 1918 Eugen Schmitz continued the negative view of *Ariadne,* especially attacking the new *Vorspiel.* "Die Neubearbeitung der Ariadne," *Hochland,* 5 (1918), 719. Another essay written in 1918 by Bernhard Diebold traced the genesis of *Ariadne* with malicious humor that is all at the expense of Hofmannsthal. "Die ironische Ariadne und der Bürger als Edelmann," *Deutsche Bühne,* 1 (1918), 219-44.
One reader he failed to amuse with such witticisms was Hofmannsthal, who lamented to Strauss: "North-German and ponderous also is this most long-winded treatise on *Ariadne* which you have sent me. My God, how dull of perception, how clumsy and heavy-handed: What can be the point of tracing the derivation of my libretto from (North-German) romanticism, when both my art and yours derive so effortlessly, so naturally from the Bavarian-Austrian baroque with its mixture of different elements and their fusion in music. And on the heart of the matter—the relation between Ariadne and Bacchus—not the slightest light is thrown throughout the whole twenty pages of these ponderous and yet complacent cogitations. What pathetic and dull-witted human beings!" (*C.*, 324).

Strauss responded in kind, indicating his pleasure over Hofmannsthal's faith in *Ariadne,* but pointing out that it had virtually disappeared from the repertoire everywhere.[16] Hofmannsthal replied that he did not feel as resigned as Strauss about the work, for he was certain that while the opera did not have the public of today, it would gain the public of tomorrow (*C.,* 303).

The poet then "humbly" suggested a change in Zerbinetta's aria that he thought was a stumbling block to success:

. . . would it by any chance be possible for you, whose steady development also extends to matters of taste and sensitivity, to compose entirely new music for one number in *Ariadne,* a single one: I mean Zerbinetta's big aria? Here, it seems to me, is a concrete obstacle in the way of the opera's future prospects: the enormous difficulty of doing justice to the coloratura which actually, half ironical as it is meant to be, fails to make any vital contribution to the over-all effect. The immense demands made by these coloratura decorations lead to peculiar difficulties in casting the part: almost every one of the younger and more attractive singers of the soubrette type, whose appearance would naturally fit them for the feminine frailty of Ariadne's unheroic counterpart, are debarred from this role because they cannot manage this elaborate aria. If, on the other hand, you were to take the words of this aria which builds up a whole feminine type, perhaps the archetype of the feminine, and were to write new music of the smooth melodiousness of *Le Bourgeois* for its various phases with their distinct variation in rhythm, the whole aria would, I imagine, all at once gain a firmer hold on people's understanding and make this understanding a delight. At the same time a perpetual obstacle to the performance of the opera, especially in smaller theatres, would be removed. I do realize how annoying suggestions of this kind always are at first sight, so I ask you in any case, to forgive me for making this one! (*C.,* 303-304)

Strauss replied that he felt no desire to tamper with Zerbinetta again, any more than he could muster any enthusiasm to rework the adaptation of the Molière comedy, even though he did not consider it so complete a failure as did Hofmannsthal: "I suppose I must endorse your judgment on *Bourgeois,* without at the same time entirely sharing its damning harshness. The whole thing, after all, is so attractive in form and content that I cannot believe that a more cultured public than exists today will not some time appreciate its value more fully—in spite of the fundamental shortcomings which you criticize and which are probably difficult to remedy at this stage. That is why I would suggest that we stop doctoring

---

[16] "I am very pleased to hear that you believe in *Ariadne* and love it: unfortunately this love and faith are shared so little by the public and the managers of German theatres that this delightful piece has vanished from the repertoire almost everywhere, with the exception of Vienna and Munich. We'll just have to put our hopes in good old posterity!" *C.,* 300.

it and why I should find difficulty in applying the surgeon's knife to Zerbinetta again" (*C.*, 306). Accordingly, the 1916 version of *Ariadne* with the revised *Vorspiel* became and remains the definitive form of the opera.

Despite all the problems connected with this troublesome creation, Hofmannsthal remained committed to *Ariadne* and repeatedly stressed his unshakable faith in the future of this opera to which he was "attached with heart and soul." He felt assured that the work would survive its authors by many years. As its success grew in various countries during the early twenties, and even before the great popularity of this work between 1924 and 1927, Hofmannsthal expressed his great pleasure in seeing his prediction for its promising future begin to come true: "*Ariadne* is, after all, my favorite among the children" (*C.*, 382).

Chapter V

The Ariadne Myths

No one has ever satisfactorily explained why Hofmannsthal became interested in Ariadne as a subject for an opera. Certainly he was thoroughly familiar with the theme from his classical training in the Akademische Gymnasium in Vienna. Throughout his career he continued an active interest in the classical period, reading extensively in the literature and about the culture of ancient Greece and writing frequently on classical themes.[1] In April 1908 a trip to Athens, Delphi, and Phokis served as the basis for three essays, collected now under the title *Augenblicke in Griechenland*.[2] This journey to Greece was exceedingly meaningful to Hofmannsthal's intellectual development; the essays describe three mystical experiences that made clear to him by direct revelation the importance of Greek culture to modern society and the relationship of his life to eternity.[3] Since the problem of time had

---

[1] One example of such reading in secondary materials is *The Rise of the Greek Epic* (2nd printing, 1911), by the classical philologist Gilbert Murray, whom Hofmannsthal counted "zu den bedeutenden reingesinnten Engländern. . . ." Hofmannsthal read this source between 22 January and 2 February 1912, while working on *Ariadne*. Other works read during this time include Murray's *A History of Ancient Greek Literature* and J. W. Makail's *Lectures on Greek Poetry;* see Michael Hamburger, "Hofmannsthal's Bibliothek," *Euphorion,* 55 (1960), 38-40. Hamburger makes no specific reference to *Ariadne* but the dates he provides place the background reading clearly in the period when this opera was being written.

[2] Part I, *Das Kloster des heiligen Lukas,* was published in 1908; Part II, *Der Wanderer,* in 1912; and Part III, *Die Statuen,* in 1917, when the three works were first published together. The collected version, *Augenblicke in Griechenland,* now forms the first essay of *Prosa* III, 3-42. A second trip to Greece in 1922 was described in an essay *Griechenland* in *Prosa* IV (Frankfurt am Main, 1955), 152-67.

[3] "Und indem ich mich immer stärker werden fühle und unter diesem einen Wort: Ewig, ewig! immer mehr meiner selbst verliere, schwingend wie die Säule erhitzter Luft über einer Brandstätte, frage ich mich, ausgehend wie die Lampe im völligen Licht des Tages: Wenn das Unerreichliche sich speist aus meinem Innern und das Ewige aus mir seine Ewigkeit sich aufbaut, was ist dann noch zwischen der Gottheit und mir?" *Augenblicke in Griechenland, Prosa* III, 42. For a more detailed interpretation of this essay see Walter Jens, *Hofmannsthal und die Griechen* (Tübingen, 1955), p. 136. According to Jens: "Die 'Augenblicke in Griechenland' analysieren, in dreifacher Variation, das Verhältnis von Erwartung und Eintreffen, Traum und jäher Erleuchtung, Dahinleben und plötzlicher Erfüllung." Another excellent analysis of these essays is to be found in Erwin Kobel, *Hugo von Hofmannsthal* (Berlin, 1970), pp. 180-200.

been of major concern to Hofmannsthal from the beginning of his career as a writer, this work became all important in helping him to find a resolution to this question which had important implications for *Ariadne*.[4]

Except for the Bacchus-Circe episode, the origin of which Hofmannsthal has documented (as will be shown), his precise literary source for *Ariadne* is not known. However, a comparison of Hofmannsthal's libretto with various classical versions of the legend suggests that he freely blended ideas from several sources in order to shape the myth to his own thematic design. Hofmannsthal was not gifted in inventing new plots, and for that reason most of his works are based on existing themes. But he always enriched his borrowed materials with his own ideas and original treatment.

His particular interest in reworking Greek myths began as early as 1893. He translated Euripides' *Alcestis*, a drama on the theme of the faithful, devoted wife, a text later used as a libretto by the composer Egon Wellesz. The power of this attraction to classical subjects is further seen in a number of other works Hofmannsthal created, many of them with Strauss who shared his enthusiasm for Greek culture. Hofmannsthal wrote the *Vorspiel zur Antigone des Sophokles* (1900), the drama *Elektra* (1904) which served as the libretto for the opera by Strauss in 1908, *Ödipus und die Sphinx* (1906), and the translation *König Ödipus* (1909).[5] Other works written in collaboration with Strauss include *Die Ruinen von Athen* (1924), a *Festspiel* with dances and choruses, and the opera *Die ägyptische Helena* (1926).[6] Hofmannsthal sought to restore these classical works to the stage by giving them contemporary values. In each instance the themes of the work chosen for revival coincided with Hofmannsthal's own ideas and outlook or at least provided a framework that would accommodate his views.[7] Such is the case with the myth of Ariadne and Bacchus which supplied him with basic materials to solve a moral problem that had intrigued and perplexed him from the time of his earliest works.

[4] For a valuable discussion of the relationship of memory and time in Hofmannsthal, see David H. Miles, *Hofmannsthal's Novel "Andreas": Memory and Self* (Princeton, 1972). Among other things Miles traces the development of these ideas to their culmination in the mythological operas.

[5] This list is by no means complete. For a fuller discussion of Hofmannsthal and Greece see Walter Jens, ibid., and Lilli Hagelberg, "Hofmannsthal und die Antike," *Zeitschrift für Aesthetik*, 17 (1923), 18-62. The most recent work on the subject and the most detailed account of Hofmannsthal's use of classical myths is Karl G. Esselborn, *Hofmannsthal und der antike Mythos* (Munich, 1969).

[6] In 1920 Hofmannsthal wrote a scenario entitled *Danae oder die Vernunftheirat*, which at the time did not attract Strauss. The composer completed this work in 1936 under the title *Die Liebe der Danae*, using a revised version of Hofmannsthal's text prepared by Joseph Gregor.

[7] With reference to a planned work based on Euripides entitled *Die Bacchen* which remained a fragment, Hofmannsthal commented in 1904 on the possibilities he saw in

88

Interest in Ariadne appears in earlier works, particularly in the drama *Der Abenteurer und die Sängerin* (1898), which in terms of plot and theme is directly parallel to the later opera. Through love and suffering, the heroine, Vittoria, is transformed into a great singer. The play ends with her singing of Ariadne:

> She is singing the great song of Ariadne,
> that she has declined for years to sing!
> The great Aria, where she stands
> on the carriage with Bacchus: O come, Lorenzo, come![8]

According to Wellesz, Hofmannsthal cited these same verses in a conversation as evidence of the importance of the Ariadne material to him and the long gestation period the subject required before he could shape it.[9]

Hofmannsthal's interest in the baroque period probably also played a role in the choice, for *Ariadne* is unquestionably one of the most famous of baroque opera plots. The numerous operatic adaptations of the Ariadne myth indicate an eternal fascination of every generation for the subject.[10]

Because of his exceedingly condensed treatment of the Ariadne-Bacchus myths, a knowledge of the orginal sources adds significantly to an understanding of Hofmannsthal's version by providing much of the background information that the poet possibly took entirely for granted in his audiences. Hofmannsthal felt, for example, that one of the least

---

using myths: "Es sind in diesem Stoff so schöne Möglichkeiten, fast ungreifbare, nie recht zu beredende Dinge allegorisch auszudrücken: als das Verhältnis des einzelnen zur Kunst oder besser, den unheimlichen Gegensatz jener beiden Verhältnisse zur Kunst, in denen eigentlich alle Menschen stehen: das des Enthusiasmus und das des wilden Hasses. Wie schön, daß dieser Mythos die Möglichkeit hergibt, das auszudrücken. Dabei ist es eine aufregende Handlung." *Briefe* II, 156.

[8] *Dramen* I (Frankfurt am Main, 1964), 272.

[9] "Wie sehr der Ariadne-Stoff aus Hofmannsthals zentraler Vorstellungswelt kam, möge die folgende Bemerkung des Dichters zeigen. Er sprach einmal davon, wie stark die Figuren seiner Dramen in ihm lebten und wie lange Zeit es oftmals brauche, bis eine sich ihm offenbarende Figur sichtbare Gestalt annähme. Er habe die erste Anregung zur Behandlung des Ariadne-Stoffes schon als junger Dichter empfangen, als er im Einakter 'Der Abenteurer und die Sängerin' die Schlußverse des Cesarino schrieb, der seine Mutter singen hört: . . ." Egon Wellesz, "Hofmannsthal und die Musik," *Hugo von Hofmannsthal*, ed. H. A. Fiechtner, p. 228.

[10] Ariadne's myth served as the basis for more than forty operas in the seventeenth and eighteenth centuries as well as for a number of cantatas and ballets. None of these operas, however, eclipsed the fame of the first setting *Arianna* (1608) by Claudio Monteverdi, which has been lost except for the superb *Lamento*. Other baroque composers among the many who wrote Ariadne operas include Provenzale, Cambert, Conradi, Kusser, Keiser, Leo, Marcello, Porpora, Pallavicini, Hasse, Benda, and Galuppi. For an interesting although incomplete study of the Ariadne legend in opera and drama see: Lilith Friedmann, *Die Gestaltung des Ariadnestoffes von der Antike bis zur Neuzeit*. (Diss. Vienna, 1933).

understood aspects of the work was that the song of Bacchus contained in brief his entire life story.[11] The character of Bacchus assumes an additional dimension when one realizes that he and Dionysus are the same person. Further, according to Heraclitus (one of Hofmannsthal's favorite authors), Hades and Dionysus are one and the same figure, thus vividly conveying the poet's idea of the interrelation of life and death. Ariadne is therefore not mistaken when she surrenders to Bacchus as the god of death. What she does not realize is that he also is, and will signify for her, a god of life.

Hofmannsthal's text is self-contained in the sense that it presents everything necessary for full understanding; however, the information often occurs in such a compressed form as to be missed or overlooked. Strauss's own reservations about the libretto's clarity and the confusion of critics up to the present day attest to the subtlety of the work.

In his attempt to pinpoint the sources used by Hofmannsthal, the critic Walter Jens suggests three choices: Hesiod, Catullus's sixty-fourth poem, or Tintoretto's painting in the Doge's Palace (Anticollegio) in Venice.[12] Of these versions, however, it would appear that Hesiod contributed little if anything, for he merely narrates succinctly the final fate of Ariadne:

> Dionysus, he of the golden hair,
> took blonde Ariadne,
> daughter of Minos, to be his
> Blossoming wife, and Kronian Zeus
> caused her likewise to be immortal and ageless.[13]

Catullus seems somewhat more related to Hofmannsthal's work, although indirectly, since his poem concentrates almost entirely on the relationship of Ariadne and Theseus, which is included in Hofmannsthal's text only by inference. Theseus never appears physically in the opera, but his presence is kept constantly in evidence by Ariadne's comments and above all by Strauss's music. Thus, a number of the details found in Catullus are noteworthy here, for they enrich the overall understanding of the opera: Thesus, son of King Aegus of Athens and Aethia, daughter of the King of Troexen, came to Cecrops, the land of Ariadne in order to prevent further human sacrifices to the Minotaur, a monster with a human body and a bull's head. The Athenians had been forced to pay tribute to King Minos of Crete by offering seven maidens and seven young men to the Minotaur each year.

---

[11] "es ist selten etwas weniger verstanden worden, als daß in dem Liedchen des Bacchus nicht nur eine Lebenssituation sondern eine ganze Lebensgeschichte darin steckt—daß er durch dieses Erlebnis gleichwertig neben Ariadne tritt. Das Entgegenkommen der mythischen Motive: Vorgeschichte des Bacchus, (Semelemotiv)." "Ad me Ipsum," *Aufzeichnungen*, p. 226.

[12] Jens, *Hofmannsthal und die Griechen*, p. 108.

[13] *The Works of Hesiod: The Theogony*, trans. Z. A. Elton (London, 1901), 1. 949.

When Theseus appeared at the palace of King Minos and offered to fight the Minotaur, Ariadne was seized by an overwhelming passion:

> Nor turned her burning glance away from him,
> Till all her inmost body caught the flame,
> And her heart's core ablaze (alas! for her)
> Woke passion in a soul unripe for love.[14]

Theseus entered the labyrinth and slew the Minotaur. Only by means of the thread provided by Ariadne was he able to escape from the labyrinth intended by King Minos to be Theseus's grave. Ariadne's love for Theseus causes her to disobey her father, turn away from her mother and sister, and to witness the slaying of her brother by Theseus. Catullus offers no motivation for Theseus's decision to leave the sleeping Ariadne on the island of Dias (Naxos), and the reader witnesses only Ariadne's tormented reaction of despair and bewilderment when she awakens and finds herself abandoned. Unlike Hofmannsthal's Ariadne who has passed beyond the stage of desperate outrage to a moribund calmness and a readiness for death, in Catullus's version passion turns to hatred, and Ariadne invokes bitter curses upon her faithless lover.[15] The God of gods grants her wish, and Theseus is punished by vengeance exacted upon his family.

None of this material concerning Theseus occurs in Hofmannsthal's version. Whereas Hofmannsthal dwells on the meeting of Bacchus and Ariadne, Catullus merely mentions his coming: ". . . there came/ Swift, bounding, blooming Bacchus, with his train/ Of Satyrs and Sileni, Nysa-born,/ Seeking thee, Ariadne, fired with love."[16]

Of Jens's three sources, the painting "Bacchus, Ariadne and Venus" found in the Doge's Palace comes closest to Hofmannsthal's conception. The portrait presents Ariadne and Bacchus, brought together by love. The youthfulness of Bacchus stressed by Hofmannsthal is fully evident in the picture, as is the idea of marriage, since Bacchus can be seen extending a ring toward Ariadne's left hand, which is held outstretched by Venus.

The fact that Ariadne subsequently marries Bacchus places the libretto into the framework of Hofmannsthal's later works, all of which stress marriage as the fundamental social unit. Discernible in the background of the painting is the ship of Bacchus, a prominent feature in Hofmannsthal's version. Also, Venus places on Ariadne's head a golden crown, which upon her death Bacchus threw into the heavens, where it formed a constellation of stars to immortalize her. Such immortality is implied in the opera in the concluding aria of Bacchus. Since this is a famous work of art and since Hofmannsthal frequently visited Venice, there is considerable probability that the painting was familiar to him.

[14] William A. Aiken, *The Poems of Catullus* (New York, 1950), p. 167.
[15] Ibid., pp. 169-70.
[16] Ibid., p. 171.

91

Another and more probable source than any of the above is not suggested by Jens; namely, the story of Ariadne found in Ovid's *Heroides and Amores*. Of all earlier versions this text most closely resembles Hofmannsthal's conception, particularly with respect to the characterization of Ariadne. Ovid's description of the heroine parallels Hofmannsthal's portrayal of Ariadne as a lost soul, existing in a languid, semi-trance condition between waking and sleeping.

In Ovid's version, Ariadne pours out her grief at having been deserted by Theseus and implores him to return. She describes her desperation and feels that she should not be left to die in this way. A major difference between the two variations is that in Ovid Ariadne is unreconciled to the thought of dying, while in Hofmannsthal she has reached the point of purifying her heart in preparation for death. Ovid also omits any mention of the arrival of Bacchus or of Ariadne's ultimate transformation.

Other sources further enrich the background story of Ariadne. One version explains that the reason Theseus deserted his bride on Naxos was possibly a magically-induced forgetfulness.[17] This important detail motivates how Theseus could abandon Ariadne after she had sacrificed her family for him and saved his life. Still another variation relates that Minerva commanded Theseus to leave Ariadne and that later he returned to Crete to marry Ariadne's sister, Phaedra.[18]

Kerenyi, in his book *The Gods of the Greeks,* relates additional variations on the Ariadne legend, which give further clues as to why the subject intrigued Hofmannsthal. Not only is the concept of marriage reinforced, but also the elevated status of Ariadne, who was mortal but virtually a goddess, made her ideal for the absolute contrast of human types that forms the basic structure of the opera:

> She was the only one who was ever spoken of as the god's wife, and her name was Ariadne. In the form in which the story of her became famous, she was the daughter of King Minos and Pasiphae, daughter of the Sun: a mortal maiden, but with the name of a goddess. "Ariadne," originally "Ariagne," meant the "holy" and "pure": it was a superlative form of Hagne, a surname of the queen of the Underworld. The goddess bearing this name was worshipped on many of our islands. Ariadne the mortal maiden had as her counterpart a sister and rival named Phaidra, "the bright," and indeed also a second, victorious lover of Theseus, her whose name was Aigle, "the shining." This second, bright aspect, however, was directly connected with Ariadne herself: she was also called Aridela, "the visible from afar," a name that she had obviously acquired after she had been raised to heaven with Dionysos.[19]

[17] *Oxford Classical Dictionary*, p. 88. It is also noteworthy that this motif of induced forgetfulness plays an important role in the later opera *Die ägyptische Helena*.
[18] Thomas Bulfinch, *The Age of Fable* (New York, 1914), pp. 125-26.
[19] C. Kerenyi, *The Gods of the Greeks* (London, 1951), p. 269.

Kerenyi provides a number of different explanations as to why Theseus abandoned Ariadne. The predominantly recurring version stresses that Theseus deserted Ariadne not out of unfaithfulness, but because Dionysos appeared to him in a dream and proclaimed that the girl was destined for himself. However, the alternative reason is also found, i.e., that Theseus forsook Ariadne because of her guilt: ". . . it is expressly stated that Ariadne was one of the great sinners, since she helped to kill her own brother."[20] Hofmannsthal ignored the idea that any guilt might be attached to Ariadne, concentrating instead exclusively on the virtue of faithfulness that sets her apart from the ordinary. Although other facets of her life and personality can be deduced from the exposition detailing her past actions, nothing detrimental to her character is mentioned. While such details would have enriched and possibly humanized her portrayal, he apparently felt that their inclusion would have made her a more ambiguous figure and thus would have distracted attention from the central thesis of the work.

Bacchus receives more attention in Hofmannsthal's retelling, and the poet makes his own original contribution to the myth by heightening the importance of this figure and stressing the relationship between Bacchus and Circe. The specific source for the meeting of Bacchus and Circe referred to in *Ariadne* is known from Hofmannsthal's earliest notes to the work, which attribute the idea and the tone for this confrontation to the following lines from Milton's famous masque *Comus* (1634):

Bacchus, that first from out the purple grape
Crushed the sweet poison of misused wine,
After the Tuscan mariners transformed,
Coasting the Tyrrhene shore, as the winds listed,
On Circe's island fell. (Who knows not Circe,
The daughter of the Sun, whose charmed cup
Whoever tasted lost his upright shape,
And downward fell into a grovelling swine?)
This Nymph, that gazed upon his clustering locks,
With ivy berries wreathed, and his blithe youth,
Had by him, ere he parted thence, a son
Much like his father, but his mother more,
Whom therefore she brought up, and Comus named.[21]

---

[20] Ibid., p. 270. None of these alternative possibilities motivating the abandonment of Ariadne by Theseus figured into Hofmannsthal's conception. Although the poet leaves the cause unexplained, Theseus fits easily into the line of adventurers (all based more or less on the archetype Casanova) in Hofmannsthal's works who are incapable of remaining faithful to any one woman.

[21] Willi Schuh, "Zu Hofmannsthals 'Ariadne'-Szenarium und -Notizen," *Die Neue Rundschau,* 71 (1960), 88-89. A recent article adds further information concerning the influence of Milton's "L'Allegro," "Il Pensoroso," and *Comus* on *Ariadne*. See Hanna B. Lewis, "Hofmannsthal and Milton," *Modern Language Notes,* 87 (1972), p. 732-41.

In his love for the mortal Ariadne, Bacchus follows the same pattern as his parents. The mother of Bacchus (or Dionysus) was Semele, a mortal woman married to Jupiter. Through the plotting of Juno, Semele was persuaded to ask Jupiter to show himself to her. Despite his protestations, Semele would not be deterred, until finally with great reluctance he granted her wish. As Jupiter and Juno had known in advance, Semele could not endure the brilliance of his godly state and was consumed in flames.

In 1901 in an outline for a *Phantastische Dichterkomödie*, Hofmannsthal had drafted a sketch entitled *Jupiter and Semele*.[22] The characterization of Semele as found in this fragment fits not only Ariadne but also a number of Hofmannsthal's other heroines such as Alkestis, Sobeide, and Elektra.[23] Women predominate as the central characters of his writings, and what Hofmannsthal calls the tragic basic motive of this brief sketch could in fact serve as a motto for many of his works: "Weibliches will hin, wo Weibliches Vernichtung findet."[24]

To return to the discussion of Ariadne myths, Kerenyi describes a wall painting in Rome which offers still another version of the theme conceivably pertinent to Hofmannsthal's conception. Since this painting concerns primarily the meeting of Ariadne and Bacchus it merits consideration as a possible source, despite the obvious differences in the characterization of the former. For here Ariadne is not a mortal, she is accompanied by a servant, and she is neither desperate nor vengeful.[25] In Kerenyi's words:

> A magnificently preserved wall-painting in Rome records the tale of how Dionysos met his divine bride—who was certainly no earthly maiden, but the risen Persephone or Aphrodite. When he found her—she was neither asleep nor forsaken. The goddess, sitting on the island crag with a servant female companion beside her, welcomed the young god as he approached unattended from the sea. She held a bowl out to him, that Dionysos might fill it and the epiphany of wine might be his doing. A later tale added that Dionysos commemorated the goddess, his companion, by setting in the heavens the famous golden wreath, the Crown of Ariadne.[26]

Another painting that deserves consideration is the well-known work by Titian in the National Gallery in London. While it contains many of

---

[22] *Dramen* II (Frankfurt am Main, 1966), 504-505.
[23] Ibid., 504. "Ihr [Semeles] dämonischer, tragischer Zug: bis zum Äußersten gehen zu wollen. So hat sie ihre Familie verlassen."
[24] Ibid., 505.
[25] Actually, Hofmannsthal's original scenario closely resembles this version. When Bacchus's arrival is heralded, Zerbinetta, acting as her maid, adorns her as if for death. The initial meeting of the couple resembles a king greeting a princess. Ariadne "bittet ihn, ihm die honneurs ihrer Grotte machen zu dürfen." Willi Schuh, "Zu Hofmannsthals 'Ariadne'-Szenarium und -Notizen," *Die Neue Rundschau,* 71 (1960), 94-95.
[26] Kerenyi, *The Gods of the Greeks,* pp. 271-72.

the same elements found in other versions of the meeting of Bacchus and Ariadne, the portrayal has the added feature of wild animals, satyrs, as well as the servants of Bacchus. Whether the satyrs were on the island or formed part of Bacchus's retinue is unclear. One can, however, speculate that possibly this combination of satyrs, revelers, and gods might have triggered Hofmannsthal's imagination to counterpose Ariadne and Bacchus by Zerbinetta and Harlekin. In the initial version of the text which was never used, he had intended Ariadne and Bacchus to be followed at the end of the opera by Zerbinetta and the dancers.

The portrayal by Guido Reni in "Bacco e Arianne" (Palazzo di Montecitorio, Rome) follows the same basic plan as Titian's version, although the divine element is much more pronounced. As the title indicates, Bacchus, the central figure in Hofmannsthal's conception, dominates the picture by being placed in the center of the action and by the darker coloring of his robe. Ariadne is being introduced to Bacchus by her maid, the role Hofmannsthal in his original scenario had intended for Zerbinetta by having her prepare Ariadne for the arrival of Bacchus. The satyrs and revelers are shown dancing around the lovers, while cherubs and angels hover in the heavens above. One of the cherubs is Amor; another holds the diadem of stars with which Ariadne is to be crowned. The two angels indicate the divine blessing on the union.

Another visual interpretation of Ariadne and Bacchus that Hofmannsthal must have known well was "The Triumph of Ariadne" by Hans Makart, possibly the foremost Austrian painter in the nineteenth century. This work, which was painted in 1873, originally served as the curtain for the Vienna Opera until it was acquired by the Vienna Imperial Gallery of Art (*Österreichische Galerie*) in 1895. The painting stresses the sensuous and erotic implications of Bacchus's arrival and contains none of the idealized emotions found in Hofmannsthal's version. Makart concentrates on the revelry between the satyrs and the compliant hand maidens in a Dionysian scene stressing music and dancing. It is possible that such a portrayal could have contributed to the decision to use the dancers in *Ariadne* to provide a contrast to the serious drama. In Makart's version, Ariadne appears indeed triumphant, but solely in the physical sense prophesied by Zerbinetta rather than in the ambiguous double meaning intended by Hofmannsthal.

As has been shown, while Hofmannsthal's version of the legend corresponds in every detail with one version of the myth or another, he has freely combined elements and omitted major details. His main contribution toward modernizing the myth was to introduce the "allomatic" element, that is, the ecstatic, magical moment of mutual transformation that forms the culmination of the opera. In *Ad me Ipsum,* his personal analysis of his works, Hofmannsthal stressed both the blending of myths as well as the "allomatic" concept in *Ariadne:* "Crossing of mythical motives. The mutual transformation. The allomatic element."[27] In keeping with his aim to revitalize earlier works, Hofmannsthal has infused this classical myth with insights of modern psychology. In earlier myths Dionysus was already a fledged god, whose character remained constant throughout. In Hofmannsthal's *Ariadne,* however, he is a young demi-god on the threshold of maturity. He and Ariadne react upon and to each other. Prepared for this moment by their past experiences and sufferings, both undergo inner changes as a result of their mutual love and both undergo transformation to a new, higher level of existence. Ariadne attains immortality and Bacchus becomes a mature full-fledged god.

In utilizing a classical theme, Hofmannsthal followed his normal inclination to work in terms of older, well-established texts. His strength, and to a certain degree his ultimate greatness as a poet, lies precisely in his ability to invest basic universal ideas with new insights and thus recharge them with new life. In general—and this by no means detracts from his importance as one of the outstanding authors of the twentieth century and perhaps the greatest Austrian writer of all times—Hofmannsthal took his inspiration from literature rather than directly from life.[28] With the exception of his poetry, many of his writings are either adaptations or translations of earlier works. Typical of his humanistic outlook, Hofmannsthal believed that every generation had the obligation to keep alive the Western heritage of ideas, rewriting the older classics in such a way that they preserve the past and at the same time contain the values and attitudes relevant to contemporary society.[29] Wellesz made much the same observation in connection with the early drama *Alkestis* which, as mentioned, he himself used as a libretto for one of his operas:

> It is the nature of the stories which the Greek poets have left to us that many different facets are contained in them, so that every age can turn to that in which it may see its own experience as in a mirror. And the characters of these dramas only take their place among our permanent possessions, only remain alive, because each age has formed them afresh, and so filled them with its own life.

[27] *Aufzeichnungen,* (Frankfurt am Main, 1959), p. 218.

[28] For further discussion of this point see Michael Hamburger, "Hofmannsthals Bibliothek," *Euphorion,* 55 (1960), 39.

[29] Hofmannsthal expressed himself explicitly on this point in connection with his now famous, though often misunderstood essay *Ein Brief.* In reply to Andrian's criticism about using a historical mask to present his ideas, Hofmannsthal justified himself as follows: "Ich denke, darin kein einziges bloß formales, kostümiertes Totengespräch zu geben—der Gehalt soll überall für mich und mir Nahestehende aktuell sein, —aber wenn Du mich wieder heißen wolltest, diesen Gehalt *direkt* zu geben, so ginge für mich aller Anreiz zu dieser Arbeit verloren, —der starke Reiz für mich ist, vergangene Zeiten nicht ganz tot sein zu lassen, oder Fernes, Fremdes als nah verwandt spüren zu machen." *Briefe* II (Vienna, 1937), p. 100.

The *Alkestis* of Hugo von Hofmannsthal is such a recreation. The poet called his work "Tragedy after Euripides." If, however, the Greek drama is compared with that of the modern poet, it is clear that Hofmannsthal handled the material very freely. With a miraculous instinct the young poet found the way back to the sources of the drama, to the stratum of myth from which it grew, and tried to prune it of later accretions, until it took the form which lies behind the drama of Euripides.[30]

In *Ariadne,* also, Hofmannsthal eliminated from the classical myths all extraneous matter in order to present in its purest state the essential idea, which he saw as the nucleus of the archetypal situation: mutual transformation through love.[31] In its stark simplicity and because of the exclusive focus on the meeting between the two lovers, this libretto resembles a work of sculpture. Like a sculptor, Hofmannsthal has picked the most fruitful moment in time for presentation, forcing the audience in its imagination to carry the action forward to its culmination. The choice of the exact moment to portray required no difficult decision for Hofmannsthal, for in his opinion the first meeting between individuals was the decisive erotic confrontation.[32] Such a meeting occurs twice in *Ariadne*, between Zerbinetta and the Composer in the *Vorspiel* and between Ariadne and Bacchus in the opera.

By using this classical subject to create a baroque opera with a modern psychological basis, Hofmannsthal has wedded together three of the most fertile literary periods in the history of man. Myths attracted him for the very reason that they enabled him to abolish the historical sense of past and present and render essential ideas in their most universal, timeless form.[33] At the same time writing in terms of

[30] Egon Wellesz, *Essays on Opera* (London, 1959), p. 146.

[31] The indestructible element in the classical works of art and in himself formed one of the bonds of communication between them, as Hofmannsthal pointed out in connection with his memory of the Greek statues that had taught him the secret of eternity: "In der Tat, ich erinnere mich ihrer, und in dem Maß, als ich mich dieser Erinnerung gebe, in dem Maß vermag ich meiner selbst zu vergessen. Dieses Selbstvergessen ist ein seltsames deutliches Geschehen: es ist ein grandioses Abwerfen, Teil um Teil, Hülle um Hülle, ins Dunkle. Es wäre wollüstig, wenn Wollust in so hohe Regionen reichte. Ungemessen mich abwerfend, auflösend, werde ich immer stärker: unzerstörbar bin ich im Kern. Unzerstörbar, so sind diese, mir gegenüber. Es wäre undenkbar, sich an ihre Oberfläche anschmiegen zu wollen. Diese Oberfläche ist ja gar nicht da—sie entsteht durch ein beständiges Kommen zu ihr, aus unerschöpflichen Tiefen. Sie sind da, und sind unerreichlich. So bin auch ich. Dadurch kommunizieren wir." *Prosa* III, 40-41.

[32] "Mich dünkt, es ist nicht die Umarmung, sondern die Begegnung die eigentliche entscheidende erotische Pantomime." "Die Wege und die Begegnungen," *Prosa* II, 306. Other important examples of this magical moment of initial encounter are found in the poem *Die Beiden,* perhaps Hofmannsthal's most dramatic poem, and in *Der Rosenkavalier,* in the first meeting between Sophie and Octavian, when he presents her with the silver rose.

[33] This sense of timelessness came to him during one of his mystical experiences in Greece: "Der eigentliche Inhalt dieses Augenblickes aber war in mir dies: ich verstand dieses Lächeln, weil ich wußte: ich sehe dies nicht zum erstenmal, auf irgendwelche Weise, in

97

myth, in which everything represents itself and its opposite simultaneously, permitted him to achieve perfect balance as well.[34] His recognition of his own achievement in *Ariadne* was possibly the main reason for his great affection for this work and his unqualified conviction that it would endure.

For the contemporary age to draw strength from the classical period was not only a desirable artistic practice from the point of view of aesthetics, but, in Hofmannsthal's opinion, was a political necessity if the Western world was to survive. In 1926, dismayed by the destruction of the values of civilization that he prized and had devoted his life to upholding, Hofmannsthal emphasized the critical state prevailing in Europe following the war and the necessity for returning to the "spirit of antiquity."[35]

irgendwelcher Welt bin ich vor diesen gestanden, habe ich mit diesen irgendwelche Gemeinschaft gepflogen, und seitdem habe alles in mir auf einen solchen Schrecken gewartet, und so furchtbar mußte ich mich in mir berühren, um wieder zu werden, der ich war.—Ich sage 'seitdem' und 'damals,' aber nichts von den Bedingtheiten der Zeit konnte anklingen in der Hingenommenheit, an die ich mich verloren hatte; sie war dauerlos und das, wovon sie erfüllt war, trug sich außerhalb der Zeit zu." *Prosa* III, 36-37.

[34] "Mythisch ist alles Erdichtete, woran du als Lebender Anteil hast. Im Mythischen ist jedes Ding durch einen Doppelsinn, der sein Gegensinn ist, getragen: Tod = Leben, Schlangenkampf = Liebesumarmung. Darum ist im Mythischen alles im Gleichgewicht." *Aufzeichnungen*, pp. 34-35.

[35] "Das, wofür Sie einstehen, ist der *Geist der Antike;* ein so großes Numen, daß kein einzelner Tempel, obwohl viele ihm geweiht sind, es faßt.

Es ist unser Denken selber; es ist das, was den europäischen Intellekt geformt hat.

Es ist die eine Grundfeste der Kirche und aus dem zur Weltreligion gewordenen Christentum nicht auszuscheiden; ohne Platon und Aristoteles nicht Augustin noch Thomas.

Es ist die Sprache der Politik, ihr geistiges Element, vermöge dessen ihre wechselnden und ewig wiederkehrenden Formen in unser geistiges Leben eingehen können.

Es ist der Mythos unseres europäischen Daseins, die Kreation unserer geistigen Welt (ohne welche die religiöse nicht sein kann), die Setzung von Kosmos gegen Chaos, und er umschließt den Helden und das Opfer, die Ordnung und die Verwandlung, das Maß und die Weihe.

Es ist kein angehäufter Vorrat, der veralten könnte, sondern eine mit Leben trächtige Geisteswelt in uns selber: unser wahrer innerer Orient, offenes, unverwesliches Geheimnis.

Es ist ein herrliches Ganzes: tragender Strom zugleich und jungfräulicher Quell, der immer rein hervorbricht. Nichts in seinem Bereich ist so alt, daß es nicht morgen als ein Neues, strahlend vor Jugend, hervortreten könnte. Homer glänzt in alter Herrlichkeit, alterslos wie das Meer, aber seinen Helden Achilleus hat Hölderlins Seelenblick getroffen, und er steht in neuem, ungeahntem Licht. Heraklit, für ein Jahrtausend nichts als ein Name, ist an den Tag getreten, und seine dunkle Lehre ist heute wieder seelenbildende Gewalt. Die dunklen ältesten Mythen, eingemauert in die Grundfesten des Werkes der Tragiker, haben in dem wunderbaren Schweizer, dem lange verkannten, ihren Deuter gefunden; noch einmal breitet sich in seinen Werken, wie einst im antiken Lebensbereich, das *Ganze* dieser Geisteswelt, vom orphischen Spruch bis zur mythischen Anekdote, die ein byzantinischer Spätling überliefert." "Vermächtnis der Antike," *Prosa* IV, 316-17.

Thus, from every standpoint—aesthetically, thematically, psychologically, socially, and politically, *Ariadne* possesses major importance as a representation of Hofmannsthal's intellectual and artistic attitudes. Once the background of the legends is known and the meaning of the opera discerned, this fragile and reputedly "thin" opera begins to reveal in addition to its extraordinary beauty the ever deepening dimensions of significance that have been buried so deceptively in the shallowest surface possible.

Chapter VI

Interpretation of the *Vorspiel*

In the original version of *Ariadne* a short prose scene provided a transition between the two-act adaptation of Molière's comedy *Le Bourgeois gentilhomme* and the opera. When Hofmannsthal decided to abandon the play and to make the opera an independent work, he retained the *Vorspiel* as an introductory act. This gave the audience the necessary exposition for understanding the opera and also made the work long enough for an entire evening in the opera house. The only alternative would have been to expand the opera itself into a longer, self-contained work. Although such a plan would have been feasible, considering the richness of the subject, the poet and composer never discussed this course of action.

The first version of the *Vorspiel,* as a transitional scene, required little internal unity of its own. At the same time, it was intended as a direct means of explaining to the audience the symbolic meaning of the characters and events in the opera. As has been seen, Reinhardt apparently thought this scene so dispensable that he deleted it at the premiere. In preparing the work for Munich in 1913, Strauss had stressed the importance of retaining what he called the dressing room scene (*C.,* 166). Yet, reviews of such performances including the *Vorspiel* showed no greater comprehension of the work.

There can be no doubt, however, that in revising the *Vorspiel* Hofmannsthal improved it. He enriched the scene aesthetically by endowing it with its own internal dramatic unity. With only minimal changes and additions he deepened the character of both Zerbinetta and the Composer, making the latter now the central focus of the act. More importantly, he also joined this scene to the opera in an ingenious manner that has not been noted previously.[1] As will be shown, the revised *Vorspiel* has been artfully constructed so that it directly parallels the opera in characterization, content, and structure. It is in essence a mirror

---

[1] The most perceptive analysis of the *Vorspiel* to date is an excellent paper by Barbara Könneker, "Die Funktion des Vorspiels in Hofmannsthals *Ariadne auf Naxos,*" *Germanisch-Romanische Monatsschrift,* NS 20 (1972), 124-41. This article, which appeared after my own interpretation was completed, is written with a different emphasis and contains only a few points of similar findings. Essentially Miss Könneker failed to see the absolute integration of the *Vorspiel* into the overall structure of the opera.

image of the opera.[2] The work, however, does not break into two separate but equal halves, for neither segment can stand alone. Rather, the *Vorspiel* and the opera together combine to form a complete, indissoluble artistic structure. Thus, the opera by its very structure becomes a symbol for the totality of existence, with the *Vorspiel* representing the mundane, everyday world of physical appearance and the opera the transcendental world.

To accomplish these new goals Hofmannsthal expanded the revised *Vorspiel* by almost one half of its former length. For greater clarity a number of textual alterations were also made in the original dialogue. One major revision involved the shift of locale from France to Vienna, a change probably resulting from Hofmannsthal's desire to eliminate any recollection of the unfortunate Molière comedy in connection with the new version of *Ariadne*. Possibly, too, Hofmannsthal felt more comfortable with an Austrian setting, having employed virtually the same background in *Der Rosenkavalier*. Although the new *Vorspiel* establishes no identifiable historical period, the milieu and the costumes indicate that the action is still set in the seventeenth century, one of Hofmannsthal's favorite periods.

The opera now takes place not in the home of Jourdain but rather in the mansion of the richest man in Vienna, who remains unnamed except to be called the Maecenas. Even though the name Jourdain has been omitted, he clearly served as the prototype for this Maecenas who is also a pretentious, socially ambitious bourgeois without taste or cultural refinement. He cannot be otherwise, for the opera with its blend of forms is predicated on the idea that only a man lacking aesthetic taste would order such an artistic mélange. The audience must deduce the character of the Maecenas through his commands, for he never appears personally, as Jourdain had in the original version, but remains in the background like an allegorical figure.

A subtle but important shift in the character of the Maecenas is achieved by his very absence from the scene. Since he is invisible, he becomes omnipresent, causing the characteristic of autocratic power to predominate over the quality of foolishness. In the first version the opposite was true of Jourdain, who was largely a buffoon. In making this significant change of emphasis, for reasons that will be discussed later, it is possible that Hofmannsthal endowed the Maecenas with some of the qualities of Louis XIV. It was Louis XIV who had originally commanded Molière to tailor *Le Bourgeois gentilhomme* to his wishes just as the Maecenas is shown here ordering an entertainment according to his own fancy. Hofmannsthal was thoroughly familiar with Molière's works, and it is quite probable that the analogous genesis for both works was consciously intended.

[2] Hofmannsthal usually preferred indirect presentation of his ideas. For an analysis of what may be the most elaborate use of the mirror image construction in Hofmannsthal's works, see D. G. Daviau, "Hugo von Hofmannsthal's Pantomime: Der Schüler, "*Modern Austrian Literature,* 1/1 (Spring, 1968), 4-30.

While the *Vorspiel* thus shows a number of alterations in content, the manner of presentation was subjected to an even more radical change. Originally designed as a prose scene in order to insure that the audience would understand the words, the dialogue was now intended largely for *secco* recitative, a style of setting words to music so as to avoid making the vocal melody more important than the words. Strauss was able to add interest to the recitatives by acquainting the audience with fragments of the music to come (largely by the orchestral accompaniment), while still keeping the musical interest subdued, so that the *Vorspiel* could fulfill its principal purpose of elucidating the meaning of the opera. This change, too, probably stemmed from the desire to make the *Vorspiel* more "operatic" and to eliminate further any suggestion of a play joined to an opera. Strauss had originally advanced the idea of using *secco* recitatives, but it was only after Hofmannsthal heard Mozart's *Marriage of Figaro* that the possibilities of this vocal style began to take substance in his mind (*C.*, 152). Mozart also figured importantly in the construction of the new *Vorspiel* in another way, for it appears almost certain on the basis of Hofmannsthal's notes that the young Mozart served as a model for the Composer.[3]

The original version exploited the idea of the play within a play, and to reinforce this device the *Vorspiel* concluded with the seating of Jourdain and his guests in boxes on the sides of the stage, where they remained during the performance of the opera. Although this arrangement added a touch of realism, the critics complained that Jourdain's asides and interjections made during the opera were annoying and distracting. As has been shown, Hofmannsthal and Strauss seriously debated whether to maintain the framework even in the new version before deciding finally to eliminate the entire stage business and to conclude the opera without returning again to the play. This open-endedness might (and has been) considered an artistic flaw, but if so, it is one that redounds to the benefit of the opera. As Hofmannsthal recognized, a return to the prosaic world with its materialistic concerns would destroy the majestic spiritual quality of the ending of the work as it now stands.

[3] Willi Schuh, who published Hofmannsthal's original scenario which contains a reference to Mozart, commented: "Zwischen den zur 'Ariadne'-Oper gehörenden Notizen von Blatt I steht unvermittelt der Satz: 'Vorspiel: siehe Mozart, Verkehr mit Sängerinnen.' Er bezieht sich auf die zwischen 'Bürger als Edelmann' und 'Ariadne auf Naxos' vermittelnde Überleitungsszene. Durch diesen Satz dürfte Martin Sterns Vermutung, Hofmannsthal habe beim 'Komponisten' zeitweilig eine Wagner-Karikatur im Sinne gehabt, in Frage gestellt sein. Der Hinweis auf Mozart erfährt übrigens durch einen handschriftlichen Zusatz in dem für den Komponisten bestimmten Maschinenexemplar des 'Vorspiels' der 'Neuen Bearbeitung' eine Bestätigung: Zu den ersten, an den Lakaien gerichteten Sätzen des Komponisten, der 'eilig von rückwärts auftritt,' fügt Hofmannsthal dort die Bemerkung: 'umflossen mit Grazie, trotz der scheinbaren Trockenheit.' Das deutet gewiß nicht Wagner, sondern auf eine dem jungen Mozart angenäherte Figur." Willi Schuh, "Zu Hofmannsthals 'Ariadne,' " *Die Neue Rundschau*, 71 (1960), 89.

Despite Hofmannsthal's efforts to the contrary, the original prose scene had a very weak curtain: the wily opportunist, Dorantes, is shown arranging a rendezvous with Dorimene. The new version of the *Vorspiel* concludes with a most effective climax. The Composer, who now dominates the action, delivers the last word at a high pitch of emotion. Recovering from a temporary trance brought on by his fascination for the seductive Zerbinetta, he explodes in a temperamental outburst at his foolishness in being deluded by such a woman. In exaggerated anger he inveighs against the music teacher for allowing him to become involved in this farcical enterprise. Finally, furious with himself, the Composer storms off the stage in despair at having acquiesced in permitting his opera to be prostituted by being performed with Zerbinetta's dance troupe. The curtain falls quickly, and at this point the intermission takes place.

Other changes involved some of the minor characters. For example, in the first version the orders of Monsieur Jourdain to the musicians and dancers are transmitted by an ordinary servant. However, since the Maecenas never appears in person in the altered version, his servant as his representative and spokesman becomes more important as the major means by which the audience obtains some notion of his character. Thus, in the new version Hofmannsthal elevated this figure to a pompous but imposing *Haushofmeister* or Major-Domo, a change which reinforces the idea that Louis XIV served now as the prototype for the Maecenas. The absolute authority of his master is expressed clearly in the imperious reply of the *Haushofmeister* to the Music Teacher, who had commented that the Composer would never permit his work to be performed as ordered: "Wer wird? Ich höre: gestatten. Ich wüßte nicht, wer außer meinem gnädigen Herrn, in dessen Palais Sie sich befinden und Ihre Kunstfertigkeiten heute zu produzieren die Ehre haben, etwas zu gestatten—geschweige denn anzuordnen hätte!"[4] [Who will—do I hear right?—not allow? Did I hear right? I would not know who would have to allow—not to mention command—anything except my noble master in whose mansion you are and where you have the honor today of exhibiting your tricks].

This speech, which has been added in the new *Vorspiel,* shows the shift in the characterization of the Maecenas from amiable buffoon to authoritarian figure.[5] In the original version the servant's manner of speaking is much less formal and commanding in tone than that of the *Haushofmeister,* who speaks in an exaggeratedly elaborate manner, announcing his master's wishes, however ludicrous, in the somber tones of unalterable pronouncements.

---

[4] *Ariadne auf Naxos, Lustspiele* III (Frankfurt am Main, 1956), 10. All translations of the opera are our own.

[5] It did not require a great deal to make this change, for the idea of absolute authority is present in the first version, although in a less conspicuous manner. Another speech in the

To accentuate and gain the fullest comic advantage from his use of involved, circuitous language, Hofmannsthal makes the *Haushofmeister* the only character who speaks his role without musical accompaniment of any kind. The dialogue for all of the remaining characters is set to music, predominantly to recitative. The *Haushofmeister* (and the Maecenas he represents) also lacks musical accompaniment because he is a wholly realistic figure. The main purpose for his spoken role is to establish immediately the difference between the pragmatic, prosaic world of the *Bourgeois gentilhomme* and the idealistic world of the creative artist. The contrast is developed additionally in smaller ways, such as by the opposing attitudes toward art. The Composer is willing to make any sacrifice for his work, while the *Haushofmeister* refers to his composition deprecatingly as *Notenarbeit* [note spinning].

The solid, ceremonial imperiousness of the *Haushofmeister,* when viewed against the seeming absurdity of his instruction, namely his Master's desire to have both the opera and the impromptu dance staged simultaneously so that the program will be finished for the nine o'clock fireworks display, introduces an added quotient of humor into the new *Vorspiel.* Similarly, the excited reaction of the Composer and the singers and the indifference of the dancers to this capricious and seemingly mad arrangement produces a greater comic effect when contrasted to the deadpan imperturbability of the *Haushofmeister* than was the case in the first version.

Although the comic vitality of the second version has thus been slightly improved, it must be admitted that in performance even this revised version hardly produces an uproarious comedy, which in any case was not Hofmannsthal's style. The animated bustling of the performers often seems much ado about very little and for the most part is not particularly amusing. The petty bickering and personal rivalry between the star singers, while possibly an accurate portrayal of backstage life among performers, is neither a novel nor exciting idea. Yet, when well performed, the *Vorspiel* does sustain the interest of the audience. Above all, the moments of musical lyricism that have been inserted, especially the splendid aria by the Composer celebrating music as the

first version (and restated in the new version), while intended primarily to stress the foolish reason for Jourdain's apparently ridiculous order to stage the tragic opera and Zerbinetta's dance simultaneously, explicitly states the extent of his power: "Es ist wohl nicht die Sache meines gnädigen Herrn, wenn er ein Spektakel bezahlt, sich auch noch damit abzugeben, wie es ausgeführt werden soll. Ein Mann wie Herr Jourdain ist gewohnt, anzuordnen und seine Anordnungen befolgt zu sehen. Zudem will ich Ihnen sagen, ist mein gnädiger Herr schon seit heute morgen ungehalten darüber, daß in einem so wohlausgestatteten Hause wie das seinige ein so jämmerlicher Schauplatz wie eine wüste Insel ihm vorgestellt werden soll, und ist eben, um dem abzuhelfen, auf den Gedanken gekommen, diese wüste Insel durch das Personal aus dem andern Stück einigermaßen anständig staffieren zu lassen." *Lustspiele* III, 151-52.

most sacred of the arts, are so spectacular that they enable the *Vorspiel* to triumph over the comic deficiencies of a plot, which without music would appear as romanticized melodrama.

On the level of dramatic construction and characterization, however, Hofmannsthal was considerably more successful; indeed, he succeeded almost too well. His attempt to interject greater substance into what was originally conceived as a relatively unimportant transition scene resulted in the employment of such subtle nuances that the full implications of this scene cannot possibly be comprehended in performance. This difficulty in appreciating the *Vorspiel,* however, does not interfere with its purpose of laying the proper groundwork for the opera, for the information needed by the audience is presented directly in readily comprehensible form. By supplying such interpretative commentary for his work—a concession on his part that went against his usual practice—Hofmannsthal indulged in a technique that modern authors have since resorted to with increasing frequency. Bertolt Brecht and Friedrich Dürrenmatt, for example, often provide interpretative hints about their writings in either a preface or postscript as well as in separate essays. However, Hofmannsthal's method of integrating the commentary into the body of the work itself is unique.

The main point is that despite its greater internal unity, the new *Vorspiel,* like its predecessor, must be judged primarily in functional rather than in strictly dramatic terms. Because audiences and critics alike failed to comprehend the original *Ariadne,* Hofmannsthal added further information to the exposition for greater clarity. While this functional purpose partly explains the artistic rationale behind the *Vorspiel,* it does not, of course, entirely overcome its theatrical deficiencies. In general it remains as true today as in Hofmannsthal's time that the ultimate appeal of *Ariadne* rests on the opera and not on the *Vorspiel.*

The elimination of Molière's play naturally necessitated a number of changes in the *Vorspiel.* All references to the play had to be deleted, while verbal and musical allusions to the opera, which had been included in the comedy, now were incorporated into the new *Vorspiel.* The beginning and the end were also changed. In the first version the scene opened with the Primadonna expecting Jourdain to pay his respects to her as was his custom.[6] This suggestion of a sub-plot hinted that there may have been an alliance between the two or at least a hope for something of the kind in her mind. The act ended with Dorantes and Dorimene preparing for their rendezvous after the opera. Both of these

---

[6] The comparison as presented here is based on the two printed versions of Hofmannsthal's text found in *Lustspiele* III. Reinhardt's *Regiebuch* (published by Fürstner; Berlin, 1912) varies slightly from both of these texts. There the Molière play runs directly to the servant's speech ordering both entertainments to be presented simultaneously. From this point on Reinhardt's text and Hofmannsthal's first version are the same.

details of the first version, rendered superfluous by the dropping of the play, were cut. Now, when the Primadonna learns of the new arrangements to have the opera and dance performed simultaneously, she demands twice to see the Count, but her statements contain none of the allusions to a possible affair between them, as was suggested by the first version.

The major change of emphasis in the new *Vorspiel* was to place the Composer firmly into the center of the action. In this way, the Composer regained some of the lines and prominence that he had possessed as a character in the Molière play. By stressing the artistic and personal conflict within the youthful musician, Hofmannsthal provides a central focus for the brief act as well as dramatic unity and interest. The Composer commands the center of the stage for most of the action and has the final word. His beautiful aria celebrating the glory of music serves as a stirring climax to the *Vorspiel* and is one of the reasons why singers cherish the part.[7] Like most other aspects of the *Vorspiel,* this aria also performs a dual function. By calling attention to the unifying capability of music as well as its power to express the inexpressible, Hofmannsthal stresses the paramount role of the music in the opera to follow. This is but one instance of how he incorporated ideas from the opera into the new *Vorspiel*. As will be seen, the same is also true of the music. It is in fact impossible to understand the full implications of the *Vorspiel* until after one has comprehended the opera.

Strauss originally offered Hofmannsthal the option of modeling the Composer after himself. He suggested, half jokingly, that the Composer could even be allowed a flirtation with Zerbinetta as long as the portrait was not too realistic. Although Hofmannsthal did not respond to either of these suggestions at the time they were made, he now fell back upon them and executed the second idea just as Strauss had proposed, although for reasons that had to do with the text rather than with Strauss. By confronting the inexperienced, idealistic Composer with the worldly coquette, Zerbinetta, Hofmannsthal enriches his character. At the same time this juxtaposition highlights the concept of contrasting worlds that forms the basic structure of both opera and *Vorspiel*. Just as we have seen this contrast earlier between the world of the rich bourgeois and that of the Composer, as symbolized by the desert island setting in the baroque mansion, now we are shown a further contrast between the idealized outlook on life of a dreamily "romantic" musician and the more realistic view of Zerbinetta. By being thrust into

[7] Lotte Lehmann, for example, who became famous overnight in this role and felt it to be decisive for her later successful career, enthusiastically endorsed the part: "I have always loved this role. Later on, when at Strauss's behest I sang Ariadne, I always used to stand backstage during the entire Prologue, listening to the Composer with longing in my heart and wishing that I could sing both roles at once." Lotte Lehmann, *Five Operas and Richard Strauss* (New York, 1964), pp. 5-6.

the performance at the express order of Maecenas, Zerbinetta later becomes the mechanism by which his pragmatic attitude is also introduced into the opera to contrast with Ariadne's ideal view. Here again Hofmannsthal worked from the opera back to the *Vorspiel,* for the Composer represents Ariadne's values and attitudes. Like her, he may be considered the rare individual among millions who is dedicated uncompromisingly to absolute standards and values. Thus the Composer *vis à vis* Zerbinetta in the *Vorspiel* is analogous to Ariadne contrasted with Zerbinetta in the opera.

Ultimately, the Composer emerges not as a portrayal of Strauss nor even of young Mozart, as Hofmannsthal originally intended, but as a composite depiction of the idealistic artist struggling to uphold his principles. There are similarities with Goethe's Werther, particularly in the tendency toward emotional excess, and in some ways, specifically in his reverence for art, the Composer even resembles an exaggerated self-portrait of Hofmannsthal himself as a young man. Possibly Hofmannsthal put some of his own feelings into this new figure, for the treatment of *Ariadne* by critics had been exceedingly distressing to him. Seeing his work profaned and misunderstood, Hofmannsthal doubtless felt some of the same disillusionment and suffering that he attributes to the young Composer. When in frustration and despair the Composer states that he has nothing in common with this world, he is to a large extent echoing Hofmannsthal's personal sentiments or at least the view of one side of his personality.

The Composer, who has not yet developed a sense of humor, at least where art is concerned, feels misunderstood, betrayed by the world, and forced to debase his talent for money. Frail in body and delicate of sensibility, he lives in a rarified world of beauty that contrasts sharply with the crass, materialistic, pleasure-seeking world represented by the Maecenas. Every obstacle to his idealism and any thought of concession or compromise in matters of art cause him to erupt in a rage. Here, too, the contrast between two types of artist is shown by the opposing attitudes of the Composer and Zerbinetta toward money. For although eventually both perform for the money they need to live, Zerbinetta does so cheerfully and willingly, while the Composer submits to the force of circumstances in a spirit of hostile resignation and only because he has no other acceptable alternative. Just as later Ariadne and Zerbinetta appear to act in the same way (that is, replace one lover by another), here the Composer and Zerbinetta likewise seem to be doing the same thing in allowing their talents to be used by the Maecenas. Yet in actuality the attitudes of the participants in both situations are diametrically opposed. This contrast of appearance and reality runs throughout the entire work and affects all of the major characters.

While the Composer remains an exaggeratedly romantic figure given to excessive self-pity, his character has been improved in this respect over the first version where, according to the stage directions, he seemed to spend much of his time proclaiming impassioned speeches on his knees. The Composer still rails over his bitter fate at having to live in such a hostile world so different from the pure spiritual world that he envisions as his own, but he no longer verges on caricature. His concluding words to the Music Teacher resound with amusing bombastic rhetoric: "Ich durfte es nicht erlauben! Du durftest mir nicht erlauben, es zu erlauben! Wer hieß dich mich zerren, mich! in diese Welt hinein? Laß mich erfrieren, verhungern, versteinen in der meinigen!"[8] [I should not have allowed it. You should not have allowed me to allow it! Who bade you to drag me—me—into this world? Let me perish of cold, hunger, and petrifaction in my own world!]. However, the innate dignity now given the Composer enables him to retain the sympathy of the audience.

In the first version the Composer paid little attention to Zerbinetta, and there was no hint of emotional contact between them. They exchanged only a few words and throughout the scene the Composer was so thoroughly absorbed by concern for his work that he was completely oblivious to her flirtatiousness. In the second version, by permitting him to succumb to Zerbinetta's obvious charms, Hofmannsthal made the Composer appear less coldly ascetic and more warmly human. This scene shows how close to the surface his youthful feelings are, making his excited behavior more understandable and more tolerable. Despite the Composer's deep-rooted antipathy toward anyone with Zerbinetta's casual, vulgar approach to art, he finds her to his own surprise an enchanting person. After witnessing how genuinely naive and unworldly the Composer is in this scene, the audience can smile indulgently at his final temper tantrum, realizing that he contains within him the substance that will enable him to outgrow this kind of behavior with maturity. The Composer emerges as a slightly ridiculous figure, as Hofmannsthal intended, but ridiculous finally in the same admirable way as most idealists appear. One may be amused by his antics, but at the same time it is impossible not to respect his sincerity and integrity. It is Hofmannsthal's intention that the Composer convey an aura of "spirituality" and "greatness" (C., 241-42); for it must be remembered that the Composer represents Ariadne on one level of his significance in the work and Bacchus on another, as will be discussed later.

A whole page of dialogue concerning Zerbinetta's flirtation with the Composer has been added, resulting in potentially new dimensions to her character as well. Zerbinetta has thus been changed into a seemingly more complex, ambivalent figure than the previous shallow stereotype. Considering every man a challenge and immediately sensing the type she is dealing with, she approaches the Composer with a demure, coy seriousness. In an ingenuous, quiet manner she states that although she plays a coquette, who is to say for certain that her heart is involved in

---

[8] *Lustspiele* III, pp. 33-34.

the act. While she gives the appearance of being a cheerful extrovert, she claims to be, like Ariadne, actually sad and lonely.

The awestruck Composer reacts by calling her a sweet, incomprehensible girl. He finds suddenly that instead of being opposites, as he had assumed from her appearance, they are both alike in being misunderstood and forced by circumstances to play a distasteful role in life. Like himself, she too is pure: "Das Irdische unvorhanden deiner Seele."[9] [The earthly does not exist in your soul]. With only minimal additions to the text Hofmannsthal has altered Zerbinetta from a one-dimensional stock figure to a complex character with considerable human appeal. Hofmannsthal's revised conception of Zerbinetta in the new *Vorspiel* admits some of Strauss's musical interpretation of her in the opera.

Egon Wellesz on the basis of a conversation with Hofmannsthal reported that one of the aims of the revised *Vorspiel* was indeed to humanize Zerbinetta: "He [Hofmannsthal] said the figure of Zerbinetta with her great coloratura aria had appeared too marionette-like to him, that she lacked the human warmth that made a figure like Philine in Goethe's 'Wilhelm Meister' so enchanting. For that reason he conceived the idea of having the opera preceded by a scene in which Zerbinetta for a moment shows a tender feeling for the young composer; this moment would suffice to humanize the figure of Zerbinetta."[10]

In a letter to Strauss, Hofmannsthal himself indicates his intention, for he refers to Zerbinetta's major aria as building up "a whole feminine type, perhaps the archetype of the feminine. . . ." (*C.*, 303-04). But does Zerbinetta really have, as she suggests, the capacity for genuine depth of feeling if only she could find the right man who could make her fall genuinely in love? Is she merely an unthinking, sexually driven, superficial girl, devoted only to sensual pleasure, or does she lead this kind of life only because fate has not as yet offered her a better choice? Is her behavior toward the Composer sincere or simply an act to serve as another test of her seductive powers? In terms of the opera the latter interpretation is necessary; for while Hofmannsthal permitted some expansion of her character in the new *Vorspiel,* he did not actually alter his theoretical conception of her character either there or in the opera itself. As far as the meaning of the opera is concerned, Zerbinetta clearly must remain the superficial character of the first version. Hofmannsthal had to adhere basically to his original conception of Zerbinetta as a person incapable of transformation, for her function in the diagrammatic structure of the opera demands this interpretation. However, because Strauss did not share Hofmannsthal's view, he failed to carry out the poet's conception of her in his music. As a result,

[9] Ibid., p. 31.
[10] Egon Wellesz, "Hofmannsthal und die Musik," in *Hugo von Hofmannsthal, Die Gestalt des Dichters im Spiegel der Freunde,* ed. H. A. Fiechtner, 2nd ed. (Bern, 1963), p. 237.

109

audiences generally overlook what Zerbinetta is supposed to represent because of the impassioned intensity and extraordinary beauty of her music and, in one of the many ironies surrounding this work, have always been attracted to her as the most appealing figure in the opera.

The changes in the Composer and Zerbinetta not only add greater dramatic interest to these characters and to the *Vorspiel* in general, but also knit this scene more closely to the opera proper. The meeting and immediate surface attraction between the young couple is Hofmannsthal's way of depicting symbolically the meeting between Bacchus and Circe, which is discussed but never actually shown in the opera. Both Bacchus and the Composer are young, unfledged men, and both are lured by a seductress without falling prey to her. Thus, the scene between the Composer and Zerbinetta provides a visual representation of Bacchus's temptation and escape, information that is essential to understand his frame of mind when he meets Ariadne. To see Zerbinetta as Circe shows her as Hofmannsthal wished, a woman devoid of the capacity to love but desirous only of enslaving men by her magical charms.

At the same time this scene has the additional purpose of contrasting Ariadne and Zerbinetta. Although the magical moment when the Composer is temporarily captivated by Zerbinetta exactly parallels the moment when Bacchus first encounters Ariadne, a world of difference separates the two incidents: the difference between the woman who only takes and never gives anything of her essential self and the woman who gives all of herself. Here again the author demonstrates how events when viewed superficially on the basis of outer appearances may seem the same, while in the realm of the invisible but equally true reality, the attitudes of the participants are revealed as being poles apart. Basically, Hofmannsthal's comedies, which include *Ariadne*, almost invariably involve the question of attitudes, for in his view, comedy juxtaposes characters in such fashion that each casts an ironic light upon the other.[11]

Lest the audience anticipate a subsequent liaison between the Composer and Zerbinetta, Hofmannsthal forces her and then him to revert to type before the end of the act. The values that they represent can never be reconciled. By introducing an element of irony through Zerbinetta's uninhibited conduct, the scene retains its comic implications and, more importantly, its parallel construction with the opera. Although the Composer has escaped from Zerbinetta as Bacchus has from Circe, the implication persists that she has left her mark on him that will have an effect when he meets the next girl. When Zerbinetta calls her dancers to

---

[11] Hofmannsthal's theory of comedy stresses the essential importance of irony: "Aber die wirkliche Komödie setzt ihre Individuen in ein tausendfach verhäkeltes Verhältnis zur Welt, sie setzt alles in ein Verhältnis zu allem und damit alles in ein Verhältnis der Ironie." *Prosa* IV, 40.

their places with a shrill whistle and the Composer witnesses these base, insensitive creatures rushing pell-mell onto the stage amidst shouts and raucous laughter, her spell over him is broken. In the realization that he has been duped by an attractive coquette, the Composer, with an outburst of furious anger, reviles his music teacher for permitting him to lend his music to the upcoming travesty of art. Hofmannsthal's intention to portray the Composer ". . . as a man in love, fooled, as guest, child, victor and vanquished in this world . . ." is successfully realized (*C.,* 153).

Although Hofmannsthal in his letters to Strauss was primarily concerned with the role of Ariadne, in the *Vorspiel* the Composer does not exchange a single word with the Primadonna who is to portray the heroine in the opera. The reason for this is that the Composer and Ariadne are intended to represent the two halves of the same figure. On the other hand, although Hofmannsthal in his letters minimizes the significance of Zerbinetta and considers her a dime-a-dozen creature, she is endowed in the *Vorspiel* with potentialities of character development that are not present in the opera libretto itself. In the opera the virtue of fidelity seems more a matter of birth or of destiny rather than something that can be achieved by individual will and resolution.

Zerbinetta claims that like Ariadne, she too could be faithful to one man, if she could find the right man who would make her want to be faithful. She would have us believe that plain bad luck rather than inclination has condemned her to a life of promiscuity. However, her subsequent behavior in the *Vorspiel,* as just recounted, as well as her long aria and conduct in the opera make clear the irony intended here by Hofmannsthal. Zerbinetta is in effect a parody of Ariadne. In the opera she describes her behavior with the same words that are appropriate to Ariadne's situation "Kommt der neue Gott gegangen,/ Hingegeben sind wir stumm" [When the new god does appear, we are his in mute surrender], yet without any similarity of meaning. This discrepancy between actions and words illustrates how the different worlds of Ariadne and Zerbinetta are united by non-comprehension. The cynical Zerbinetta believes that she knows the solution to Ariadne's dilemma when in reality she does not even understand the problem.

Possibly, if Hofmannsthal had endowed Zerbinetta in the opera with the qualities suggested by the *Vorspiel* and had similarly humanized Ariadne more, the opera might have been more immediately appealing. The major objection against the libretto, even by Strauss, was that it seemed cold and remote. To call it abstract would be more accurate, for these figures have been idealized as extreme possibilities for symbolic purposes. Much of Hofmannsthal's work exhibits the qualities of abstraction and symbolism not only because he disliked all realism in art[12]

---

[12] When Strauss sent Hofmannsthal the draft of the libretto for *Intermezzo,* which he had written himself, the latter replied: "Have received you know what I mean and shall do

but also because he believed that realism was incapable of rendering the complexity of the world. Only myth made this possible, and for that reason he favored mythological opera as the truest of all forms. [13] Yet, the popularity of *Ariadne* has suffered because audiences failed to appreciate that this allegedly contrived, remote theatrical situation invented by Hofmannsthal is actually a more accurate representation of the reality of existence than artistic realism could ever accomplish.

The character of Ariadne contributes to the problem, for despite her obvious moral worth, it is difficult to relate to her except as a symbol that appeals to the intellect. Although Hofmannsthal considered her a well-drawn, rounded figure, [14] she exerts little emotional appeal as a woman, possibly because of her exalted status and the intentional stylization of her portrayal. On the surface it seems strange and even paradoxical that in the *Vorspiel* the Primadonna, who is to represent Ariadne, the symbol of human steadfastness, is portrayed in a most unattractive light as a petty, vain, scheming woman, while Zerbinetta is shown from her most appealing side, even if only for a brief moment. The difference in the presentation of the two women reinforces the kind of theater each represents and typifies the extraordinary subtlety prevailing in this work. On the basis of the *Vorspiel* it is clear that the Primadonna is a singer who is capable of transforming into the role she plays in the opera just as Ariadne is endowed with the potential for

my best to read it through, but I must say right away that I am not the public nor, since I lack all sympathy for the genre of realism, a competent judge of the whole thing" (*C.*, 287).

[13] "Es sind die Kunstmittel des lyrischen Dramas, und sie scheinen mir die einzigen, durch welche die Atmosphäre der Gegenwart ausgedrückt werden kann. Denn wenn sie etwas ist, diese Gegenwart, so ist sie mythisch—ich weiß keinen anderen Ausdruck für eine Existenz, die sich vor so ungeheuren Horizonten vollzieht—für dieses Umgebensein mit Jahrtausenden, für dies Hereinfluten von Orient und Okzident in unser Ich, für diese ungeheure innere Weite, diese rasenden inneren Spannungen, dieses Hier und Anderswo, das die Signatur unseres Lebens ist. Es ist nicht möglich, dies in bürgerlichen Dialogen aufzufangen. Machen wir mythologische Opern, es ist die wahrste aller Formen. Sie können mir glauben." *Prosa* IV, 459-60.

[14] "That Ariadne is a decidedly well-rounded figure, in the music and in the poetry, far better fashioned and rounded than many thousand Miss Müllers or Mrs. Meiers we get on the stage whose addresses and incomes we are told in detail, no less 'round' than Electra or Salome, this is something which these louts cannot comprehend." (*C.*, 147). Possibly Hofmannsthal misjudged the character of Ariadne so badly because he had vividly fixed in his own mind many of the various myths concerning Ariadne. If one considers Ariadne as portrayed in this opera in the context of her earlier experiences, she does take on the richness of character that he claims for her. The only problem is that little of this richness is explicitly stated in the opera but only implied. Yet Hofmannsthal considered her ". . . altogether *real*, as real as the Marschallin" (*C.*, 80). See also the letter of 23 June 1912 (*C.*, 133).

transformation.[15] By contrast, Zerbinetta, who is incapable of transformation and can only play herself, remains the same person in both
the *Vorspiel* and the opera.

Thus, the dissimilarity between the two women, insisted upon by the
Primadonna who exclaims that a world separates her from Zerbinetta, is
true both of the *Vorspiel* and the opera.[16] At the same time the
similarity of the two women is revealed at the other end of the spectrum, for the Primadonna surpasses Zerbinetta in unsympathetic
behavior. Each woman has been shown to be capable at least potentially
of the full range of conduct of the other. This was even truer of the first
version where it was hinted that the Primadonna might be having an affair with Jourdain. While this overlapping of characteristics is true of
the *Vorspiel,* it is not true of the opera. Here only Ariadne possesses the
full gamut of human possibility, while Zerbinetta is restricted to a life
based on her elementary level of understanding. The same situation is
true of the tenor who is to play Bacchus as opposed to Harlekin. The
unsympathetic tenor is able to transform into his role, while Harlekin
remains the same in both *Vorspiel* and opera.

One of the major criticisms of *Ariadne* was the purported in-
compatible mixture of art forms, the supposed impossible marriage of
contrasting styles within the frame of a single work. That Hofmannsthal
had an aesthetic purpose in this carefully integrated and balanced blend
of contrasting styles was either overlooked or ignored by critics and
audiences alike who refused to enter into the comic spirit of the work.
Even his attempt to motivate this aspect of his work in credible fashion,
possibly to forestall such criticism, proved ineffective. The blame, if
any, belongs to the Maecenas, who in his ignorance of the rules of

[15] Elsbeth Pulver, discussing Hofmannsthal's attraction to the actor's gift of transformation, comments: "Mit der Gabe der Verwandlung verbindet sich aber eine zweite
Fähigkeit, die Hofmannsthal oft geradezu die 'mimische' genannt hat. Der Schauspieler
nämlich vermag, durch Mimik und Gestik, durch sein ganzes Spiel, die Bewegung der
Seele nach außen zu projizieren und darzustellen. Auch diese Fähigkeit war für Hofmannsthal von großer Bedeutung: denn hier sah er ja den ganzen Menschen, Außen und
Innen, als untrennbar Eines, hier sah er zugleich eine Weise der Darstellung, die dem
Psychologisch-Analytischen denkbar fern ist und sein ästhetisches Bedürfnis nach
sinnenhaft Dargestelltem befriedigt." Elsbeth Pulver, *Hofmannsthal's Schriften zur
Literatur* (Bern, 1956), p. 68. By having those performers capable of transformation
perform Ariadne and Bacchus, while Zerbinetta and Harlekin remain constant, Hofmannsthal points out the difference between the two worlds, and the spiritual dimension
missing in the dancers.

[16] In terms which foreshadow the antithetical structure of the opera, the Music Teacher
states to the Primadonna: "Wo hätten Sie eine schönere Gelegenheit als auf der Bühne,
ihr zu zeigen, welch unermeßlicher Abstand zwischen Ihnen befestigt ist!" To this the
Primadonna answers: "Abstand! Ha! Eine Welt, hoffe ich." The reply of the Music
Teacher emphasizes the importance of gestures in the opera: "Legen Sie diese Welt in
jede Gebärde und—man wird Ihnen anbetend zu Füßen sinken." *Lustspiele* III, 32.

aesthetics provides the rationale for this allegedly grotesque artistic mixture of forms. This wealthy though untutored bourgeois can afford to have his every whim satisfied. Since he is blissfully unaware of critical insistence on rigid separation of art forms and of the requirement for purity and consistency of styles, he can dictate the form he desires on the basis of sheer practical expediency. If the result should be an offense against good taste, he is oblivious to his error, for he possesses none himself. The only concern of the Maecenas is that the entertainment he has arranged will fit into a convenient time schedule. The fireworks at nine o'clock are much more to his taste and hence more important to him than either of the other performances that he is staging to impress his guests rather than for his own amusement. Thus, the fireworks take priority. Since at heart he is a thrifty bourgeois, he does not want to omit anything he is paying for—which results in the command for both groups to present their act simultaneously. He also has been distressed at the sight of a desert island in his opulent mansion and hopes to enliven it with the dancers.

The critics failed to see or refused to accept the comic spirit inherent in this situation and censured Hofmannsthal for violating their preconceived artistic code. They seemed to judge the work according to their own values and standards rather than on its own terms. Actually *Ariadne* with its bold sense of formal innovation was far ahead of its time. Yet today it seems extraordinarily mild by comparison with the extravagances of the contemporary theater of the absurd which, with its stress on the grotesque,[17] has demolished all rigidity in matters of form. Ironically, the joke at the heart of *Ariadne* turned out temporarily to be on Hofmannsthal himself. The very breach of good taste that Hofmannsthal was satirizing in *Ariadne* became one of the most serious stumbling blocks to its artistic success.

Hofmannsthal had further attempted to anticipate the critics and to emphasize the concept of a joke by including caustic observations on the boring nature of the opera.[18] The critics were not deterred by this

---

[17] It is interesting to note in this connection that in his original draft of the scenario, Hofmannsthal emphasized the grotesque in connection with the four dancers: "Nicht zu vergessen, daß die vier groteske Gestalten sind: Arlekin ein Gauner, Brighella ein Tölpel, Scaramuccio ein Charlatan und Truffaldin ein grotesker Alter." Willi Schuh, "Zu Hofmannsthals 'Ariadne'-Szenarium und -Notizen," *Die Neue Rundschau,* 71 (1960), 93.

[18] "Es sind gerade die Striche, durch welche eine Oper sich empfiehlt, und die vorzüglichsten Theater rechnen es sich zum Verdienst an, durch ihre Striche mindestens ebensoviel zum bleibenden Erfolg eines musikalischen Werkes beigetragen zu haben, als der Komponist durch das, was er an Arbeit hineingetan hat. Das erste, wonach der Herr Generalintendant der Königlichen Vergnügungen zu fragen pflegt, ist, ob eine Oper auch recht gute Striche enthält, und es wäre an der Zeit, daß ein geschickter Musikus die Bequemlichkeit annähme und komponierte ein gut Teil ordentlicher Striche von Anfang an in die Partitur hinein." *Lustspiele* III, 153-54.

preemptive device. Instead, they tended to accept these comments on the work at face value, quoting them in their reviews and gleefully turning them against the authors themselves with devastating effect.

Since in 1912 the opera had been received with such confused reaction and discrepancy of opinion, Hofmannsthal made every effort in the new *Vorspiel* to clarify its meaning. Among the important additions are comments by the Composer who now carefully explains to each of the leading characters the meaning of his role. The Composer is even given an opportunity to repeat his explanatory interpretative comments to correct the misconceptions of both the Dance Master and Zerbinetta. Presumably by the end of the *Vorspiel* every member of the cast and simultaneously of the audience has been thoroughly rehearsed in the plot of the opera and the significance of the characters.

When the Composer first learns that a dance improvisation will follow his opera, he expresses his contempt of the wealthy bourgeois and his guests by stating: "Das Geheimnis des Lebens tritt an sie heran, nimmt sie bei der Hand—und sie bestellen sich eine Affenkomödie, um das Nachgefühl der Ewigkeit aus ihrem unsagbar leichtfertigen Schädel fortzuspülen!"[19] [The mystery of life touches their lives, takes them by the hand—and they order a foolish comedy to wash away the afterglow of eternity from their unspeakably empty heads!]. Possibly, since these lines did not appear in the first version, Hofmannsthal was availing himself of an opportunity to reproach critics of his work as well as to convey information. This statement that *Ariadne* reveals the holiest mysteries of life was taken from Hofmannsthal's letter explaining his conception at length to the musician. Although at that time Strauss had enthusiastically urged that the full contents of the letter be included in the *Vorspiel,* Hofmannsthal, in full confidence that the work was clear enough, rejected the proposal. Now, by returning to this earlier suggestion, Hofmannsthal tacitly admitted the correctness of Strauss's judgment.

Of paramount importance are the interpretative guidelines given to the two principals. The Composer especially tries to impress the Tenor with the range of his role, stressing that he must convey the idea that Bacchus is at the same time boy, child, and god. It is particularly important for Bacchus to understand that he is a god, "kein selbstgefälliger Hanswurst mit einem Pantherfell".[20] [no conceited clown wearing a panther skin].

While turning to Ariadne in order to explain her role to her, the Composer overhears the Dancing Master explicate the plot of the opera to his troupe. The latter, echoing the criticism of the Maecenas, ridicules the desert island setting of the opera, noting: "Es gibt nichts Geschmackloseres als eine wüste Insel."[21] [There is nothing in poorer

[19] *Ariadne auf Naxos, Lustspiele* III, 17.
[20] Ibid., p. 14.
[21] Ibid., p. 24

taste than a desert island]. The representatives of the real world are not attuned to symbolism and fail to comprehend the meaning of the setting in anything but literal terms. From a practical point of view the Dancing Master sees only that such a dreary setting will work to the dancer's advantage. Zerbinetta will have an easy time of conquering the audience after it has been so bored by the opera. In defense of his work the Composer interjects that the setting must be an isolated place, since Ariadne is the symbol of "menschliche Einsamkeit"[22] [human loneliness]. In the first version Hofmannsthal had called her the symbol of "menschliche Verzweiflung" [human despair].[23]

Hofmannsthal seems to have been trapped here between alternatives with neither choice entirely satisfactory. The change to solitude from despair relates more closely to the following speech: "Sieht sie ein menschliches Gesicht, wird meine Musik sinnlos."[24] [If she sees a human face, my music will be meaningless]. However, in terms of her characterization despair makes more sense, for Ariadne is suffering from disillusionment at being abandoned by Theseus, not from loneliness as such. Contrary to the Composer's view, the presence of the dancers does not in itself nullify the idea of loneliness, for Ariadne is oblivious to their presence and remains as isolated with them around her as if they were not present. This change seems to have produced a minor discrepancy in these lines.

Since the dancers were not originally an integral part of the opera as conceived by the Composer, they are encouraged to improvise their roles as they find an opportunity amidst the formal plot. This necessitates acquainting the dancers with the plot of the opera, a device that enables Hofmannsthal to outline the action for the audience in a natural, plausible manner. Most importantly, this technique makes evident the contrasting viewpoints of the various characters who reveal their own nature through the way they describe the plot. The breezy, irreverent recapitulation of the narrative line first by the Dancing Master and then by Zerbinetta contrasts sharply with the solemn, almost reverential attitude of the Composer toward his work. In this way Hofmannsthal foreshadows the difference between Ariadne and Zerbinetta whose opposing views on life form the basic construction of the opera.

The Dancing Master explains that Ariadne is the daughter of a king, who has run away with a certain Theseus whose life she saved previously only to be abandoned by him. She is being consumed by anguish and wishes for death. Zerbinetta, appraising Ariadne in her own terms, interjects that naturally Ariadne is only pretending to yearn for death, while in reality she is awaiting her next admirer (*Verehrer*). This word has been changed from the word lover (*Liebhaber*) used in the

[22] Ibid.
[23] Ibid., p. 152.
[24] Ibid., p. 24.

116

first version as a means of intensifying the cynicism still present in Zerbinetta's character. By this means Zerbinetta tries to abolish the social difference between herself and Ariadne, a difference that she acknowledges but does not really accept. The term *Verehrer,* which is natural for Ariadne, sounds artificial when used by Zerbinetta. This change also represents another effort to show how the same word assumes a different meaning, depending on the quality and personal outlook of the person using it.

The Composer objects to Zerbinetta's crass interpretation, explaining that Ariadne is one of those rare women who belong to only one man in life and afterward to no other except death. He strengthens his argument that her fate cannot be otherwise by further characterizing her as a woman who cannot forget. Zerbinetta is not at all impressed by these qualities of Ariadne and persists in her opinion that it will not be death who arrives, but a pale, dark-eyed lad. Both prove to be correct, for it is not death *per se* but the youthful god Bacchus who comes. However, for Ariadne he represents death, and symbolically her belief is vindicated. As the Composer stresses, only Ariadne's absolute conviction that Bacchus is the god of death makes it possible for her to be receptive to him. She not only believes that she is to die, but the Composer even corrects himself to insist emphatically that she really does die. He grows angry when Zerbinetta mockingly states: "Tata. Du wirst mich meinesgleichen kennen lehren."[25] [Do you think you can teach me about women like myself]. He emphatically repudiates the notion that Ariadne and Zerbinetta are alike.

At this point Zerbinetta turns her back on the Composer and proceeds to translate his lofty plot to the other dancers in her own pragmatic fashion. She believes, as she later states to the Composer, that her presence will introduce reason into the extravagance, as she terms the opera.[26] Meanwhile, to heighten the contrasting styles and outlooks further by direct juxtaposition, the Composer, who has become enraptured by his own poetic conception, continues throughout Zerbinetta's discussion to rhapsodize on the implications of Ariadne's fate: "Sie gibt sich dem Tod hin—ist nicht mehr da—weggewischt—stürzt sich hinein ins Geheimnis der Verwandlung—wird neu geboren—entsteht wieder in

25 Ibid., p. 29.
26 Hofmannsthal shortened this scene considerably from the first version where the contrast between the Composer and Zerbinetta was made more explicit: "Sie machen mir eine wahnwitzige Posse aus dem einzigen Traum meiner Seele. Schütten den Kehricht der Straße in ein himmlisches Gemach. Ich muß mich zur Wehr setzen. . . . Ein Lebendiges ist es, ein Atmendes, fließend geschmiedet Glied an Glied—wie das da—. . . und Ihr wollts auseinanderreißen. Eure infamen Affenstreiche dazwischen treiben. Mörder seid ihr alle miteinander." Zerbinetta replies: "Besser wirds. Vernunft kommt in die Verstiegenheit." *Lustspiele* III, 158. By replacing the words "Besser wirds" with "Courage," Hofmannsthal retains the same meaning, only now by implication and not by direct statement. The word "Courage" has the additional function of anticipating the use of the word *Mut* by the Composer in the climactic aria.

seinen Armen!—Daran wird er zum Gott. Worüber in der Welt könnte eins zum Gott werden als über diesem Erlebnis?"[27] [She surrenders herself to death, is no longer there, obliterated, engulfed in the mystery of transformation. She is born anew, is created again in his arms!—Thus he becomes a god. How else in the world could one become a god except through this experience?].

In this way the significance of the opera is explicitly stated with particular emphasis given to the essential facts basic to a full comprehension of the work: that Bacchus is a demi-god who becomes a god through the love of Ariadne; that Ariadne, the woman who cannot forget, and who can love only once, through the total surrender to her fate (death) dies as one self and is reborn as another, demonstrating the miracle of transformation. Hofmannsthal now felt confident that there could be no further possibility of misunderstanding the revised *Vorspiel,* for the meaning of the work is now "driven into the heads of the audience with a sledge-hammer, point for point" (*C.,* 135).

In *reading* the libretto, one must agree with Hofmannsthal on the issue of clarity. The information needed for comprehension of the opera is present, and Strauss succeeded with particular accomplishment in setting the words, so that they are clearly intelligible. Nevertheless, it is questionable, despite the quantity of repetition and the use of *secco* recitative to restrain the impact of the music, how much of this information is absorbed by audiences who hear *Ariadne* sung. Opera audiences always were and still are expected to learn the details of the plot in advance. The sale of the libretto in the opera house is a traditional practice as old as opera itself. Although an opera can and often does hold an audience in dramatic suspense, that is not its primary aim. One does not attend opera to be surprised by clever twists of plot, but to enjoy the performance as a combination of intellectual, emotional, and aesthetic experience.

By its very nature of conveying information musically, the emphasis of opera is on the performance rather than on the development of the plot. Therefore, to acquaint the audience with the details of the action in advance, increases rather than diminishes the effectiveness of an opera. This is, perhaps, the major difference between opera and drama which needs to be taken into account by a librettist. The revised version of the *Vorspiel* shows how much Hofmannsthal had learned about the art of writing for a musician. He provides all of the information needed for understanding the surface action in a clear, relatively straightforward fashion, and allows the music to add depth to the meaning, dimension to the characters, and emotional warmth to the subject.

The original version of the *Vorspiel* was spoken without musical accompaniment, which presumably enabled audiences to understand every word. Yet, there was still apparently insufficient information to make

[27] *Ariadne auf Naxos, Lustspiele* III, 30.

118

the work comprehensible, at least judging from the baffled reactions of the professional critics and the lack of enthusiasm for the work by the general public. The second version of the *Vorspiel* is absolutely lucid, containing unmistakably precise statements about the meaning of the work. For Hofmannsthal, whose forte was the mysterious, the shadowy, and the ambiguous, this elucidation of his intentions became the most straightforward commentary he ever made about any of his writings within the content of the work itself.

Hofmannsthal made one final significant addition to the new *Vorspiel,* the brief but spectacular aria glorifying music above all of the other arts. The Composer voices Hofmannsthal's heartfelt conviction when he sings:

> Seien wir wieder gut! Ich sehe jetzt alles mit anderen Augen! Die Tiefen des Daseins sind unermeßlich!— Mein lieber Freund, es gibt manches auf der Welt, das läßt sich nicht sagen. Die Dichter unterlegen ja recht gute Worte, recht gute— jedoch, jedoch, jedoch, jedoch, jedoch! —Mut ist in mir, Freund. —Die Welt ist lieblich und nicht fürchterlich dem Mutigen— und was ist denn Musik? Musik ist heilige Kunst, zu versammeln alle Arten von Mut wie Cherubim um einen strahlenden Thron! Das ist Musik, und darum ist sie die heilige unter den Künsten![28]
>
> [Let us be friends again. I now see everything differently!
> The depths of existence are immeasurable!
> My dear friend, there are many things in this world,
> That cannot be expressed in words.
> The poets can provide many very good words,
> Very good words, yet-yet-yet-yet-yet!—
> I am filled with courage, friend.
> The world is lovely and not fearful for those who are courageous—
> And what is music?

[28] Ibid., pp. 32-33. The use of the word *Mut* is unusual and striking. While the basic meaning is courage, it has the effect in this context of meaning attitudes or convictions. The image of gathering all kinds of courage around the throne suggests that differences of opinion are not actually reconciled or synthesized by music but brought into a harmonious pattern which allows each viewpoint its place in the world. The Composer sings this aria when the impact of Zerbinetta upon him is at its greatest force. Deceived for the moment by her manner and charm, he expresses his enthusiasm and optimism that the situation is not as he had feared. Immediately after this aria, the Composer discovers the truth about Zerbinetta and reverts to his pessimistic outlook. However, the ideas of the aria are not impaired by this temporary relapse, for the Composer's view of music's importance is correct. His present understanding is still limited, and his attitude is wrong. He believes in music, but at the moment his belief is not strong enough to overcome disappointment. He will grow up, however, to embody his principles and not simply espouse them. This is the beginning of his artistic and personal maturity, which is foreshadowed in the following exchanges: Komponist: "Ich überlebe diese Stunde nicht!" Zerbinetta: "Du wirst noch ganz andere überleben." Ibid., p. 30. Earlier the Dancing Master had pointed out to the Composer that many famous musicians began their careers with similar sacrifices: "Hundert große Meister, die wir auf den Knien bewundern, haben sich ihre erste Aufführung mit noch ganz anderen Opfern erkauft." Ibid., p. 26.

Music is a sacred art which unites all forms of courage like
Cherubim around a radiant throne!
And therefore it is the most sacred among all the arts!].

This aria stresses the unifying capability of music and forms the
climax and resolution of the *Vorspiel,* which like the opera is constructed of seemingly imcompatible differences of opinion. Through the
harmonizing effect of music the opposing viewpoints of the various
characters—authoritarianism and materialism (Maecenas), hedonism
and shallow opportunism (Zerbinetta), steadfastness and idealism (the
Composer)—can be brought together into a workable unity. Through
the magic of music artists with totally different outlooks can join
together to create a work of art like the opera to follow. By this means
Hofmannsthal justifies in advance the blend of forms in the opera,
demonstrating that through the unifying effect of music the seemingly
discrepant styles of classical tragedy and seventeenth-century *commedia
dell'arte*—purity of form as opposed to improvisation—can be reconciled to create a new, harmonious unity. In this sense it can be seen that
one of the unique features of this work is that its very structure becomes
part of the means by which the "message" of the work is conveyed.

The parallel construction of the *Vorspiel* and the opera becomes
evident in another way as well. What music is in terms of the *Vorspiel,*
the concept of transformation is in the opera—the means of breaching a
seeming impasse in life. The difference is that while music makes it
possible to surmount differences between individuals and even between
art forms, the miracle of transformation makes it possible for a
dichotomy within a single individual to be resolved. In both cases
religious overtones are present. Music is called sacred because it has the
capability of producing unity out of the opposing contrasts that form the
basic construction of life.

If Hofmannsthal had ended the *Vorspiel* with this brilliant aria or
returned to the world of the Maecenas at the end of the opera as had
been the original plan, the symmetry between the two halves of this
work would have been absolute. Since, as has been mentioned, the two
parts do stand in a mirror image relationship, and since the aria of the
Composer would have made an outstanding curtain scene, Hofmannsthal clearly intended something different by vitiating the sublime
moment of the Composer to end the scene with him in violent despair.
Only by understanding the significance of this conclusion to the *Vorspiel* is it possible to fathom the work's overall structure. For Hofmannsthal did not intend this work to fall into two more or less separate
but equal entities. Although each part is complete within itself and at
the same time reflects the other half of the work, ultimately they con-
stitute an indissoluble unity that relates one single life story from beginning to end. Once recognized, the form of *Ariadne* cannot but be admired as a masterpiece of virtuosity.

The *Vorspiel* presents the background exposition for the opera symbolically as well as literally. The proof of this connection lies in the identification of the Composer and Ariadne. By ending the *Vorspiel* with the Composer in a paroxysm of despair, Hofmannsthal prepares the audience for the condition of Ariadne when the curtain rises on the opera. At the same time the similarity of their emotional state helps the audience make the connection between them which alone makes the entire work understandable on a deeper level of meaning. Even here, however, a progression is indicated. The Composer's frenzy, which must have been Ariadne's reaction upon finding herself abandoned, has subsided now. Her moribund state depicts the calmness of resignation which has replaced frustrated anger.

Thus, the pattern of the work becomes clear. The Composer represents both himself and Ariadne at an earlier stage of her development. Ariadne, by the same token represents herself and the Composer's life in the future. The Composer's desperation at the end of the *Vorspiel,* motivated partly by his disappointment in Zerbinetta, reflects the response of Ariadne to her deception by Theseus.

Simultaneously, on another level of meaning the Composer represents Bacchus. The disenchantment of the Composer with Zerbinetta signifies Bacchus's escape from Circe. Thus, as a key example of the telescoping and overlapping of symbols, the episode between the Composer and Zerbinetta represents itself on the literal level, symbolizes the affair between Bacchus and Circe, which is never shown but is only alluded to, and foreshadows the meeting between Bacchus and Ariadne in the opera.

Not only does the *Vorspiel* anticipate the opera, but the opera in turn also refers back to the events at the beginning. The eventual transformation and triumph of Ariadne at the end of the opera adumbrates the future success of the Composer as well. While seemingly victimized at the moment, as Ariadne felt after Theseus deserted her, the Composer, because of his character and the values he espouses, will eventually prevail.

This triumph in anticipation serves as a testament of Hofmannsthal's unwavering faith in the power of the spirit to survive in the world, if individuals remain true to themselves. Despite financial pressures, which Hofmannsthal felt keenly, living as he did in financially precarious circumstances all of his life, he nevertheless refused to compromise his works. He was sustained by the conviction that ultimately the true qualities of his writings would be recognized and appreciated. Viewing the opera in these terms, as Hofmannsthal's own personal testament to his art, may possibly explain the deep attachment he felt for *Ariadne.* His confident belief in its future success, which he constantly reiterated to Strauss, quite likely expressed his unswerving faith in the imperishable nature of the values it contains as much as his conviction concerning the work's quality.

121

To recognize the composition of this text as one straight line of development from beginning to end clarifies some of the smaller revisions that were mentioned earlier. One example is the change of the Maecenas from a foolish dupe to an imposing, authoritative figure, still basically foolish to be sure. This change of focus was necessitated by the new identification of the Composer with Ariadne which was not true of the first version. Just as Ariadne felt destroyed in life and prepares for death only to be saved against her will by the intervention of God through the miracle of transformation, the Composer is similarly being helped by the Maecenas, although he does not recognize the fact and rails against his fate. What God is for Ariadne in the higher, idealized world of the opera, the Maecenas represents for the Composer in the everyday, materialistic world of the *Vorspiel*. For this performance will provide the Composer with the money to write more works, enabling him eventually to succeed. Subconsciously he must recognize this fact, for he could withdraw the work and carry out his threat to starve in purity rather than profane himself. Discounting the exaggerated tone which can be attributed to his youthfulness, something within him must be telling him that such a step would benefit neither himself nor his art. The evident irony in the final speech of the Composer is necessary to enable the *Vorspiel* to retain its comic character, for without the obviously excessive rhetoric, the scene would end on a serious note.

There also seems to be in both the Composer and Ariadne a remote but nevertheless detectable overtone of Goethe's *Faust* with its idea that paradoxically the way to goodness and salvation often leads through error.[29] Like Ariadne, the Composer must first be subjected to suffering before he can transform to a higher level of insight and maturity.[30] On another level the Composer has to learn, as did Hofmannsthal, that to some degree he must work in the world's terms in order to improve it.

In this sense Hofmannsthal's text for the Composer's aria might also conceivably be interpreted as a firm rebuttal to those friends and colleagues who felt that he was wasting his time writing librettos. Possibly, too, he intended it as a generous and heartfelt tribute to his colleague, Strauss. At any rate, it represents his true opinion; for Hofmannsthal believed that music represented the best possibility for expressing the inexpressible, for conveying the mystery of existence that cannot be documented positivistically but must be felt as direct experience. There are religious, mystical overtones in this approach to art and life, and these features are paramount in his work. A mystical,

---

[29] Variants of the ideas in *Ariadne* are found in more orthodox Christian terms in both *Jedermann*, which was written at the same time in 1911, and in the later baroque allegorical drama adapted from Calderón, *Das Salzburger große Welttheater* (1922).

[30] The relationship of suffering to insight was most clearly shown in Hofmannsthal's essay "Der Wanderer," written just prior to the revised version of *Ariadne* in 1912. This essay concludes with the words: "Einmal offenbart sich jedes Lebende, einmal jede Landschaft, und völlig: aber nur einem erschütterten Herzen." *Prosa* III, 26.

ritualistic quality, which crosses over at times into the purely religious . sphere, is present in many of Hofmannsthal's works immediately prior to *Ariadne*, for example in *Elektra, Ödipus und die Sphinx,* and *Der Rosenkavalier.* Above all, this element is present in *Jedermann,* his adaptation of the famous morality play *Everyman,* which he was completing at the time he began *Ariadne.*

Not only does Hofmannsthal's acknowledgment of the supremacy of music undercut the earlier criticism he had jokingly presented in the *Vorspiel,* but it also directs the audience's attention to the predominant role of the music in *Ariadne.* The aria magnificently focuses attention on the music as the bearer of the meaning, placing the music and libretto in proper perspective. Now that the audience has been apprised of the meaning of the plot, what it witnesses in terms of the action and the stage is merely the symbolical representation of this verbal statement. The true meaning, the miracle of transformation, is to be revealed and can only be rendered through the language of music.

Chapter VII

Interpretation of the Opera

Strauss's cool response to Hofmannsthal's completed libretto for *Ariadne*—"The whole of *Ariadne* is now safely in my hands and I like it well enough: I think there'll be some good use for everything" (*C.,* 92)—elicited from the poet a lengthy letter explaining the quality and meaning of his text, which he thought had escaped the musician. Since this unique appraisal by Hofmannsthal of his own work is one of the most important letters in their correspondence, it will be partially quoted here as the basis for the following interpretation:

> What it [*Ariadne*] is about is one of the straightforward and stupendous problems of life: fidelity; whether to hold fast to that which is lost, to cling to it even unto death—or to live, to live on, to get over it, to transform oneself, to sacrifice the integrity of the soul and yet in this transmutation to preserve one's essence, to remain a human being and not to sink to the level of the beast, which is without recollection. It is the fundamental theme of *Elektra,* the voice of Electra opposed to the voice of Chrysothemis, the heroic voice against the human. In the present case we have the group of heroes, demi-gods, gods—Ariadne, Bacchus, (Theseus)—facing the human, the merely human group consisting of the frivolous Zerbinetta and her companions, all of them base figures in life's masquerade. Zerbinetta is in her element drifting out of the arms of one man into the arms of another; Ariadne could be the wife or mistress of *one* man only, just as she can be only *one* man's widow, can be forsaken only by *one* man. One thing, however, is still left even for her: the miracle, the God. To him she gives herself, for she believes him to be Death: he is both Death and Life at once; he it is who reveals to her the immeasurable depths in her own nature, who makes of her an enchantress, the sorceress who herself transforms the poor little Ariadne; he it is who conjures up for her in this world another world beyond, who preserves her for us and at the same time transforms her.
>
> But what to divine souls is a real miracle, is to the earth-bound nature of Zerbinetta just an everyday love-affair. She sees in Ariadne's experience the only thing she *can* see: the exchange of an old lover for a new one. And so these two spiritual worlds are in the end ironically brought together in the only way in which they can be brought together: in non-comprehension.

In this experience of Ariadne's, which is really the monologue of her lonely soul, Bacchus represents no mere *deus ex machina;* for him, too, the experience is vital. Innocent, young and unaware of his own divinity he travels where the wind takes him from island to island. His first affair was typical, with a woman of easy virtue, you may say or you may call her Circe. To his youth and innocence with its infinite potentialities the shock has been tremendous: were he Harlekin, this would be merely the beginning of one long round of love affairs. But he is Bacchus; confronted with the enormity of erotic experience all is laid bare to him in a flash—the assimilation with the animal, the transformation, his own divinity. So he escapes from Circe's embraces still unchanged, but not without a wound, a longing, not without knowledge. The impact on him now of this meeting with a being whom he can love, who is mistaken about him but is enabled by this very mistake to give herself to him wholly and to reveal herself to him in all her loveliness, who entrusts herself to him completely, exactly as one entrusts oneself to Death, this impact I need not expound further to an artist such as you. (*C.,* 94-95)

This letter makes clear that the action in *Ariadne* transpires almost entirely within the minds of the characters. External action in *Ariadne* is minimal, occurring only in the meetings of the Composer and Zerbinetta and of Bacchus and Ariadne. The remainder of the plot must be surmised from the repeated explanations about the previous lives of Bacchus and Ariadne both in the *Vorspiel* and in the opera. The psychological effect of these events on the characters is witnessed, but the miraculous process of this spiritual transformation can only be felt, not explained.

The thinness of plot in *Ariadne* reflects Hofmannsthal's intention to strip the classical myth of all embellishment in order to present its universality in the clearest manner possible. At the same time, in avoiding complexity Hofmannsthal returns to the lyricism of his early works, the style from which he had never really departed.[1] Despite his avowed desire to write action-filled tragedies, the particular orientation of his unique talent precluded this possibility. Throughout his career he worked almost exclusively within the realm of psychological drama.[2]

While the technique of conventional drama usually stresses plot in order to develop character, Hofmannsthal preferred from the beginning of his career as a dramatist to depict moments of "heightened vision" that

[1] To an inquiry by Bodenhausen's wife as to why he no longer wrote poems, Hofmannsthal replied as follows: "Sie fragten einmal oder zweimal, warum ich keine Gedichte mehr schriebe—ich weiß es ja nicht, Mädi—aber sind diese kleinen Lieder in der 'Ariadne,' das Liedchen des Harlekins und der Zerbinetta und des Bacchus, nicht richtige kleine Gedichte von mir? oder fehlt Ihnen etwas an diesen?" Hugo von Hofmannsthal, *Briefe der Freundschaft* (Düsseldorf, 1953), p. 128.
[2] Hofmannsthal's adaptation of Otway's *Venice Preserved* is a case in point. He expanded this tragedy by about one third and in the process changed it from a drama of action into a psychological study of the hero Jaffier.

125

produced inner change.[3] Accordingly, his dramas generally consist of situations exposing the main character to intense experiences that produce sudden flashes of insight into the meaning of his own life or of life in general.[4]

Because of its technique, the libretto for *Ariadne* could be considered one of the forerunners of Expressionist drama and Hofmannsthal one of the pioneers of this form. For like the majority of Expressionist plays that appeared between 1910 and 1920, *Ariadne* (written during 1911 and 1912) illustrates a theme rather than presents a plot. The flow of

[3] Hofmannsthal stressed the concept of vision not only for the writer but also for the intelligent reader, who must read creatively to make in his own mind the synthesis required for understanding the poet's symbolic presentation: "Für ihn [den Lesenden] gibt es *ein* Zeichen, das dem dichterischen Gebilde aufgeprägt ist: daß es geboren ist aus der Vision. . . . Er wartet nicht, daß die Zeit in einem beredten Dichter, einem Beantworter aller Fragen, einem Herold und einem Anwalt, ihre für immer gültige Synthese finde. Denn in ihm und seinesgleichen, an tausend verborgenen Punkten vollzieht sich diese Synthese: und da er sich bewußt ist, die Zeit in sich zu tragen, einer zu sein wie alle, einer für alle, ein Mensch, ein einzelner und ein Symbol zugleich, so dünkt ihm, daß, wo er trinkt, auch das Dürsten der Zeit sich stillen muß. Ja, indem er der Vision sich hingibt und zu glauben vermag an das, was ein Dichter ihn schauen läßt—sei es menschliche Gestalt, dumpfe Materie des Lebens, innig durchdrungen, oder ungeheuere Erscheinung orphischen Gesichtes—, indem er symbolhaft zu erleben vermag die geheimnisvollste Ausgeburt der Zeit, das Entstandene unter dem Druck der ganzen Welt, das, worauf der Schatten der Vergangenheit liegt und was zuckt unter dem Geheimnis der drängenden Gegenwart, indem er es erlebt, das Gedicht, das seismographische Gebilde, das heimliche Werk dessen, der ein Sklave ist aller lebendigen Dinge und ein Spiel von jedem Druck der Luft: indem er an solchem innersten Gebilde der Zeit die Beglückung erlebt, sein Ich sich selber gleich zu fühlen und sicher zu schweben im Sturz des Daseins, entschwindet ihm der Begriff der Zeit und Zukunft geht ihm wie Vergangenheit in einzige Gegenwart herüber." *Prosa* II (Frankfurt am Main, 1951), 297-98.

[4] *Der weiße Fächer* (1897), a play that is a direct forebear of *Ariadne*, expressed this idea clearly: "Es gibt Augenblicke, die einen um ein großes Stück weiterbringen, Augenblicke, in denen sich sehr viel zusammendrängt. Es sind die Augenblicke, in denen man sich und sein Schicksal als etwas unerbittlich Zusammengehöriges empfindet." Hofmannsthal, *Gedichte und Lyrische Dramen* (Stockholm, 1946), p. 312. Hofmannsthal expressed the same idea in broader terms in a letter to Schnitzler: "Es ist mir eine außerordentliche Wohltat, einmal durch sprunghafte Visionen vorwärts gebracht zu werden und nicht, wie man es gewöhnt ist, bloß durch Entwicklung der Charaktere. Aber ich glaube, wenn diese Kette von bildhaften Momenten, die zugleich Ballungen des Seelischen sind, richtig von einem Publikum soll genossen werden, so müssen Sie mit aller Härte hineinschneiden bis (ungefähr) ein normaler Theaterabend herauskommt." *Briefe* II (Vienna, 1937), 350. This view of drama corresponds closely to Goethe's definition of opera as "significant situations in artificially arranged sequences," as Hofmannsthal reported to Strauss after reading Houston Stewart Chamberlain's book on Goethe published in 1912 (*C.,* 154). The impact of Chamberlain's book on Hofmannsthal is conveyed by his comment to Bodenhausen in a letter of 21 January 1913, the period when he was considering revising *Ariadne:* "Das Buch von Chamberlain über Goethe ist mir ein rechter Gewinn. Es kommt immer wieder jemand, dem man Dank schuldig wird." *Briefe der Freundschaft,* p. 150. Hofmannsthal himself experienced such illuminating moments or epiphanies, as he recorded in "Augenblicke in Griechenland," *Prosa* III. (Frankfurt am Main, 1952), 7-42.

the action can be charted graphically by the straight upward thrust of a single line. There are no subplots, no turning points, digressions or dramatic twists, and very little occurs in the way of retarding elements to impede the forward flow of development leading to the celebration of the miracle at the end.

This text, which Hofmannsthal admitted was rather "thin" or "possibly a little too rectilinear," can perhaps be most appropriately characterized as essentially an elaborate metaphor glorifying transformation as *the* fundamental and universal phenomenon of human existence. In all of his works Hofmannsthal attempted to define the values and the processes that make possible a meaningful life in human terms. In *Ariadne* he focused on one aspect of the problem; namely, how it is possible for the human being to overcome a potentially tragic circumstance in his life. He believed he had finally discovered the answer to this problem in the phenomenon of transformation, recognizing this as the fundamental mystery of life containing all other human mysteries.

Ariadne is intended primarily as a glorification of the miracle of life which, under the proper circumstances, enables a human being to become transformed from one level of existence to another, or in less grandiose terms to replace one set of attitudes with another. Only this human quality enables the individual to be reborn, to regain hope after his life has reached such an impasse that it no longer seems worth living. *Ariadne* is a paradigmatic description of the prerequisites and processes leading up to transformation. First Hofmannsthal describes a set of conditions that could produce the state of transformation, and then he concludes with an actual demonstration of the miracle itself. The opera progresses in virtually an unbroken line from its static, prosaic beginning to the final transcendent moment of inner change that forms the climax and the focus of the entire work.[5]

Since inner transformation is one of the intangible qualities of human life, neither Hofmannsthal nor anyone else can define it in precise terms. It cannot be proved empirically but only demonstrated metaphorically. His depiction of the event is not to explain but rather to glorify the beauty, the mystery, and the majesty of transformation. Hofmannsthal considered the overemphasis on rationalism to be one of the weaknesses of his generation: "Situations are symbolic; it is the weakness of people today that they treat them analytically and in so doing dissipate the element of magic."[6]

---

[5] Similarly, Expressionist drama proceeds by means of scenes called *Bilder* or *Stationen* and builds to a climax at the end, which usually involves an inner transformation of the main character.

[6] *Aufzeichnungen* (Frankfurt am Main, 1959), p. 14.

By virtue of its theme and manner of presentation, *Ariadne auf Naxos* might be considered a twentieth-century counterpart of the medieval morality and miracle play. Hofmannsthal was well versed in this tradition in German, French, and Spanish literature,[7] and in 1911 actually suspended temporarily his work on an adaptation of the fourteenth-century morality play *Everyman* in order to complete *Ariadne.* The overlapping of *Ariadne* and *Everyman* shows Hofmannsthal's preoccupation with the theme of transformation and the medieval Christian dramatic tradition while he worked out his libretto.

There is little doubt that Hofmannsthal's adaptation of *Everyman* influenced his writing of *Ariadne.*[8] The two works are similar in theme and execution. Even the religious dimension of *Everyman* is present in *Ariadne,* although in a more subtle way. Both the drama and the opera establish through a series of confrontations a set of preconditions leading to the miracle of inner transformation. Both works stress that when man is deserted by all others in this world, there still remains God and His miracle.[9] In each instance the climax appears at the end of the drama as an ecstatic glorification of the miracle itself. One reason why

[7] In 1902 when introduced to *Everyman* by his friend Franckenstein, Hofmannsthal wrote: "ich danke Dir vielmals. *Everyman* hat mir einen sehr großen Eindruck gemacht, nicht so sehr der Text, weil ich ziemlich viele wunderschöne solche Moralitäten und 'mystères' kenne (mittelhochdeutsch, altfranzösisch, und besonders die in der Erfindung wundervollen 'autos' von Calderon), aber diesmal hab' ich einen besonderen Genuß gehabt durch Deine genauen szenischen Angaben, die mir ein fortwährendes Bühnenbild gegeben haben." *Briefe* II, 71.

[8] In a letter to Bodenhausen, Hofmannsthal brought *Everyman, Faust,* Greek myth, and *Ariadne* into relationship: "Für jetzt nur dies: über die allegorische Linie kommt ja das alte Gedicht nicht hinaus und ich hab ja doch nichts weiteres gethan, als mit einer nicht schlechten Hand—das alte Gedichte restauriert. Es scheint mir das Wesen dieser Kunstform—des morality play—daß sie zweidimensional ist, sich ihre dritte Dimension durch den Bezug auf ein außerhalb Seiendes—die Glaubenswahrheiten—beschafft. Was Du in dem Gedicht suchst, scheint mir aber jene Dreidimensionalität—Du nennst sie Symbolhaftigkeit—wie das Antike Drama sie hat, und wie, von verwandten, religiösen Dramen, der 'Faust' sie wieder hat. Vielleicht aber meinst Du etwas anderes und ich habe mich im tieferen Sinn, als ich jetzt erfassen kann—unzulänglich erwiesen—dann möchte ich es jetzt nicht wissen—sondern erst später.

"Daß die kleine 'Ariadne' Dreidimensionalität, Welt, Symbol, Polarität hat—hoffe ich—nur freilich liegt ja diese Arbeit viel mehr auf der Hauptlinie meiner Production, die auch noch den 'Rosenkavalier' näher berührt als 'Jedermann'—an dem ich und an dessen noch nicht ganz entschiedenem Schicksal ich trotzdem sehr hänge." *Briefe der Freundschaft,* p. 138.

[9] Grete Schaeder sees the relationship of these two works from a slightly different, but important perspective: "Das Bindeglied zwischen beiden Werken ist das Außerkraftsetzen der falschen Ordnung, die den Menschen auf sich stellt und in die Mitte der Dinge rückt. Hofmannsthal mußte an das Wunder glauben lernen, das sich an Bacchus und Ariadne, vom Ich zum Du hin vollzog, damit er die christlichen Gedanken der Bruderliebe und Gottesfurcht mit der Kraft des Gemütes in sich hervorbringen konnte, mit der sie vom mittelalterlichen Menschen gedacht wurden. Schicksalhaft notwendig geht die Auseinandersetzung zwischen dem Lebens- und Todesmotiv in seiner Dichtung weiter, aber seit

Hofmannsthal desired to work in terms of familiar myths was the opportunity they gave him to subordinate characters to events. The major difference between *Ariadne* and *Everyman* is the absence of moralizing in the opera. This same difference also sets *Ariadne* apart from Expressionist drama.

Because of its emphasis on the mysterious and the miraculous, *Ariadne* should ultimately be appreciated by the audience with the awe displayed by Zerbinetta as she witnesses the miracle. While *Ariadne* does have a clear surface meaning, as Hofmannsthal pointed out—the contrasting of the heroic world with the ordinary world in terms of fidelity—the final depiction of the transformation on the stage must be felt by the spectator. Like Expressionist drama, which it resembles in technique and basic theme of transformation, *Ariadne,* while providing a rational basis for understanding, makes its ultimate appeal to feeling rather than to reason. Since the miracle cannot be explained totally in words, it is conveyed by the expressive techniques of the actors and above all by the music.[10]

Failure to see the work in these terms caused much of the widespread hostility of early critics who attempted to judge the work by conventional operatic standards of plot and character development. To a generation of critics schooled in the techniques of realism, followed by naturalism and impressionism—all rational and deterministic approaches to art—this opera came as a complete surprise. Hofmannsthal in a letter to Strauss tried to pinpoint the critics' source of dissatisfaction. Confessing his puzzlement over the "almost unbelievable degree of antagonism this light and poetic work of art has aroused among the scribbling race," he states: "Is it that these people sense in it what they apparently hate more than anything else: this turning away from merely ephemeral effects, from the mere *semblance* of reality, this search for transcendental meaning?" (*C.,* 158). Actually, the principal difficulty for the critics, as has been shown earlier, was their failure to penetrate the symbolism of the work. They overlooked the connections between the characters that clarify the overall structure of contrasts and lead to a proper understanding of the opera.

The opera opens with Ariadne, motionless, on the ground in front of a cave, the symbol of a woman who has reached the nadir of her

---

dem 'Jedermann' hat sie ein neues Gesicht bekommen, sie wird gleichbedeutend mit der Erkenntnis, daß die christliche Wahrheit tiefer ist als die 'höchste Schönheit,' wie er sie in seiner Jugend sah. Hofmannsthal mißtraut nun jeder Schönheit, die das Leben aus sich selber hervorbringt, allem, was dem Dasein Schmuck und Glanz gibt." *Hugo von Hofmannsthal und Goethe* (Hameln, 1947), pp. 57-58.

[10] Hofmannsthal commented in 1923: "Die Sprache, ja, sie ist Alles; aber darüber hinaus, dahinter ist noch etwas: die Wahrheit und das Geheimnis." "Neue deutsche Beiträge," *Prosa* IV, 142. In this connection, too, the words of the Composer in the *Vorspiel,* cited on p. 119, should be recalled.

existence. Since she represents the Composer as well as herself, Ariadne's depressed condition indicates that considerable time has elapsed since her frenzied outburst at first discovering her betrayal by Theseus, the situation symbolized by the impassioned speech of the Composer at the conclusion of the *Vorspiel*. The gloomy darkness of the stage explicitly emphasizes the blackness of her despair and her feelings of hopelessness. She has lapsed from the initial paroxysms of despair into mute resignation, and now with her inner resources exhausted, she wishes only for death.

The visual expression of Ariadne's state of mind is reinforced by Naiad, Dryad, and Echo, the uninvolved, elemental life forces who stress the misfortunes of Ariadne. Soon Zerbinetta, Harlekin and company appear and attempt to console Ariadne. They are not subject to attacks of despondency and cannot understand such sadness, particularly in one so young and beautiful. Their sympathetic but uncomprehending remarks are another means of projecting the lamentable state of Ariadne, for the superficial levity of the dancers contrasts sharply with the latter's genuine grief.

Ariadne is so pitiable that even these normally joyous, carefree figures seem sincerely moved by her distraught condition. Harlekin attempts to restore her cheerfulness by singing a gay song that is filled with practical advice about living. He sings about the complexity of life, the ability of the heart to withstand tribulations of all kinds, and the necessity to live again, even if it means new suffering.

Mußt dich aus dem Dunkel heben,	You must raise yourself out of the darkness,
Wär es auch um neue Qual,	Even if to new torment.
Leben mußt du, liebes Leben,	You must live, lovely creature,
Leben noch dies eine Mal![11]	Live again this one time!

A little later, Harlekin, joined by the other dancers, stresses the power of forgetting as well as the restorative powers of nature:

Was immer Böses widerfuhr,	Whatever misfortune did occur,
Die Zeit geht hin und tilgt die Spur.[12]	Time will pass and its traces erase.

Thus, almost from the very beginning, Hofmannsthal contrasts the two worlds of the opera that are held together by irony and by the harmonizing effect of music, as was anticipated in the *Vorspiel*. The diverse styles—the lofty emotions of the *opera seria* and the grotesque buffoonery of *commedia dell'arte*—oppose and at the same time supplement each other in a logical and consistent manner. As a result the opera embodies in its very structure the union of opposites, the *coincidentia oppositorum*, which in Hofmannsthal's opinion constituted the fundamental unity of the world.

[11] *Ariadne auf Naxos, Lustspiele* III (Frankfurt am Main, 1956), 38-39.
[12] Ibid., p. 41.

Ariadne is totally immersed in herself and her grief and ignores the lighthearted but well-meant, common-sense advice of the dancers. Her opening monologue, while lying on the ground, reveals how completely she has withdrawn from the world and how oblivious she is to her surroundings. She has suffered a loss of perspective, for she wonders whether she had been dead and now lives again. Her confusion makes it impossible for her to remember whether her experiences were real or merely a dream. Past events have become obscured in the dark shadows of her mind. This blurring of reality and dream show that the process of forgetting, a crucial aspect of her transformation, has already begun. Hofmannsthal stresses not only what is going to happen—the rebirth of Ariadne from the threshold of death to renewed life—but also the means: by overcoming the past. The inability of the dancers to assist her recovery emphasizes that the healing or regenerative process must first occur within the individual alone and cannot be initiated from outside forces. First Ariadne must find and return to herself before she is capable of recovery.[13] Throughout the initial half of the opera, Ariadne is engaged in the process of trying to return to her earlier, happier self as a means of overcoming her personal dilemma: "Man muß sich schütteln: ja, dies muß ich finden: Das Mädchen, das ich war![14] [I must arouse myself, indeed, this I must find: the girl I once was!].

Actually Ariadne must forget the past, for only by breaking all ties with her previous unhappy experiences can she be restored to life. As Hofmannsthal demonstrated previously in *Elektra,* the refusal or the inability to forget the past condemns the individual to certain unhappiness and even death. Even the virtue of fidelity if carried to an extreme, as Elektra does, may become a dehumanizing, destructive force. Although Ariadne is the spiritual twin of Elektra in her unswerving fidelity, she possesses neither the latter's demonic quality nor her capacity for bitterness and revenge. Thus Ariadne, who is capable of transformation, survives, while Elektra must die. The central problem of both works is the obligation to reconcile the dual necessity of being (*Sein*) and becoming (*Werden*).[15]

The solution to this problem lay in the concept of transformation, as Hofmannsthal now recognized:

> Thus here anew Ariadne stands opposed to Zerbinetta, as previously
> Elektra stood contrasted to Chrysothemis. Chrysothemis wanted to
> live, nothing more; and she knew that whoever wants to live must

---

[13] Hofmannsthal considered this idea of finding oneself a basic idea of his writings: "Grundthema: Sich selbst finden." *Aufzeichnungen,* p. 222.

[14] *Lustspiele* III, 37.

[15] In *Aufzeichnungen,* p. 217, Hofmannsthal indicated the connection between *Elektra* and *Ariadne:* "Eigentliche Antinomie von Sein und Werden. Elektra—Chrysothemis. Variation: Ariadne—Zerbinetta."

forget. Elektra forgets nothing. How could the two sisters understand each other? Zerbinetta is in her element, when she drifts from one man to another, Ariadne could only be one man's wife, she can only be forsaken by one man. She gathers her dress about her: it is the gesture of those who want to flee from the world.

"Here one thing soon leads to another," she says, which is just as sorrowful, even if not as harsh as much said by Electra, for whom Klytemnestra's bedroom is the world and the world Klytemnestra's bedroom. For Elektra nothing remained except death; here however the theme is carried further. Ariadne, too, believes she is giving herself to death; here "her boat sinks and sinks to new oceans." This is transformation, the miracle of all miracles, the actual mystery of love. The immeasurable depths of her own nature, the bond between us and an unnamable eternity that from our childhood, indeed from the period before we were born was in and near us, can be enclosed from within into a lasting, painful rigidity: shortly before death we sense, these depths would open: something of this kind that can scarcely be expressed, is announced in the minutes which precede the death of Elektra. But in a life not so marked by destiny a softer power than death will also unlock these depths: love is spread throughout existence; when it grips a human being with its entire force, this person is released from his rigidity to the depths of his being: the world is restored to him, indeed, the world emerges as a magical unity consisting of this world and the transcendental world at the same time. When Ariadne before her transformed self sees also the cave of her sufferings transformed into a joyous temple, when the mother's eye gazes upon her from the cloak of Bacchus and the island changes from a prison to an Elysium—what else is she proclaiming, but that she loves and lives.[16]

Like Elektra, Ariadne as the woman without a peer among millions, the woman who cannot forget, is a victim of her own character. As long as she remembers Theseus, she must remain faithful to him even though he has repudiated her, just as Elektra must remain faithful to the memory of the dead Agamemnon. In neither case does the faithfulness bring any benefits, for Theseus will not and Agamemnon cannot return. Although Ariadne and Elektra have no choice but to accept their fate, nevertheless there is a major difference in their response. Ariadne does not will her destiny of faithfulness as does Elektra, who uses every available means to keep the memory of her murdered father alive and to nourish her consuming passion for vengeance on his murderers. While Elektra becomes a pathological monomaniac, Ariadne, who is not demonically afflicted, has a divided mind. She remembers Theseus, but her innate, healthy common sense tells her she must forget him for her own survival. She wonders why she cannot forget this experience; in-

[16] *Prosa* III, 138-40.

deed she feels she *must* forget it, for she considers her present distraught condition shameful:

Ein Schönes war, hieß Theseus-Ariadne	There was something beautiful called Theseus-Ariadne
Und ging im Licht und freute sich des Lebens!	Who walked in light and rejoiced in life!
Warum weiß ich davon? ich will vergessen!	Why do I remember this? I want to forget!
Dies muß ich nur noch finden: es ist Schmach,	Only this must I still find: it is shameful
Zerrüttet sein, wie ich![17]	To be so distraught as I!

She tries to recall her girlhood, feeling instinctively that she would regain peace of mind if she could blot out the affair with Theseus and return to the memory of her earlier, happier life.[18] However, she finds it impossible to bypass the experience with Theseus, for

---

[17] *Lustspiele* III, 37. Hofmannsthal was expressing his own attitude toward suffering in this speech by Ariadne. In a letter to Henriette von Lieben he wrote: "Seine Eltern zu verlieren ist das Schwerste, was das Leben in sich schließt, und doch muß man es ertragen und seine Haltung wiederzugewinnen trachten, denn auch durch den Schmerz darf man sich nicht zerrütten lassen, es straft sich hart, wie jede Zerrüttung . . . Man kann von sich selber die richtige Entwicklung erzwingen, das glaube ich fest, und glauben Sie es auch mir, wenn ich es Ihnen in einer so ernsten Stunde ausspreche. Nur nachlässig darf man nicht sein, nicht unter dem zurückbleiben, was man sich selber in starken und klaren Stunden vorgesetzt hat, und nicht dem Kleinmut und der häßlichen Verzweiflung sich ausliefern, deren unheimlicher Kern die Freude an der Selbstzerstörung ist." *Briefe* II, 39-40. Hofmannsthal reiterated this deeply held conviction in a letter to Andrian: "Verzweiflung aber ist das häßlichste, das gemeinste, der wahre Meuchelmord, an der eigenen Seele begangen." Hugo von Hofmannsthal—Leopold von Andrian, *Briefwechsel,* ed. Walter Perl (Frankfurt am Main, 1958), p. 91.

[18] The scene presents in a sense the reverse situation found in *Der Rosenkavalier,* when the *Marschallin* wonders with dismay how the young girl that she was has grown into the aging woman that she is now:

Wo ist die jetzt? Ja, such dir den Schnee vom vergangenen Jahr.
Das sag ich so:
Aber wie kann das wirklich sein,
daß ich die kleine Resi war
und daß ich auch einmal die alte Frau sein werd! . . .
Die alte Frau, die alte Marschallin!
"Siehst es, da gehts', die alte Fürstin Resi!"
Wie kann denn das geschehen?
Wie macht denn das der liebe Gott?
Wo ich doch immer die gleiche bin.
Und wenn ers schon so machen muß,
warum läßt er mich denn zuschaun dabei,
mit gar so klarem Sinn? Warum versteckt ers nicht vor mir?
Das alles ist geheim, so viel geheim.
Und man ist dazu da, daß mans ertragt.
Und in dem "Wie" da liegt der ganze Unterschied—.
Lustspiele I (Stockholm, 1959), 301-302.

Jetzt hab ichs—Götter! daß ichs nur behalte!	Now I have it—gods! If I may only retain it!
Den Namen nicht—der Name ist verwachsen	Not the name—the name has grown intertwined
Mit einem anderen Namen, ein Ding wächst	With another name, one thing grows
So leicht ins andere, wehe![19]	So easily into another, alas!

Strauss was puzzled by this passage and asked for a clarification which the poet supplied as follows: "As for the obscure passage in the text: Ariadne endeavors to recall in her bewildered brain the picture of her own innocent self, of the young girl she once was (and who, she fancies, is now living again, here in the cave), but she refuses to employ the actual name of Ariadne in this process of recollection, because that name is for her all too closely bound up, grown together with Theseus; she wants the vision but without the name and therefore, when the three nymphs call her by that name, she fights shy of it: 'Not again! Do not let me hear that name again!'" (*C.*, 90).[20]

---

[19] *Lustspiele* III, 37.

[20] It is interesting to compare Hofmannsthal's explanation of this passage with the ideas of Marianne Winder who, in an article entitled, "The Psychological Significance of Hofmannsthal's *Ariadne auf Naxos*," *German Life and Letters*, 15 (1961), 104, attempted a Jungian interpretation of *Ariadne*. She feels that in this speech "Light is a symbol of consciousness, rationality. Theseus represents the rational function with which the conscious mind had exclusively identified itself. The part of the myth which is not used in the opera is where Theseus kills the Minotaur symbolizing the irrational element in the soul in its most animal form, the natural instincts. Reason when no longer complemented by the free play of the instincts has to desert the soul and leave it barren and desolate." Winder continues: "Ariadne lives in a cave by the sea. Jung says: 'Cave and sea refer to the unconscious state with its darkness and secrecy.'" Since Hofmannsthal's work does deal with archetypal situations, there is naturally a parallelism with Jungian ideas. Even though Winder indicates that Hofmannsthal had Jung's *Wandlungen und Symbole der Libido* in his library, she offers no evidence to support the suggestion of influence. As has been shown in the present analysis, the entire thrust behind Hofmannsthal's work came from other directions and was not an attempt to dramatize Jungian theory. While Winder's article is imaginative and holds together in its own terms, it simply violates the spirit behind the work and is thus ultimately false. Her conclusion is in error: "In one work only did he [Hofmannsthal] dare to deal with the central problem of human existence, and though, perhaps characteristically, *Ariadne auf Naxos* was prefaced by and mingled with buffoonery, it became and remained his favourite work" (108-109). This quotation shows that Winder did not understand the role of the buffoonery at all and thus judged the entire work solely in terms of Ariadne, which resulted in her one-sided analysis. It also shows that she did not understand the position of *Ariadne* in terms of Hofmannsthal's development, for both *Der weiße Fächer* and *Der Abenteurer und die Sängerin* as well as many of his other works deal with this same theme. As Hofmannsthal himself commented: "Man hat mir nachgewiesen, daß ich mein ganzes Leben lang über das ewige Geheimnis dieses Widerspruches mich zu erstaunen nicht aufhöre." *Prosa* III, 138. The indirection was not because Hofmannsthal feared insanity, which Winder erroneously presents as the reason he avoided this theme, but because he had not clearly worked out the essential focus of the problem until *Ariadne*.

Although Ariadne had eloped with Theseus, only to be abandoned by him (for reasons which are unessential to Hofmannsthal's theme and therefore never explained in the text), she still feels pure in heart and able therefore to die with a clear conscience:

Ihr Schlaf ist rein, ihr Sinn ist klar,	Her sleep is serene, her mind is clear,
Ihr Herz ist lauter wie der Quell:	Her heart is as pure as the spring!
Sie hält sich gut, drum kommt auch bald der Tag,	She lives in purity, thus soon the day will come,
Da darf sie sich in ihren Mantel wickeln,	When she may wrap her cloak about her,
Darf ihr Gesicht mit einem Tuch bedecken	May cover her face with a shroud
Und darf da drinnen liegen Und eine Tote sein![21]	And may lie in her cave and be dead.

She resolves to die because she recognizes that she cannot continue in her present state of existence, and yet she cannot imagine any possibility for renewed life without Theseus who will never return. Despite her acceptance of her own purity, she sees no possibility of returning to a happy life, for her character dictates that she can love only once. Yet, paradoxically, only the complete openness and receptiveness of mind resulting from her willingness to die enables Ariadne to feel love again and to be reborn.[22]

At this point Ariadne still loves Theseus, and he is uppermost in her thoughts, as the music emphasizes. She could continue to languish and to suffer while yearning in vain for his return, but as her past actions indicate, she is a woman of strength and determination. Without remorse or self-pity she recognizes the futility of wasting away in a state of non-life and calmly prepares herself for death. Having surrendered herself totally to Theseus in complete trust and innocence only to be betrayed and forsaken by him, she, like the Composer in the *Vorspiel,* feels now that nothing in this life is pure: "Hier ist nichts rein! / Hier kam alles zu allem!"[23] [Here nothing is pure! / Here everything became involved with everything else!]. Her affair with Theseus, which has seemingly ended so tragically, has disillusioned her about life. She does not realize that because in life everything can come to everything, the miracle is still

---

[21] *Lustspiele* III, 37.
[22] Hofmannsthal used this same idea in the later unfinished work *Semiramis:* "Der geheimnisvolle Dialog, den sie im Zelt austauschen: daß nur der lebt, der den Tod in sich aufgenommen hat. . . . Semiramis und der Tod: erst da sie weiß, daß sie stirbt, vermag sie Liebe zu fühlen, die anderen Geschöpfe zu fühlen, nun erst *lebt* sie." *Dramen* III, 454.
[23] *Lustspiele* III, 39.

possible to her.[24] Therefore she is ready to enter the kingdom of death where everything is pure.[25]

In Hofmannsthal's view, the way into life was through the deed.[26] Ariadne's inner resolve is rendered through gesture, for her words here are accompanied by her rising from the ground for the first time since the beginning of the opera. This positive action of getting to her feet represents visually the beginning of her changed outlook that will make possible her eventual transformation. Paradoxically, she arises to die but instead discovers life anew.

By voluntarily willing death, Ariadne accomplishes the deed that makes her transformation possible. As Hofmannsthal wrote in *Ad me Ipsum:* "The transformation through the deed. To act is to surrender oneself." Hofmannsthal adds that "the decisive aspect lies not in the deed but in fidelity. Identity of fidelity and destiny."[27] The fact that she acts does not set Ariadne apart, but rather her quality of faithfulness or of not forgetting makes her unique among millions of women and is important in making possible her final transformation. Because Ariadne remains faithful to herself, the circumstances of life make possible her rebirth through Bacchus to a new level of existence, thus exemplifying the paradox of self-preservation through change. As Hofmannsthal noted in the Ariadne letter: "He [Bacchus] preserves her for us and at the same time transforms her." Although Elektra apparently should be capable of the same transformation, she differs from Ariadne in that she is capable only of hate and thoughts of revenge. Consequently she precludes the possibility of love and the opportunity to be transformed.

[24] The idea that everything leads to everything else in life relates to Hofmannsthal's view of the unity of the world, as he described in his essay on Balzac: "Und es ist das Wesen der Welt, in dieser grandiosen und epischen Weise gesehen, daß *alles zu allem* kommt. Es sind überall Übergänge, und nichts als Übergänge, in der sittlichen Welt so gut wie in der sozialen. Die Übergänge zwischen Tugend und Laster—zwei mythische Begriffe, die niemand recht zu fassen weiß—sind ebenso fein abgestuft und ebenso kontinuierlich wie die zwischen reich und arm. Es stecken in den auseinanderliegendsten und widerstreitendsten Dingen gewisse geheime Verwandtschaften, wodurch *alles mit allem* zusammenhängt." *Prosa* II, 391. (Emphasis added).

[25] *Lustspiele* III, 39.

[26] In one of his essays on D'Annunzio Hofmannsthal stated: "Ins Leben kommt ein Mensch dadurch, daß er etwas tut. . . . Es hängt aber das ganze Leben an der geheimnisvollen Verknüpfung von Denken und Tun. Nur wer etwas will, erkennt das Leben. Von dem Willenlosen und Untätigen kann es gar nicht erkannt werden, so wenig also eine Frau von einer Frau. Und gerade auf den Willenlosen und Untätigen haben die Dichter, welche die letzten zwei Jahrzehnte traurig und niedrig wiederspiegeln, ihre Welt gestellt. Und doch stehen seit zweitausend Jahren diese Zeilen in der 'Poetik' des Aristoteles: '. . . auch das Leben ist (wie das Drama) auf das Tun gestellt, und das Lebensziel ist ein Tun, nicht eine Beschaffenheit. Die Charaktere begründen die Verschiedenheit, das Tun aber Glück oder Unglück.'" "Der neue Roman von D'Annunzio," *Prosa* I (Frankfurt am Main, 1950), 274.

[27] *Aufzeichnungen,* p. 217.

Ariadne yearns for Hermes, the messenger of death, to release her from life. However, in order to be acceptable to him, her heart must first be purified of all violent sufferings: "Ach, von allen wilden Schmerzen/ Muß das Herz gereinigt sein. . . ."[28] [Alas, from all wild torments/ Must my heart be purified]. She intends the cave to be her grave, and while waiting for Death's arrival she adorns herself in finery given to her by her mother.[29] Her soul, however, will follow Hermes. Death will mean not only release from this now burdensome physical existence, but it will also restore the peace of mind, equanimity, and purity of soul she possessed before she met Theseus:

Du wirst mich befreien,	You will free me,
Mir selber mich geben,	Return me to myself.
Dies lastende Leben,	This burdensome life,
Du nimmst es von mir.	You will take it from me.
An dich werd ich mich ganz verlieren,	To you I will lose myself completely,
Bei dir wird Ariadne sein.[30]	With you will Ariadne be.

This speech exemplifies the double-level of meaning found throughout this work, for what Ariadne says is true and will come to pass, but in a totally different way than she foresees.

In preparing herself mentally to resolve the dilemma of her existence, Ariadne is in a trance-like state. She remains in this condition throughout the first half of the opera, passively aware of the events occurring around her. When the voices of Zerbinetta and the other danc-

---

[28] *Lustspiele* III, 40.

[29] In this way Hofmannsthal motivated Ariadne's adornment. In the earlier version Zerbinetta not only announces the arrival of Bacchus with a lengthy description of him to Ariadne but proceeds to act as a maid, helping Ariadne to dress in suitable finery to meet him as a bride: *Sie schmücken die Willenlose—Unbewußte/* "Kein Wunder, wenn sie seine Stimme hörte!/ Und noch hat sie ihn nicht gesehn!/ Die Spangen schnell, den Mantel nun herbei!/ Sandalen an den hübschen Fuß!/ Könnt ihr nicht fühlen: Er ist nah!/ Beflügelt euch denn nicht, was hier geschehen muß?!" (*Lustspiele* III, 376). In the revised version Naiad, Dryad and Echo herald Bacchus's coming, while the adornment scene is related strictly in terms of Ariadne's preparation for death: "In den schönen Feierkleidern,/ Die mir meine Mutter gab,/ Diese Glieder werden bleiben,/ Schön geschmückt und ganz allein,/ Stille Höhle wird mein Grab./ Aber lautlos meine Seele/ Folgt ihrem neuen Herrn,/ Wie ein leichtes Blatt im Winde,/ Folgt hinunter, folgt so gern." (Ibid., p. 40).

[30] *Lustspiele* III, 40. This scene is almost a sequel of the earlier drama, *Der Tor und der Tod,* where the appearance of Death similarly awakened new feelings in Claudio after demonstrating to him the meaninglessness of the way he had lived. At the moment of dying, Claudio was reborn in understanding and purity: "Da tot mein Leben war, sei du mein Leben, Tod!/ Was zwingt mich, der ich beides nicht erkenne,/ Daß ich dich Tod und jenes Leben nenne?/ In eine Stunde kannst du Leben pressen,/ Mehr als das ganze Leben konnte halten,/ Das schattenhafte will ich ganz vergessen/ Und weih mich deinen Wundern und Gewalten." (Hugo von Hofmannsthal, *Gedichte und Lyrische Dramen* [Stockholm, 1946], p. 291). Ariadne, too, will be transformed and reborn beyond life: "Verwandlung.—Aber jenseits des Lebens: Ariadne. Wiedergeburt." *Ad me Ipsum, Aufzeichnungen*, p. 217.

ers penetrate her consciousness, certain key words strike chords of comprehension within her. She responds to these thoughts in her mind and incorporates them into her monologue. However, she never awakens from her reverie to confront the people around her directly. When, for example, Naiad, Dryad, and Echo call her name, Ariadne raises her arm to ward them off, exclaiming: "Nay, call no more." The calling of her name reminds her of how she had responded to such a summons in the past. This reaction causes the dancers to comment: "Ganz sicher, sie ist toll." [Most surely, she is mad]. To this Ariadne responds to herself, without turning her head, as if she had heard these last words in her dream: "Toll, aber weise, ja!— Ich weiß was gut ist, wenn man es fernhält von dem armen Herzen."[31] [Mad but wise, too!—I know what is good, when one holds it distant from his poor heart].

Since the other members of her company fail to obtain a response from Ariadne, Zerbinetta, who has been watching from the wings, dismisses them and undertakes the task herself. Love after all is her specialty. To ingratiate herself with Ariadne, Zerbinetta ironically pretends to acknowledge the distance of class between them by addressing her as "Most gracious princess." As was true of Harlekin's earlier speech, her cynically pompous and artificial language and tone contrast vividly with the sincerity of Ariadne. In mock deference Zerbinetta explains that she realizes Ariadne's grief must be judged by a different measure than is used for common mortals. However, the irony concealed in this remark strikes at Zerbinetta herself rather than at Ariadne; for while Zerbinetta does not for a moment believe what she is saying, unwittingly she is speaking the truth.

When Ariadne fails to respond to her exaggerated politeness, Zerbinetta in her adaptable way changes her approach and as woman to woman discusses Ariadne's problems as one common to all members of their sex:

Wer ist die Frau, die es nicht durchgelitten hätte?	Who is the woman who hasn't suffered this?
Verlassen! in Verzweiflung! ausgesetzt!	Abandoned! In despair! Desolate!
Ach, solcher wüsten Inseln sind unzählige	Alas, such desert isles are countless
Auch mitten unter Menschen, ich—ich selber	Even in the midst of people. I—I myself
Ich habe ihrer mehrere bewohnt—	Have lived on a number of them—
Und habe nicht gelernt, die Männer zu verfluchen![32]	And have not learned to curse men!

[31] *Lustspiele* III, 38.
[32] Ibid., pp. 43-44.

As in the *Vorspiel* Zerbinetta interprets Ariadne's fate in terms of her own experience. They have both suffered rejection and desertion at the hands of faithless men. Yet, the possibility of transformation, or, what she calls transformation—replacing one man by another—has saved her from extended suffering. Even though she tries to be faithful to one man, she never succeeds:

Doch niemals Launen,	But never capricious,
Immer ein Müssen!	Always necessity!
Immer ein neues	Always a new,
Beklommenes Staunen.	Anguishing amazement.
Daß ein Herz so gar sich selber,	That a heart itself so little,
Gar sich selber nicht versteht![33]	Itself so little understands!

Zerbinetta not only uses the same vocabulary to describe her transformation but also considers each new man who produces this change in her to be a god, completing the analogy to Ariadne's forthcoming experience. Zerbinetta claims that when the new god appears, she has no alternative except silent surrender:

Als ein Gott kam jeder gegangen,	Like a God came each one to me,
Und sein Schritt schon machte mich stumm,	And his very walk filled me with awe.
Küßte er mir Stirn und Wangen,	Kissed he my forehead and cheeks,
War ich von dem Gott gefangen	I was captivated by the God and
Und gewandelt um und um!	Thoroughly transformed!
Als ein Gott kam jeder gegangen,	Like a God came each one to me,
Jeder wandelte mich um,	And transformed me thoroughly.
Küßte er mir Mund und Wangen,	Kissed he my mouth and cheeks
Hingegeben war ich stumm!	I was his in mute surrender!
Hingegeben war ich stumm!	I was his in mute surrender!
Hingegeben war ich stumm!	I was his in mute surrender!
Kam der neue Gott gegangen,	When the new God came to me,
Hingegeben war ich stumm![34]	I was his in mute surrender!

Again parallel to the *Vorspiel,* where her version of the opera contained the same plot outline but with a completely different emphasis and meaning than the Composer's version, so here too everything that Zerbinetta says about herself is true outwardly with respect to Ariadne while being false in essence. The same compulsion to fall in love again that drives Zerbinetta also holds true for Ariadne. The appearance of Bacchus does make her love and live again, for she is subject to the same conditions of existence as Zerbinetta.[35] To cancel the effect of

---

[33] Ibid., p. 45.
[34] Ibid., p. 45.
[35] It is possible to view the opera as an exceedingly subtle distillation of the idea that all human beings are puppets in the hands of God or destiny. Hofmannsthal carried out this idea more explicitly in his adaptation of Calderón's *Das große Welttheater,* where God is shown assigning the roles that people must play. Hofmannsthal's friend Schnitzler of-

will, for given her character Ariadne could not knowingly love again, Hofmannsthal has purposely shown her in a trance-like state with no further hopes for this life. In this passive condition her will offers no resistance to change, and therefore the miracle of transformation can occur spontaneously.

The difference between the two women lies in their attitude and in their character. Zerbinetta's use of the term transformation is a parody of its application to Ariadne and represents but one of the ways in which the contrast between them is indicated. Transformation for Zerbinetta means merely the physical exchange of one man for another. For Ariadne, however, transformation signifies not the outer object causing the change but the actual changes occurring within her, making her a different person than she was. Although outwardly resembling each other in their actions, the two women represent the opposite ends, the A and the Z of the female spectrum, a relationship symbolized by their very names.[36]

Zerbinetta's witty and knowledgeable advice elicits no greater response from Ariadne than had the songs and dances of Harlekin and the others. Ariadne, who withdrew into her cave during Zerbinetta's recital, remains immersed in her own thoughts, prompting the latter to comment, again with more truth than she recognizes, that she and Ariadne appear to speak different languages. In Zerbinetta's view, the question is whether Ariadne will finally learn to express herself in Zerbinetta's terms, that is, whether Ariadne will not finally adopt a more realistic attitude toward life. This statement coincides with her earlier confident remark to the Composer that she, Zerbinetta, would introduce reason into his work of exaggerated fancy. While Zerbinetta's simplified analysis of Ariadne's problem and its solution—surrender to another man—proves eventually to be correct, there is a qualitative difference in the occurrence far beyond her comprehension.

Zerbinetta and her troupe are featured throughout the first half of the opera in order to establish the ideas of love and life as seen through the eyes of the "realistic" elements of society. For, as established in the discussion of the *Vorspiel*, Zerbinetta and her dancers are in Hofmannsthal's terms "base figures in life's masquerade," and are intended to symbolize the lowest common denominator of man. They are the personification of man in his natural, uninhibited state, providing the con-

ten used this theme, most explicitly in the three plays comprising the dramatic cycle *Marionetten*.

[36] Whether Hofmannsthal chose the name Zerbinetta to convey this idea of absolute opposites is not clear. However, Zerbinetta was originally called Smeraldina, a name that Hofmannsthal possibly borrowed from Molière's comedy *Les Fourberies de Scapin*. Smeraldina was used later as the name of Barak's wife in *Die Frau ohne Schatten*. See Willi Schuh, "Zu Hofmannsthal's 'Ariadne'-Szenarium und -Notizen," *Die Neue Rundschau*, 71 (1960), 89.

trast with the world of Ariadne, Bacchus (and the Composer), who embody the ideal, transcendent view of life. The major difference between the two groups lies in the fact that the latter figures combine both worlds within them, whereas the dancers are only one-dimensional figures. This overlapping is responsible for the outward similarity of action, while the difference in the dimensions of the characters causes the contrasting interpretations that show how far their inner worlds are removed from one another.

Despite the supposed impromptu appearance of Zerbinetta and the spontaneous buffoonery of her dance troupe, nothing has actually been left to chance. In every instance the interweaving of the *commedia dell'arte* and the classical drama has been artfully constructed to achieve a highly intricate and subtle juxtaposition of diametrically opposed types, joined together by the elements of irony and misunderstanding. Each world, because of the similarities and the differences between them, reflects and illuminates the other. Viewed together, they provide an insight into the nature of the world which is composed entirely in terms of such contrasts.

Since Ariadne refuses to heed their common-sense advice on how to live,[37] Zerbinetta and her group cease their attempts to cheer her and resume their frivolous activities. This final appearance in the opera for all of these figures except Zerbinetta develops into a major production number of song and dance. Not only does it provide a contrast for the scene to come between Bacchus and Ariadne, but it also completes the true characterization of Zerbinetta. She reverts to her natural role as a universal flirt, playing one man off against the other. After all, she asks wistfully as well as rhetorically, if God had intended women to resist men, why did he make them all so different?[38] At the same time she stresses the ambivalence of her nature, stating that the human heart does not understand itself at all.[39] The four male dancers put on masks and try to catch Zerbinetta, who encourages their pursuit while eluding their grasp. After she finally chooses Harlekin to the annoyance of the others, all exit. While Zerbinetta dances from one partner to another, she again sings the part of her earlier rondo with special application to the forthcoming encounter between Bacchus and Ariadne:

---

[37] Karl-Joachim Krüger states that Ariadne is in danger of succumbing to Zerbinetta's blandishments: "Wie Ariadne in Versuchung geraten soll, durch die Tröstungen Zerbinettas sich zu verlieren, so tut es für einen Augenblick Bacchus in den Armen Circes." *Hugo von Hofmannsthal und Richard Strauss* (Berlin, 1935), p. 135. While this is true of Bacchus, it is not at all true in the case of Ariadne, who ignores Zerbinetta and her friends and never displays the slightest inclination to succumb to their overtures.

[38] *Lustspiele* III, 47.

[39] Ibid., p. 45.

Immer ein Müssen,	Always necessity,
Niemals Launen,	Never capricious,
Immer ein neues	Always a new,
Unsägliches Staunen![40]	Inexpressible wonder!

With these verses and by having the dancers wear masks during their pursuit of Zerbinetta, Hofmannsthal was apparently suggesting that something mysterious and incomprehensible lies at the heart of even the most commonplace erotic encounter. At the same time both the use of masks and the dance form indicate that the pursuit of the eternal feminine forms the universal round dance of life, and that human beings are often no more than puppets being made to dance on the strings of their erotic desires.[41]

With the stage suddenly empty (Ariadne had remained in her cave to avoid the dancers) there is an abrupt shift from the carnival atmosphere surrounding Zerbinetta to the serious world of Ariadne. Despite the intention to blend art forms, the libretto falls into two main sections of almost equal length, with the first half also sub-divided into two parts. The opening segment is devoted almost exclusively to Ariadne, while Zerbinetta's world dominates the second section. However, the second half of the opera belongs almost exclusively to Ariadne and Bacchus. The lower world, represented by the dancers, makes only a token appearance near the end, when Zerbinetta alone returns briefly to repeat two lines of her earlier rondo. However, as will be seen in the discussion of the music, Strauss has constructed the musical form in tripartite divisions of almost equal length.

Just as Dryad, Naiad, and Echo introduce Ariadne at the beginning of the opera, they reappear and prepare the audience for the arrival of Bacchus. They narrate in simple statements the pertinent information necessary to understand Bacchus, in case anyone has forgotten what he learned from the *Vorspiel:* namely, that Bacchus's mother was mortal and died at his birth, while his father was a god. They emphasize particularly that Bacchus is on the threshold of manhood. He is a demi-god who is about to become a god. He has had one major adventure in his life with Circe, but, despite her seductive powers and magic potions, he has escaped from her unharmed and, most importantly, untransformed. This encounter is the essential experience preparing him for his subsequent meeting with Ariadne. Hofmannsthal's desire to present the most salient information about Bacchus takes the form of considerable repetition in the text. Immediately prior to Bacchus's entrance there are thirteen references to Bacchus as a young god, seven to his youthfulness, and six repetitions of the fact that he has escaped from Circe untransformed.

---

[40] Ibid., p. 48.
[41] In this connection see Arthur Schnitzler's drama, *Reigen* (1900). See also n. 35.

The orchestra heralds Bacchus's entrance, creating an aura of excitement. Hofmannsthal wanted this music introducing Bacchus to be "thoroughly strange and unique, mysterious." In his opinion, the music should suggest Bacchus's agitated state of mind because of his recent adventure with Circe, as well as his godlike quality. Hofmannsthal, in writing to Strauss about the second half of the opera, pointed out specifically the connotations of word and tone that must emanate from the music rather than the text: ". . . the second part of the text is sure to suggest to you certain themes: the strange aura of the fabulous East which surrounds Bacchus, the vibrating sense of the realm of death and shadow, that delicate, lyrical, unearthly atmosphere to which Ariadne still clings—and all this in most distinct contrast to the melodically pellucid world in which Zerbinetta and Harlekin have their being" (*C.*, 90). This is an example of the way in which Hofmannsthal considered his libretto merely as a basis for the music that was to convey the actual meaning. Strauss, however, chose to ignore most of Hofmannsthal's recommendations, which led to some of the discrepancies between text and music in the final version.

Circe as an experience in Bacchus's life parallels the vital role of Theseus in Ariadne's life. Although the Circe-Bacchus relationship was foreshadowed in the scene between Zerbinetta and the Composer, Circe was not mentioned by name in the *Vorspiel*. Therefore, Bacchus immediately relates the details of his adventure with the sorceress, describing how she attempted to transform him into an animal. This idea of physical transformation from a higher to a lower order of existence provides a reverse variation on the principal theme. However, because of his birthright as a god, Circe was unable to control him just as Zerbinetta could not long fool the Composer who likewise escaped from the seductress untransformed.

Nevertheless, the experience with Circe has profoundly influenced the youthful god. He is jubilant over having survived this first serious challenge in his life and, without knowing why, Bacchus finds himself in an agitated state of anticipation. He feels drugged, as if Circe's potions were acting on him, and, foreshadowing the impact that Ariadne will have on him, he asks whether the transformation which Circe could not effect is still going to happen to him:

Doch da ich unverwandelt	But since I escaped you
Von dir gegangen bin,	Untransformed,
Was haften die schwülen Gefühle	Why do these uneasy feelings
An dem benommenen Sinn?	Cling to my numbed senses?
Als wär ich von schläfernden Kräutern	As if I were a forest beast,
Betäubt, ein Waldestier!—	Benumbed by sleeping potions!—
Circe—was du nicht durftest,	Circe—what you could not do,
Geschieht es doch an mir?[42]	Is it going to happen to me after all?

[42] *Lustspiele* III, 59.

The sound of Bacchus's voice draws Ariadne out of her cave under the assumption that Hermes has arrived in response to her wishes for death. Yet, when she first sees Bacchus she starts in fright and cries out the name Theseus,[43] revealing that she has not yet completely forgotten the past and that her former lover is still uppermost in her mind. The music at this point makes clear in a simultaneous manner that words alone could not achieve, how Theseus, Hermes, and Bacchus are all blended into one in her mind (see pp. 199-203). Recovering from her initial shock, Ariadne corrects her mistake and unquestioningly accepts the attractive god before her as Hermes.

In the ensuing dialogue Ariadne and Bacchus talk past one another, indicating that because each of them is still under the influence of his previous experience, they totally misconceive the present situation with its altered conditions. Here again the music expresses the duality which exists in their minds. Ariadne, believing that Bacchus is the God of Death, addresses him in terms of this misunderstanding. Bacchus, still apprehensive after his narrow escape from Circe, wonders suspiciously whether Ariadne is another sorceress who will attempt to transform him. The entire conversation proceeds on this double level, accurate and meaningful in one sense, for they are going to transform each other, but not in the terms in which they are thinking. When, for example, Ariadne asks whether Bacchus is the master of a dark ship, the latter admits only that he is master of a ship.[44] She is too absorbed in her thoughts of death to notice the omission of the adjective and accepts his answer as a confirmation of her belief that he is Hermes. When Ariadne questions him about the means he will employ to bring about her transformation into death—by using his hands, his staff, or by means of a potion—she is subconsciously recalling references to the magic tricks of Circe, remembered from Bacchus's own earlier song.

Bacchus becomes so charmed by Ariadne that he falls into a trance similar to Ariadne's condition at the opening of the opera and the Composer's state of mind in his scene with Zerbinetta in the *Vorspiel*. In this dreamlike state he begins to forget his experience with Circe and overcomes his initial suspicions. This archetypal situation of two young people falling in love at first sight is genuinely moving in its naive simplicity and forms one of the great moments of the opera.

Ariadne seizes upon the idea of forgetting, to show that she understands the meaning of death, for she interprets Bacchus's disconcerted behavior and enigmatic responses to her questions as his test of her readiness to go with him. In this way Hofmannsthal keeps before the audience the concept of forgetting that is essential to the eventual transformation:

[43] Ibid., p. 60.
[44] Ibid., p. 61.

144

Ich weiß, so ist es dort, wohin du mich führest!	I know, so it is there, where you will lead me!
Wer dort verweilet, der vergißt gar schnell!	Whoever abides there, will forget very quickly!
Das Wort, der Atemzug ist gleich dahin!	Speaking even breathing will cease to exist!
Man ruht und ruht vom Ruhen wieder aus;	One rests and rests for evermore;
Denn dort ist keiner matt vom Weinen,—	For there no one is exhausted from weeping,—
Er hat vergessen, was ihn schmerzen sollte:	One has forgotten what was causing grief:
Nichts gilt, was hier gegolten hat, ich weiß—[45]	Nothing matters there that counted here, I know—

Although initially suspicious of Ariadne because of the Circe episode, Bacchus becomes passionately aroused when she expresses her wish to accompany him without making any demands on him. Ariadne is capable of this unreserved surrender of self because of her inherent genuineness (as opposed to the deceitfulness of Circe and Zerbinetta) and because she expects death and is resigned to it. This is the kind of total yielding of self found only at times of love or death. Circe gave nothing of herself but only wanted to dominate and demean Bacchus. As mentioned, her attempted transformation of Bacchus was the precise opposite of that worked by Ariadne, for she would have turned him into an animal, while through Ariadne he will become a God. Zerbinetta is a variant of Circe, giving bits of herself ("Mine the shoe! Mine the glance! Mine the hand!") or even all of herself at times as with Harlekin, to dominate men. However, even her total surrender involves only her physical being and never her inner self as is the case with Ariadne. The latter, because of her uncompromising nature which demands that she give all of herself, could only love once, until through the miracle of transformation she is reborn and can love again. Zerbinetta can undergo repeated "transformations" because her essential self is never committed or surrendered, and she remains on the same level of existence.

Under the impact of his experience with Circe, Bacchus first became aware of his godly nature.[46] He recognizes now for the first time that Circe's magic failed, because he has divine blood in his veins. Although his mother perished in flames when, in response to her demands his all powerful father showed himself to her in all his godly splendor, Bacchus, with the confidence of his new insight into life, assures Ariadne explicitly that she will never die because of him.

---

[45] Ibid., p. 62.
[46] "Ariadnes Verwandlung durch Bacchus / verstärkendes Gegenmotiv: sein Nicht-verwandelt-werden durch Circe, wodurch erst seine Auserwählung ihm selber bewußt wird. Circe, wie Zerbinetta, ist der Weltdämon, Tyche, ein Element gleich dem Efrit." *Aufzeichnungen*, p. 222.

Ariadne fails to comprehend the implication of Bacchus's words. She is only aware that there is no turning back from her decision to die. She has no regrets about dying, except that she wonders whether the sufferings of this world are going to be taken from her forever. Will she be separated from everything, the sun, the stars, even herself? She asks, "Bleibt nichts von Ariadne als ein Hauch?"[47] [Will nothing remain of Ariadne but a breath?] Now she even laments the loss of her sufferings, for they are inextricably connected with her richest experiences. Hofmannsthal never resolves in the opera the question of whether transformation permits a continuity of the ego or whether the former self is completely forgotten. It can be assumed on the basis of the *Vorspiel,* where the Composer emphatically insists that Ariadne really dies in order to be reborn, that the process of forgetting is intended to be complete. Hofmannsthal seems to have taken over the Goethean idea of "stirb und werde" [die and become] to mean literally the death of one self and the rebirth of another. The individual's outlook on life is transformed, a "new" person created, but the essence of the individual remains intact. In actual practice then the forgetting process is shown to be selective; for at the moment of transformation, Theseus is "forgotten," but Ariadne at the same time is able to recall the memory of her girlhood and her mother, showing that there has been a new connection with the past rather than a complete break. Ariadne's sufferings are not lost but have become buried in her subconscious, so that they no longer inhibit her continuous existence. Although Ariadne believes that she is descending from this world into the realm of death, in reality fate is moving her in the opposite direction, as the changes in the stage setting indicate. Over the young couple a star-filled sky magically appears, and Bacchus proclaims that life is just beginning for Ariadne and himself. All vestiges of the prosaic, "real" world of the Maecenas disappear and with them the idea of the play within the play. The dimensions of the opera expand into the ideal, infinite realm of the gods.

Ariadne cannot understand what is happening within her but correctly attributes her changed outlook to Hermes (Bacchus), whom she calls sorcerer and transformer, again unconsciously using words from his earlier song. Her willing acceptance of him is made complete, when she believes to perceive her mother's eye looking at her from the shadows of Bacchus's cloak:

Du Zauberer, du! Verwandler, du!	You sorcerer, you! Transformer, you!
Blickt nicht aus dem Schatten deines Mantels	Do not my mother's eyes look out
Der Mutter Auge auf mich her?	Upon me from the shadow of your cloak?

[47] *Lustspiele* III, 63.

146

| Ist so dein Schattenland! Also gesegnet! | Is it so in your shadowy realm? Thus blessed! |
| So unbedürftig der irdischen Welt?[48] | So free from the needs of this earthly world? |

Ariadne interprets this sign as her mother's blessing on her decision to accompany Hermes (Bacchus). The memory of her mother also signifies that Ariadne has now made the connection with her girlhood and earlier self which she was striving unsuccessfully to attain at the beginning of the opera. By implication, the memory of Theseus has now been forgotten or at least assimilated to the point of being neutralized as a factor in Ariadne's life, showing that Ariadne is being or has been transformed by Bacchus, who serves as the catalyst for the process:

Gibts kein Hinüber?	Is there no crossing over?
Sind wir schon drüben?	Are we already on the other side?
Sind wir schon da?	Are we there already?
Wie konnt es geschehen?	How could it have occurred?
Auch meine Höhle, schön! gewölbt	Even my cave, beautiful, arched over
Über ein seliges Lager,	A blissful bed,
Einen heiligen Altar!	A sacred altar!
Wie wunder-, wunderbar verwandelst du![49]	How wonderfully, wonderfully you transform!

Her sufferings have not been lost but are largely responsible for her new state of being. Only through them was she made ready for death and totally receptive to Bacchus and her subsequent transformation. Later her sufferings are assimilated and effaced by the altered state which they produced. Hofmannsthal's explanation in the Ariadne letter quoted earlier may be repeated here for emphasis:

> Ariadne could be the wife or mistress of *one* man only, just as she can be only *one* man's widow, can be forsaken only by *one* man. One thing, however, is still left even for her: the miracle, the God. To him she gives herself, for she believes him to be Death: he is both Death and Life at once; he it is who reveals to her the immeasurable depths in her own nature, who makes of her an enchantress, the sorceress who herself transforms the poor little Ariadne; he it is who conjures up for her in this world another world beyond, who preserves her for us and at the same time transforms her. (*C.*, 94-95)

Ariadne's transformation is demonstrated concretely by her changed attitude toward her cave. Instead of an uninviting place of withdrawal from the world, she now considers it beautiful. Formerly she had lain on the ground amidst nettles, worms, and insects, feeling still lower than

[48] Ibid., p. 64.
[49] Ibid.

these creatures. Now, however, the cave forms an arch over a wonderful bed which she regards as a sacred altar.[50]

The cave as well as Ariadne's sufferings have important significance for Bacchus as well. He wishes to draw this cave around him, for he yearns to immerse himself in Ariadne's sufferings and absorb her as completely as he now feels he has surrendered to her. Through his love for Ariadne, he recognizes that he, too, has become transformed. He considers the changes within him the means by which he can totally grasp Ariadne's being:

Du! Alles du!	You! Everything you!
Ich bin ein anderer, als ich war!	I am a different person than I was!
Der Sinn des Gottes ist wach in mir,	The feeling of a god is awake in me,
Dein herrlich Wesen ganz zu fassen!	In order to grasp completely your splendid being!
Die Glieder reg ich in göttlicher Lust!	My whole being stirs in godly desire!
Die Höhle da! Laß mich, die Höhle deiner Schmerzen	Let me draw the cave there,
Zieh ich zur tiefsten Lust um dich und mich![51]	The cave of your sufferings, about You and me with greatest pleasure.

Despite the references to the cave and its nuptial bed, the two are actually enclosed by a Baldachin—a canopy—which is lowered over them by an invisible force. This avoidance of the cave by the lovers is one of the discrepancies of the text, as discussed earlier. Possibly Hofmannsthal felt that overtly stressing the erotic implications of this final scene might vitiate the idealized ending he preferred.

At this point Zerbinetta returns briefly to gloat that, from her standpoint, Ariadne has fulfilled precisely the destiny Zerbinetta had predicted for her. Ariadne repeats once more her apprehensions about the effects of losing her sufferings, before she finally surrenders to the rapture of the moment. Bacchus joyously proclaims that through Ariadne's sufferings he has become a different person and concludes the opera by reassuring Ariadne that the eternal stars will die before she will perish in his arms.

The opera presents what Hofmannsthal called the allomatic solution, that is, the mutual transformation of two people through love. Love alone, however, is not enough in Hofmannsthal's view. Both Ariadne and Bacchus have been prepared for this unique moment in their life by a previous unhappy experience. Suffering, either actual or potential (as in the case of Bacchus) was necessary in order to condition them for this moment of fulfillment. Ariadne's sufferings were not lost, as she feared, but played a vital role in making possible her own and, eventually, Bac-

---

[50] In *Ad me Ipsum* Hofmannsthal commented: "Die Wiedergeburt eines neuen genießen aus der Höhle der Schmerzen. Ariadne-Elektra." *Aufzeichnungen*, p. 225.

[51] *Ariadne auf Naxos*, p. 64. In Freudian terms it might be possible to interpret the cave as representing the womb, and Ariadne's sufferings as symbolizing the labor pains involved in "giving birth" to her own new self and to the new Bacchus.

chus's transformation. Without the previous attempt of Circe to enslave him, Bacchus, whose youthfulness is stressed, would not have been sufficiently matured to be receptive for the experience with Ariadne. In the letter to Strauss quoted earlier (p. 125), Hofmannsthal had stressed the importance of this experience to Bacchus's development.

Similarly, Ariadne's experience with Theseus, resulting in her preparedness for death, produces within her the purity of heart and openness of mind to be receptive to Bacchus by mistaking him for Hermes. Since she is that woman in a million who can love only once, she could not consciously fall in love with another man after Theseus. By meeting Bacchus in unsuspecting innocence, love can work its miracle before she is aware of what has happened. Mutual transformation thus accomplishes the important additional function of restoring contact with the world or, in Hofmannsthalian terms, of enabling the individual to proceed from preexistence to existence.[52] Actually Ariadne is not deceived, for Bacchus does represent death for her in the sense that he helps bring about her transformation to a new level of existence. At the same time she remains true to her character as the woman who can only love once, for her memory of Theseus has been suppressed, and she is released from the bondage of her own character. Without the possibility of transformation, Ariadne would have had to perish like Elektra.

The same double meaning based on misunderstanding is found also in Zerbinetta's reaction to the romantic scene between Ariadne and Bacchus. She had asserted that Ariadne would learn to express herself in her language, that is, find solace in the arms of a new lover. Her belief now, that the union of souls she is witnessing represents the confirmation of her former prediction, is true and not true at the same time. Zerbinetta naturally interprets the actions of Ariadne in terms of her own understanding, and in one sense she is right. Like Zerbinetta, Ariadne is transformed, at least partly, by the physical attractiveness of a new lover. Ariadne's references to the nuptial bed and Bacchus's comments ("Die Glieder reg ich in göttlicher Lust") make fully evident the erotic implications of their love. Bacchus changes after all not only from demi-god to god but also from youthfulness to manhood. Yet, what a contrast exists between Zerbinetta's common flirtation with Harlekin and Ariadne's references to her bed as a sacred altar! For Zerbinetta love is a pleasant pastime for self-gratification, while for Ariadne it represents total yielding of herself to another person.

[52] Hofmannsthal commented in *Ad me Ipsum:* "Hinzutretendes Hauptmotiv: (mit welchem die Auflösung erfolgt) mit dem Sich-verwandeln das Verwandeln eines Andern—Verknüpfung mit der Welt durch Verknüpfung zweier Individuen." *Aufzeichnungen*, p. 222. Hofmannsthal had previously employed the theme of transformation ironically in *Der weiße Fächer*, where he depicted two young people who had lost their respective mates. Each has vowed to renounce life in order to remain forever faithful to his dead spouse. Meeting in the cemetery, the two cannot suppress their normal, healthy youthful nature. By the end of the play it is evident that they will learn to love and live again through each other.

Ariadne auf Naxos is a study in attitudes, showing repeatedly how the same act can be interpreted in opposing ways, depending on the attitude of the participant or onlooker.

Ariadne's renewed capacity for love, in the mind of the Composer (and Hofmannsthal), represents *the* miracle of existence. That Zerbinetta sees the same event as a commonplace, trivial exchange of lovers is a comment on her outlook, not on the event itself. Love (or sex) like beauty is in the mind of the beholder or participant. Their fully human emotional responses show Ariadne and Bacchus to be creatures with the same flesh and blood as Zerbinetta and her companions, rather than disembodied, idealized abstractions employed to make a theoretical commentary on life. Hofmannsthal also wished to show that the transcendental and "real" worlds are not widely separated but are interrelated and may be found in the same person. *Ariadne* expresses Hofmannsthal's general poetic intent, namely, to make one aware of the mysterious and miraculous nature of life.[53]

What Zerbinetta cannot possibly understand because of her limited perspective is the fact that Ariadne's transformation elevates her to a new level of existence, whereas her own "transformations" always take place on the same level. This capacity for rebirth differentiates Ariadne from Zerbinetta, for the latter, as conceived by Hofmannsthal, was incapable of transformation and condemned to remain forever on one level of existence. While Ariadne—and by analogy Bacchus—encompasses the full range of human capability, Zerbinetta, like Harlekin, in Hofmannsthal's conception, is severely limited in her potential. Although his portrayal of Zerbinetta accords with his theory of life, the opera possibly would have been enriched in human terms if Zerbinetta, like Ariadne, had been granted at least the potential for the full range of personal development, including transformation.[54]

Strauss and Hofmannsthal differed radically on the interpretation of Zerbinetta. Hofmannsthal insisted that the mocking presence of Zerbinetta be included near the end of the opera, in order to reemphasize through the use of irony the contrast of the two worlds that constituted the premise of the work. In the original libretto used by Reinhardt, Zerbinetta repeated a long section of her main aria at the end of the opera, while Harlekin and the other members of the troupe performed a dance.

[53] ". . . das Geheimnis des Lebens ist überall, nicht bloß im ersten Lächeln eines Neugeborenen oder im ersten Strähnlein weißer Haare auf dem Kopf einer Frau, die noch jung ist—es umgibt uns überall und drängt sich so dicht um uns herum, daß es einem manchmal fast den Athem nimmt. Nichts, aber auch gar nichts ist selbstverständlich, alles ist zum Staunen und *hinter* allem ist ein Höheres, noch geheimer aber auch lichter, nirgends ist Festes, worauf wir ruhen könnten, wir meinen zu stehen und sinken, meinen zu sinken und werden gehoben und getragen." *Briefe der Freundschaft*, p. 118.

[54] Hofmannsthal carried out this idea in the following opera *Die Frau ohne Schatten*, where the representatives of both the "lower" and "higher" worlds undergo transformation.

Although Hofmannsthal insisted that this ending was right and artistically necessary, he compromised in the face of Strauss's strong objections and settled for a token reappearance of Zerbinetta singing just two lines of her rondo.

Even here the two men disagreed on the manner of rendition. Hofmannsthal's stage direction states explicitly that Zerbinetta is to deliver her remarks in a mocking tone. By using such a tone he expected to overcome the severe reduction of the text sung by Zerbinetta and still stress the irony he felt must be present at the end. Strauss, however, partly because of his greater attraction to Zerbinetta as a character, but mainly because he desired a theatrically effective ending, remained unconcerned over the dramatic necessity for irony here in terms of the work's construction and eliminated the ironic quality of Zerbinetta's appearance in his music. Instead, Zerbinetta sings the same words from her earlier rondo "Kommt der neue Gott gegangen,/ Hingegeben sind wir stumm!" but this time with a subdued, almost reverent expression. Strauss's musical interpretation (see p. 217) implies a richer, more ambivalent character for Zerbinetta than Hofmannsthal intended. As shown previously, Hofmannsthal partially accepted this idea, for he incorporated a suggestion of this ambivalence into the confrontation between Zerbinetta and the Composer in the revised version of the *Vorspiel*. However, Hofmannsthal vitiated the ambiguity by causing Zerbinetta immediately to revert to type, showing that he had not altered his original conception of her as a one-dimensional Circe-like figure.

Despite the difference in the interpretation of Zerbinetta's final appearance, no harm was actually done to the overall structure of the work. Strauss's judgment is defensible: to juxtapose irony with the musical setting of a miracle would be distracting and disruptive of the delicate mood and soaring quality of the ending. Although the contrast of attitudes that lies at the heart of the work is not as strongly reemphasized as Hofmannsthal wished, the point is not lost. At the same time, her subdued attitude blends naturally into the theatrically effective conclusion. Zerbinetta by no means comprehends the nature of the miracle she beholds in the love of Ariadne and Bacchus, yet she is deeply moved by it. She senses intuitively the presence of a wonderful though inexplicable mystery which is beyond her understanding. Her reaction is that of a spectator, and it should be shared by the audience if *Ariadne* is properly performed. [55] Only when the opera can engender in

---

[55] In the first version of *Ariadne*, Hofmannsthal had expressly stated to Strauss that Jourdain was intended to symbolize the public. *C.*, 107. Jourdain and his guests were seated along the sides of the stage and made comments throughout the early part of the opera. However, when the scene shifts to the larger world, Jourdain and his guests fall silent, indicating that against their will and without their fully understanding what is happening on stage, they have been captivated by the miracle occurring between Ariadne and Bacchus. Since Zerbinetta is the representative of the Maecenas in the opera in the revised

an audience this feeling of wonderment at having beheld the miracle of life's greatest mystery has it achieved the effect and purpose intended by Hofmannsthal.

Since the entire opera is focused on a single theme, Ariadne derives its complexity from Hofmannsthal's use of contrasts. The libretto is carefully worked out in the narrowest space in terms of opposing values which have been judiciously selected and juxtaposed in order to encompass the full range of human possibilities. In this method of using contrasts to provide the internal unity as well as richness of his text Hofmannsthal saw his particular merit as librettist. [56]

Consider the opposing forces and values within Ariadne which provide its dramatic tension and effectiveness: the action expands in gradual stages from microcosm to macrocosm, from confining present to the infinite, from the materialistic world of the Maecenas to the transcendental realm of the gods, from *commedia dell'arte* to classical drama, from the temporal to the eternal, from recited dialogue to rapturous song, from prosaic reality to sublime miracle. In terms of the opera alone, the development proceeds from the somberness of absolute depair to the joyous exaltation of love, from expectation of death to the ecstatic moment of transformation, from mortality to immortality, from dream state to waking, from static rigidity to eternal becoming, from the playful burlesque world of Harlekin and Zerbinetta to the serious, divine world of Bacchus, from a superficial flirtatious affair to genuine love. Thus, measured in terms of theatrical effectiveness, the revised *Ariadne* represents a distinct improvement over the earlier version, where these upward progressions were largely nullified by the return at the end of the opera to the crass world of the *Vorspiel*.

This same technique of antithetical contrast can be found in the characters as well. Not only do they represent the two opposing worlds of the opera, but antithetical contrasts also occur within the individuals. Zerbinetta's cynicism highlights Ariadne's faith and sentimentality, her frivolity, the latter's seriousness, her artificiality, Ariadne's genuineness, and her infidelity, Ariadne's faithfulness. Ariadne desires to die and is reborn. She thinks she is surrendering and losing herself and regains her inner unity. Bacchus at first regards Ariadne suspiciously and mistakenly as another Circe. Yet, while Circe cannot effect his transformation, Ariadne does. Zerbinetta believes she understands Ariadne but does not comprehend even herself. The Composer thinks he has been corrupted by being forced to present his work together with Zerbinetta's dancers but is actually learning a lesson about life that will make him a better, stronger person in the future. The Maecenas is ap-

version, her reaction retains the same symbolic value originally attached to Jourdain.
[56] "My special qualities as librettist are perhaps not so hard to define—I build on contrasts to discover, above these contrasts, the harmony of the whole; that is to say they are perhaps of a general artistic order (and such artistic qualities are rare among Germans)." *C.*, 90.

parently creating chaos by his whimsical order to put on both entertainments at once, but actually creates the means to capture the miracle of life. This paradoxical situation holds true for the entire work, for although highly contrived, it encompasses reality in a way never achieved by so-called naturalistic or realistic works, where the realism is a matter of the surface. Finally, while *Ariadne* appears to be a delicate, fragile work, it is actually indestructible in the sense that it grows stronger the more one analyzes it critically. It is almost as intangible as the human spirit to which it is a tribute and promises to endure as long as human values are prized.

These contrasts as well as the upward soaring quality of the plot are conveyed and reinforced by every aspect of the work, so that the point of the text, the ultimate harmony of life created by this very contrasting of the heroic and base worlds, is inescapable. The *Vorspiel* with its petty bickering and rough humor and the antics of the buffo elements in the opera offer the precise reverse of the ecstatic ceremonial conclusion. These contrasts are also reflected in the music, as will be seen, and are further accentuated by the gestures and positioning of the actors—Ariadne resurrected from a prone to a vertical position—and by the staging, which proceeds from darkness to light, from an artificial desert island temporarily set in a large room of a rich man's palace to the infinite setting of a star-studded firmament and the realm of the limitless imagination.

Through the polar opposites of Ariadne and Zerbinetta, the woman who cannot forget and therefore can love only once with the woman who cannot be faithful to one man, and by the contrasts of the god, Bacchus, with Harlekin, a representative of the Casanova-type of predatory male, Hofmannsthal has created a situation that is all-encompassing of the human situation in the world. This text can be diagrammed as a perfect square with Ariadne and Bacchus as the top two corners and Zerbinetta and Harlekin the bottom two.[57] By conceiving his characters in terms of the lowest and the highest examples of human beings, Hofmannsthal has created a work that is universal in its validity and application, for every other individual must fall somewhere on the human scale between these two extremes.

The poet measures the moral quality of his characters by their attitude toward the concept of faithfulness. The inner difference between Ariadne and Zerbinetta, reflected by their character and general attitude toward life, is extreme and complete, at least in Hofmannsthal's mind and intention. Zerbinetta lacks the potential for transformation

---

[57] Hofmannsthal presented this same format in visual terms in *Die Frau ohne Schatten*, which may be considered a more ambitious sequel to *Ariadne*. At the end of this opera the princess and the prince stand on an elevated platform with Barak and his wife at the base, to show how the two different worlds are united but separate. In Hofmannsthal's opinion, *Die Frau ohne Schatten* represented the "Triumph des Allomatischen. Allegorie des Sozialen." *Aufzeichnungen*, p. 218.

because she is not endowed with the requisite depth of character which is needed in order to experience this miracle of existence. Ariadne is capable of transformation through love by virtue of her faithful character and because of her past sufferings. Because she is capable of falling to the depths of despair, she is capable of achieving the heights of bliss.

Transformation is only possible through suffering, through the pains which can give birth to it. The opposite is also true. Zerbinetta does not transform because she does not possess the quality of faithfulness and because she does not suffer. She is totally superficial in her approach to life, incapable of deep feelings, and consequently cut off from achieving transformation to another level of existence. Since she is unconnected to anyone or anything beyond herself, she represents a woman condemned to a shallow life of the senses with no possibility of breaking out of the essentially meaningless round dance of sensuality. She cannot fall genuinely in love and hence change her character, nor can she change her character so that she could fall in love. Hofmannsthal equated the capability for spiritual growth with the quality of fidelity: "Identity of fidelity and destiny."[58] Since Zerbinetta cannot be faithful, she is, in Hofmannsthal's view, without destiny ("schicksalslos"), condemned forever to life on one level. However, Ariadne, the personification of fidelity, is "schicksalsvoll" or capable of inner growth.[59] Audiences, nevertheless, find great appeal in Zerbinetta, who accepts graciously, though with wistful resignation, the destiny of leading the unwanted but unavoidable flirtatious life of a coquette, passing aimlessly from one man to another. Hofmannsthal explicitly created Zerbinetta so that she should be incapable of transformation and hence of understanding Ariadne. That these two worlds are united ultimately in the only way they can be, through misunderstanding, forms the underlying irony and antithesis on which the opera is based.

Because of this purpose to contrast opposite types, Hofmannsthal, who liked to work in terms of absolute ideas, contrived a hypothetical situation that would encompass the limits of the theoretically possible range of human beings. If one can suspend disbelief to accept the premise of a mortal becoming a goddess, then the premise of an individual incapable of love and suffering and hence potentially incapable of change should also be acceptable. The abstract design of the text may possibly be one of the reasons why people find it difficult to identify with this work.[60]

---

[58] Ibid., p. 217.

[59] This contrasting of responsible and irresponsible individuals runs throughout Hofmannsthal's works. For a detailed list of examples see Walter Naumann, "Drei Wege der Erlösung in Hofmannsthals Werken," *The Germanic Review,* 19 (1944), 153 ff.

[60] The critic Richard Specht regards the abstract quality of the characters as a weakness of the opera: "Aber ich muß schon gestehen, daß ich all diese Antithesen mit ihrem gedankenschweren Sinn ganz rein und stark nur aus der Musik heraus verstehe—oder besser gesagt, empfinde; denn die Dichtung ist vielleicht wirklich zu abstrakt

One important problem regarding this text is that of clarity of ideas. Is the information necessary for understanding the opera present in the work in a manner clearly discernible to the audience? While the climax is a miracle that must be directly experienced, nevertheless, the text does provide the needed preparation for this event. As has been shown, the elements necessary for comprehension are explicitly presented not only in the *Vorspiel* but also in the opera itself by repetition of the key ideas, while the total number of words has been held to a minimum. From the point at which Bacchus is introduced by the orchestral interlude, the libretto shows the highly repetitive content that is necessary for the conveyance of ideas in opera. Hofmannsthal made every effort to stress repeatedly the fundamental concepts necessary to appreciate the miraculous event about to take place. The word *Gott* occurs seventeen times, and *göttlich* three times. *Verwandeln* appears eight times, while other forms, *Verwandlung, unverwandelt, Verwandler* occur once. *Vergessen* is used twice and *Vergessenheit* once. *Schmerzen* is repeated seven times. The word *Zauber* and variants such as *Zauberer, Zauberin, Zauberworte, Zauberlieder, Zaubertrank,* and *Zauberlippen* appear ten times.

Despite this clarity it is doubtful that anyone can understand more than the surface details on first seeing this opera.[61] In part this difficulty is attributable to the extreme subtlety of the text and in part to the fact

maskenhaft, um menschlich nahe, warm, anteilweckend zu wirken. Kürzer: um dramatisch zu wirken. Mag sein übrigens, daß hier ein auffallendes Beispiel für die Tendenz des heutigen Tondramas ist, das Stoffliche auszuschalten, die äußerlichen Vorgänge auf ein nebensächliches Maß zu konzentrieren und nur das Innerliche durch die ihm einzig gemäße Sprache der Musik andeuten zu lassen. Nur daß man dem großen Dichter, der diese 'Ariadne' geschrieben hat, doch vorwerfen muß, daß hier eben keine inneren Vorgänge mehr sind, sondern nur Abstraktionen, wandelnde Ideen. Darin übrigens vieldeutig genug: man könnte die beiden ineinandergeschobenen Spiele ebenso gut als das Symbol unsrer eigenen hohen und skurrilen Stunden auffassen, die einander ablösen und durchdringen . . . Was mir hier fehlt, sind Menschen, die mir nahe sind, die mein Erleben leben, die ich lieb haben und für die ich zittern kann. Wie im 'Rosenkavalier'. Hier sind nur mehr Begriffe; für mich wenigstens." *Richard Strauss und sein Werk,* II (Vienna, 1921), 275-76. Later Specht repeated his attack on the undramatic nature of this text in even stronger terms: "Ihre Wirkung, die fleckenloseste, die er geübt hat, ist vollkommen die der reinen Musik. Die dramatische schweigt. Ich habe die Empfindung: ein Vokalkonzert im Kostüm. Ich bedarf der Szene nicht, ja sie stört mich eher in ihren Barock-Velleitäten—ich schließe die Augen und öffne die Seele so weit ich kann, um die edlen Worte und die erlauchte Musik über sie hin- und tief in sie hineinfluten zu lassen. Ariadne, die Gestalt, das dramatische Schicksal—all das geht mich im Grunde nichts an. Der Musiker spricht; und ich werde heiß. Der Dramatiker bleibt stumm. Das macht: die *Ariadne* ist ein Maskenspiel, bringt abstrakte Symbole auf die Szene, singende Figurinen, die nicht sind, sondern bedeuten. Hofmannsthal ist vielleicht niemals tiefer in die Gleichnisse des Lebens hinabgetaucht, aber er war auch niemals weniger Dramatiker. Man sieht Sinnbilder des Daseins, die das Hohe und Niedere aller Existenz verkörpern, hört Sinnsprüche und parabolische Lyrik, Metaphern des Daseins in Wort und Ton—und sehnt sich nach einem unmittelbaren menschlichen Laut." Ibid., p. 286.

[61] Hofmannsthal had expressed this view to Strauss: "No, my dear Friend, the essence of poetic meaning comes to be understood only gradually, very gradually; this un-

that the relationship of the opera to the *Vorspiel* can only be understood in retrospect. However, these complexities are not a permanent barrier to enjoyment of the opera, which ultimately is not meant to be understood in rational terms. The intent of this opera is not to explicate but to demonstrate, indeed, to celebrate a miracle. Hofmannsthal constantly emphasized the mysterious element involved in the concept of transformation that could only be rendered through music and not through words alone. He stated to Strauss, in the version of his letter published in the *Almanach für die musikalische Welt*, that the idea behind Ariadne is difficult to grasp. ". . . like all the open secrets of life, which it is not given to us to approach with words; with tones however they can be drawn into our heart, and it is exactly here where music is called upon by the arts of writing, and their union is fully justified and sealed."[62]

Near the conclusion of this same letter he states again that the essential meaning of his text is beyond the possibility of words to express. After describing the mutual transformation of Ariadne and Bacchus he remarks: "I needn't continue to describe the situation for you—by this time you have either long thrown your pen from your hand, or you have felt the most profound and most secret powers of music released within you and are in a region where the words of the text have become hieroglyphics for you for something impossible to state in words."[63]

Not only must the music convey the magical and miraculous message of Ariadne but also, as we have previously stressed, the staging and the set design must contribute to the utmost: "Here the painter and the regisseur must, if we are ever to bring this on to the stage, extend all their powers, in order not to reveal but to glorify a true mystery; here the small stage must grow into the infinite. . . . everything which has gone before must be forgotten and the spectator must remember these things as whoever lies in a deep dream knows anything about his bed."[64]

There is an element of ritual in *Ariadne* that must be rendered by the acting and staging. The characters Ariadne and Bacchus are highly

derstanding emanates from a very few people who are in close touch with the world of poetry, and it takes decades to spread. But it is equally true that the poet's text must possess yet another attraction, through which it can effectively reach even the non-comprehending majority, and such attraction lies in the fact that it exhibits something which is neither insubstantial nor commonplace. . . . I have, what is more, been at pains to treat the main action in such a manner that it is something thoroughly familiar to the average spectator: Ariadne, deserted by Theseus, consoled by Bacchus, *Ariadne auf Naxos* is in fact, like *Amor und Psyche*, something everybody can picture to himself, even if it be only as a plaster of Paris ornament on the mantelpiece." *C.*, 98-99. This relationship in Hofmannsthal's works between the visual surface and the plastic content has been discussed in an excellent article by Walter Naumann: "Das Visuelle und das Plastische bei Hofmannsthal," *Monatshefte*, 37 (1945), 159-69.

[62] *Prosa* III, 138.
[63] Ibid., 142.
[64] Ibid.

stylized, with every gesture calculated as in dance. The singers must employ all of their acting resources such as facial expressions and gestures in addition to vocal quality to convey their feelings.[65] For this reason *Ariadne* belongs only in small opera houses. Hofmannsthal himself compared *Ariadne* to a dance and insisted that in performance the work in essence needed to be choreographed:

> . . . even if I think only of the opera, only of the two groups: Ariadne-Bacchus, Zerbinetta and the four men—even then I must tell myself that they need a mysterious power higher than music alone in order to reveal their ultimate significance at all. The subtly conceived exiguity of this play, these two groups acting beside each other in the narrowest space, this most careful calculation of each gesture, each step, the whole like a concert and at the same time like a ballet—it will be lost, meaningless, a tattered rag in incompetent hands; only in Reinhardt's, yours and mine, can it grow into a singing flower, the incarnation of dance. *Love* is what it needs, enthusiasm, improvisation; it needs a theatre conscious of its ability to achieve something which is today altogether out of the ordinary; it needs a real man at the conductor's desk whose heart and soul is in it—not that appalling atmosphere of the commonplace, the drab routine, the conductor with the cold heart, the opera singers who get through their music somehow. Everyone concerned must stake his life, the impossible must become possible. . . . (*C.,* 109-110)

From the moment of Bacchus's entrance the opera enters the world of great poetry and impassioned music. Everything else fades away, and the two principal characters have the stage entirely to themselves. Their final apotheosis forms the climax and the point of the entire work, which can only become meaningful in performance. By uniting all art forms, Hofmannsthal and Strauss succeeded in celebrating the mystery of transformation, that miraculous phenomenon of existence which enables a vanquished, dispirited human being to be elevated from the depths of despair, from the acceptance of death as the only solution to life's problems, to renewed hope, love, and life.

[65] Hofmannsthal's interest in pantomime, which was particularly strong in 1901, was renewed in the period coincident with the writing of *Ariadne,* possibly because of his work with the young dancer Grete Wiesenthal, with whom he collaborated on several dances. In a revealing letter to Reinhardt, Hofmannsthal in March 1914 indicated his attitude toward words, gestures, and ceremonial: ". . . es ist in dieser stummen Form jetzt eine namenlose Fascination für mich—fast scheint mir das heroische und das tragische Sujet nur *so* möglich, die Worte lösen mir alles auf, in Worten kann ich nur die Comödie fühlen, wo die Worte eben Masken vor den Gesichtern sind und in dieser Weise mit dazugehören, in den Tragödien brechen die Worte lauter Löcher, und (?) so ist mir das Wort im Sophokles schon zu viel—im Euripides ganz unerträglich zu viel—man müßte in einem Pentheus fast alle Worte von den Figuren wegheben und in ein Ceremoniell hinauf, bei den Figuren nur die notwendigsten, kaum articulierten Worte halten." Wolfgang Nehring, *Die Tat bei Hofmannsthal* (Stuttgart, 1966), p. 140. Hofmannsthal's fondness for the impact of wordless ceremonial may be seen particularly in the presentation of the silver rose in *Der Rosenkavalier,* a ceremony that he himself invented for use in this work. Another example is the ceremony of the glass of water in *Arabella.*

Chapter VIII

Ariadne auf Naxos—The Music

Even though the correspondence between Hofmannsthal and Strauss implies that the composer was not enthusiastic about the dramatic basis of *Ariadne auf Naxos,* the musical implications of Hofmannsthal's little baroque opera eventually stimulated the composer's imagination. The result, an opera unique among the fifteen works by Richard Strauss, includes a variety of musical innovations that were influential in determining aspects of style in his later operas. To write an opera in a pseudo-seventeenth-century setting, Strauss altered considerably many of the musical characteristics of previous operatic successes. The libretto suggested to him the sound of a chamber orchestra. Since the poetic structure relied on clearly marked musico-poetical forms of recitative, aria, and various ensembles, these opened the way for Strauss, with his predominantly lyrical genius, to write an extended work without recourse to even a hint of the Wagnerian style of "endless melody." Of course, already in *Der Rosenkavalier* one hears evidence of Strauss's natural inclination towards composing lyrical, self-contained arias, duets, and trios, as well as a new approach to recitative-like musical conversation. This development on the part of a composer whose greatest musical god was Mozart, "the most sublime of all composers"[1] finds its purest realization in *Ariadne*. It remained a prominent feature of Strauss's later works and was eventually recapitulated in his final opera, *Capriccio*.

The orchestral concept is first among the innovations of *Ariadne*. The decision to score the opera for a chamber orchestra undoubtedly originated in Strauss's search for a suitable modern imitation of a French baroque opera orchestra. The composer did not, however, attempt to imitate a seventeenth-century ensemble; rather, he discovered in the older musical practice the basis of a very new orchestral sound, one of the early twentieth-century neo-classical adaptations of the orchestra.

Strauss originally planned to write *Ariadne* for fifteen to twenty players, including two violins, viola, cello, double bass, flute, oboe, clarinet, bassoon, one or two horns, harpsichord, harp, celesta, har-

[1] Richard Strauss, *Betrachtungen und Erinnerungen,* trans. L. J. Lawrence as: *Recollections and Reflections* (London, 1953), p. 75.

monium, and perhaps a trumpet and some percussion instruments (*C.*, 83). This list hardly suggests a seventeenth-century orchestra, in which clarinet, celesta, and harmonium would have been historically out of place. In the final version, however, Strauss strengthens the ensemble by increasing the number of string players (six violins, four violas, four cellos, two double basses), by doubling the woodwinds (two flutes, two oboes, two clarinets, two bassoons), and by adding in the brass group two horns, a trumpet, trombone, and tenor tuba. In addition the score employs two harps, celesta, timpani, percussion instruments (glockenspiel, tambourine, triangle, and snare drum).

The most distinctive and most original change is the substitution of a piano for the harpsichord. Throughout the opera the sound of the piano symbolizes the common vulgarity of the world belonging to Zerbinetta and her friends. With one deft instrumental touch, Strauss found an ingenious musical means to contrast the two planes of action interwoven in the opera.

The orchestral ensemble requires thirty-seven performers, but Strauss employs this corps of musicians sparingly, carefully reserving the full impact of the instruments for a few climactic moments: the end of Ariadne's first scene, the arrival of Bacchus in the final scene, and the whole of the final duet between Ariadne and Bacchus. For the greater portion of the score, the chamber orchestra is reduced to two violins, two violas, two cellos, and one double bass; trombone and percussion are largely absent. The woodwinds and French horn are generally given solo passages. In fact, the score demands the very best instrumental soloists, since the transparency of the sound allows no technical inadequacy to be covered up. Strauss fully realized the technical difficulties of his work and insisted that first-rate people from the Royal Court Orchestra in Berlin perform at the premiere (*C.*, 82).

Another original feature of the score is Strauss's use of the harmonium, an instrument similar to the American reed organ. The harmonium serves four important functions: (1) to contribute a dark, bass color to the orchestra, especially in Ariadne's opening scene; (2) to substitute for the more conventional bass woodwind instruments missing in the score; (3) to supply the harmonic framework, freeing woodwinds and French horns from their traditional role of providing harmonic solidarity to the score (in conjunction with the brass choir, which is largely absent in *Ariadne*); (4) to add (together with the piano) reserve resources of tonal strength in climactic passages. Strauss, who was accustomed to drawing upon the huge decibel bank of a symphonic orchestra for his musical climaxes, expressed concern initially that his small chamber ensemble would fail him at the moments of crucial dramatic impact. At one point he even suggested to Hofmannsthal (foolishly, as he admitted later) that the final operatic climax might make use of a second orchestra hidden behind the scene.[2]

[2] Ibid., pp. 161-62.

159

Strauss's original doubts, however, were not without substance. Performances of *Ariadne* in the typically large opera houses of the world prove that the chamber orchestra does not fully realize the musical climax at the end of the score. In attempting to play very loud, the instruments frequently sound forced in tone. Of course, Strauss recognized this danger, and he hoped that the opera would be given only in small theaters—one of his favorites being the Residenztheater of Munich with its four hundred and fifty seats.

The classical simplicity of Hofmannsthal's libretto for *Ariadne* shapes many details of the score. As Strauss once suggested to his librettist: "The interplay of forms: the formal garden must come into its own here." This is an extraordinary statement coming from a composer frequently grouped with the arch-romantics in music. Yet, as the formal design of the score as a whole indicates (see Table I, pp. 162-65), the opera has a markedly classical ternary superstructure: three distinct divisions and a preface consisting of an overture and introductory music for three sopranos: the sounds of Nature personified by the three nymphs, Naiad, Dryad, and Echo.

Structure is paramount in Strauss's mind, and he makes no attempt to hide the seams between sections, but rather assures the musical independence of each section. This technique keeps the dramatic contrasts that characterize Hofmannsthal's libretto clearly in focus. Moreover, this sectional independence requires the almost total rejection of a Wagnerian type of motive system (in which brief thematic ideas associated with characters, objects, events, states of mind, etc. are stated and developed throughout the course of the work). Melodic motives occur in *Ariadne,* but they are limited in overall application. Subtle interconnections of melodic ideas are found between Parts I and III, although these reminiscences are confined to the opening bars of the Overture, the music for Ariadne's theme of Ecstasy, and the more complex Bacchus-Theseus motive (to be discussed later).

The sparse use of melodic motives delineates another aspect of *Ariadne* that had great importance for Strauss's future musical development. It is true that both the nature of the libretto, with its non-Wagnerian, classical setting, and the stark poetic contrasts between the worlds of Ariadne-Bacchus and Zerbinetta-Harlekin influenced the musical course taken by Strauss; nevertheless, the turning away from Wagner and the embracing of a neo-classical musical language were momentous in their impact on musical history. Music historians frequently write that twentieth-century neo-classicism occurred first in the music of Hindemith and Stravinsky. While the history of the neo-classical movement certainly includes these composers, as well as

Schoenberg, in actual fact Richard Strauss also belongs at the top of the list of neo-classicists.[3]

When Strauss asked Hofmannsthal if his prose transition from the play to the opera (in the original version of *Ariadne auf Naxos* —*Ariadne* I) would allow the orchestra to play an overture, the poet replied:

> The transition to the actual opera takes place on the stage. . . . The lights are being lit, the musicians are tuning their instruments, Zerbinetta tries a few roulades, Jourdain and his guests appear and take their seats in the fauteuils—and at this point, I must say, a little overture seems to be stylistically indispensable; a little symphony of the old kind which brings together the main themes from the opera would, I feel, be charming. Perhaps, however, it might be better to leave the writing of this to the very end, for the second part of the text is sure to suggest to you certain themes. . . . (*C.*, 90)

Despite Hofmannsthal's suggestion, Strauss's instrumental introduction—the label "overture" notwithstanding—has nothing in common with a conventional opera overture. Strauss's overture is not an independent composition, a "little symphony," as would have prefaced operas of the late seventeenth and early eighteenth centuries. Nor does Strauss derive the thematic material of the overture from the score as a whole, for neither the middle part (Zerbinetta's music) nor the final part (the music of Bacchus and Ariadne) appear in the overture. The greatest part of the introduction comes from Ariadne's first aria, and it is introduced by an opening section quite independent of the thematic material of the work as a whole. The overture, then, is an extended instrumental passage (the only one in the entire opera) intended to prepare the audience for the first scene. The music depicts the state of Ariadne's mind, and emotions which fluctuate between abject despair and her love for Theseus.

[3] William Mann, in *Richard Strauss: A Critical Study of the Operas* (London, 1964), p. 147, states that Hofmannsthal "was anxious to develop the importance of separate musical numbers connected by *secco* recitatives—precisely the concept of opera which Strauss, following Wagner, was developing away from." This viewpoint totally misreads the available evidence in the correspondence as well as the distinctive tendencies in Strauss's music. At no time does Hofmannsthal suggest to Strauss that set numbers would be desirable in either *Der Rosenkavalier* or *Ariadne;* quite the contrary, it is Strauss who urges repeatedly that Hofmannsthal provide him with words for arias or aria-like passages (the latter he frequently refers to as "contemplative ensembles"). One example, among several, to prove Strauss's ever-growing desire for more opportunities for set numbers: In writing *Der Rosenkavalier* Strauss told Hofmannsthal that he needed a text for the closing duet, a set number for which he had already created the music *before* having text in hand (*C.*, 35). It is Hofmannsthal who tells Strauss he hopes to learn in *Ariadne* how to construct a dramatic piece as a whole so that set numbers can regain more and more importance (ibid., p. 77). Such a passage hardly suggests that Hofmannsthal is attempting to incorporate into his work that very element Strauss missed most seriously. Finally, one need only remember that Hofmannsthal (ibid., p. 80) asks Strauss to suggest places for duets, trios, quartets, sextets, etc. in *Ariadne;* here again, quite obviously, Hofmannsthal is not leading but following Strauss's desires.

161

TABLE I

Basic Structure of *ARIADNE AUF NAXOS*

Part I [Ariadne + Commedia players]

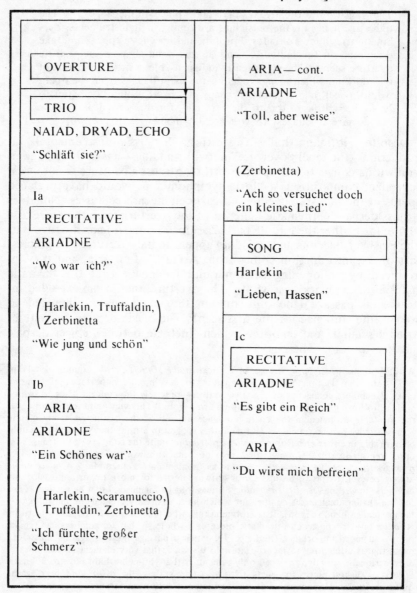

OVERTURE

TRIO

NAIAD, DRYAD, ECHO

"Schläft sie?"

Ia

RECITATIVE

ARIADNE

"Wo war ich?"

⎛Harlekin, Truffaldin,⎞
⎝Zerbinetta   ⎠

"Wie jung und schön"

Ib

ARIA

ARIADNE

"Ein Schönes war"

⎛Harlekin, Scaramuccio,⎞
⎝Truffaldin, Zerbinetta ⎠

"Ich fürchte, großer Schmerz"

ARIA—cont.

ARIADNE

"Toll, aber weise"

(Zerbinetta)

"Ach so versuchet doch ein kleines Lied"

SONG

Harlekin

"Lieben, Hassen"

Ic

RECITATIVE

ARIADNE

"Es gibt ein Reich"

ARIA

"Du wirst mich befreien"

Part II [Commedia players]

IIa

QUARTET

Brighella, Scaramuccio, Harlekin, Truffaldin

"Die Dame gibt mit trübem Sinn"

SONG—DANCE

"Es gilt, ob Tanzen, ob Singen tauge"

QUINTET

\+ Zerbinetta

"Wie sie sich schwingen, Tanzen und singen"

IIb

RECITATIVE

ZERBINETTA

"Großmächtige Prinzessin"

ARIA

"Noch glaub' ich"

RONDO

"Als ein Gott kam Jeder gegangen"

IIc

RECITATIVE

Harlekin, Zerbinetta

"Hübsch gepredigt aber tauben Ohren"

FINALE

\+ Brighella, Scaramuccio, Truffaldin

"Eine Störrische zu trösten"

Part III [Bacchus and Ariadne]

IIIa

TRIO

NAIAD, DRYAD, ECHO

"Ein schönes Wunder"

STROPHE 1

BACCHUS

"Circe, Circe"

ARIADNE

"Es greift durch alle Schmerzen"

1. TRIO

"Töne, töne süße Stimme"

STROPHE 2

BACCHUS

"Doch da ich unverwandelt"

ARIADNE

"O Todesbote"

2. TRIO

"Töne, töne süße Stimme"

STROPHE 3

BACCHUS

"Circe, Circe"

ARIADNE

"Belade nicht zu üppig"

CLIMAX

ARIADNE
BACCHUS

Encounter

IIIb

ARIADNE

"Ich grüße dich"

BACCHUS

"Du schönes Wesen"

ARIADNE

"Ich weiß nicht, was du redest"

BACCHUS	**ARIADNE**
"Wie? kennst du mich denn?"	"Gibt es kein Hinüber?"
ARIADNE + BACCHUS	**BACCHUS**
A "Nein, nein" B "Wer bin ich denn?"	"Du! alles du"
IIIc	**3. TRIO**
BACCHUS	"Töne, töne süße Stimme"
"Bin ich ein Gott"	**ARIADNE**
ARIADNE	"Laß meine Schmerzen"
"Das waren Zauberworte"	**ZERBINETTA**
BACCHUS	**DUET:** **ARIADNE + BACCHUS**
"Ich sage dir"	A. "Laß meine Schmerzen" B. "Deiner hab ich um alles bedurft"
BACCHUS + ARIADNE	
A. "Lag nicht die Welt auf meiner Brust?"	

Transformation

165

The Overture

The music of the overture proper, leading to the curtain raising, has three brief parts. The musical matrix of these sections consists of eight major melodies or melodic groups, all of which are interrelated by a simple rhythmic motive (♪. ♪ ♩). The opening theme in g minor (see ex. 1) serves to create a bleak musical atmosphere of brooding sadness for the entire first part; the melancholy of the melody and its accompaniment results in part from the numerous harmonic and melodic dissonances: the first eight measures incorporate dissonances such as augmented seconds and fourths, and sevenths, in disregard for conventional concepts of good melodic structure.

In a continuing mood of melancholia, the second thematic idea further exploits the "painful" dissonances, which now emphasize the rhythm ♪. ♪ ♩ . Strauss adds an archaic—or perhaps he thought non-Western—sound by accompanying the melody in parallel fourths (see ex. 2). This section ends with an especially striking cadence that proceeds melodically from A♭ to F#, an interval of a diminished third helping also to add a remote color to the music; a particularly expressive cross-relation occurs between the A♭ and the A♮ in the penultimate chord. The succeeding material, the final portion of this initial section, concludes with a suitably sad chromatic melody (see ex. 3), to occur later in the opera with a textual reference to Ariadne's crying. Although brief, the music exquisitely casts a mood of strangeness and poignancy and that remoteness from everyday reality demanded by Hofmannsthal's text.

The subtlety and refinement of this music can best be judged from its orchestration. The radical departure from a whole tradition of German practice stands out from the opening page of the overture. Strauss effects the intimacy of the sound by imposing austere limitations upon himself. Of the thirty-seven performers at his disposal he uses only nine in the first seventeen measures (and the double bass has but a single note in the passage). The extreme disjunctiveness of the string sextet texture punctuates the chordal nature of the music (by subordinating the melodic line of each part) as well as lending richness to the strings despite their limited number. Coupled to the general sadness is a bleak unrealness that comes from the weightlessness of the orchestral sound. Most of the section has little bass support; it uses a single cello, which for the most part is maintained in a very high range. Even the few measures given to the bassoon are generally high, until the important sectional cadence. Thus, the desolate state of Ariadne's mind and her feeling of abandonment on an isolated island are captured musically by this combination of compositional forces.

Just as g minor expresses the tonal world of Ariadne's present tragic state, the tonality of E♭, in which the second section of the overture

Ex. 1

Ex. 2

Ex. 3

opens, symbolizes Ariadne's previous world of love and happiness with Theseus. Strauss lifted this entire middle section almost note for note from that portion of Ariadne's first aria beginning *Ein Schönes war*. In this music Ariadne relives her love for Theseus, and as example 4 indicates, Strauss provides a double melody combining an Ariadne motive (see ex. 4b) and a Theseus motive (see ex. 4a). The section concludes (see ex. 5) with music taken from a further portion of the same aria: example 5a is music from the words [*und ging im*] *Licht und freute sich des Lebens;* example 5b is a different melodic idea used with the former text, and example 5c the melody to *Ein Schönes war*. The entire passage concludes with an exact repetition of the cadence that closed example 2a, bringing the overture back to the original g minor tonality. However, unless the audience has already heard the opera, these interrelationships of themes cannot be appreciated. Nevertheless, the occurrence of such important melodic material in the overture serves to condition the listener to react more actively when the same music is heard later in the opera. This kind of musical underscoring, of course, has been a favorite device of composers from almost the beginning of operatic history.

The orchestral sound changes from the previous somberness and remoteness to a sensuous glow expressive of the love of Ariadne for Theseus: Ariadne's melody in a sudden outburst from a clarinet and Theseus's theme, first by the incandescent sound of a French horn, and then with even greater expressiveness by a solo cello. Strauss adds to the orchestra, leading the music to a climax (see ex. 5b), with a relatively full, unmistakably passionate sound of the strings, harmonium, woodwinds, and French horn.

Ex. 4

The mood is broken violently, as it will be in the first scene in the opera from which the preceding music was borrowed, with the thematic material of Ariadne's aria, *Ich will vergessen* (see ex. 6a-6b). The latter half of the thematic material is based on both the rhythm and parallel fourths of example two. The section continues briefly in a furious four bar development of the mótives through a series of chromatic progressions, until the g minor of the overture's opening again returns. At this moment the powerful dotted rhythm associated with Ariadne—one is tempted to say, with Ariadne's deranged mind—dissipates and eventually vanishes, preparing us musically for the appearance of the three nymphs. This section as well as the overture

169

Ex. 6

6a

6b

proper concludes with the same harmonic cross-relation occurring at the end of section one (emphasizing the closed form of the overture). The music, however, continues without pause, as a long, wavy melodic line arises out of the g minor chord until it halts abruptly in the sudden attack of woodwind chords with harmonium (see ex. 7) associated with Ariadne's outcry.

The curtain rises on this musical outcry, but the music continues with what is a concluding—not a beginning—section of mood music in preparation for Ariadne's first scene. The trio of nymphs sings simple yet superbly colorful music that flows along like the elements of wind and water. The questions of Naiad and Dryad as to whether Ariadne still sleeps are supported with orchestral references to the opening theme of the overture (see ex. 1). (In a sense this part of the introductory music functions as a very free recapitulation of the whole overture.) The answer of *Nein, sie weinet* [No, she weeps], brings back a further restatement of the overture material of example three. Another important melodic idea found in the orchestra (see ex. 8) underlines the words *Tag um Tag in starrer Trauer* [Day after day in benumbed mourning]. Finally, one hears to the words *Ewig neue bittre Klagen* [Eternally new, bitter laments] the sound of Ariadne's outcry, the same sound that opened this section.

Ex. 7

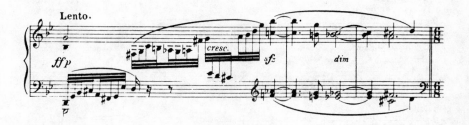

Ex. 8

The first half of the soprano trio concludes with *ewig unversöhnt* [eternally unreconciled] and the orchestra restates the entire opening theme of the overture, but with a surprise ending in G major. The gloomy pall of predominantly minor music is dispelled and the nymphs begin their magically beautiful lullaby: *Ach, wir sind es eingewöhnet. Wie der Wellen sanftes Gaukeln, wie der Blätter leichtes Schaukeln* [Alas, we are accustomed to it, like the waves' soft ripples, like the leaves' light motion] (see ex. 9). The lower strings of the orchestra imitate the rustling sounds of leaves referred to in the text. This trio melody returns twice in ever more elaborate vocal variations. In the

171

Ex. 9

first variation the motive of example 8 is repeated twice as Strauss reminds us of Ariadne's *starre Trauer* in the midst of the lovely sounds of nature. The next line of text, *Ihre Tränen, ihre Klagen* [her tears, her laments], is reflected in the music with the outcry of Ariadne. The vocal variation concludes with an orchestral reference to the opening of the overture to stress once again Ariadne's continuing despair.

The second variation of this trio begins with seventeen measures of vocal zephyrs, coloratura wanderings of the three spirit voices to the word *Ach*.[4] The variation and the entire introduction in its complete dimension as both instrumental and vocal description ends with a final statement of the beginning theme of the overture. This time the music leads directly to a new form of Ariadne's outcry, reduced to two powerfully effective chords, filled with harmonic confusion and entailing striking contrasts of orchestral color: the first scored for woodwinds and horns, the second only for the bleak emptiness of the harmonium.

---

[4] Exception needs to be taken to William Mann's statement that this trio is "reminiscent of Wagner's Rhinemaidens" (*Richard Strauss*, p. 160). The trio resembles Wagner's Rhinemaidens neither in melodic shape nor phrase patterns; nor is tonality or harmony similar.

Scene I: Ariadne's Monologue

The first third of the opera proper belongs to Ariadne, forsaken by Theseus, abandoned on the island of Naxos, awaiting salvation in death. Strauss initially conceived this scene as a recitative and aria; Hofmannsthal's text, however, provided the composer with sufficient material to expand the plan into two arias, each prefaced by recitative-like passages. The contrasting world of Zerbinetta and Harlekin intrudes musically in two structurally significant places: first, following Ariadne's opening recitative and preceding the opening aria; second, following this aria and preceding the next major recitative-aria complex. In other words, the appearances of the comic figures divide the structure of the whole scene into three parts. Also, the musical contrast of these intrusions serves the purpose of emphasizing the despair and futility of Ariadne's existence. Musically, as well as poetically, the two worlds collide head on, but Ariadne buried in her grief remains unresponsive and unaffected.

The essential key plan (see Table II below) shows a steady progression from an initially unclear—"confused"—tonality, to Eb major, and gradually in an upward direction to the climactic key of Bb major. The effect of these key changes fulfills the dramatic rise in Ariadne's emotions from despondency, to joy in love remembered, and finally the ecstasy found in anticipating her release in death.

TABLE II

Scene I (Ariadne and Naiad, Dryad, Echo; Zerbinetta-Harlekin and Friends)

	Primary Tonalities
Section I (Ariadne):	
Recitative:	
a. *(Ach, Wo war ich?)*	?-E^b
b. (*Was hab' ich denn geträumt?*)	c#
c. (*Ach*) Echo (*Ach*)	(E^b)
Harlekin-Zerbinetta-Truffaldin	(d)
Section II (Ariadne):	
Aria:	
a. (*Ein Schönes war*)	E^b
b. (*Ich will vergessen*) Trio (*Ariadne*)	g
c. (*Sie lebt hier ganz allein*)	G^b-E^b-g

Section III (Ariadne):

    Recitative (*Es gibt ein Reich*) G^b
    Aria:
      a. (*Bald aber naht ein Bote*) B^b-g
      b. (*Du wirst mich befreien*) B^b

Ariadne's *Ach* (see ex. 10), set to the unsettled interval of a
diminished fifth, is sustained by the striking juxtaposition of harmonies;
the first chord (D^b, F^b, A^b, B^b) has no functional connection with the
preceding harmonies. Further harmonic uncertainty involves the suc-

Ex. 10

ceeding chord and its lack of harmonic relationship with the antecedent
chord on D^b. Note Strauss's dramatic use of a cross-relationship:

The harmonic contrast of these two chords, strengthened by the difference in orchestral color for each, fits the moment of the action. The music, by its obscure tonal wanderings, vascillating between the key areas of E♭ and E, stresses Ariadne's distress and mental confusion: *Wo war ich? Tot? Und lebe wieder und lebe noch?* [Where was I? Dead? And live again and live still?]. The diminished fifth of the actual outcry returns emphatically in the violas. Following *und lebe noch?* the violins and lower strings refer to example 4b. This melodic motive, already heard in the overture, is discovered later to be connected with Ariadne's love for Theseus.

The voice part is recitative-like in character, almost spoken, with a continual repetition of a few pitches placed in the lower register of the soprano range. The deep tones of the soprano accentuate the illusion of darkness that veils the whole passage (at one point Ariadne descends to a low G, the very bottom extreme of the soprano range). To the words *zerstückelt Herz* [broken heart] Strauss takes pleasure in a bit of musical tone painting as the orchestra gives a syncopated, broken pattern of heart beating. Suddenly the vagueness of tonality vanishes, as a c# minor triad introduces two new melodic motives and the orchestra comes alive. The harps play for the first time and the instrumental background sounds less weighty for a moment as Ariadne suddenly remembers a dream: *Was hab' ich denn geträumt?* [What was it then I dreamed?]. The orchestra fills in details of the dream, although the point must be lost on those who have not heard the work previously, for the rapidly rising perfect fourths are associated with the music of Theseus (see ex. 11a), which appears only in the last part of the opera. The dream and its music vanishes (to another dream motive, a falling line with the characteristic dotted rhythm found throughout the overture and painful, diminished fifth intervals—example 11b). A sudden silence and then nothing but the unaccompanied notes of example 11b fading into the bottom of the orchestra as Ariadne's dream evaporates. She returns to the same musical *Ach* that opened her recitative, which is softly repeated by the soulless voice of Echo. The two desolate chords accompanying the echo have hardly sounded when we are startled with the appearance of Harlekin and Zerbinetta coming from behind the curtains.

Harlekin sings *Wie jung und schön und maßlos traurig* [How young and beautiful and how great her sorrow] to the same diminished fifth of Ariadne's outcry but supported by a totally new rhythm associated with this new character (see ex. 12). The color of the orchestra is altered momentarily to hint at the light-hearted music of Harlekin, Zerbinetta, and the rest of their group, a change brought about by the first use of the piano, the catchy rhythm of Harlekin in the bassoon, and the high, clear flute melody frequently associated with Zerbinetta. The orchestra quietly laughs with Zerbinetta, Harlekin, and Truffaldin when they say *und schwer, sehr schwer zu trösten* [and hard, most hard to comfort].

Ex. 12

Just as quickly the orchestra fabric changes again as the accompaniment shimmers with the magnificently warm sounds of the French horn as it states the entire Theseus theme. This instrumental prelude introduces Ariadne's aria, beginning with a long, expressive melisma on *Schönes*. Hofmannsthal's original text for the aria reads: *Ein Schönes war: hieß Theseus-Ariadne und ging im Licht und freute sich des Lebens* [There was something beautiful called Theseus-Ariadne, who walked in light and rejoiced in life]. Strauss, however, found these words totally inadequate for the emotionally expansive, lyrical plateau he wished to establish at this place in the opera. Therefore, he extended the text by word repetition to add twenty-eight additional measures. This is the first of several cases in *Ariadne* in which Strauss required greater poetic expansion of an idea to fit his urge for a musically climactic section. These passages in the libretto were without question great disappointments for Strauss and were clearly the basis for the composer's prodding of his librettist to "spur your Pegasus a bit, so that the ring of the verses should stimulate me a little" (*C.*, 85).

176

A portion of this aria occurs in the E^b major section of the overture (see ex. 5a, b, c) although the melodic ideas are reordered and expanded in the aria. The following section, *Warum weiß ich davon, ich will vergessen* [Why do I remember that, I want to forget], similarly is the musical substance of the concluding g minor portion of the overture (see ex. 6a). When Ariadne says: *Den Namen nicht—der Name ist verwachsen mit einem anderen Namen* [Not the name—the name has grown intertwined with another name], the orchestra softly reminds us of the Theseus theme. With *Ein Ding wächst so leicht ins andere* [One thing grows so easily into another], the chord of Ariadne's outcry (see ex. 10) is succeeded by the nymphs' cry of *Ariadne,* to remind her of her own name. Subtly this time the strident chord of pain melts away into Ariadne's own motive of love (as she says *nicht noch einmal* [not again]), and Strauss achieves an effective tonal shift into G♭ major and a new section of the aria.

With an orchestral color based on the highest ranges of the violins and viola, a crystaline, weightless texture paints Ariadne's reminiscences of her youth (see ex. 13)—*Sie lebt hier ganz allein* [She lives here all alone]. With a return to the E^b tonal center apparently associated

Ex. 13

in Strauss's mind with Ariadne's past, a clarinet weaves a peaceful sound around Ariadne's own lullaby to *ihr Schlaf ist rein, ihr Sinn ist klar* [her sleep is serene, her mind is clear] (see ex. 14). At the conclusion of the section *da darf sie sich in ihren Mantel wickeln, darf ihr Gesicht mit einem Tuch bedecken und darf da drinnen liegen und eine Tote sein* [Then she may wrap her cloak about her, may cover her face with a shroud, and may lie in the cave and be dead], Strauss cuts off the sounds of her childlike reminiscences by plunging tonally from G♭ major to the somber color of g minor on the words *eine Tote sein,* and by restating example 13 in the minor mode.

A second, very brief intrusion by Zerbinetta and her friends *(Ich fürchte, großer Schmerz hat ihren Sinn verwirrt—Ganz sicher sie ist toll* [I fear great pain has confused her mind—surely she is mad]), permits Ariadne to pick up the word *toll* and to add *aber weise: Ich weiß was gut ist, wenn man es fern hält von dem armen Herzen* [but wise: I know what is good, when one holds it distant from his poor heart]. Zer-

Ex. 14

binetta urges Harlekin to attempt a little song to cheer Ariadne, and he breaks Ariadne's monologue in half with the totally contrasted song *Lieben, Hassen, Hoffen, Zagen, alle Lust und alle Qual* [Love, hate, hope, fear, all pleasure and all pain]. Harlekin's song is a tuneful, catchy ditty, accompanied by piano, clarinet, bassoon, and an occasional passage for French horns, all supported by guitar-like imitation of pizzicato strings. To connect this song with the main dramatic action of the scene, Echo, in a musically beautiful touch, repeats the final phrase of Harlekin's song. Half way through the song Echo substitutes an A♮ for the use of a minor A♭ by Harlekin on the word *Qual,* and at the end of the song, Echo repeats the phrase, singing first an A♭ and then quickly changing to an A♮. Finally, as a postlude, Echo repeats the melody another time, in a slightly varied form, but this time ending on the minor A♭, as if even the soulless Echo has been moved to sadness by the song. Only Ariadne remains untouched. Harlekin finishes his song and, after a few comments by his friends and a brief reference to another motive to be developed later with Zerbinetta's music (see ex. 15), Ariadne resumes her monologue as if nothing had been sung by Harlekin.

Ex. 15

The second part of the great monologue begins in a quasi-recitative passage in G♭ with a description of Death. The motive of death (see ex. 16) is a simple outlining of a triad. Strauss enjoys the musical description of the word *Totenreich* [realm of death] by forcing Ariadne to sing a low A♭. The word is darkened further by the blackest sounds of an orchestra: harmonium, bassoon, horns, and the first use of the tenor trombone (with a pedal tone).

Ex. 16

As Ariadne sings in joyful anticipation of the arrival of Death's messenger, Hermes, the orchestra adds a new dimension to the death motive, now played twice as fast and transformed melodically to become Hermes' music. The orchestra quivers excitedly with tremolos in the strings and with the sound of harps (see ex. 17).

Strauss hints at the approaching climax of the aria by references to the final melody of the scene, which will form the joyful outpourings of Ariadne's ecstatic greeting to death (see ex. 18). The recitative-like section develops both the death and Hermes ideas until we reach the aria, *Du wirst mich befreien* [You will free me], with one of Strauss's great vocal passages, a long, wordless, impassioned melody on the word *befreien*. Also in this section Strauss repeats several lines of text in order to expand the poetic material. For the first time in the opera more instruments are added to the orchestra, until on the climactic *mir* of the line *du nimmst es von mir* [You will take it from me], set to the highest

Ex. 17

Ex. 18

note, Bb, of the entire scene, the full orchestra (excepting piano and various percussion instruments) surges forth with the resplendent tonal climax of this impressive scene. A postlude closes the aria to the words *An dich werd' ich mich ganz verlieren, bei dir wird Ariadne sein* [To you I will lose myself completely, with you will Ariadne be]. To a repetition of *bei dir . . .* Strauss completes the scene with a memorable cadence, a distinctive musical punctuation of indelible musical magic, leaving the listener transported into the firmly established new key of Bb major (see ex. 19).

Ex. 19

Scene II: Zerbinetta and Her Companions

The second section of Hofmannsthal's libretto opposes "the merely human group consisting of the frivolous Zerbinetta and her companions, all of them base figures in life's masquerade" (*C.,* 94), to the preceding scene of Ariadne's dark, unwordly atmosphere of resignation and death. As discussed earlier, Hofmannsthal's favorite technique was to build on contrasts to reveal the higher unity of life. Consciously intended on his part, this world of pleasure and light-heartedness, a non-comprehending world of stock figures from the *commedia dell'arte,* belongs to the baroque operatic tradition. In the late seventeenth and early eighteenth century it was not uncommon to find a two-act comic intermezzo interspersed between the three acts of an *opera seria.* However, the baroque enjoyment of comic relief (with plots unrelated to the surrounding work) interjected into operatic tragedy was transformed by Hofmannsthal to serve his own poetic-symbolic purpose. Although not widely appreciated by critics of his day, the poet's idea of mixing together within a single opera the mythological-tragic and the *maschere*-comic and pseudo-improvisational was a felicitous invention of striking originality.

Strauss possessed a natural genius for the comic in music. Few composers in the nineteenth and twentieth centuries have written as many genuinely funny moments in music to match *Till Eulenspiegel,* sections of *Don Quixote,* large portions of *Der Rosenkavalier,* as well as parts of the operas *Intermezzo* and *Die schweigsame Frau.* The comedy of *Ariadne* in the second scene of the opera is as fresh and vital today as when it was first heard in 1912.

The whole scene develops as a series of vocal and dance ensembles (see Table III, p. 182) that surround the central delight of the entire opera, the spectacularly difficult recitative, aria, and rondo for Zerbinetta, a *pièce de résistance* in Strauss's word (*C.,* 94), intended to portray the frivolity and shallowness of her character.[5] We are abruptly introduced to the scene: Ariadne has hardly completed her ecstatic paean to Death when the score plunges from Bb major into an f minor triad and the quartet of voices (Brighella, Scaramuccio, Harlekin, and Truffaldin) begin *Die Dame gibt mit trübem Sinn* [The lady gives herself with troubled mind] (see ex. 20).

---

[5] Strauss originally intended the role for Frieda Hempel, who possessed a uniquely high coloratura range.

Ex. 20

TABLE III

Scene II (Zerbinetta and Her Friends)

	Primary Tonalities
Section I:	
a. Men's Quartet (*Die Dame gibt mit trübem Sinn*)	f
b. Song-Dance for Quartet (*Es gilt, ob Tanzen*)	F
c. Quintet (Zerbinetta plus men) (*Wie sie sich schwingen*)	F
Section II (Zerbinetta)	
a. Recitative (*Großmächtige Prinzessin*)	F
b. Aria:	
1. (*Noch glaub' ich dem einen*)	D^b
2. (*So war es mit Pagliazzo*)	D
c. Rondo (*Als ein Gott kam jeder gegangen*)	D
Section III	
a. Recitative (Harlekin and Zerbinetta)	E
b. Quintet-Dance Finale	E-D

Although Ariadne remains on stage, she is unmoved by anything the four comedians say or do. The vocal quartet is simply constructed with a regular rhythmic dance beat of eighth notes in 2/4 meter. The melodic material of the opening quartet as well as of Zerbinetta's aria and rondo and the concluding dance quintet recall the café music of early twentieth-century Vienna. The tunefulness borders on, though never quite

182

descends to, the vulgar, and there is an overall *Schwung* to the dances. This new tonal world contrasts with the more formal, intricate, and heroic vocal style of Ariadne's music. It emphasizes both in musical style and musical humor the anachronism of the comic figures within an *opera seria*. In addition, the orchestra surrounds each world in a colorfully contrasted web of sound. The harps, percussion, trumpet, trombone, and harmonium that were significant elements in Ariadne's scene do not appear (with the exception of a very brief passage for trumpet) in scene II. In their place the overtly vulgar-sounding piano—an element of Viennese cabaret music—becomes the main support of the voices and orchestra. With a single instrument, the piano, Strauss tips the balance of the orchestra into a new world, the crass, mundane world on the lowest level of triviality.

Quickly following Brighella's comment: *Wir wissen zu achten der Liebe Leiden, doch trübes Schmachten, das wollen wir meiden* [We know how to heed the pains of love, but gloomy pining we would shun] (see ex. 21), the quartet strikes up a vigorously catchy dance tune, a melody of real Straussian flavor, to the words: *Es gilt, ob Tanzen, ob*

Ex. 21

Singen tauge, von Tränen zu trocknen ein schönes Auge [We want to test whether dancing and singing can serve to dry tears from a lovely eye] (see ex. 22). The dance, which continues for 161 measures, is joined almost immediately with Zerbinetta's chromatically uncertain melody to: *Wie sie sich schwingen, tanzen und singen, gefiele der eine oder der andre, gefiele mir schon* [the way they swing, dance, and sing, the one or the other would certainly please me] (see ex. 23). Following a brief dance tune, *Es gilt ob Tanzen. . . . .* Zerbinetta's part begins to soar above the men's quartet in an ever-expanding vocal display of her upper range, including the lovely turn of phrase on the word *singen*.

The dance grows progressively more complex as each of the parts proceeds with more and more musical independence, creating a fine example of Strauss's love of contrapuntal variety. With fragments of the theme of *Es gilt ob Tanzen . . .* tossed about from one dancing figure to another, the music closes with Zerbinetta's gentle admonition: *Drum laßt das Singen, zieht euch zurück!* [So cease your singing and withdraw!]. The four men dance off into the wings, while Zerbinetta is left face to face with her regal counterpart, Ariadne.

The moment has arrived for which all those familiar with the opera wait with anticipation. The great scene for Zerbinetta, one of the most

Ex. 22

Ex. 23

challenging vocal parts ever created for coloratura soprano, demonstrates Strauss's virtuoso style at its most extraordinary. In her music Zerbinetta projects a personality that is flashily brilliant, witty, yet surprisingly compassionate. Strauss shows, by the central placement of this scene (making it the musical axis of the whole opera) and his memorable music, that in his mind Zerbinetta was or should have been the star of the opera. He had suggested as much to Hofmannsthal at one point. Without doubt this character aroused Strauss to an intensity and spontaneity of musical ideas that he found nowhere else in the libretto. Essentially a man of the world, who did not identify with Hofmannsthal's spiritual realm of ideas and gods, Strauss understood the very real character of this woman of the world, a Viennese soubrette, perhaps, just as he had understood the Marschallin, Elektra, and

Salome. There was no need for him to interpret Zerbinetta in an aura of obscure symbolism, and consequently his musical inspiration flowed unimpeded.

Hofmannsthal, however, was shocked to learn of the composer's immediate decision to emphasize Zerbinetta in a way fully beyond the poet's intentions: "That you intend to place Zerbinetta so distinctively in the musical limelight surprised me at first . . ." (*C.*, 83). Four years later when they were collaborating on *Frau ohne Schatten,* Hofmannsthal again referred to his disappointment that Strauss had altered his original dramatic intentions in *Ariadne:* "For we would run risks if we were to be at cross purposes anywhere in this work [*Frau ohne Schatten*] as happened for instance, as you know, more than once over *Ariadne,* where what I had meant to be subordinate and even unimportant was often emphasized and drawn out by the music, so that the final product as a whole has about it something of a convex mirror" (*C.*, 214).

The allusion here is undoubtedly to the role of Zerbinetta. Strauss knew as soon as he saw Hofmannsthal's sketch that Zerbinetta would be well-suited to a virtuoso operatic scene. The composer suggested in May 1911 that Hofmannsthal should try to learn something about the poetic form of well-known coloratura arias, perhaps by having Selma Kurz (of the Vienna Opera) sing to him the best known ones from Bellini's *La Sonnambula,* Donizetti's *Lucia,* Hérold's *Zweikampf (Le Pré aux clercs),* Verdi's *Rigoletto* or some of Mozart's rondos (*C.*, 82). The poet worried excessively about writing suitable words for the Zerbinetta scene, even though Strauss attempted to assure him that nothing special would be required by him as text. In other words, the musical side of the problem was in a sense not closely dependent on the words.

Just as the musical form of the opera as a whole is tripartite, as is Ariadne's monologue, so too is Zerbinetta's scene which is also essentially a monologue. Although Ariadne remains on stage, she deliberately pays no attention to Zerbinetta's words and at the end of the recitative (significantly to Zerbinetta's outburst of *die Männer zu verfluchen. Treulos—sie sinds!* [all men to curse. Faithless they are!]) Ariadne suddenly disappears into the cave where she remains for the rest of scene II.

Zerbinetta's music is divided into recitative, aria (in two parts), and rondo (with variation). The recitative begins with a simple chordal accompaniment by piano (in imitation of eighteenth-century keyboard accompaniments to recitatives), but quickly the keyboard becomes part of an orchestral ensemble. This ensemble is exceedingly delicate in its expressive power, consisting of single woodwinds (flute, clarinet, bassoon), one horn, and a solo string ensemble.

The opening words *Großmächtige Prinzessin* [Most gracious princess] (see ex. 24) are followed by a phrase of Hofmannsthal's memorable text, which Strauss carefully sets to music so as to reinforce the meaning. He colors the *unbegreiflich Herz* [incomprehensible heart] (see ex. 25a) with a sudden, "incomprehensible" harmonic surprise by shifting from F major to E major. This passage is followed by an important motive (see ex. 25b) with a jaunty rhythm ♩♪♫ ♩♪♫ cleverly representing Zerbinetta's curtsy to Ariadne. Another motive (see ex. 25c) follows immediately Zerbinetta's *von unsrer Schwachheit sprechen* [to speak of our weakness], and seems to refer back to this line, i.e., "woman's weakness," in several other places in the recitative. The mood is changed again for Zerbinetta's description of Ariadne, *schön und stolz und regungslos, als wären Sie die Statue auf Ihrer eignen Gruft* [fair and proud and motionless, as if you were a statue on your own grave]. A shift to the "noble" tonality of E♭ major (originally associated with Ariadne's first aria), and a solemn rather pompous set of chords in the piano and lower strings, adds these feelings to the meaning of the words. Then, to Zerbinetta's words, *Sie wollen keine andere Vertraute als diesen Fels und diese Wellen haben?* [You would have no other confidant than these rocks and waves?], we are reminded by the sudden appearance of Hermes' melody (see ex. 17) of the earlier monologue of Ariadne and her greeting Hermes, whom she envisioned in her mind as the messenger of Death. In a new section of the recitative, Zerbinetta's speech becomes agitated, breathless, as the words *Verlassen, in Verzweiflung, ausgesetzt* [Abandoned, in despair, desolated], are interjected between brief chromatic sixteenth note passages in the piano and strings. And in a dramatic joining of the word and tone, for *Ach, solcher wüsten Inseln sind unzählige auch mitten unter Menschen, ich, ich, selber ich habe ihrer mehrere bewohnt* [Alas, such desert isles are countless even in the midst of people. I, I, myself, I have lived on a number of them], the words, *Ach unzählige* and *mehrere* are all struck incessantly on high A-flats to help drive home Zerbinetta's position in Hofmannsthal's parable of existence.

The rapid rhetorical outbursts continue for *Treulos sie sinds, ungeheure, ohne Grenzen* [Faithless they are, monstrous, without measure]. Suddenly, chromatically shifting piano arpeggios underscore the brevity and fleeting uncertainty of: *Eine kurze Nacht, ein hastiger Tag, ein Wehen Luft, ein fließender Blick verwandelt ihr Herz* [a brief night, a feverish day, the sigh of a breeze, a passing glance transforms their heart].

The recitative ends with a picturesque and seemingly ironical musical interpretation of the word *Verwandlungen?*, a long coloratura passage that incorporates the musical motive heard first to the expression of "woman's weakness" (see ex. 26). Zerbinetta's inability to comprehend transformation is amusingly stressed with the single staccato octave F of the piano—the musical equivalent of Zerbinetta's raised eyebrow.

Her two-part aria begins in D♭ major, with a broadly lyrical, tuneful melody. The style is Mozartian, distinctly divisible into component phrases, and it forms one of the memorable melodic inventions of the opera. It is the kind of melody, one feels, that occurred to Strauss quite independently of the individual words of the text. The independence of the melody from the text also stands out in Strauss's free adaptation of Hofmannsthal's libretto. Strauss sets the entire text to music:

(1) Noch glaub' ich dem einen ganz mich gehörend,
(2) Noch mein' ich mir selber so sicher zu sein,
(3) Da mischt sich im Herzen leise betörend
(4) Schon einer niegekosteten Freiheit
(5) Schon einer neuen verstohlenen Liebe
(6) Schweifendes freches Gefühle sich ein!
(7) Noch bin ich wahr und doch ist es gelogen,
(8) Ich halte mich treu und bin schon schlecht.
(9) Mit falschen Gewichten wird alles gewogen—
(10) Und halb mich wissend und halb im Taumel,
(11) Betrüg' ich ihn endlich und lieb' ihn noch recht!
(12) Ja, halb mich wissend und halb im Taumel,
(13) Betrüge ich endlich und liebe noch recht!

The music hints at the coloratura style that will be prominent in the second half of the aria, particularly the fanciful roulades that decorate words such as *gelogen* and *schlecht*. The climax of this portion of the aria occurs on the significant words *betrüg' ich ihn endlich* [finally I deceive him], which Strauss repeats for emphasis with a soaring melody

Ex. 25

Ex. 26

(to high B♭), a dramatic (and typically Straussian) return to the opening D♭ major tonality, and a fortissimo repetition of the initial melody (see ex. 27a, first four measures). The orchestra having in effect restated the opening line, *Noch glaub' ich dem einen ganz mich gehörend* [While still believing that I fully belong to the one], Zerbinetta continues the repetition of the melody with line two of the text. The aria closes,

Ex. 27

In *Ariadne* II, with line five (line four is omitted by Strauss in this freely conceived reprise-like section).

This aria is the first important example of major surgery in the composer's effort to reduce the overall length of the opera, when it was joined to the newly-composed *Vorspiel*. In this particular section of the opera Strauss saw the need to shorten the taxing length of the exceedingly difficult role he had written originally for the soprano part of Zerbinetta.[6] In *Ariadne* I Strauss repeated all of the remaining text and also developed the aria to a rather more brilliant conclusion with a high C# on the final *liebe noch recht* [loving him still]. Further change involved the concluding tonality that prepares for the second part of the aria. In *Ariadne* I the music concludes in E major, the tonality for the remainder of the scene II in the original version. In *Ariadne* II, the music concludes one whole tone lower, in D major, a solution Strauss employed to eliminate the high F#'s of the original coloratura line, which now become high E's. While the latter notes are hardly a great

---

[6] The only revision Strauss made in the preceding scene, Ariadne's monologue, was to cut out the spoken interjections of Jourdain and his guests, who, in the original version, sat on the stage and watched the performance of the opera. Other major revisions in *Ariadne* II include incisions in Zerbinetta's rondo, the arrival of Bacchus in scene III, and the conclusion of the opera, all to be discussed later.

simplification of the singer's vocal hurdles, there are more sopranos capable of reaching an adequately produced high E than a high F#.

Part II of the aria, *So war es mit Pagliazzo* [Thus it was with Pagliazzo], gives Strauss an opportunity to portray the frivolity as well as a certain perplexed uncertainty and wistfulness in Zerbinetta's character. The gayness and carefree spirit are fully realized in the coloratura roulades. The vocal motive on *mit Pagliazzo* (see ex. 28) is particularly important to the aria's structure and also to a later section of scene II. Here again Strauss's musical plans require textual adaptation. The last line, (which follows *Daß ein Herz so gar sich selber nicht versteht* [That a heart understands itself so little]), is repeated to a series of brilliant ascending scales, until the aria concludes with the purely musical virtuosity (unaccompanied) of a breathtaking cadenza (see ex. 29) that propels us directly into the concluding part of Zerbinetta's music, the rondo.

A rondo is simply defined as a musical form based in principle on the repetition of a musical section, A, the repetitions of which are separated by the insertion of new materials. The formal scheme of a rondo is normally represented by the scheme, A B A C A, etc. Strauss intended Zerbinetta's *tour de force* to conclude with a rondo with variations, or in other words a rondo in which the repetitions of the A section would not be literal, but musical variations of the original A. In *Ariadne* I, this rondo section consisted of a form that can be represented as:

var. 1   var. 2

A B A   C A   Coda (=A)

Ex. 28

190

Ex. 29

In *Ariadne* II, in his drastic and, at least to some musicians, regrettable reduction of this section of the opera, more than eighty measures are eliminated. The form is destroyed and now becomes:

                        var. 1
          A B A   Coda (=A)

The original rondo structure becomes a modified ternary form, which lessens somewhat the exaggerated emphasis on Zerbinetta's role in *Ariadne* I. Strauss's revised version came closer to Hofmannsthal's original dramatic plan, although the part in total duration is still longer than Hofmannsthal had intended and consequently out of balance with the main characters and action of the play.

The rondo theme is a jaunty tune (see ex. 30a), the concluding portion of which is given over to the orchestra (see ex. 30b). The whole idea is light-hearted and flavored with the sounds of Viennese coffee house ensembles. The subtlety and refinement of the rondo evolves from the ever-increasing complexity of the vocal line as Zerbinetta weaves a coloratura melody around the basic musical idea. The A section closes in D, and the contrasting B section that follows in a darker, more tranquil flat key of Bb (and marked *tranquillo* by the composer), becomes a reflective and quiet, although repeating exactly the text of the opening rondo: *Als ein Gott kam jeder gegangen, jeder wandelte mich um, küßte er mir Stirn und Wangen, war ich von dem Gott gefangen, hingegeben war ich stumm* [Like a god came each one to me, and transformed me thoroughly; when he kissed my forehead and cheek, I was captivated by the god, I was his in mute surrender]. A solo cello

Ex. 30

tenderly supports Zerbinetta's reflective *jeder wandelte mich um*. The
strings pause in quiet sustained chords as solo woodwinds softly imitate
Zerbinetta's vocally elaborate line. There is an overall pause in the
humor of the rondo, the frivolity seems to evaporate, the satire melts
away. Strauss, in a revealing moment, exposes a tender and reflective
side of Zerbinetta's personality. She becomes a more truly human and
comprehending character than Hofmannsthal ever wished her to be. On
the basis of this music one feels instinctively that Zerbinetta at least
momentarily both longs for and is capable of that quality of faithfulness,
which is Ariadne's distinguishing and enobling feature.

The B section concluded, Strauss continues (in *Ariadne* II) with a
variation on the opening *Rondo* theme in which vocal virtuosity is
paramount. The complexity of the voice part develops through to the
conclusion of the section with a cadenza in the rarified heights of the
soprano range (see ex. 31).

The last high D, however, does not conclude the *Rondo,* but rather this stunning display of vocal gymnastics is followed by a brief reprise of the opening rondo theme and the hesitant, questioning, almost puzzled statement of Zerbinetta: *Kam der neue Gott gegangen------hingegeben------war------ich------stumm-----stumm.*

The third part of scene II begins with considerable impact as Harlekin jumps out from behind the curtains, immediately following Zerbinetta's final *stumm,* with *Hübsch gepredigt aber tauben Ohren!* [Pretty sermon, but on deaf ears!]. The spell is broken and Zerbinetta is thrust back into her own world. The ensuing discussion between the two characters in recitative-like vocal style is supported largely by Zerbinetta's motive first sung to *So war es mit Pagliazzo* (see ex. 28). As Zerbinetta repulses Harlekin's advances, a new motive occurs in the orchestra (see ex. 32) supporting her lines: *Zu denken, daß es Frauen gibt, denen er eben darum gefiele* [To think that there are women who find him pleasing for this very reason] and also Harlekin's reply: *Und zu denken, daß du von oben bis unten eine solche Frau bist!* [And to think that you, from head to toe, are such a woman]. The other *commedia* players, Brighella, Scaramuccio, and Truffaldin stick their heads out from behind the curtains to attract Zerbinetta's attention, and she concludes the preparatory recitative section of this third part with a long cadenza passage, an amusing musical picture of the word *verschieden* [different] in the line, *Männer . . . warum hast du sie so verschieden geschaffen?* [Men . . . why have you created them in so many forms?] (see ex. 33).

Ex. 32

Ex. 33

The conclusion, a large, complex dance scene, evolves around the central symbol of Zerbinetta's attraction for the various members of the comedy troupe and her flirtations with all of them. The musical style is closer to that of Viennese popular music than any other part of scene II. Strauss makes use of rather obvious dance rhythms, particularly the waltz, and simple, catchy tunes to drive home to the audience the extraordinary commonness—or vulgarity—of the stage drama. Beginning with the rhythmically spirited idea of ex. 34a, the men's quartet enters with *Eine Störrische zu trösten, laßt das peinliche Geschäft!* [To comfort a stubborn woman is hopeless, give up that painful business!] to ex. 34b. Zerbinetta, back in true character, begins flirting, dancing from one man to another with a Viennese lilting tune in the orchestra (see ex. 35a), as the men pick up the motive of ex. 35b for words such as *Doch ich bin störrisch nicht, gibst du ein gut Gesicht* [But I am not stubborn, if you look kindly upon me]. When Harlekin observes: *Wie sie vergeudet Augen und Hände, laur' ich im Stillen hier auf das Ende* [While she wastes eyes and hands, I lurk here quietly for the outcome], the orchestra comments with a new, very expressive soaring melody (see ex. 36).

Ex. 34

Ex. 35

Ex. 36

The next part of the scene returns momentarily to ex. 34a. For the most part, however, the music is based on a splendid development of Zerbinetta's melody originally sung to *So war es mit Pagliazzo,* which is woven throughout the orchestra and Zerbinetta's vocal part as the three men (without Harlekin) pursue her. The third part of this scene opens with a climactic outburst of the dance motive (see ex. 34a) in E^b major as Zerbinetta loses a shoe. Scaramuccio picks it up and kisses it, considering it a symbol of encouragement to his designs on Zerbinetta. Truffaldin and Brighella also are encouraged to think that Zerbinetta has chosen each of them, and the orchestra chuckles to itself. The dance grows progressively more animated and crude, with a new waltz tune in the orchestra (see ex. 37). While the three men dance around the stage in eager anticipation, Zerbinetta and Harlekin slip off hand in hand. Thus, Harlekin's previous assessment of Zerbinetta proves correct after all, and despite the instant of heightened pathos, she now musically and dramatically embodies her role as Hofmannsthal conceived it. The three comedians find themselves alone, and in a confusion of interjections

196

humorously set to awkward, stumbling chords (see ex. 38), they repeat *mir die Hand, mir der Schuh, mir der Blick* [to me the hand, the shoe, the glance].

Ex. 38

The conclusion (somewhat shortened in length in *Ariadne* II) descends to overt buffoonery, as the three men dance around the stage bumping into one another, searching for Zerbinetta. The orchestra again laughs out loud and picks up a new melody from Zerbinetta, who sings from behind the scenes. Her voice soars expressively over the heads of the comedians with *Daß ein Herz so gar sich selber nicht versteht* (see ex. 39) and Harlekin, also unseen, replies *Ach wie reizend fein gegliedert!* [Ah, how delicious, delicately formed!]. The cries of

Ex. 39

ai, ai, ai and *Der Dieb, Der Dieb* [the thief] are the final despairing sentiments of the comedians when they discover that they have been duped by Zerbinetta and Harlekin. These words stand in comical, musical opposition to the love duet of Zerbinetta and Harlekin sung to ex. 39. The scene closes effectively with the trio dancing out in comic confusion and angry disappointment.

Scene III: Naiad, Dryad, Echo-Trio, Ariadne, Bacchus, Zerbinetta

The final scene of the opera is also cast into a general tripartite form: (1) the announcement of Bacchus's approach to Naxos by the trio of nymphs, (2) Bacchus's arrival, and (3) the confrontation of Bacchus and Ariadne and the denouement. The scene as a whole is considerably more complex than either of the preceding parts of the opera. The final section in particular has an intricate poetical-musical give and take between Ariadne and Bacchus as they progress from their meeting through transformation to the stirring musical apotheosis (see Table IV below).

Immediately following the exit of the comic figures, the orchestra quickens in tempo, violins engage in excited tremolos, harps replace the piano, and a trumpet calls out an important three-note motive (see ex. 40a), which was heard (as a fourth rather than a third) in scene I when Ariadne related her dream of Theseus (see ex. 11a). The nymphs reappear to herald the approach of the young god—Bacchus. Because they sing an excited, almost breathlessly quick music, much of what they say cannot be understood. Apparently Strauss did not feel that Hofmannsthal's exposition of Bacchus's lineage was especially important, and he substituted a mood of general excitement rather than textual details. The *vivace* tempo and the intertwining, relatively complex melodic texture does force one to listen with a new sense of urgency after the boisterousness and relaxed musical framework of the final portion of scene II. In addition, Strauss subtly employs a subliminal method of thematic statement by which he implants new melodic ideas in our mind, even though they pass by so rapidly that we are not aware of their importance at the moment.

Two major thematic ideas occur in the initial pages of scene III: Bacchus's melody (see ex. 40b) as well as a motive of chords in triplets associated with Bacchus's godliness (see ex. 41). The Bacchus melody in particular recurs in the orchestral texture throughout the opening trio, flashing by like a shadow of its true form. We do not feel the full impact of this splendid theme until the nymphs relate—in their flash-back story—that Bacchus has just escaped from the arms of Circe (*Aus den Armen ihr entwunden;* ex. 44).

The form of Bacchus's theme necessitates a digression. In examining Strauss's choice of thematic ideas for the three male figures surrounding Ariadne, Theseus, Hermes (Death's messenger) and Bacchus, one discovers (see musical illustration) that each of the melodies shares a strong resemblance with the others. In a musically symbolic sense each representative of the heroic world develops from the same melodic formula: The structure of the Theseus theme divides itself into three melodic segments: the falling interval of a fourth at the opening (a), the longer melodic section rising to G and falling back to E (b), and finally

Ex. 40

Ex. 41

TABLE IV

Scene III (Naiad, Dryad, Echo, Ariadne, Bacchus)

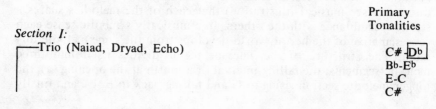

Section I:

Primary
Tonalities

┌─Trio (Naiad, Dryad, Echo)

C#-D♭
B♭-E♭
E-C
C#

200

Section II:
1. verse 1a. Bacchus (*Circe, Circe*) — c#-A
        1b. Ariadne (*Es greift durch alle Schmerzen*) — f#
└─────── 1c. Trio (*Töne, töne, süße Stimme*) — D♭
2. verse 2a. Bacchus (*Doch da ich unverwandelt*) — A-E
        2b. Ariadne (*Todesbote*) — bb-B♭
└─────── 2c. Trio (*Töne, töne, süße Stimme*) — B♭
3. verse 3a. Bacchus (*Circe, Circe*) — B♭-C#
        3b. Ariadne (*Belade nicht zu üppig*) — A-b
Transition   Bacchus's Arrival — C-F

Section III:
    1a. Ariadne (*Ich grüße dich*) — B♭
    1b. Bacchus (*Du schönes Wesen*) — B♭
    1c. Ariadne (*Ich weiß nicht, was du redest*) — g
    1d. Bacchus (*Wie kennst du mich denn?*) — g-b
    2.   *The Transformation*
        Ariadne (*Nein, nein*) — g
        Bacchus (*Wer bin ich denn?*) — b
        Ariadne (*Du bist der Herr*) — b
        Bacchus (*Ich bin der Herr*) — g
        Ariadne (*Nimm mich hinüber*) — ?
        Bacchus (*So willst du mit mir gehen auf mein Schiff*) — ?
        Ariadne (*Ich bin bereit*) — D♭-f
        Bacchus (*Sprach ich von einem Trank?*) — ?
        Ariadne (*Ich weiß, so ist es dort*) — A♭-D♭
        Bacchus (*Bin ich ein Gott*) — A D♭
        Ariadne (*Das waren Zauberworte*) — c#-E
        Bacchus (*Ich sage dir*) — b
        Ariadne (*Lag nicht die Welt auf meiner Brust?*) — E♭-F
        Ariadne (*Gibt es kein Hinüber*) — C-?
        Bacchus (*Du, alles du*) — A
    3a. Bacchus (*Höhle deiner Schmerzen*) — D♭
└─────── 3b. Ariadne + Trio (*Töne, Töne*) — D♭
    3c. Zerbinetta (*Kommt der neue Gott gegangen*) — D♭
    3d. Ariadne, Bacchus Duet — D♭
    3e. Bacchus (*Durch deine Schmerzen bin ich reich*) — D♭
    3f. Orchestral coda — D♭

the overall thrusting motion up to E and then back to D-C (c). The character of Theseus's theme is strong in its forward, upward force, yet paradoxically weak—or more lyrical—in the sense that it falls back to C, which drains away some of the power of the ascending motion.

In contrast the motive for Death literally consists of the first part of the Theseus theme, but with the third note D omitted. The motive is broken apart by the intervening rest. Hermes, as Death's messenger, takes his melody from the Death motive, but instead of continuing in an ascending direction as had been true of the original Theseus idea, this melody descends with strong symbolic implications of death to low E. Most intriguing of the four interrelated themes is the Bacchus melody. The notes of the originally falling fourth at the beginning of the Theseus subject (a) are reversed in order to become an ascending fourth. The b section of the Theseus melody remains intact, but the thrusting motion to high E has been lessened so that, in effect, the whole melody is stronger with its steady, unyielding ascent to D, where the theme remains, perhaps Strauss's musical expression of the strength of the young god versus the flaw in the character and ultimate weakness of the mortal Theseus. Strauss clearly considered Theseus, Hermes (Death), and Bacchus all aspects of one male archetype and his careful choice of melodic structure adds both musical and symbolic unity to the character of the male figures in Ariadne's world.

ILLUSTRATION I

Thematic Relationships Between Theseus—Hermes (Death)—Bacchus

Theseus (Ex. 4a)

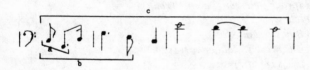

Death (Ex. 16).

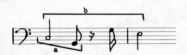

Hermes (Ex. 17).

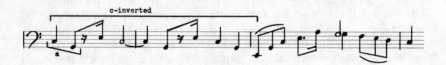

Bacchus (Ex. 40b).

Returning to the nymphs' narration, we learn that Bacchus was raised by nymphs (see ex. 42). They describe his encounter with Circe,

Ex. 42

whom Strauss surrounds with a passionate, chromatic melody (see ex. 43) given with full instrumental strength of the orchestra. For the

Ex. 43

description of Circe's magic potion, he uses another melodic fragment of a surging, strikingly dissonant character, rather close to a parody of the magic potion motive of Wagner's *Tristan und Isolde* (see. 44). We learn that the potion fails, that Bacchus does not become an animal as

Ex. 44

have other previous victims of Circe, and that he escapes. Now Strauss slows down the tempo and for the first time allows the theme of Bacchus to sing out richly in horns, violas, and cellos. The theme "matures," just as Bacchus has matured. The nymphs confirm this by emphasizing that he stands before Ariadne as a young god. Thus, through the music Strauss reenforces the text, showing Bacchus well advanced in his transformation from demi-god to god (see ex. 45).

Ex. 45

In the continuing excitement the nymphs call out to Ariadne (bringing back a fleeting recollection of their trio at the beginning of the opera). The latter emerges from the cave just as Bacchus arrives on a cliff at the edge of the sea (though he still is not visible to Ariadne). With Bacchus's cries of *Circe,* we enter the second section of scene III, formed by three verses of dialogue between Bacchus and Ariadne of which the first two are concluded with a quiet, hymn-like trio by the nymphs. In the first verse Bacchus calls out to Circe (see ex. 46), showing that his mind is still grappling with the implications of his narrow escape from her. Strauss employs the same falling interval of the fourth promi-

Ex. 46

nent at the beginning of the themes of Theseus and Hermes and, in reverse, the Theseus motive occurring in Ariadne's dream. Bacchus asks *was war dein Wille, an mir zu tun?* [what was your wish to do to me?]. These words are combined in the orchestra with references to Circe's magic potion, triplet figure of chords representing Bacchus's godliness, as well as the Circe theme. His song elicits Ariadne's introspective, dreamy response: *Es greift durch alle Schmerzen, auflösend alte Qual* [It strikes through all pain, dissolving old woe], supported musically by Circe's theme in the strings and then in the oboes. Suddenly the music shifts into low gear as the nymphs interrupt with mysterious, hymn-like music (see ex. 47) to:

Töne, töne, süße Stimme,	Sounds, sounds, sweet voice,
Fremder Vogel, singe wieder!	Strange bird, sing on!
Deine Klagen, sie beleben!	Your laments, they enliven!
Uns entzücken solche Lieder!	Such songs captivate us!

The atmosphere is unreal, the musical effect magical, and the tonality Db major, the most exalted key in the Straussian palette of tonal colors. The spirits of Nature prepare the setting for the impending love scene. The melody of this trio resembles in mood, though not in actual notes, the Octavian—Sophie duet in the final act of *Der Rosenkavalier.*

The utter simplicity of the idea is rooted in Strauss's inclination toward the music of Mozart and Schubert and other great melodists of the classic and early romantic periods.[7]

Ex. 47

[7] Either consciously or subconsciously Strauss took the opening measure of this trio melody from the Schubert song, *Wiegenlied (Schlafe, schlafe, holder, süßer Knabe);* see Otto Erich Deutsch, *Schubert Thematic Catalogue of All His Works* (New York, 1951), p. 221. See also *Franz Schuberts Werke*, Serie 20, III (Leipzig, 1895; repr. New York, 1965), p. 239.

Just as the exalted mood of the forces of Nature broke into the music of Bacchus and Ariadne, now Bacchus shatters the lovely mood created by the nymphs. Beginning his second verse with an intense outburst to *Doch da ich unverwandelt von dir gegangen bin* [But since I escaped from you untransformed] his high A in the bright key of A major is almost shocking, following directly upon the previous Db major. The orchestra continues to allude to the magic of Circe's potion, and again Bacchus asks the enchantress: *was du nicht durftest, geschieht es doch an mir?* [what you were unable to do, does it happen nevertheless to me?] Ariadne interrupts, again with no apparent relationship to Bacchus's question, in a gloomy Bb minor with the words *O Todesbote, süß ist deine Stimme* [O messenger of death, sweet is your voice]. The orchestra recalls the ecstasy of Ariadne's original greeting to Death in the first scene (see ex. 18), but the joy of that first welcoming has been reduced to sadness as the melody becomes minor this time. For the words *süß ist deine Stimme,* the strings of the orchestra, richly divided into several parts, present a totally transformed, expansive, and most expressive version of Circe's magic potion (see ex. 48), which melts into Ariadne's next words, *Balsam ins Blut* [balm to my blood], as if somehow Circe's magic had invaded Ariadne's soul.

Ex. 48

The nymphs repeat their hymn as before, except that the tonality has been raised to a brighter Bb major, emphasizing their mood of expectation. To accentuate this mood still further, the orchestration, which in the first statement consisted of all the darker string instruments (viola, cello, bass) plus the gloomy harmonium, becomes definitely brighter with the addition of two harps and the omission of all of the lower strings.

For the third verse Bacchus returns to his outcry of *Circe, Circe,* but in the key of B♭ major established by the Nymphs' hymn. As he asks Circe his question, for the third time, *Was war dein Wille an mir zu tun?* (with repeated strains of the magic potion theme), Ariadne cuts him off with rapturous, soaring response of *Belade nicht zu üppig mit nächtlichem Entzücken* [Do not burden too sumptuously with nocturnal charms], sung to the new version of Circe's magic potion, which we might now label Ariadne's *Balsam ins Blut.*

Ex. 49

208

Ariadne stands with open arms awaiting Death. The entire orchestra joins together for a shattering climax built upon the Bacchus melody in the bass, to which are added mysterious, tonally confusing, yet exciting chords in parallel fourths (see ex. 49). For the first time in the opera Strauss resorts to percussion instruments (timpani, tambourine, snare drum, glockenspiel) to aid this climax with appropriately exciting sounds. Bacchus suddenly stands before us, and Ariadne in fright screams *Theseus,* for she thinks momentarily that her former lover has indeed returned.

In *Ariadne* I, Strauss and Hofmannsthal had carefully led up to this climax by a very long transitional passage in which Zerbinetta returned to the stage and had an opportunity to describe with considerable emotion the approaching god. She also helped the nymphs dress Ariadne appropriately for her meeting with destiny, while Ariadne spoke fervently of her anticipated encounter with Death. Strauss's drastic cut in the score at this point eliminated 336 measures of unquestionably beautiful music, certainly the greatest single loss to the opera in the revision and a cut that is strongly felt in performance. (One would like to suggest that some enterprising conductor restore these impressive pages of music, for the elimination of this cut would clearly improve the continuity of the opera at this point).

Faced with Bacchus, Ariadne quickly collects herself and in music (see ex. 50) of peace and pastoral atmosphere, constructed from the Hermes motive (see ex. 17) joined to the second half of the magic potion motive, she greets him as Death, *du Bote aller Boten!* [messenger of all messengers!]. These words are sung to Ariadne's theme of ecstasy

Ex. 50

(see ex. 18) to which she sang originally, *Du wirst mich befreien* [You will free me]. Thus, through this musical interrelationship of scenes I and III, Strauss establishes the fact that Ariadne thinks that Death has responded to her earlier plea. Bacchus, to an accompaniment of the same magically shifting chords in fourths that carried him onto the scene (but now greatly subdued), asks if Ariadne is the *Göttin dieser Insel* [Goddess of this island], suggesting that his thoughts still dwell on his experience with Circe. The orchestra similarly recalls the episode by hinting softly at Circe's magic potion. Ariadne is utterly confused by Bacchus's words:

Ich weiß nicht, was du redest.	I know not, of what you speak.
Ist es, Herr, daß du mich prüfen willst?	Is it, Lord, that you wish to test me?
Mein Sinn ist wirr von vielem Liegen ohne Trost!	My mind is confused from lying prostrate for so long without comfort!
Ich lebe hier und harre deiner, deiner harre ich	I have been living here and awaiting thee, thee awaiting
Seit Nächten, Tagen, seit wie vielen ach, ich	For nights, days, for how many, alas, I
weiß es nicht mehr!	know no longer!

With touching musical expressiveness, Strauss composes the words, *Mein Sinn ist wirr von vielem Liegen,* to the same music first experienced at the outset of Ariadne's monologue in scene I (to *Wo war ich, tot? und lebe, lebe wieder?*). With a power of recall possible only through the medium of music, Ariadne recalls her thoughts at the opening of the opera. Strauss further connects this scene to the beginning by setting *Ich weiß es nicht mehr* to the first theme of the overture and by using the same tonality (g minor) found at the opening of the overture.

When the last notes of the theme to the overture conclude, Bacchus, surprised by Ariadne's apparent recognition of him, asks if she knows him. His own theme rises from the bottom of the orchestra, very quietly in the cellos and then the violas. As has occurred with the introduction of other thematic ideas in this portion of the opera, the effect here is felt more subliminally than consciously. When Bacchus asks *Wer bin ich denn?* [Who am I then?], the horn replies with the rising motive heard first in Ariadne's dream in scene I. Again the relationship of Theseus (of Ariadne's dream) and Bacchus is emphasized.

Ariadne, mistaking Bacchus for Hermes, replies that he is the *Herr über ein dunkles Schiff* [Master of a dark ship]. Her inner joy at the thought of death and release from her sufferings is reflected in the flutes and oboes as once more the theme of ecstasy is heard in minor. Although bewildered by her remarks as she is by his, Bacchus confirms that he has a ship and asks if she really wishes to leave with him. The theme of Ariadne's ecstasy, now in joyful major, returns, as Ariadne says

Ich bin bereit. Du fragst? Ist es, daß du mich prüfen willst? [I am prepared. You ask? Is it, that you wish to test me?].

The moment of transformation arrives for both Bacchus and Ariadne. Strauss creates ever greater musical confusion by writing succeeding passages in an indeterminate tonality and also by constantly placing the words of the two in opposing key centers. This lends the ensuing music a feeling of incessant shifts and breaks, like a fragmentation of the musical train of thought, which, as Strauss planned, emphasizes the total lack of communication between Ariadne and Bacchus, until the moment of transformation and apotheosis when the two are joined together in a soaring emotional climax in D♭ major. The goal of the music beginning at this point is to create the impression of confusion. Even the motive of the rising fourth is distinctly heard in clarinets, bassoon, and horn, turned upside down. When Ariadne asks if Bacchus will achieve her transformation (she means her death) by a drink, we are reminded, as is Bacchus, of Circe; for the motive of the magic potion returns in the viola, oboes, and muted trumpet.

Bacchus begins to forget his own past: *Sprach ich von einem Trank, ich weiß nicht mehr?* [Did I speak of a drink; I no longer remember?]. Strauss artfully depicts his forgetting of the past by allowing the magic potion melody to appear in the harmonium where, instead of repeating itself several times as in the past, the motive disintegrates by slowly collapsing and fading away into the bass register of the keyboard. Ariadne's next reply, *Ich weiß, so ist es dort: wohin du mich führest* [I know, so it is there, where you will lead me], is lightly surrounded by the transformed Bacchus melody in two clarinets. Some strangely elusive, chromatically inflected sixths color her words, *wer dort verweilet, der vergißt gar schnell* [whoever abides there will forget very quickly], as if to emphasize further the confusion in her mind as she gropes for comprehension.

In an extended passage beginning *Bin ich ein Gott* [Am I a god] (see ex. 51), Strauss develops a splendid setting for the motive of Bacchus's

Ex. 51

211

godliness (see ex. 41), first heard at the beginning of this scene, but now predominating in woodwinds and harps, while strings and the magical bell-like sound of the celesta lightly tremble around it and Bacchus's words. The music grows more assertive and in tonality seems about to enter the key of transformation, D♭ major, as Bacchus proclaims: *Dann sterben eher die ewigen Sterne, als daß du stürbest aus meinen Armen* [The eternal stars will die before you would perish and leave my arms] (see ex. 52)—which in a most effective poetic touch Hofmannsthal will repeat as Bacchus's final words in the opera.

Ex. 52

But Ariadne remains perplexed; the music fails to reach D♭ major as the preceding passage had forecast, but turns to an unsettled, sound of C# minor, as Bacchus's godliness motive wanders uncertainly through various chromatic variations. Ariadne asks if she is already dead and wonders if forgetting could be achieved so quickly. Suddenly an expressive new theme appears in the violins, the love theme of Ariadne-Bacchus (see ex. 53), as she sings *Entfernt sich alles von mir?* [Does everything withdraw from me?].

The remainder of the transformation evolves in a series of lines between the two lovers, set musically to the abrupt fluctuation between the Bacchus theme (see ex. 40) and the love theme (see ex. 53), as the two lovers express themselves always in opposing tonalities. Especially effective and touching are Bacchus's words *Ich sage dir, nun hebt sich erst das Leben an für dich und mich!* [I say to you, now only does life begin for you and me!]. The stage setting transforms, and a starry heaven appears above the lovers. The music returns to the magically shifting chords in fourths in the harps, the rising fourth motive and its altered form, the rising third, occur in the bassoon and clarinet, while the theme of Bacchus softly but quite distinctly ascends in the solo cello and viola.

The love music comes back in the contrastingly darker key of E♭ as Ariadne replies, *Lag nicht die Welt auf meiner Brust? hast du sie fortgeblasen?* [Lay not the world on my breast? Have you blown it away?]. The music reverts again to the same mood of the preceding lines for Bacchus as the two join together in a duet: Ariadne looks back to her cave saying, *Da innen lag die arme Hündin, an' Boden gedrückt, auf*

kalten Nesseln mit Wurm und Assel und ärmer als sie [There, within, lay the poor wretch, pressed to the ground, on cold nettles with worms and lice and poorer than they], while simultaneously Bacchus literally overwhelms her with his own magnificent theme (see ex. 40) sung to *Nun steigt deiner Schmerzen innerste Lust in dein und meinem Herzen auf!* [Now your sorrow's deepest joy arises in your heart and mine!]. Ariadne has one more confused, bewildered comment: *Du Zauberer du! Verwandler, du! Blickt nicht aus dem Schatten deines Mantels der Mutter Augen auf mich her? Ist so dein Schattenland! also gesegnet? so unbedürftig der irdischen Welt?* [You sorcerer, you! Transformer, you! Do not my mother's eyes look out upon me from the shadow of your cloak? Is it so in your shadowy realm! Thus blessed? So free of the needs of this earthly world?]. The music based on the love melody disintegrates into fragments; the instability of the tonality becomes more marked in chromaticism, and very delicately a motive heard during Ariadne's dream sequence (see 11b) accompanies *der Mutter Augen auf mich her?* in bassoons and violas. In forgetting, Ariadne seems to retain her past only in the form of a musical dream.

Bacchus replies in an outburst of passion, *Du selber! du bist unbedürftig, du meine Zauberin* [You yourself, you are free of earthly needs, my sorceress], and at that moment the orchestra grows tranquil. The harmonic uncertainties vanish like evaporating mists as the tonality becomes C major, the purest and simplest of keys. As the violins and cellos quietly sing out with the Bacchus theme, the harp and piano create a flowing current of sound as background to Ariadne's words: *Gibt es kein Hinüber?* [Is there no crossing over?] (see ex. 54). *Sind*

wir schon da? Wie konnt' es geschehen? Sind wir schon drüben? Auch
meine Höhle, schön, gewölbt [Are we there already? How could it have
occurred? Are we already on the other side? Even my cave, beautiful,

Ex. 54

arched], sung to one long soaring melodic phrase. Once again, but for
the last time, the music lapses into less positive tonality as Ariadne
prophetically states: *Wie wunderbar verwandelst du* [How miraculously
you transform] (see ex. 55). Now Bacchus interrupts with a blazing A
major version of the love theme: *Du! Alles Du! Ich bin ein anderer als
ich war! Der Sinn des Gottes ist wach in mir, dein herrlich Wesen ganz
zu fassen!* [You! Everything, you! I am a different person than I was!
The feeling of a god is awake in me, in order to grasp completely your
splendid being!]. The final transformation of the Bacchus theme, which
has been only hinted at previously, results in the direct and passionate
theme as sung by Bacchus to *Die Glieder reg' ich in göttlicher Lust!*
[My whole being stirs in godly desire!].

This remarkable Strauss melody, which has been developed during
the final third of the opera from a very vague, almost unheard melody at
the beginning of the scene, demonstrates Strauss's masterful ability with
symphonic transformations of themes, a talent apparently ideal for Hofmannsthal's poetic purpose of showing the transformation of his characters. The Bacchus theme has arrived in B♭ major, the orchestra bursts
out in a tremendous climax built on this melody, in which the full
thirty-six man orchestra strains to produce the dynamics required by the
score (see ex. 56). The transformation as music is brilliantly uplifting.
Thematic expansion, orchestral volume and color, vocal excitement of a
soaring tenor melody enable Strauss to give Hofmannsthal's illusive
literary idea of human transformation a musical interpretation of extraordinary emotional impact. But just as Hofmannsthal's transformation remained an ideal inherently inexpressible in words, so too
Strauss's musical transformation adds nothing to the literary impact of
the libretto and its symbols. This Straussian musical climax remains a
purely musical achievement, and only secondarily does its relationship
to the text seem significant. It takes a great deal of concentration while

Ex. 55

Ex. 56

listening to this music to remember that at this point Hofmannsthal hoped Strauss would create that magical moment of transformation between two human beings. The whole of the scene is magical, but primarily as music rather than as drama.

The climax of the opera, however, is not its conclusion. As a canopy descends over the heads of Ariadne and Bacchus, the music grows quiet, and from somewhere behind the scenes the voices of nature sing their now familiar hymn of love *(Töne, töne, süße Stimme)* to which Ariadne joins her own voice in continuing perplexity: *Was hängt von mir in deinem Arm? O, was von mir, die ich vergehe, fingest du Geheimes mit deines Mundes Hauch? Was bleibt von Ariadne?* [What is left clinging of me in your arm? O, which mysteries of me, who is languishing, did you inhale with the breath of your mouth? What remains of Ariadne?].

The return of the nymphs' trio does not appear in Hofmannsthal's libretto, and again we have evidence that Strauss wielded a powerful influence in adapting his librettist's idea, both for dramatic and musical reasons. The trio not only adds a substantial element of musical form to the third scene, in the three-fold appearance of the music and text rather than the two isolated appearances Hofmannsthal had planned, but the repetition also gives Strauss an opportunity to remind his audience, musically, of Bacchus's arrival, which initially inspired this music. The nymphs add not only a lovely parenthetical passage of serene, non-human praise to the love, but they also remind us that we have experienced the culmination of a musical-dramatic action that began with the first appearance of this music. It is an exceedingly effective moment musically, the kind of purely musical joy that a librettist can never anticipate or plan simply because the operatic form remains essentially a musical, not a poetic experience.

At this point in *Ariadne* I Strauss began the final Db major love duet. With its conclusion and the enclosing of Ariadne and Bacchus within the canopy, the *commedia* figures reappeared on the stage. Zerbinetta in a "mocking tone of triumph," according to Hofmannsthal's stage directions, sang portions of her rondo, *Kommt der neue Gott gegangen, hingegeben sind wir stumm* . . . , as well as a considerable recapitulation of her aria from scene II. The four men also joined in with part of their dance quartet, singing *daß ein Herz so gar sich selber nicht verstehet*. As they danced off the stage in laughter, the opera ended with a few brief words by Monsieur Jourdain, who mused to himself over his ill fate in not having been born a true nobleman.

All of these developments were removed in *Ariadne* II. Since Jourdain of the Molière play was eliminated from the revised *Vorspiel,* he and his guests no longer take part in the opera performance. Strauss also suggested to Hofmannsthal that for a better curtain Zerbinetta and the comedians should be eliminated, an idea that shocked the poet, as he makes clear to Strauss in a letter dated 15 May 1916:

. . . . it would be a shameless betrayal of the work and its future for me to concede—out of pusillanimity—that the human counterpart (Zerbinetta) should be deprived of some last word!

This would be, allow me to say so, deliberately and openly sacrificing the fundamental idea, the spiritual meaning of the whole work for the sake of an effective curtain. . . .

Where then is the compromise between your legitimate proposal and my: "Thus far and no further!" I believe it is here: I will only insist that the counter-voice, represented by the sole figure of Zerbinetta, should be heard at the end for a second. Something like this: while to the rear of the stage the couple step down towards the sea, and before the orchestra opens the epilogue, Zerbinetta appears in front right, in the wings, but visible, waves her fan mockingly over her shoulder towards the back and proceeds to sing her couplet:

Kommt der neue Gott gegangen, hingegeben sind
wir stumm, Und er küßt uns Stirn und Wangen,
etc. . . . gefangen . . . Hingegeben sind wir stumm.

If need be let her only begin to sing, sing the first line—then let the orchestra drown her, so that the rest is to be found only in the libretto: I am satisfied with her symbolic mocking presence and exit. . . . (*C.*, 246-47)

Strauss appears to agree entirely with Hofmannsthal, for in a letter dated 18 May 1916 he replies: "Your wish is my command: At Number 326 Zerbinetta shall softly step from the wings and sing mockingly: 'Kommt der neue Gott gegangen, hingegeben sind wir stumm-stumm—'; the bassoon hints at the rondo theme from her aria. . . " (*C.*, 247).

But the final result in *Ariadne* II is not what Hofmannsthal thought he had made clear to Strauss. With Ariadne's words *Laß meine Schmerzen nicht verloren sein,* Zerbinetta steps out from behind the curtain. In a soft and, Strauss indicates, "peaceful" passage of exceedingly sensitive beauty (faint, tinkling chords in harps, celesta, and piano) with "tenderly emphasized" (again Strauss's words) fragments of Zerbinetta's rondo theme in the bassoon, she sings *Kommt der neue Gott gegangen, hingegeben sind wir stumm, stumm.* The passage has a tone of sentimentality, as if Zerbinetta were awestruck and deeply, sincerely moved by the event she has witnessed. Certainly, there is no hint of a "symbolic mocking presence." In fact, despite Hofmannsthal's efforts to emphasize the word "mocking" (*spöttisch*) in libretto as well as in his correspondence, Strauss omits the word in the score. Zerbinetta as a creation of Strauss has also been at least momentarily transformed. She clearly shows a visible change in character as reflected by her music, a change brought about by witnessing the transformation of Ariadne and Bacchus. Zerbinetta leaves the stage in a musical sense as a wiser woman, who perhaps still hopes to find her own Bacchus who could transform her. She is, however, far removed from the figure that Hofmannsthal had created and required for the balanced construction of the libretto. As mentioned, this discrepancy remained one of the major unresolved differences of opinion between the two men with the composer having the last word. As Zerbinetta exits, the opera in its revised form quickly resumes the passionate music of Ariadne and Bacchus, who sing a brief though overtly operatic duet to their love music. The final words of Bacchus, which he had already sung during the scene of transformation, *Durch deine Schmerzen bin ich reich, nun reg' ich die Glieder in göttlicher Lust! Und eher sterben die ewigen Sterne, eh denn du stürbest aus meinem Arm,* are now repeated to his own transformed, exalted theme, as the orchestra in the full splendor of its D^b major glory soars to unprecedented heights of rapture.

With Bacchus's last word, the lovers disappear within the canopy, and a brief orchestral coda continues the mood of Bacchus's triumph. His earlier theme (see ex. 40) pours out of the orchestral brass and woodwinds, followed by a momentarily perplexed, uncertain statement of the death motive. But death vanishes, overcome by the transformation tonality of D^b and the love music triumphs to its greatest climax. The music rapidly subsides for a tranquil, beautiful final statement of Bacchus's godliness motive, and the curtain descends as the sound fades away to nothing on the last D^b major triad.

Chapter IX

The *Vorspiel*—The Music

Strauss's reluctance to consider revising *Ariadne auf Naxos* is not surprising. He clung to his conviction that the original work, including the Molière play in Hofmannsthal's adaptation and the incidental music, was an artistic success that eventually would find its place in the German repertoire. Moreover, Strauss in general probably found the thought of revision distasteful, for his career offers little evidence of rewritings or adaptations of his music. His genius was quite opposed to tampering with works that he had shaped in the creative act of composition. Strauss preferred the stimulation of new ideas; however, a greater challenge faced him in writing an introductory act for *Ariadne auf Naxos:* he would be forced to work backwards, to write what would amount to a first act after he had already completed the finale.

In the composition of lengthy dramatic works composers normally write from the beginning to the end. The reason is simple: music, no matter what the period or style, is a temporal art. The meaning conveyed by a formal musical organization grows logically and of necessity from the first page of the score to the last. Musical developments, musical-poetical relationships, musical-dramatic climaxes, all depend on the planning of the route each score takes in its temporal journey. No matter how carefully a composer plans the thematic content of an opera, maps out key relationships, organizes the form, or predetermines any other facet of the music, an opera demands the logical development of music leading from one measure to the next, one scene to the following scene, and one act of the work to subsequent acts.

When Hofmannsthal broached the idea of the new version of *Ariadne*, he was in a sense asking Strauss to ignore these limitations on his craft. The thought of composing a *Vorspiel* after he had already completed a self-contained opera was unthinkable, at least during the years from 1913 to 1916. Yet, Strauss eventually warmed to the task for artistic as well as practical reasons.[1] To appreciate Strauss's accomplishment, we need to review a few of the difficulties he overcame:

---

[1] Another persuasive argument and more practical reason leading Strauss to think about revising *Ariadne* perhaps was his interest in performing the work in the United States, an important source of royalties for him. The original version with its lengthy Molière play in a German translation precluded any hope of American performances. As early as the

1. As the previous chapter shows, the original *Ariadne auf Naxos* was composed as a highly integrated and complex form. Strauss's musical design was essentially a tripartite structure in which each section grows musically from a relatively quiet beginning to a climax. Each of the three climaxes is more impressive than the preceding one, until the opera ends in the climactic scene of mutual transformation brought about through the love of Bacchus for Ariadne. In considering a new *Vorspiel,* Strauss faced the task of writing an act of music to preface what was planned as a self-contained, one-act *Ariadne.* If this new act were to be successful, it must not distract the audience from the ultimate goal to be reached in *Ariadne,* nor must it make the opera proper seem anticlimactic.

2. There was a problem of musical integration. Strauss needed a musical means for interrelating the music of the new *Vorspiel* to the opera *Ariadne* if he wished to achieve some degree of musical unity for the entire work. The solution would necessarily involve the insertion into the new act of themes and aspects of the musical style found in *Ariadne.* Here, however, lay danger as Strauss must have realized: to emphasize these thematic materials in the *Vorspiel* could drain their freshness and vitality to the degree that they would lose their effectiveness in the opera.

3. An additional difficulty was posed by the reversed order of composing a two-act opera. If he used thematic ideas connected with characters and dramatic events in the opera, Strauss would create a *Vorspiel* with an inner structure and meaning that would be largely incomprehensible to audiences not already familiar with the opera. Yet this is what happened; quotations from *Ariadne auf Naxos* in the *Vorspiel* are meant to convey to the audience many subtle relationships in the music between the *Vorspiel* and the opera. However, these musical interrelationships are lost until one has heard the complete score more

first part of 1913, Strauss makes clear his intentions to write a *Vorspiel* in secco recitative primarily for the American opera stage. In a letter published only in the German edition of the Strauss-Hofmannsthal correspondence he informs the poet: ". . . Die Bearbeitung der 'Ariadne' zu Seccorezitativ eilt gar nicht. Es genügt mir, sie zum Mai zu haben. Bitte nur dringendst, gegen Niemand—Niemand, besonders nicht in Wien, ein Wort davon verlauten zu lassen. Wenn wir im Herbst die Sache an die Amerikaner geben, ist's früh genug, daß die Welt es erfährt. Bis dahin mindestens und hoffentlich auch weiterhin soll die 'Ariadne' in Deutschland in der jetzigen Form laufen." See Strauss-Hofmannsthal, *Briefwechsel* (Zürich, 1964), p. 211. Curiously, even this idea seems to have been abandoned by Strauss later in the year for on 15 December of the same year he writes to Hofmannsthal: ". . . I am against any re-arrangement or separation of the opera from the comedy, and negotiations are now taking place with America to have the piece performed there next winter, in English, in a small theatre, in the way we've written it" *C.,* 180-81. Quite likely the English version was the one prepared by Somerset Maugham and performed by Sir Thomas Beecham in London on 27 May 1913. Unfortunately, the production in the United States did not take place, no doubt cancelled because of the outbreak of the war (during which anti-German sentiments led to the cancelling of performances of music by many German composers).

than once. Certainly this very fact stood in the way of an immediate general audience acceptance of the revised version. For the attentive listener all opera involves an educational process, that is, the recognition of the statement, development, and restatement of musical materials; but in Strauss's *Vorspiel* one does not learn the musical content and its development as the drama unfolds. For this reason *Ariadne* II is a rare example in the literature of opera that demands repeated listening before one can begin to appreciate its "formal garden," to borrow Strauss's expression. For this same reason, the authors of this book have chosen to reverse their examination of the two parts of the opera.

One may recall from the previous chapter that Strauss had asked Hofmannsthal if he might preface *Ariadne auf Naxos* with some form of overture. As has been shown, Strauss completely disregarded the details of Hofmannsthal's suggestion that "a little overture seems . . . stylistically indispensable; a little symphony of the old kind which brings together the main themes from the opera" (see p. 161).

Though Strauss ignored Hofmannsthal's advice at the time, he must have filed it away in the back of his mind, for the instrumental introduction to the *Vorspiel* does in fact resemble "a little overture" in miniature. The 64-bar instrumental preface not only states several major themes to the *Vorspiel* proper, but it also presents for the first time significant melodic ideas of the opera *Ariadne*. Strauss is careful, however, not to use any of the *Ariadne* themes found in the overture to the opera itself.

The introduction has the character of a symphonic sketch: the themes come quickly and often fall pell-mell on top of one another without apparent dramatic meaning. The score begins in the key of C major, the basic tonality of the entire *Vorspiel* and the key that Strauss chose to represent the prosaic, bourgeois world of the "richest man in Vienna."[2] The *Vorspiel* opens with a roll of the timpani, C major triads in the violas, and a bombastic measure of timpani beats on the notes C,G,C,G,C (see ex. 57). The pomposity of the timpani, which later serves to introduce the Major-domo (*Haushofmeister*), is combined with the most important theme of the *Vorspiel* (see ex. 58a), the stormy, rhythmically impulsive, powerfully ascending theme of the Composer. Against the ordinary background of C major triads and the thumping of the Major-Domo's timpani motive, the Composer's theme is impetuously nervous, brashly discordant, and full of élan. The third repetition of this theme soars to high C, but suddenly the melody

---

[2] C major originally was the all-encompassing key of the incidental music to the Molière play, where it represented M. Jourdain's own simple tonal world. In *Ariadne* I, the end of the opera proper returned to C major (as M. Jourdain was left alone on the stage). This cohesion of tonality enclosing the entire play-opera in a frame of C major was lost when Strauss cut the final music of *Ariadne* and ended the opera in the key of D♭ major, the tonality of the transformation of Ariadne and Bacchus.

changes into a kind of thematic alter-ego and becomes a gentle, hesitant, descending motive, more feminine and reflective, which establishes the poetic side of the young Composer's youthful masculinity (see ex. 58b).

Ex. 57, 58a & 58b

The general melodic contour from its low G to the peak of e and falling back to c, show how closely this theme also belongs to the other masculine characters as outlined in the previous chapter (see pp. 202-03). As a thematic complex, the Composer's music is one of Strauss's great successes in portraying musically the personality of one of his opera characters.

Those who have heard *Ariadne* previously will notice the quiet though very distinct appearance of the theme of Bacchus in the bassoons and solo horn, combined contrapuntally with the Composer's music, Strauss's method of reenforcing Hofmannsthal's idea that Bacchus was another aspect of the Composer's personality (see ex. 58c). As the Composer's melody subsides with its gentle rocking figure, Strauss takes an unexpected tonal detour into E♭ major for a full statement of the love music of Ariadne and Bacchus (see ex. 53). This in turn is interrupted by a two measure statement of the comedians' dance theme occurring in *Ariadne* to the words, *Es gilt ob Tanzen, ob Singen* (see ex. 22). This material frequently recurs in the *Vorspiel* and in its many varied guises will be referred to simply as the "Comedians' " melody. The F major tonality for this passage is the same as when the tune is sung completely in the opera. In very quick order then, the Composer's passionate melody has been enmeshed with strikingly disjointed references to the Comedians' dance melody.

Just as suddenly the music breaks out in a brief though sumptuous reference to Bacchus's great transformation melody found at the end of the opera. In both instances Strauss maintains the unifying tonality of the D♭ major (see ex. 56). However, again the music returns to the Composer with a reference to the most reflective part of his melody, only to be followed almost immediately by one of the waltz tunes from the middle part of the opera (see ex. 37).

From this point through to the raising of the curtain, carefully organized musical chaos reigns. An exciting contrapuntal interweaving of ideas combines the Composer's melodies with references to the Comedians' dance melody, Bacchus's godliness and also Zerbinetta's Rondo. A great scurrying in the orchestra leads directly into the scene as the Music Teacher rushes onto the stage.

Although quite succinct, the instrumental introduction is a radiant gem among Strauss's orchestral achievements. The masterful expressiveness of the chamber orchestra, the brilliant contrapuntal handling of several major themes, and the overall vitality introduce the audience to the *Vorspiel* with a musical potpourri of great originality. This music fully belies any notion that once he began to compose Strauss lacked enthusiasm for the task at hand.

As we have already shown (see p. 70), Strauss envisioned Hofmannsthal's introductory prose scene to *Ariadne* in a musical version set largely to secco recitatives. The *secco* ("dry") recitative developed originally as an aspect of late baroque opera and became a prominent stylistic feature of works of the great Classic opera composers, including Strauss's god Mozart. Secco recitatives are meant to present the narrative part of an opera libretto as quickly and with as little musical lyricism as possible. In concept such recitatives are a form of musically heightened speech, sung usually to simple chords from a harpsichord. In the hands of lesser masters, the secco recitative often became tedious, and audiences frequently suffered through these seemingly endless passages of narrative declamation in order to enjoy the arias waiting at their end.

In the nineteenth century several composers experimented with numerous means to revitalize or even to eliminate recitatives from opera. Some composers attempted to inject more interest into

223

recitatives by adding orchestral accompaniments of greater variety. Others wrote more interesting melodic lines (which, of course, destroyed to some extent the narrative and declamatory impact of these passages). Wagner perfected a form of "endless melody" that shifted subtly between declamatory and lyrical melodic interest, without making a formal distinction between the styles. Although arias as such are largely absent from Wagner's mature works, his vocal lines are always more intensely melodic and musically effective than would be true of secco recitative. With Wagner's narrative style, the orchestra often equals the voices in importance, and in the music dramas the classical characteristics of opera tend to become inverted. As the orchestra shakes off its subservient role of accompanying the voices, so too the vocal parts surrender their former domination over the music. In Wagner's hands the orchestra frequently tends to control the dramatic forces and to subjugate the voices. Strauss, on the other hand, seldom permitted his orchestra to dominate the vocal writing; the only real exceptions occur in his early masterworks, *Salome* and *Elektra*.

The Wagnerian solution to opera narration became the most widely adopted method of later nineteenth-century opera composers, and Strauss tended to follow this same path in his early operas. However, overtly aria-like forms were always a prominent feature of his stage works beginning with his first opera *Guntram*. In *Rosenkavalier* Strauss developed a different style that frequently approaches a more conversational tone for dialogue. Such a return to a musically-supported rhetoric could in many instances be labelled traditional recitative if the orchestra were not so prominent. Recitative stands out prominently in *Ariadne* during Zerbinetta's solo, which became the source of inspiration for the recitative style employed in a large portion of the *Vorspiel*.

Both Strauss and Hofmannsthal agreed that the *Vorspiel* should help clarify for the audience the less than obvious poetic meaning of the opera. To convey the necessary information required a recitative style placing more emphasis on words than on music. The result was a new act of music that balances narration with sufficient melodic lyricism (songs, arias, duets) to relieve the austerity of the recitative style. Not until his final opera, *Capriccio* (which he called a conversation piece in music), did Strauss write as felicitous a combination of recitatives. Although the word is the paramount element in the *Vorspiel,* one never grows weary of the musical lines supporting the text and, in addition, one is constantly entertained by the charm and wit of the orchestral commentary.

The *Vorspiel* opens with the impassioned conversation between the Music Teacher and the Major-domo, who has the only spoken role in the opera. The spoken lines seem particularly pompous within the musical milieu of sung recitative, and this pomposity is heavily underscored by the Major-domo's verbosity. The Music Teacher in great agitation asks if he could have heard correctly that his student's opera *Ariadne* is to appear on the same program with a *Singspiel* in the "Italian buffo style," an event, he insists, his student will never permit. His words spill out in a torrent as the strings of the orchestra hint at the Comedians' dance melody. For the Music Teacher's references to the title of his student's work, Strauss accompanies the words *Ariadne auf Naxos* with harmonium alone. This deft touch of instrumental color relates to the opera's opening mood of desolation and sadness where the harmonium has an important role in setting the scene. After several indignant comments by the Music Teacher to the Major-domo (including the line, *Zu diesen die Verdauung fördernden Genüssen rechnen Sie demnach die heroische Opera: Ariadne?* [To these entertainments promoting digestion do you reckon the heroic opera: *Ariadne*?] sung to the opening portion of the Comedians' melody), both leave the stage.

Following a suitably tragic (F minor) version of the Composer's theme, a brief parenthetical action involves the entrance of an Officer (otherwise unidentified), led by a lackey who knocks on Zerbinetta's dressing room door (to horn knocks). As the Officer enters the dressing room, the Composer, introduced by the opening notes of his theme, comes on stage. The next statement of the same theme, suddenly all sixteenth notes and rushing up the normal two-octave span of the melody (see ex. 59), is the musical result of his excitement and impatience.

Ex. 59

Thwarted in his plan to rehearse the orchestra that is busy performing dinner music for the guests, the Composer decides to visit the Prima donna who will sing the role of Ariadne. As he approaches the dressing room, the strings lightly support a gentle statement of the Hermes motive in the clarinet, a nicely humorous allusion to the approach of Bacchus to Ariadne in the opera. Denied entry by the lackey, the Composer is perplexed, and (to another though broken off statement of the Hermes motive in the oboe, bassoon, violins, and cellos) he proclaims: *Weiß er, wer ich bin? Wer in meiner Oper singt, ist für mich jederzeit zu sprechen!* [Does he know who I am? Whoever sings in my opera, is always available to speak with me]. He knocks on the door, also to horn knocks, but receives no answer—for this is the dressing room of Zerbinetta, who at the moment is entertaining the Officer—and the orchestra and the lackey both chuckle in amusement. The Composer angrily dismisses the lackey while the Composer's melody surges furiously in all the strings but is prevented from moving by the E pedalpoint.

Quickly the mood changes from fury to calm, as the Composer is transfixed by a new musical idea passing through his mind. The orchestra reveals this new theme, as the flute, accompanied by a lightly flowing passage of sixteenth notes in the violas, presents the opening bars of the melody that later is identified as a song describing Bacchus: *Du Venussohn gibst süßen Lohn für unser Sehnen und Schmachten* . . . [Thou, son of Venus, bringst sweet recompense for our longing and anguish]. The theme breaks off abruptly. The Composer despairs that there is so much he would still like to change in his opera, and again the orchestra returns to the Hermes motive.

Taking up his new inspiration again, the Composer, while searching in his pocket for a piece of music paper, sings the melody and words to the conclusion of the song, *Du allmächtiger Gott* [Thou omnipotent god]. Just as quickly he crushes the music paper and decides to speak with the Tenor playing the part of Bacchus. The Composer feels he must stress that *Bacchus ein Gott ist, ein seliger Knabe* [Bacchus is a god, a blessed youth]. Simultaneously, the orchestra introduces the melody of Bacchus's godliness by referring to the triplet motive found in the opera. As the Composer knocks on the door (again with French horn knocks), he sings out in full voice the final lines of his new song, *O du Knabe, du Kind, du allmächtiger Gott!* (see ex. 60).

After this very brief though splendid lyrical moment that captures the Composer's musical image of his young god-hero, the succeeding action and music comically contrasts with his vision, as the balding Tenor and the Wigmaker come out of the dressing room engaged in a violent argument over Bacchus's wig. While the Composer tries to speak with the Tenor, the orchestra attempts to bring forward the Bacchus godliness motive, but to no avail, for the Tenor slams the door.

The Composer again returns to his new musical idea, which comes forward tenderly from the cellos, and he asks the Wigmaker if he has a piece of music paper. The latter ignores his question and runs off, and suddenly we hear the frivolous descending melody connected with Zerbinetta (see ex. 15) as she comes from her dressing room with the Officer. She explains in recitative that her troupe will appear after the opera in order to make the audience laugh again after being bored. The first chord of the piano accompaniment forcefully emphasizes how effective the sound of this instrument has become as a symbol of Zer-

Ex. 60

binetta's world. For those who know the opera, the piano sound recalls the whole central scene of the opera *Ariadne*. Similarly, Strauss uses the harp to surround the Prima donna Ariadne in the symbolic sound frequently associated with her role in the opera.

The Composer learns about Zerbinetta from the Dancing Master. His question, *Wer ist dieses entzückende Mädchen?* [Who is this entrancing young girl?], is sung to a tenderly expressive solo violin statement of his own impassioned melody. When the Music Teacher responds that Zerbinetta *singt und tanzt mit vier Partnern* [sings and dances with four partners], his vocal line incorporates the Comedians' melody. The Composer's angry retort, *nach meiner Oper? Ein lustiges Nachspiel? Tänze und Triller, freche Gebärden und zweideut'ge Reden nach Ariadne?* [after my opera? A comic epilogue? Dances and trills, insolent gestures and off-color speeches after Ariadne?] permits Strauss a moment of contrapuntal virtuosity. In addition to numerous "trills" referred to in the texts, the orchestra combines the music of the Comedians with the Dance Quintet waltz theme while the opening notes

227

of the overture to *Ariadne* occur three times. With the second of these statements the Composer sings the word Ariadne to these notes (see ex. 61 and ex. 35a). The Composer's lofty philosophy of *Das Geheimnis des Lebens tritt an sie heran* [The mystery of life touches their lives] is

Ex. 61

set to the theme of Bacchus's transformation. By equating the mystery of life to transformation, Strauss demonstrates that he has learned well his lessons from Hofmannsthal. The Composer's continuing tirade unites an angry variant of his own theme with the melody of the Comedians, as well as with a vocal and orchestral return to the opening notes of the overture.

The Composer's rage again dissipates as he returns to his earlier musical inspiration, which he says had been interrupted when the Tenor (the word is underscored with the godliness motive) gave the Wigmaker a box on the ear. This time the Composer sings for his teacher's benefit the entire song, *Du Venussohn* (see ex. 62).[3] As frequently occurs in Strauss's operas, this moment of lyricism has been prepared by two separate introductory statements of the melody. The realization of those tantalizing fragments does not disappoint the listener in this, the first great soprano melody to be heard in the score.

Ex. 62

At this instant we are jolted by another of the kaleidoscopic musical surprises that mark the first three quarters of this act. A woodwind and brass march (minus trumpet) of overt crudeness introduces the four comedians, Harlekin, Scaramuccio, Brighella, and Truffaldin. Zerbinetta requests a mirror, rouge, make-up pencil, and the four comedians run into the dressing room to find them. When the Composer angrily reproaches his Teacher, *Und du hast es gewußt* [and you knew it all along], the latter replies philosophically (to a bassoon and viola accompaniment) that he is some thirty years older than his student and has learned to conform to the world. The Composer responds, *Wer so an mir handelt, der ist mein Freund gewesen, gewesen* [Whoever treats me like this was, was my friend], each of the words *gewesen* given finality by hammer-blow chords. With this he tears up his previously notated song.

---

[3] This song originally appeared in Strauss's incidental music to the Molière play. In the opening scene of the play, the Composer improvises at the keyboard. His Teacher later tells Jourdain that his pupil has just composed a new song, and the melody is sung for him. The music was preserved by Hofmannsthal, who carefully planned the figure of the Composer around this melody. See *C.*, 169-70.

A sweeping arpeggio on the harp reintroduces the Prima donna, who makes insulting comments about Zerbinetta and her group: *Pfui, was gibt's denn da für Erscheinungen? Uns mit dieser Sorte von Leuten in einen Topf?* [Ugh, what are those strange creatures over there? We are to be in same pot with such sorts?] (More harp arpeggios). *Weiß man hier nicht, wer ich bin?* [Doesn't one know here who I am?]. Zerbinetta cuts into these remarks with a brief solo of exceedingly brisk music, accompanied entirely by the solo piano. The tempo, piano sound, and the triteness of the music all add to our impression of a shallow, vulgar coquette—the popular entertainer certainly out of place in these surroundings. She hopes that her troupe will be allowed to perform before the audience has become too bored, for otherwise she insists it will be twice as hard to make people laugh.

The Dancing Master suggests that the audience, having just dined, will probably sleep through the opera, only to awaken expectantly for the concluding part of the program, *Die ungetreue Zerbinetta und ihre vier Liebhaber* [The fickle Zerbinetta and her four lovers]. His remarks are composed to an *Ariette,* a charming song that Strauss lifted bodily from the incidental music that accompanied the dinner served to Jourdain and his guests during the Molière play (see ex. 63). The dance-like character *à la Couperin* nicely fits the Dancing Master's character—as well as his words—and evokes a momentary feeling of French court milieu, one of the rare occasions in the entire work that carries over the atmosphere of the first version. Strauss also works in references to Zerbinetta's motive when the Dancing Master mentions her name, and the line quoted above, *Die ungetreue Zerbinetta . . .* is sung to the Comedians' dance melody. The *Ariette* is a miniature *da capo* form, with the opening tune of the orchestra returning *forte* at the end and sung by the Dancing Master to the line, *Und wenn sie in ihren Karossen sitzen, wissen sie überhaupt nichts mehr, als daß sie die unvergleichliche Zerbinetta haben tanzen sehn* [And when they are in their coaches, they will remember nothing else but that they have seen the incomparable Zerbinetta dance].

Quite naturally the Music Teacher disagrees with the Dancing Master's viewpoint, and accompanied by repeated references to the opening notes to the overture of *Ariadne,* he proclaims: *Ariadne ist das Ereignis des Abends, um Ariadne zu hören versammeln sich Kenner und vornehme Personen im Hause eines reichen Mäcens. Ariadne ist das Losungswort. Sie sind Ariadne. . . .* [Ariadne is the event of the evening, to hear Ariadne connoisseurs and distinguished people have gathered in the home of a rich Maecenas. Ariadne is the redeeming word. You are Ariadne]. Strauss appropriately underscores the word *Mäcens* to a C major triad (that is, the tonal center of the opening of the *Vorspiel*), but two measures later the words, *Sie sind Ariadne,* have been lifted up in tonality and emotion to D^b major, the key of the future transformation. The end of the Music Teacher's speech includes a fur-

Ex. 63

ther statement of the Hermes theme, which is one more thematic link anticipating the music of the opera.

These artistic polemics end when a lackey reports that the audience is about to enter the theater from the dining salon. The Music Teacher orders the players to take their places; one hears the Hermes theme combined with the Comedians' melody, and then, to everyone's astonishment, the timpani bangs out the opening music of the *Vorspiel* (see ex. 57) as the Major-domo returns to the stage. His announcement that the Master of the house has decided to change the program elicits agitated comments from the assembled performers all of which are marked humorously by Strauss. The Prima donna's *Was ist das?* [What is this?] is literally engulfed in a regal sweep of the harp; the Dancing Master asks, *Was wünscht man von mir?* [What does one want from me?] to a piano embellishment; the Music Teacher says, *Jetzt im letzten Moment?* [Now, at the last moment?] to sinister-sounding viola tremolos. The

Dancing Master thinks he knows what will be asked: *Das Nachspiel wird Vorspiel, wir geben zuerst die ungetreue Zerbinetta* [The epilogue becomes prologue; we are to perform the fickle Zerbinetta first], which he sings to the Comedians' melody. However, the Major-domo's command to perform both the opera and dance masquerade simultaneously shocks everyone so greatly that the immediate reaction of the orchestra is silence broken only by a few nervous beats of the timpani.

When the Dancing Master agrees with the Major-domo's report that the Master does not feel a desert island is a tasteful sight *in einem so wohlausgestatteten Hause* [in such a magnificently furnished mansion], the Composer bursts out with one of Hofmannsthal's most significant declarations: *Ariadne auf Naxos, Herr. Sie ist das Sinnbild der menschlichen Einsamkeit* [*Ariadne auf Naxos*, sir, she is the symbol of human loneliness]. Two frenetic statements of the Composer's theme accompany his continuing statement, *Nichts um sich als das Meer, die Steine, die Bäume, das fühllose Echo* [Nothing around but the sea, rocks, trees, and unfeeling Echo]. Strauss adds a subtle musical twist to the words, *Sieht sie ein menschliches Gesicht, wird meine Musik sinnlos* [If she sees a human face, my music becomes meaningless], by a quick intrusion of the Comedians' melody on *ein menschliches Gesicht*. The Dancing Master ends the argument with *So wie es jetzt ist* [As it now exists] (with a faint, perhaps ironic, allusion to Ariadne's theme of ecstasy), *ist es um stehend einzuschlafen* [it will put everyone to sleep]. Further conversation is cut off by the order of the Major-domo to begin the performance.

The next several pages of the score are the most complex of the *Vorspiel;* for as the players undertake the joining of the two entertainments, there is an involved display of musical ideas connected with the characters in the argument and interwoven with allusions to the opera about to be performed. As the Composer chides his Teacher that they have nothing to lose and should leave, the Music Teacher replies that they would lose fifty ducats. Strauss cannot resist orchestrating the words with the tinkling sounds of money suggested by trills on flutes, clarinets, and the triangle.

The Dancing Master counsels the Music Teacher that the performance of the two works will be very simple. First, the various monotonous stretches of the opera should be cut, and we hear another reference to the theme of Ariadne's ecstasy. The Dancing Master points out that Zerbinetta and her group know how to improvise, and the orchestra quotes Zerbinetta's aria melody, *So war es mit Pagliazzo*. The Dancing Master urges his colleague to take a red pencil, ink and pen and to instruct the Composer to make whatever changes are necessary to save the work. Here the theme of Hermes and the Comedians' melody collide. The Composer's outraged reaction, *Lieber ins Feuer* [rather into the fire], brings a bit of philosophy from his Teacher that Strauss sets in learned contrapuntal style: *Hundert große Meister, die wir auf*

den Knien bewundern, haben ihre erste Aufführung mit noch ganz an-
dern Opfern erkauft [Hundreds of great masters, to whom on our knees
we pay homage, have bought their first performance by even greater
sacrifices] (see ex. 64).

Ex. 64

Relenting in his determination to abandon his work, the Composer
(accompanied by soft references to his own theme) sets about the task of
revisions and deletions. In an exciting and exceedingly intricate passage
the Tenor and Prima donna attempt to keep their own roles intact at the
expense of their partner. The Tenor approaches the Composer to urge
cutting Ariadne's music and we hear Ariadne's motive from the opera,
Ich will vergessen (see ex. 6a). Ariadne asks the Music Teacher to see
that Bacchus's role is reduced and the orchestra plays a rather
humorously over-extended development of the Bacchus godliness
motive. The Music Teacher assures Ariadne that her part will remain
intact, and the motive of Hermes occurs in the orchestra. At the same
time, the Tenor is advising the Composer that no one will endure "this
woman's continuous presence on the stage," and the orchestra plays
briefly the melody of Ariadne's ecstasy. At this point the Music Teacher
reports to the Tenor that two arias of Ariadne have been cut; then he
tells Ariadne that Bacchus's role has been reduced by half. All of this
conversation takes place rapidly in the space of ten concentrated
measures. The melodic motives are fused into a symphonic fabric of
considerable intensity. However, it is impossible to absorb the symphonic treatment of various motives in a single listening experience.
This passage, like many in the *Vorspiel,* is meant for the connoisseur of
the work who has learned to absorb its intricate beauty through
repeated listening. What Hofmannsthal had intended as low comic
relief, Strauss casts in such complicated musical interpretation that the
comedy is all but crushed. What was textual cliché is redeemed by compositional virtuosity.

We reach the dramatic crux of the *Vorspiel*, the actual describing of
the plot and meaning of the opera, by which Hofmannsthal hoped the
audience would gain a clear insight into the poetical and philosophical
values of *Ariadne*. The Dancing Master explains to Zerbinetta that

Ariadne wishes death after having been abandoned by Theseus. She responds characteristically, *Den Tod! das sagt man so. Natürlich meint sie einen andern Verehrer* [She longs for death! That's what they say. Naturally she means another admirer]. Her words, *das sagt man so,* are colored by a brief reference to her own theme, *So war es mit Pagliazzo,* showing that she regards Ariadne as just another woman like herself, waiting for the next man. When the Dancing Master agrees, *Natürlich so kommts ja auch* [Naturally, and so it turns out], the Composer contradicts this interpretation, *Nein, Herr, so kommt es nicht. Denn Herr, sie ist eine von den Frauen, die nur einem im Leben gehören und danach keinem mehr als dem Tod* [No Sir, it is not so. For Sir, she is one of those women who belongs to only one man in life and then no one other than death]. Strauss reenforces the difference between the women by shifting the orchestra into D^b major to state calmly the Hermes motive. From this motive is born the opening to the final transformed melody of Bacchus, which is rudely interrupted by a trill and roulade from Zerbinetta.

Unaffected by the Composer's viewpoint, Zerbinetta continues her explanation, predicting that it will not be Death who comes but more likely *ein blasser, dunkeläugiger Bursche wie du einer bist* [a pale-faced, dark-eyed young lad just like you]. The Composer is oblivious to her pointed reference to him, for he has fallen into a trance brought on by his own poetic inspiration regarding Ariadne. The Music Teacher continues the explanation, telling Zerbinetta that she has guessed correctly, that it is the young god Bacchus (accompanied by repeated musical references to the Bacchus godliness motive) who comes to Ariadne. Almost triumphantly Zerbinetta says mockingly: *als ob man das nicht wüßte! Nun hat sie fürs Nächste ja was sie braucht* [as if one did not know it! Now she has everything she needs for the moment].

The Composer, however, still in his transported mood, explains: *Sie hält ihn für den Todesgott. In ihren Augen, in ihrer Seele ist er es, und darum, einzig darum. . . .* [She thinks he is the god of death. In her eyes, in her soul, he is Death, and therefore, only for this reason . . .]. The tonality is again D^b major, and the orchestra gives us a touching preview of the transformation scene at the end of the opera. Bacchus's theme dominates this passage, and the words of the Composer's continuing reverie are surrounded by the magically shifting chords that later create the basic mood of the transformation. The Composer sings in awe-struck reverence: *Einzig nur darum geht sie mit ihm auf sein Schiff. Sie meint zu sterben. Nein! Sie stirbt wirklich* [Only for this reason she goes with him on his ship. She expects to die. No! She really dies]. Strauss has been especially careful to duplicate the mood and sound of the transformation in the opera. Clearly he hoped that we would remember these key words: *Sie meint zu sterben. Nein! Sie stirbt wirklich,* when we experience this moment in the action of the opera. But Zerbinetta is not impressed. Again she attempts to equate Ariadne to herself: *Ta, ta!*

Du wirst mich meinesgleichen kennen lernen [Ta, ta! You think you can teach me about women like myself], a notion that the Composer vigorously repudiates: *Sie ist nicht Ihresgleichen. Ich weiß es, daß sie stirbt. Ariadne ist die eine unter Millionen, sie ist die Frau, die nicht vergißt* [She is not like you. I know that she does die. Ariadne is the one in a million; she is the woman who never forgets]. The violins pour forth passionately with Ariadne's love theme.

While Zerbinetta then narrates in recitative with piano accompaniment her version of the plot to her companions, the Composer remains lost in his own thoughts just as Ariadne will be found at the opening of the opera. In a somber, mysterious musical passage mixing together the Hermes motive with the reflective final portion of the Composer's theme, he sings to himself: *Sie gibt sich dem Tod hin, ist nicht mehr da, weggewischt, stürzt sich hinein ins Geheimnis der Verwandlung* [She surrenders herself to death, is no longer there, obliterated, engulfed in the mystery of transformation]. The final words are accompanied by Bacchus's theme, very softly and expressively in clarinets, bassoons, and horn. The orchestral and vocal lines grow more and more expansive in their warmth and emotionality. As the Composer sings *wird neu geboren* [will be born anew], the orchestra breaks out with the love duet of Bacchus and Ariadne. With *wieder* of *entsteht wieder* [arises again], the vocal line soars to a high A, and at the end of *in seinen Armen* [in his arms], a climax is reached with the prominent entrance of the Bacchus theme of transformation, that great sweeping scale theme to be heard again only at the close of the opera. It is joined also to the Composer's vocal line as he says, *Daran wird er zum Gott* [Thus he becomes a god], reaching high B♭ (see ex. 65) on the final word.

The Composer, in the warm emotional glow of his own poetical inspiration, becomes caught in Zerbinetta's web of womanly charms. The music expands the gentle, rocking, reflective portion of the Composer's theme and then quietly settles down to prepare for the climax of the *Vorspiel,* an outpouring of such beautiful lyricism that one forgets the *Vorspiel* had been planned as a narrative introduction to the opera and not necessarily as a richly emotional experience of its own.

A masterful cadence prepares us for Zerbinetta's response to the Composer's question: *Was wollen Sie damit—in diesem Augenblick—sagen?* [What are you trying to say at this moment?]. The entire thirteen measures are a rich intensification of the dominant chord leading to the E major of Zerbinetta's aria. Throughout these measures, and over the dominant pedal note B, the reflective portion of the Composer's theme wends its way through warmly tender chromaticism; the puzzled inquiry of the Composer seems to grow and grow, filling the orchestra with an ever-expanding emotional attachment to Zerbinetta. The text to Zerbinetta's aria, with the Composer's interruptions is as follows:

235

Zerbinetta: *Ein Augenblick ist wenig, ein Blick ist viel. Viele meinen, daß sie mich kennen, aber ihr Auge ist stumpf. Auf dem Theater spiele ich die Kokette, wer sagt, daß mein Herz dabei im Spiele ist? Ich scheine munter, und bin doch traurig, gelte für gesellig, und bin doch so einsam.* [A moment is little, a glance is much. Many believe that they know me, but their eye is unperceptive. In the theater I play the coquette, but who says that my heart is part of the act? I seem merry, and yet I am sad. I am considered gregarious and am yet so lonely].

Composer: *Süßes unbegreifliches Mädchen!* [Sweet incomprehensible girl!]

Zerbinetta: *Törichtes Mädchen, mußt du sagen, das sich manchmal zu sehnen verstünde nach dem einen, dem sie treu sein könnte, treu bis ans Ende.* [Foolish girl you must say, one who might know how to yearn for the man to whom she could be faithful forever].

Composer: *Wer es sein dürfte, den du ersehnest! Du bist wie ich—das Irdische unvorhanden deiner Seele.* [Whoever it may be for whom you long, you are as I—the earthly does not exist in your soul].

Zerbinetta: *Du sprichst, was ich fühle.—ich muß fort. Vergißt du gleich wieder diesen einen Augenblick?* [You speak what I feel—I must go. Will you forget this one moment right away?]

Composer: *Vergißt sich in Aeonen ein einziger Augenblick?* [Can a single moment be forgotten in eternity?]

Ex. 65

The brief love scene between Zerbinetta and the Composer which, as explained earlier, is analogous to the encounter between Ariadne and Bacchus, inspired Strauss to music that ranks with the very greatest of

236

his achievements. It is another of those occasions where Strauss operated independently. Although Hofmannsthal clearly indicates that Zerbinetta's response should be *scheinbar ganz schlicht, mit äußerster Coquetterie* [ostensibly very simple, with utmost coquetry] thus keeping Zerbinetta in character, the aria is neither simple nor coquettish. Rather the music is incandescently sensuous, and the aria is the most passionate and compelling of its type in either act. The long flowing melodic line in the voice is characteristic of Strauss's most reflective melodies, and the harmonic color demonstrates the composer's mastery in commanding our emotions through chord progessions.

The aria falls into a three-part form. The musical setting of Zerbinetta's opening lines establishes the mood of the aria and forms the A section. The Composer's first and last comments embrace the B or middle section, and the final lines of Zerbinetta beginning *Du sprichst, was ich fühle* as well as the Composer's concluding remark, *Vergißt sich in Aeonen ein einziger Augenblick,* consist of a freely conceived repetition of the musical elements used earlier in both the A and B parts of the aria. Ex. 66 shows several important aspects of this aria: (1) The long sustained tones of the melodic lines. (2) Four major thematic ideas: (a) the exceptionally poignant non-harmonic octave leaps (unresolved appoggiaturas) that bathe Zerbinetta's line in emotionally vibrant orchestral sounds; (b) the melodic turn and ascending melody that is actually Zerbinetta's tune, *So war es mit Pagliazzo,* but so completely transformed as to be almost unrecognizable and certainly not frivolous in mood; (c) the use of the Composer's own theme, transformed through the use of longer sustained tones that drain away its nervousness and rhythmic drive and substitute the lyricism of Zerbinetta's melody; and finally (d) the descending, gently rocking melodic portion of the Composer's theme (not shown in example, but found in two subsequent measures).

The remaining lines of the first portion of the aria are set to a repetition of the Composer's theme (c), a further and typically Straussian intensification of the sensuousness of the descending portion of the theme (d) through the use of parallel thirds in the violins, and a soaring and then falling repetition of Zerbinetta's motive (b). The aria comes to a rest with Zerbinetta's words, *und bin doch so einsam,* as the same cadence that preceded the aria is repeated in a slightly intensified version. To the Composer's own theme in its new version (c) he sings his *Süßes, unbegreifliches Mädchen,* and as the orchestra proceeds with a long descending chromatic passage based on the second half of his theme (d), she says *törichtes Mädchen mußt du sagen.* A new and again exceedingly moving musical idea is introduced to emphasize her feelings as expressed in the lines, *das sich manchmal zu sehnen verstünde nach dem einen* (see ex. 67). This motive of "longing" rests solidly on the tonality of D♭ major. The use of D♭ seems to show that in Strauss's mind, Zerbinetta momentarily resembles Ariadne, for this is

Ex. 66

the key of Ariadne's transformation. Hofmannsthal could of course never have agreed to this view of Zerbinetta. The word *Treu* is further accented by the same longing motive as Zerbinetta sustains the word on a high G♭.

The Composer responds to the same motive, but the orchestra climbs into its highest region (with Zerbinetta's motive [b]), only to descend again with the reflective side of the Composer's theme as he says: *das Ir-*

Ex. 67

dische unvorhanden deiner Seele. The return of the aria to a free type of recapitulation of the ideas begins with Zerbinetta's line, *Du sprichst, was ich fühle,* and she sings these words to that most seductive of melodies in the aria, the motive (a) of soaring, sensuously colored dissonant octave leaps, which began the aria in the orchestral part. No one having heard this motive at the beginning of the aria and then repeated by Zerbinetta at this point can fail to feel the musical rapture that triumphs here in Strauss's music. We are carried away with Zerbinetta's charms, for she has become what she was not meant to be: a genuinely tender, misunderstood woman whose magnetic personality is more than anyone could resist. Because of the music, the audience cannot make the necessary distinction between what she appears to be and what Hofmannsthal intended her to be.

Zerbinetta's final words, *Vergißt du gleich wieder diesen einen Augenblick* round out the aria with a long, flowing vocal line immersed both in the motive of longing and the ascending dissonant octaves. The longing motive continues to be embedded in the sensuality of Zerbinetta's music as the Composer's melody reaches the first of two climaxes, one on *Aeonen,* only to be followed by an even greater soaring vocal climax on *ein einziger Augenblick.* The Composer's own theme ascends higher and higher, fading away in a totally transported melodic line that seems to have no end, for before we can determine how high it will go, the Music Teacher and other figures of the opera company come scurrying back onto the stage. (In reality this moment of broken transformation is restored and completed in the final scene of the opera.) The mood of transformation that had swept up the Composer (and the audience) in his momentary passionate attachment to Zerbinetta collapses with this sudden plunge back into the reality of preparations for performance.

The Composer, in a state of momentary transformation induced by love, bursts out with his exalted hymn of praise to the art of Music:

> *Seien wir wieder gut. Ich sehe jetzt alles mit anderen Augen!* [Let us be friends again. I now see everything differently!]/ *Die Tiefen des Daseins sind unermeßlich!* [The depths of existence are bottomless!]/ *Mein lieber Freund, es gibt manches auf der Welt,* [My dear friend, there are many things in this world,]/ *Das läßt sich nicht sagen.* [That cannot be expressed in words.]/ *Die Dichter unterlegen ja recht gute Worte.* [Poets can provide many very good words.]/ *Recht gute—jedoch—jedoch—jedoch—jedoch* [Very good words, yet—yet—yet—]/ *Mut ist in mir, Freund!* [I am filled with courage, friend!]/ *Die Welt ist lieblich und nicht fürchterlich dem Mutigen—* [The world is lovely and not fearful for those who are courageous—]/ *Was ist denn Musik?* [And what is music?]/ *Musik ist eine heilige Kunst, zu versammeln alle Arten von Mut wie Cherubim um einen strahlenden Thron!* [Music is a sacred art which unites all forms of courage like Cherubim around a radiant throne!]/ *Und darum ist sie die heilige unter den Künsten* [And therefore it is the sacred one of the arts]/ *Die heilige Musik!* [Sacred music!]

This aria serves as a recapitulation of the entire *Vorspiel,* for the orchestra returns to Composer's theme almost exactly as it was found at the opening of the opera (see ex. 68). However, one subtle change has occurred: both parts of the thematic identity are combined simultaneously, as the fourth measure of example 68 shows; the falling reflective portion follows immediately upon the bold ascending idea.

The emotional outburst at the beginning of the aria quiets down for the words, *Die Dichter unterlegen ja recht gute Worte.* An impressively sudden modulation to E^b major introduces in the bassoon the love music of Bacchus and Ariadne. For the fivefold statement of *jedoch,* Strauss uses a splendidly affirmative version of the "longing" motive from Zerbinetta's preceding aria. The tender, hesitant quality of the idea is changed into a positive, clearly masculine musical expression. As the aria reaches its first melodic climax, *Mut ist in mir, Freund,* the orchestra returns to the Composer's melody, *Du Venussohn gibst süßen Lohn,* perhaps to recall for us the Composer's inventiveness and his previous lack of courage, since we know the melody was abandoned and not used in the opera. The Composer reflects on *Was ist denn Musik,* and Strauss creates music of radiant beauty for a sentiment obviously very close to his heart. In the darker and quieter key of A^b major, the lovely words of this final section of the Composer's aria begin with veneration (see Ex. 69). On the word *Mut* Strauss begins to accompany

240

Ex. 68

the text with yet another meaningful contrapuntal interpretation of the
Composer's thematic materials: the reflective falling portion is placed
uppermost in the orchestra and the youthful, brash, passionate theme,
underneath, in a subordinate position (see ex. 69). The climax of this
aria, and indeed the climax of the whole role of the Composer is arrived
at with the words, *ist sie die heilige unter den Künsten, die heilige
Musik.* The orchestra pours forth with all of its tonal resources and includes in its thematic fabric the transformed Bacchus theme as it supports the Composer's high G on the word *Künsten*. This is followed by
a drawn out final cadence climbing to the Composer's highest note, a
B♭, a passage that will always remain one of the most thrilling moments
in the music of Strauss.

The *Vorspiel*, however, does not end in this state of emotional
exaltation. The final syllable of *Musik* brings forth a shrill whistle from
Zerbinetta as she and her partners rush onto the stage. This sight and
sound quickly restores the Composer to reality. The orchestra rushes
headlong into a triplet passage as the Composer cries, *Was ist das?
Wohin? Diese Kreaturen! In mein Heiligtum hinein* [What is this?
Where are they going? These creatures! Into my holy work]. When the
Music Teacher says, *Du hast es erlaubt* [You have permitted it], the or-
chestra refers for the last time to the original version of the Composer's
theme, and the Major-domo's timpani motive from the opening of the
Vorspiel is also heard, reminding us of the place and occasion. The
Composer's final words begin: *Ich durfte es nicht erlauben, du durftest*

mir nicht erlauben, es zu erlauben! Wer hieß dich mich zerren, mich! in diese Welt hinein? [I should not have allowed it. You should not have allowed me to allow it! Who bade you to drag me—me—into this world]. Then, without accompaniment except for crashing chords from the orchestra between commas, he shouts: *Laß mich erfrieren, verhungern, versteinen in der meinigen!* [Let me perish of cold, hunger, and petrifaction in my own world]. A whirlwind orchestral postlude accompanies the Composer's flight from the stage. The music, interestingly enough, is the same reflective, poetic motive of the Composer's original theme, now stuck in its tracks, moving nowhere yet going around and around in circles of terrifying derangement (see ex. 70).

Ex. 70

(läuft ab, verzweifelt. Musiklehrer sieht ihm nach, schüttelt den Kopf)

Sehr schnell

(Der Vorhang fällt rasch)

For those who know the *Vorspiel* well, Strauss's accomplishment will always be a favorite among his many works. At the same time this delicately balanced masterwork of recitative and aria, narration and overt musical emotionalism remains a striking paradox in operatic history. Like all of the Strauss compositions, the music is complex and highly organized in all of its elements. The effect of the *Vorspiel* is that of one great crescendo of musical values that begin at lowest ebb with the raising of the curtain and are carefully permitted to grow and intensify up to the Composer's aria. Each entrance of the Composer is rigorously controlled by Strauss to allow for the gradual musical buildup. Beginning with the initial secco recitative with the Lackey, through the glimpses at and then the completed version of his *Du Venussohn* song, the music slowly gathers momentum, as the Composer's emotions become more and more involved in his reflective interpretation of the opera *Ariadne*. The climax results from his meeting with and subsequent partial transformation through Zerbinetta. The thematic content of the Composer's music is in every sense the synthesis of himself as a human being: initially an incomplete young man with a split music personality of youthful brashness and quiet, artistic reflectiveness, he becomes musically complete with his two thematic sides combined as one, a poetic transformation in which the artistic or reflective side is most prominent. Finally, through the reality of the world

243

around him, the Composer returns to his opening status, but just as Bacchus seemed the same but was changed by Circe, the Composer is a more mature person after his encounter with Zerbinetta than he was at the beginning.

Thus, the *Vorspiel* is clearly a microcosm of Strauss's great genius in combining the dramatic, the lyrical, and the symphonic sides of his art. Paradoxically, audiences find the *Vorspiel* hard to understand, despite all that is inherently so perfect about the plan and balance of the work. The fault lies, as has been stated earlier, in the demands made upon the listener by the composer. Until one has had an opportunity to absorb and become truly familiar with the opera *Ariadne,* one cannot decipher the miraculous web of ideas or the overall musical plan of the *Vorspiel*.

Epilogue

The Hofmannsthal-Strauss collaboration on *Ariadne auf Naxos* seemed to have no end. Even before the premiere in Vienna in 1916 of *Ariadne* II, Hofmannsthal had suggested to Strauss that they reconsider the Molière comedy which had been abandoned in the revision. The poet was especially fond of Strauss's incidental music to the play, considering it his best work. This admiration, plus the encouragement of several friends including Hermann Bahr, convinced Hofmannsthal that he must save the music, and accordingly he set about revising his Molière adaptation under the new title *Der Bürger als Edelmann*.

This project, like everything else connected with *Ariadne auf Naxos,* was characterized by wide areas of disagreement between the collaborators. Strauss voiced deep concern that the new play with "Incidental music by Richard Strauss," would be theatrically a failure because Hofmannsthal seemed determined to avoid every good opportunity for the use of music. In many ways, this attempt to salvage something from the effort originally expended on the Molière play gave rise to more bitter confrontation than had occurred in their previous work together. It is a sad tale, leading to failure, just as Strauss foresaw. Hofmannsthal created a three-act play out of his original two-act version of *Le Bourgeois gentilhomme,* but the result was neither Molière nor effective comedy. Hofmannsthal successfully defeated Strauss's efforts at every turn. The production in Berlin on 9 April 1918, even with Reinhardt as director, was generally condemned, and it was withdrawn after a minimum number of performances.[1] The parallel with the original premiere of 1912 was complete: critics still dismissed the work as a bad play with good music. It also reemphasizes that Hofmannsthal's excessive confidence in Reinhardt's directorial genius was misplaced.

This epic struggle over the salvaging of all of the original *Ariadne auf Naxos* was finally closed when Strauss decided to arrange as an independent orchestral suite a major part of the incidental music, partly drawn from his music for the Molière play of *Ariadne* I and partly from

[1] For details of the lengthy verbal sparring between Hofmannsthal and Strauss during the work on *Der Bürger als Edelmann*, see Norman Del Mar's excellent discussion in his *Richard Strauss*, II (London 1969), 78-101. See also Hofmannsthal's letter to Strauss in which he condemns *Der Bürger als Edelmann* as a failure (*C.,* 304). The Vienna premiere on 1 October 1924 with Strauss himself conducting was likewise unsuccessful.

the new music he added to *Der Bürger als Edelmann*. This suite received its first performance in Vienna in January 1920 with Strauss conducting, and it has subsequently become accepted as one of the composer's major orchestral compositions. Thus, the incidental music, or at least the major part of it, was reclaimed from the debacle of Hofmannsthal's final attempt to preserve his original concept of the Molière.

Without doubt, no other opera by a major composer has had such an extraordinarily protracted, painful gestation and realization. Not even Beethoven's extensive labors in revising *Fidelio* can be compared to the struggles of these two artists to create a successful theater piece out of Hofmannsthal's original idea to experiment with a brief interim work, partly to occupy Strauss between major operatic ventures and partly to discover for himself how better to write a libretto. Equally protracted has been the public acceptance of the opera in major opera houses of the world. Among the many paradoxes of this great literary-musical masterpiece has been the fate of *Ariadne* II, a fate that could not be controlled by its authors.

Strauss as a practical artist and experienced man of the theater certainly foresaw from the beginning that the combination of a French classical play and an opera based on Greek myth would not receive the audience approval that had greeted a work such as *Der Rosenkavalier*. Nor could *Ariadne* II stimulate the kind of controversy and literary furor leading to the box office successes of *Salome* and *Elektra*. Nevertheless, Strauss plunged into the tasks of writing *Ariadne* the opera, and later the *Vorspiel,* with the best of his creative energy, and in the final analysis this curious work called forth from Strauss some of his most beautiful music.

Strauss as well as Hofmannsthal had good reason to be disappointed by the failure of *Ariadne* I, for it is a unique creation, an experiment of sheer ingenuity and originality, introducing to the theater new potentialities of expression and meaning hardly realized by any of their contemporaries or successors. It is impossible at this distance in time and without the opportunity to see the work on the stage to speculate on all the reasons for its failure. As has been shown, audiences and critics alike did not respond to the interweaving of forms and ideas. Conceivably, the unsuccessful nature of the comedy itself, evidenced by its later fate when performed alone, acted as a deterrent to the enjoyment of the opera. It is also true that there was a general failure to understand the work's deeper implications, but it seems unreasonable to attribute the lack of appeal primarily to this cause. How many spectators really grasp the musical and philosophical significance of Wagner's operas, and yet their popularity has never suffered on this account.

The final proof that there must be another explanation for the failure of *Ariadne* I is the continuing success of *Ariadne* II, which now forms part of the regular repertoire of most major opera houses. Even in this final version, the meaning of the plot is hardly obvious, as we have shown, and it is certain that opera audiences today do not understand its full implications any better than the contemporary audiences which received it coolly at the premiere in 1916. However, during the twenties the opera grew in popularity and continued to gain acceptance until today it ranks next to *Der Rosenkavalier* as one of the most popular of the Strauss-Hofmannsthal operas.

One historical development that must have adversely affected the initial success of *Ariadne* was the collapsing social and cultural patterns of Europe in the period before and after World War I. Strauss, at the time of composing *Ariadne auf Naxos*, witnessed the main stream of music taking new directions totally unsympathetic to his own musical convictions. In 1913 Stravinsky completed *Le sacre du printemps,* Schönberg's path was already leading him towards twelve-tone principles in his *Chamber Symphony* completed in 1906 and in the Op. 16, *Five Orchestra Pieces* of 1909. Bartok's own natural style, to some extent influenced by Strauss, had become both nationalistic and uncompromisingly dissonant, and Debussy's impressionism seemed to lead in yet another direction. Strauss was assaulted from all sides with an incredible variety of new trends; and it should be remembered that as one of the most prominent conductors of the time, he was fully aware of every musical trend even if he refused to conduct certain, to him, excessively modern scores.

Some may consider it presumptuous to compare Richard Strauss the composer in the period beginning about 1910 to Johann Sebastian Bach as he came to Leipzig in 1723. But there are similarities: both composers had reached the peak of their careers, both fully realized the magnitude of their previous work and looked for further acknowledgement of their abilities. Neither composer was particularly interested in the extraordinarily fluid musical world around him. In each case, a lengthy historical development had clearly entered the last stages of its decline: for Bach, the Baroque period, for Strauss, the Romantic age. Johann Sebastian Bach died in Leipzig largely ignored as a composer. Richard Strauss would also live to see himself passed by, becoming a historical figure—indeed, to some, a curiosity—in his own lifetime. But with Richard Strauss, fate was nevertheless not as cruel as with Bach, for in the early decades of this century he maintained vast influence, both through his conducting and through a legion of admirers and powerful musical friends, and his music was kept before the public. Nevertheless, time was working against him; critics began to whittle away at his reputation, attacking him for lacking a new style to match the most recent fads as well as genuine musical developments.

As our perspective begins to deepen into the history of music of this century, we can appreciate that Strauss was a giant among composers, with few equals in his lifetime. However, he suffered the consequences of historical change. Changing musical taste, changing social and political structures, these were part of the basis for the poor critical and audience receptions to Strauss's operas written after *Der Rosenkavalier*, not the composer's flagging musical inspiration. As the entire twentieth century becomes music history, and as part of our musical culture remains committed to past rather than contemporary musical achievements, and as we find that so many apparently radical musical departures no longer seem so radical, it becomes easier to accept Strauss's entire *œuvre* on its own terms, rather than in terms of what we think it should have been. In a sense, only now can the substance and genius of his scores stand in their own right, and it is hardly surprising that every major opera house of the world now performs regularly all of the major operas of Strauss, not just those written up to and including *Der Rosenkavalier*.

It is to be hoped that this book has shown *Ariadne auf Naxos* to be a work of its own time. It is one of the earliest neo-classical works in music, the first modern chamber opera, and it initiates stylistic elements of neo-classicism which dominate many of Richard Strauss's later compositions. Finally, it contains new aspects of musical style which Strauss continued to incorporate into later compositions. In the operas *Intermezzo, Die schweigsame Frau, Daphne,* and *Capriccio,* as well as the masterful final orchestral composition for strings, *Metamorphosen,* the neo-classical elements are direct outgrowths of the music style first explored in *Ariadne. Die Frau ohne Schatten* employs much of the *Ariadne* orchestra for the parts of that complicated work dealing with the unreal world of the Emperor and his wife. Both for Hofmannsthal's libretto, the most complex and abstract work written for Strauss, and for Strauss's music, *Die Frau ohne Schatten* becomes comprehensible only after one understands the substance of *Ariadne*.

Of course, for Strauss audiences earlier in the century, the shock of *Ariadne* was the totality of his musical about-face, which they had not anticipated, despite some of the clues to be found in *Der Rosenkavalier*. Every new opera by Strauss had become a European musical sensation. Yet what were audiences to think of an opera by Strauss, the commander of great orchestral forces found both in the famous tone poems and the earlier operas, the writer of the shockingly dissonant scores to *Salome* and *Elektra,* the composer of Viennese waltzes, not to mention the earthy, very real musical humor of *Der Rosenkavalier,* when this composer suddenly restricted himself to the austere orchestral resources of just thirty-six solo instrumentalists to produce an apparently confusing blend of static, pseudo-Baroque and pseudo-popular, Viennese-like music hall tunes? The shock to the audience resulted from its inability to assimilate the experience.

The more one hears and studies the score of *Ariadne auf Naxos,* the more one must marvel at the perfection and originality of the work. Even taking for granted that the actual surgery performed by the authors in revising the opera to fit together with the new *Vorspiel* left minor scars (especially in the scene of Bacchus's arrival), the opera must be evaluated as among Strauss's most vital and continually inspired creations. The originality has been frequently referred to: the genius of new effects for small orchestra, the freshness of approach to the whole problem of setting poetry in recitative style, the intensifying of the formal planning of a theater piece without unnecessarily relying on Wagner's leading motive organization, the sensitivity to vocal expressiveness, and the knowledge of the voice permitting the composer to create so masterfully the sheer virtuosity of Zerbinetta's coloratura aria.

Similarly, Hofmannsthal's libretto with its brilliant integration of the *Vorspiel* into the overall design of the opera, cannot but awaken profound appreciation at this demonstration of artistic skill. While the poet later felt that the text ultimately was too light to support the weight of Strauss's musical structure, nevertheless he considered the work worthy of acceptance in its final form.[2]

Despite its inauspicious beginnings, *Ariadne auf Naxos* grew into a work of major significance in the development of both artists. For Hofmannsthal, as for Strauss, this work is pivotal, not only in time[3] but also within the thematic and formal context of his overall production. This opera represents a plateau of achievement, climaxing the early years of growth and artistic experimentation and at the same time serving as the basis of the direction pursued in his later works. Almost all of Hofmannsthal's fundamental ideas occur in *Ariadne,* and its ultimate value lies in the fact that much of Hofmannsthal's mature world view is contained in this one work. His works, when analyzed in sequence, reveal an interlocking connection, as the young author struggled in successive writings to master certain problems pertaining to life and art that were his primary concern.

[2] "Ich habe die Ariadne sehr lieb, es ist doch ein Wesen besonderer Art. Sie hätte leicht viel schöner werden können, wenn ich mehr Verständnis für die besonderen Bedingungen der modernen Musik—meine Fantasie verweilt immer bei den alten, historisch gewordenen Formen—oder wenn Strauss mehr Voraussicht und Einsicht in das Ganze eines Kunstwerks besäße. Manches war berechnet, spieluhrhaft vorbeizuklingen, und nun da es große wenn auch nicht laute Musikstücke geworden sind, hat der Text nicht den Gehalt u. die Tragkraft, es ist wie wenn man ein Vogelhaus mit seinen dünnen Stäbchen u. Drahtzierarten zu den Dimensionen eines von Menschen bewohnten Lusthauses vergrößerte, das ist nicht schön. Es hätte der Musiker voraussehen müssen, daß er ein großes Menschenlusthaus, daraus zu machen nicht umhin können würde—dann hätte man das Project, den Bauplan ändern müssen, und alles wäre schöner geworden. Immerhin ist es ja so, daß man es wohl liebgewinnen kann." Quoted in Rudolf Hirsch "*Auf dem Weg zu Ariadne," Neue Zürcher Zeitung* (15 November 1970), 50.

[3] As the third of the six librettos completed by Hofmannsthal, *Ariadne* holds approximately the central position among his opera texts. This centrality is further underscored when one considers that the fourth opera, *Die Frau ohne Schatten,* is essentially an extension of the ideas worked out in *Ariadne* and thus may be viewed as a "sequel." Moreover, since Hofmannsthal's writings extend from 1890 to 1929, the period from 1911 to 1912, during which *Ariadne* was created, forms almost the precise chronological midpoint of his career.

By extracting the key terms from the interpretation of *Ariadne,* it becomes evident that the concepts of fidelity, transformation, human being versus the gods, remembering, forgetting, mutual love, death, life, non-comprehension between individuals, and the unity of life as a coincidence of opposites are central to the opera. How these basic qualities and problems of human existence came to be harmonized and reconciled in a meaningful way in *Ariadne* constitutes the history of Hofmannsthal's early work. These attributes of life had been present in various forms and under various guises in all of his writings from the beginning. Not until the discovery of the proper combination of these key phenomena in *Ariadne* was Hofmannsthal able to present a solution to the problem of fidelity (*Treue*), that had been central to his life and work from the outset of his career.[4] Thus, this opera attains a position of major significance in the framework of his writings, for it not only combines all of the important facets and dimensions of Hofmannsthal as artist and man but also unites them in such an integral, unified manner as to endow them with universal value. In view of this central importance of *Ariadne* to an understanding of Hofmannsthal, it is ironic that his name is hardly associated with the opera beyond the field of literary scholars. Musicians and audiences alike generally refer to *Ariadne,* and the other five operas as well, as Strauss operas, and the considerable contribution of Hofmannsthal to these works goes largely unrecognized.

One of the questions remaining to be considered is the role Hofmannsthal played in determining the musical style of *Ariadne.* Was his influence on Strauss decisive in forcing him to turn away from his previous compositional manner, as exhibited in *Elektra* and *Der Rosenkavalier?* Actually, there is nothing in the available sources to suggest that Strauss felt Hofmannsthal had forced him to take an artistic path not totally natural to him. The thesis of both recent English writers on Strauss, Norman Del Mar and William Mann,[5] that this was the case is a conjecture built primarily on the assumption that Strauss's compositional sympathies were more oriented to Wagner's literary and musical achievements. Yet, as has already been shown more than once,

---

[4] While Hofmannsthal's preoccupation with the theme of faithfulness has been documented in terms of one work or another by almost all of the major studies on Hofmannsthal, the most thorough examination of this theme to date has been made by Katharina Mommsen, "Treue und Untreue in Hofmannsthals Frühwerk," *Germanisch-Romansiche Monatsschrift,* NS 13 (1963), 306-34. Although she enumerates twenty-four specific works, ranging from *Gestern* (1891) to *Die ägyptische Helena* (1928), in which the theme of faithfulness or unfaithfulness plays an essential role, her detailed analysis of the theme is limited to the early works. She apparently failed to recognize the importance of its occurrence in *Ariadne,* where for the first time Hofmannsthal discovered the means to resolve the problem to his own satisfaction, and she failed to show that *Ariadne* represents the culmination of this theme in his works.

[5] William Mann, *Richard Strauss: A Critical Study of the Operas* (London, 1964), p. 167; Norman Del Mar, *Richard Strauss,* II, 3.

Strauss was not anxious to follow in Wagner's footsteps, but, quite on the contrary, sought a viable way around the masterworks of Wagner so that opera as an art form might continue to live. It is true that Hofmannsthal felt certain aspects of Strauss's operas prior to *Ariadne* had been detrimental to the understanding of the texts—which Strauss certainly agreed with—and that Hofmannsthal equated these problems with an over-all label of Wagnerism. Strauss himself humored Hofmannsthal's view and, for example, when Strauss announced the completion of *Frau ohne Schatten,* he told his poet: "Your *cri-de-coeur* against Wagnerian 'note-spinning' has touched my heart and has thrust open a door to an entirely new landscape where, guided by Ariadne and in particular the new Vorspiel, I hope to move forward wholly into the realm of un-Wagnerian emotional and human comic opera. . . . I promise you that I have now definitely stripped off the Wagnerian musical armour" (C., p. 262). This comment, like so many coming from Strauss is both jest and truth, encouragement and window dressing for his frequently hypersensitive, sometimes reluctant librettist. For Richard Strauss was not a Wagnerian composer, and obviously did not wear Wagnerian musical armour. Even his first and most nearly Wagnerian opera, *Guntram,* is more Wagnerian in story and poetic mood than actual compositional practices. Neither *Salome* nor *Elektra,* despite their large orchestra and considerable use of leading motives, resembles Wagner's concept of opera, nor does the musical style grow out of Wagnerian style.

Already in *Der Rosenkavalier,* Strauss's immersion in classical music, in which his own roots were deep, came to the fore, and there is in *Ariadne auf Naxos* a great deal that is Mozartian as well as reminiscent of French baroque music. It is just as possible to explain both the interest of Hofmannsthal in baroque theatrical style and Strauss's love of baroque and classical music as the result of the powerful cultural forces energizing the arts at the beginning of this century, rather than to ascribe Strauss's stylistic changes to the demands of his librettist. Strauss's reverence for Mozart, Beethoven, and Schubert, as well as other classic masters, was deeply engrained in his natural musical consciousness. In fact, quite clearly from the evidence in all of the operas succeeding *Der Rosenkavalier,* with the possible exception of *Arabella,* Strauss never again returned fully to the musical styles of his early works, and from this point his development was largely consistent with the musical implications of *Ariadne auf Naxos.* The classical frame—the aria forms, recitative, reduced orchestral forces, overt lyricism, and, after *Frau ohne Schatten* and *Arabella,* stories largely drawn from classical or other early historical periods—all show that Strauss could not have pursued the remainder of his career as a composer differently, with or without Hofmannsthal.[6]

[6] A final word about the classical foundation of Strauss's genius comes from his own pen,

In the final analysis, of course, it was with Hofmannsthal that Strauss made this change in direction,[7] and because it was Hofmannsthal, Strauss was able to work with stimulating poetry of literary quality. Even though the genesis of *Ariadne* was long and continuously frustrating, Strauss found the inner strength and inspiration to return each time to this work with renewed enthusiasm.

On the basis of its extenuated genesis, its daring blend of *commedia dell'arte* and grand opera, its central importance in the individual careers of both Hofmannsthal and Strauss as well as in their collaborations, and its ultimate success in the theater, *Ariadne auf Naxos* is a uniquely significant work of art. The final question is whether this work created a new genre, as Hofmannsthal hoped it

in a letter that has not previously been noted for its importance. In the summer of 1945 Strauss, in reflecting on his career in a letter to a local school director, Ernst Reisinger, said: ". . . die Liebe zu Griechenland und zur Antike ist mir geblieben und hat sich immer gesteigert, seit ich durch die Munifizenz meines braven Onkels: des Bierbrauers Georg Pschorr, im Jahre 1891 zur Herstellung meiner durch zwei Lungenentzündungen gefährdeten Gesundheit auf acht Monate nach Ägypten reisen durfte und vorher drei Wochen in Griechenland verbrachte. Von dem Augenblick an, als ich, von Brindisi kommend, auf dem italienischen Dampfer Corfu die blauen Berge Albaniens erblickte, bin ich germanischer Grieche geblieben bis heute, da ich auf künstlerische Arbeiten zurückblicken kann, die wie "Ariadne", "Ägyptische Helena", "Elektra", "Daphne" und die "Liebe der Danae" dem Genius des griechischen Volkes huldigen und mit Stolz unterschriebe ich mich mit dem vor etwa 20 Jahren verliehenen Titel: 'Ehrenbürger der Insel Naxos' und trage gerne das Großkreuz des hohen griechischen Christus-Ordens." Franz Grasberger ed., *Der Strom der Töne trug mich fort: Die Welt um Richard Strauss in Briefen* (Tutzing, 1967), p. 439.

[7] Hofmannsthal did credit himself for forcing Strauss to a changed style: "It does me good to think that I, who hardly consider myself as standing even at the extreme periphery of your art, should have found—with that instinct which is the common bond between all creative artists, over the heads, so to speak, of the rest of the crowd—the right thing to do in producing this particular work which literally forced upon you a definite style, only to give you back your freedom more fully on a higher plane; and that I should in this way have fulfilled the promise I made to myself in devising this plot, a promise affecting the musician . . ."(*C.,* 132-33). Later Hofmannsthal stated ". . . I still draw lasting pleasure from the thought that I forced upon you so unusual and important a work" (*C.,* 147). In 1924 in discussing the successful premiere of Strauss's own opera *Intermezzo* Hofmannsthal commented: "What affects me especially in this matter is this: you have striven here for a new style (starting from what is suggested in the *Ariadne Vorspiel* and to some extent also of course from *Rosenkavalier*), and you have achieved what you wanted. That is very much. From your conversation fourteen months ago, as we walked up and down one evening at Ischl, I was able to gather very clearly what you had been trying to do, and today I know that it has been realized. This immediately gives me great confidence and hope for *Helena,* to which I am much attached. Although you will not be spared there the necessity of having to search once more for a new style (since one can never rest on one's laurels), certain features of what you have done can in the future be relied upon as vested and indefeasible qualities. This is the real point of artistic development and in this sense one can speak of a master, indeed a master above all, learning and growing through what he has learnt. Among the features from which Helena will reap vast gain I count your wise and mature attitude towards the libretto which shows itself in the fact that every single word can be understood (this is stressed unanimously by all critics). This must be the result of your having learnt to achieve the desired effect with fewer means, a hallmark of every masterly 'final' style" (*C.,* 393).

would, renewing in modern garb features of the Austro-Bavarian baroque tradition, in which the art of both himself and Strauss were rooted. The answer is negative, and *Ariadne* remained, as Hofmannsthal termed it, "an unrepeatable experiment" (*C.,* 149). Actually, he was convinced in principle that nothing in the realm of art should ever be repeated. Despite the poet's expectations that the new *Vorspiel* pointed the direction that their collaboration should follow in the future (*C.,* 258) and his hope that Strauss's new technique might "develop into a 'third manner' and perhaps produce works of lasting value in a yet almost unknown genre" (*C.,* 263), none of these promises were fulfilled. While stylistic features of the *Vorspiel* were continued in *Daphne, Die schweigsame Frau, Intermezzo,* and possibly to a lesser degree in *Die ägyptische Helena* and *Arabella,* no attempt was made to continue the search for a new genre and no echo was awakened in the works of other writers and composers.

Nevertheless, in its blending of poetic and musical forms, and in its successful recreation of a historical milieu both poetic and musical in terms of absolutely modern technique and style, *Ariadne auf Naxos* is a masterwork of twentieth-century theater. One sees elements of the modern grotesque drama as well as certain logical outcomes of Wagner's concept of the totally unified theatrical experience, the so-called *Gesamtkunstwerk.* Most importantly, *Ariadne auf Naxos* combines two worlds of art: the exalted poetry of Greek myth, the impassioned noble musical style at once reminiscent of baroque opera and the previous superb Straussian vocal lyricism; but there is also the popular cultural forms of the dance hall figures, the street plays of the *commedia dell'arte,* the coffee house instrumental ensembles, the theater soubrette, and Italian eighteenth-century comic opera. Not surprisingly, such daring and imaginative innovations all at one time mystified audiences.

Today it is easy to recognize that Hofmannsthal's dramatic concept and Strauss's brilliant musical realization were far in advance of theatrical developments of their generation, and only since World War II have these elements become commonplace in the theaters of the world. It is not surprising, therefore, that during the same period *Ariadne auf Naxos* has been received with ever-growing popularity in both Europe and the United States. The very success Hofmannsthal and Strauss knew in their hearts and minds would one day come to this work has occurred,[8] ironically, after the collapse of Austria and Germany, and has been only possible in a new artistic climate characterized by the very cultural collision Hofmannsthal and Strauss had poetized with such eloquence decades earlier.

[8] In 1918, before *Ariadne* had yet achieved any noteworthy success, Hofmannsthal wrote to Strauss ". . . of all these works, this is the one which, believe me, *possesses the strongest guarantee that it will endure.* From this point the road leads on, even for me, when I think of you; not one road but several." (*C.,* 299).

Hugo von Hofmannsthal

A Select Bibliography

The fifteen-volume set *Gesammelte Werke in Einzelausgaben* edited by Herbert Steiner and published by S. Fischer Verlag, Frankfurt am Main, 1945—1960 is the source of all quotations from Hofmannsthal's works. The text of *Ariadne auf Naxos* used as the basis for the present work is contained in *Lustspiele* III. Other primary sources include Max Reinhardt's *Regiebuch, Ariadne auf Naxos* (Berlin, 1912), and Hofmannsthal's adaptation *Der Bürger als Edelmann* (Berlin, 1918), which also appears in *Lustspiele* III. The various correspondences of Strauss and Hofmannsthal that have been consulted will be found listed under the respective entries for the composer and the poet.

Alewyn, Richard. *Über Hugo von Hofmannsthal.* Göttingen, 1958.

Anstett, Jean Jacques. "A Propos d'*Ariadne auf Naxos.*" In *Un Dialog des Nations.* Munich, Paris, 1967, 159-89.

Auernheimer, Raoul. "Hugo von Hofmannsthal als österreichische Erscheinung," *Die Neue Rundschau,* 40 (1929), 660-66.

-----. "Der Bürger als Edelmann," *Neue Freie Presse* (3 October 1924), 1-2.

Baker, George M. "Hofmannsthal and Greek Tragedy," *Journal of English and Germanic Philology,* 12 (1913), 383-406.

Baumann, Gerhart. "Hugo von Hofmannsthal: Betrachtungen zu seiner dramatischen Dichtung," *Der Deutschunterricht,* 5 (1957), 36-55.

-----. "Hugo von Hofmannsthal: 'Elektra'," *Germanisch-Romanische Monatsschrift,* 40 (1959), 157-82.

-----. *Rudolf Kassner, Hugo von Hofmannsthal: Kreuzwege des Geistes.* Stuttgart, 1964.

Beau, Albin Eduard. "Hofmannsthals Wendung zur Oper," *Libris et Litteris: Festschrift für Hermann Tiemann zum 60. Geburtstag,* eds. Christian Voigt and Erich Zimmermann, pp. 318-24. Hamburg, 1959.

Berendsohn, Walter A. *Der Impressionismus Hofmannsthals als Zeiterscheinung.* Hamburg, 1920.

Berger, Dorothea. "Hugo von Hofmannsthals Gestalt im Wandel der Jahre," *Wort in der Zeit,* 2 (1956), 385-99.

Bergstraesser, Arnold. "Hofmannsthal und der europäische Gedanke," *Kieler Universitätsreden,* II (1951), 5-24.

-----. "The Holy Beggar: Religion and Society in Hugo von Hofmannsthal's 'Great World Theatre of Salzburg'," *The Germanic Review*, 20 (1945), 261-86.

Bianquis, Geneviève. "Hofmannsthal et la France," *Revue de Littérature Comparée*, 27 (1953), 301-18.

-----. "L'Image de Venise dans l'Oeuvre de Hofmannsthal," *Revue de Littérature Comparée*, 32 (1958), 321-26.

Bie, Oskar. "Elektra," *Die Neue Rundschau*, 20 (1909), 589-93.

Blei, Franz. "Aus einer Schrift: Hofmannsthal und diese Zeit," *Hyperion* (Series II), 2 (1909), 47-62.

Block, Haskell M. "Hugo von Hofmannsthal and the Symbolist Drama," *Wisconsin Academy of Sciences, Arts and Letters*, 48 (1959), 161-78.

Bollnow, Otto F. "Zum Lebensbegriff des jungen Hugo von Hofmannsthal," *Archiv für Literatur und Volksdichtung*, 1 (1949), 50-62.

Borchardt, Rudolf. *Prosa*, I. Stuttgart, 1957.

Brand, Olga. *Traum und Wirklichkeit bei Hugo von Hofmannsthal*. Diss. Münster, 1932.

Brandes, Georg. "Griechische Gestalten in neuerer Poesie." *Nord und Süd*, 125 (1908), 5-24.

Braun, Felix. *Das musische Land*. Innsbruck, 1952.

Brecht, Erika. *Erinnerungen an Hugo von Hofmannsthal*. Innsbruck, 1946.

Brecht, Walther. "Grundlinien im Werke Hugo von Hofmannsthals." *Euphorion* (Suppl.), 15-16 (1923), 164-79.

-----. "Hugo von Hofmannsthals 'Ad me ipsum' und seine Bedeutung," *Jahrbuch des Freien Deutschen Hochstifts* (1930), 319-53.

-----. "Über Hugo von Hofmannsthals *Bergwerk zu Falun*," *Corona*, 3 (1932-1933), 210-35.

Brinkmann, Richard. "Hofmannsthal und die Sprache," *Deutsche Vierteljahrsschrift*, 35 (1961), 69-95.

Broch, Hermann. *Hofmannsthal und seine Zeit*. Munich, 1964.

Burckhardt, Carl J. *Erinnerungen an Hofmannsthal und Briefe des Dichters*. Basel, 1949.

-----. "Begegnungen mit Hugo von Hofmannsthal," *Die Neue Rundschau*, 65 (1914), 341-57.

-----. "Zu Hugo von Hofmannsthals Lustspiel *Der Schwierige*," *Die Neue Rundschau*, 71 (1960), 133-37.

Burger, Hilde. "French Influences on Hugo von Hofmannsthal," *Comparative Literature*, 2 (1959), 691-97.

-----. "Hofmannsthal's Debt to Molière," *Modern Languages*, 39 (1958), 56-61.

Butler, E. M. "Hugo von Hofmannsthal's *Elektra*: A Graeco-Freudian Myth," *Journal of the Warburg Institute*, 2 (1938), 164-75.

Chelius-Göbbels, Annemarie. *Formen mittelbarer Darstellung im dramatischen Werk Hugo von Hofmannsthals*. Deutsche Studien, 6.

Meisenheim am Glan, 1968.

Cohn, Hilde D. "Hofmannsthals Libretti," *The German Quarterly,* 35 (1962), 149-64.

-----. "Mehr als schlanke Leier: Zur Entwicklung dramatischer Formen in Hugo von Hofmannsthals Dichtung," *Jahrbuch der Deutschen Schiller-Gesellschaft,* 8 (1964), 280-308.

Corrigan, Robert W. "Character as Destiny in Hofmannsthal's *Elektra,*" *Modern Drama,* 2 (1959), 17-28.

Coughlan, Brian. "The Cultural-Political Development of Hugo von Hofmannsthal During the First World War." *Publications of the English Goethe Society,* NS 27 (1958), 1-32.

-----. *Hofmannsthal's Festival Dramas.* Cambridge, 1964.

-----. "Traditionelle Form und eigener Stil im Spätwerk Hugo von Hofmannsthals," *Stil- und Formprobleme in der Literatur: Vorträge des VII. Kongresses der Internationalen Vereinigung für moderne Sprachen und Literaturen in Heidelberg,* pp. 492-98. Heidelberg, 1959.

Curtius, Ernst Robert. "Hofmannsthal und die Romanität," *Die Neue Rundschau,* 40 (1929), 654-59.

Curtius, Ludwig. *Deutsche und antike Welt.* Stuttgart, 1958.

Dabatschek, Heinz H. *Hugo von Hofmannsthal als Dramatiker.* Diss. Vienna, 1957.

Daviau, Donald G. "Hugo von Hofmannsthal's Pantomime: *Der Schüler,*" *Modern Austrian Literature,* 1/1 (1968), 4-30.

-----. "Hugo von Hofmannsthal and the Chandos Letter," *Modern Austrian Literature,* 4/2 (1971), 28-44.

Diebold, Bernhard. "Die ironische *Ariadne* und der *Bürger als Edelmann,*" *Deutsche Bühne. Jahrbuch der Frankfurter Städtischen Bühnen,* 1 (1919), 219-44.

Dieckmann, Liselotte. "The Dancing Electra," *Texas Studies in Language and Literature,* 2 (1960), 3-16.

Eberlein, Kurt Karl. "Das Problem des Neubarock: Bemerkungen zur *Ariadne auf Naxos,*" *Das Nationaltheater,* 5 (1932), 12-19.

Erken, Günther. "Hofmannsthal-Chronik," *Literaturwissenschaftliches Jahrbuch,* NS 3 (1962), 239-313.

-----. *Hofmannsthals dramatischer Stil.* Tübingen, 1967.

Ernst, Erhard. "Hugo von Hofmannsthal und der Begriff 'Asien'," *Wirkendes Wort,* 16/4 (1966), 266-73.

Esselborn, Karl G. *Hofmannsthal und der antike Mythos.* Munich, 1969.

Exner, Richard. *Hugo von Hofmannsthals "Lebenslied": Eine Studie.* Heidelberg, 1964.

von Faber du Faur, Curt. "Der Abstieg in den Berg—Zu Hofmannsthals *Bergwerk zu Falun,*" *Monatshefte,* 42 (1951), 1-14.

Fahrner, Rudolf. *Dichterische Visionen menschlicher Urbilder in Hofmannsthals Werk.* Ankara, 1956.

Feise, Ernst. "Gestalt und Problem des Toren in Hugo von Hofmannsthals Werk." *The Germanic Review,* 3 (1928), 218-61.

-----. "Philosophische Motive im Werk des jungen Hofmannsthal," *Monatshefte,* 37 (1945), 31-39.

Fiechtner, Helmut A. "Hofmannsthal der Europäer," *Wort in der Zeit,* 2 (1956), 33-40.

-----, ed. *Hugo von Hofmannsthal, die Gestalt des Dichters im Spiegel der Freunde.* 2nd ed. Bern, 1963.

Fiedler, Leonard M. "Hofmannsthal, Reinhardt und Molière," *Hofmannsthal-Forschungen,* 1 (Basel, 1957), 48-58.

-----. *Max Reinhardt und Molière.* Salzburg, 1972.

Fleischmann, Benno. *Max Reinhardt: Die Wiedererweckung des Barocktheaters.* Vienna, 1948.

Freudenberg, Günther. *Die Zeit als dichterische Erscheinung im Werke Hugo von Hofmannsthals.* Diss. Freiburg im Breisgau, 1951.

Friedmann, Lilith. *Die Gestaltung des Ariadnestoffes von der Antike bis zur Neuzeit.* Diss. Vienna, 1933.

Garten, Hugh F. "Hofmannsthal as a Librettist," *Opera,* 1 (1950), 15-21.

Gilbert, Mary E. "Hugo von Hofmannsthal and England," *German Life and Letters,* 1 (1936-1937), 182-92.

Goff, Penrith B. "Poetry and Life in the Early Criticism of Hugo von Hofmannsthal." In: *Literature and Society,* ed. Bernice Slote. Lincoln: University of Nebraska Press, 1963, 213-26.

Goldschmit, Rudolf. *Die Erfahrung der Vergänglichkeit bei Hofmannsthal.* Diss. Munich, 1952.

Gräwe, Karl Dietrich. *Sprache, Musik und Szene in "Ariadne auf Naxos" von Hugo von Hofmannsthal und Richard Strauss.* Diss. Munich, 1969.

Gregor, Joseph, ed. *Meister und Meisterbriefe um Hermann Bahr.* Vienna, 1947.

Grether, Ewald. "Die Abenteurergestalt bei Hugo von Hofmannsthal," *Euphorion,* 48 (1954), 171-209.

Guddat, Kurt Herbert. "Hugo von Hofmannsthal: Eine Studie zur dichterischen Schaffensweise." Diss. Ohio State University, 1959.

Haas, Willy. *Hugo von Hofmannsthal.* Berlin, 1964.

Hagelberg, Lilli. "Hofmannsthal und die Antike." *Zeitschrift für Aesthetik und Allgemeine Kunstwissenschaft,* 17 (1923-1924), 18-62.

Hamburger, Michael. "Hofmannsthals Bibliothek: Ein Bericht," *Euphorion,* 55 (1960), 15-76.

-----. *Hugo von Hofmannsthal: Zwei Studien.* Göttingen, 1964.

-----. "Hofmannsthal und England." *Zwischen den Sprachen: Essays und Gedichte.* Frankfurt am Main, 1966, 102-120.

Hammelmann, Hanns. *Hugo von Hofmannsthal.* London, 1957.

Harden, Maximilian. *"Elektra," Die Zukunft,* 12 (1904), 349-58.

Heberle, Johannes A. *Hugo von Hofmannsthal: Beobachtungen über seinen Stil.* Enschede, 1937.

Hederer, Edgar. *Hugo von Hofmannsthal.* Frankfurt am Main, 1960.

Hering, Gerhard F. "Hofmannsthal der Lehrer," *Deutsche Beiträge,* 3 (1949), 4-13.

-----. "Hofmannsthal und das Theater," *Der Ruf zur Leidenschaft.* Cologne, 1959, 43-82.

Heuschele, Otto. *Hugo von Hofmannsthal: Dank und Gedächtnis.* Freiburg im Breisgau, 1949.

Hill, Claude. "Hugo von Hofmannsthal: A Classic of German Poetry in the Twentieth Century," *Universitas,* 4 (1961), 63-77.

Hillard, Gustav. "Casanova und ein Ende," *Merkur,* 19 (1965), 997-99.

Hilpert, Constantin. "Eine stilpsychologische Untersuchung an Hugo von Hofmannsthal," *Zeitschrift für Aesthetik und Allgemeine Kunstwissenschaft,* 3 (1908), 361-93.

Hinrichs, Else. *Das Verhältnis von Kunst und Leben in der österreichischen Dichtung von Franz Grillparzer bis Hugo von Hofmannsthal.* Diss. Hannover, 1954.

Hirsch, Rudolf. "Auf dem Weg zu 'Ariadne'," *Neue Zürcher Zeitung* (15 November 1970), 49-50.

Hladny, Ernst. "Hugo von Hofmannsthals Griechenstücke," *Jahresbericht des königlichen Staatsgymnasiums in Loeben,* 13 (1910-1911), 5-26.

Höck, Wilhelm. *Das Problem von Formen und Form bei Hugo von Hofmannsthal.* Diss. Munich, 1954.

Hofmann, Werner. "Hofmannsthal als Kunstkritiker," *Wort in der Zeit,* 1 (1955), 39-45.

von Hofmannsthal, Hugo. *Gesammelte Werke in Einzelausgaben,* ed. Herbert Steiner. 15 vols. Frankfurt am Main, 1945-1960.

-----. *Briefe 1890-1909,* 2 vols. Berlin, Vienna, 1935, 1937.

-----. and Leopold von Andrian. *Briefwechsel,* ed. Walter H. Perl. Frankfurt am Main, 1968.

----- and Edgar Karg von Bebenburg. *Briefwechsel,* ed. Mary J. Gilbert. Frankfurt am Main, 1966.

----- and Eberhard von Bodenhausen. *Briefe der Freundschaft,* ed. Dora Freifrau von Bodenhausen. Düsseldorf, 1953.

----- and Rudolf Borchardt. *Briefwechsel,* ed. Herbert Steiner. Frankfurt am Main, 1954.

----- and Carl J. Burckhardt. *Briefwechsel,* ed. Carl J. Burckhardt. Frankfurt am Main, 1956.

----- and Stefan George. *Briefwechsel zwischen George und Hofmannsthal,* ed. Robert Boehringer. 2nd ed. Munich, 1953.

----- and Willy Haas. *Ein Briefwechsel,* ed. Rolf Italiander. Frankfurt am Main, 1968.

----- and Harry Graf Kessler. *Briefwechsel 1898-1929,* ed. Hilde Burger. Frankfurt am Main, 1968.

258

----- and Helene von Nostitz. *Briefwechsel*, ed. Oswald von Nostitz. Frankfurt am Main, 1965.

----- and Richard Strauss. *Briefwechsel*, ed. Willi Schuh. Zürich, 1964.

----- and Richard Strauss. *The Correspondence between Richard Strauss and Hugo von Hofmannsthal*, ed. Franz and Alice Strauss, trans. Hanns Hammelmann and Ewald Osers. London, 1961.

Hohoff, Curt. "Hofmannsthals Lustspiele," *Akzente*, 2 (1955), 369-83.

Holländer, Hans. "Hugo von Hofmannsthal als Opernlibrettist," *Zeitschrift für Musik*, 96 (1929), 551-54.

Hubalek, Elisabeth. *Hermann Bahr im Kreise Hofmannsthals und Reinhardts*. Diss. Vienna, 1953.

Jacoby, Karl. *Hugo von Hofmannsthal Bibliographie*. Berlin, 1936.

Jászi, Andrew. "Die Idee des Lebens in Hofmannsthals Jugendwerk 1890-1900," *Germanic Review*, 24 (1949), 81-107.

Jens, Walter. *Hofmannsthal und die Griechen*. Tübingen, 1955.

Joubert, M. "Hofmannsthal and his Collaboration with Strauss," *Contemporary Review*, 136 (1929), 632-37.

Kessler, Walter. *Hugo von Hofmannsthals Beziehungen zur bildenden Kunst*. Diss. Freiburg, Switzerland, 1948.

Kikuchi, Takehiro. "Der Dichter Hugo von Hofmannsthal und sein Lebenswerk in der geistigen Situation unserer Zeit," *Universitas*, 20 (1965), 499-506.

Knaus, Jakob. *Hofmannsthals Weg zur Oper "Die Frau ohne Schatten."* Berlin, 1971.

Kobel, Erwin. *Hugo von Hofmannsthal*. Frankfurt am Main, 1970.

Koch, Franz. "Hofmannsthals Lebens- und Weltgefühl," *Jahrbuch des freien deutschen Hochstifts* (1930), 257-318.

Kommerell, Max. *Hugo von Hofmannsthal: Eine Rede*. Frankfurt am Main, 1930.

Könneker, Barbara. "Die Funktion des Vorspiels in Hofmannsthals *Ariadne auf Naxos*," *Germanisch-Romanische Monatschrift*, NS 20 (1972), 124-41.

Konrad, Gustav. "Österreichische Bewahrung in der Essayistik Hofmannsthals," *Festschrift zum 75. Geburtstag von Hermann August Korff*, ed. Joachim Müller. Leipzig, 1957, 279-90.

Krumbach, Wilhelm. "Hofmannsthal über das Wesen der Oper," *Neue Zeitschrift für Musik*, 120 (1959), 13-15.

Kuna, F. M. "Wie modern ist Hugo von Hofmannsthal," *Literatur und Kritik*, 9-10 (Dec., 1966), 77-88.

Laubach, Jakob. "Hofmannsthals Turm der Selbstbewahrung," *Wirkendes Wort*, 4 (1954), 257-68.

Lehn, Marie Therese. "Tragedy and Comedy in Hofmannsthal's Dramatic Works." Diss. Washington University, 1959.

Lenz, Eva-Marie. *Hugo von Hofmannsthals mythologische Oper "Die Ägyptische Helena."* Tübingen, 1972.

Lewis, Hanna Ballin. "Hofmannsthal and Browning," *Comparative*

Literature, 19 (1967), 142-59.

-----. "Hofmannsthal and Milton," *Modern Language Notes,* 87 (1972), 731-42.

Llewellyn, R. T. "Hofmannsthal's Nihilism," *Modern Language Review,* 61 (1966), 250-59.

Mauser, Wolfram. *Bild und Gebärde in der Sprache Hofmannsthals.* Vienna, 1961.

-----. "Hofmannsthal und Molière," *Innsbrucker Beiträge zur Kulturwissenschaft,* Sonderheft 20 (Innsbruck, 1964), 1-16.

Mayer, Hans. "Hugo von Hofmannsthal und Richard Strauss," *Ansichten zur Literatur der Zeit.* Hamburg, 1962, 9-32.

Mehring, Franz. "Hofmannsthals *Die Hochzeit der Sobeide* und 'Der Abenteurer'," *Neue Zeit,* 17 (1898-1899), 22-24; repr. in *Gesammelte Schriften,* XI (Berlin, 1961), 527-30.

Mell, Max. "Hofmannsthals Werk," *Die Neue Rundschau,* 40 (1929), 634-47.

Metzeler, Werner. *Ursprung und Krise von Hofmannsthals Mystik.* Munich, 1956.

Meyer-Benfey, Heinrich. "Die Elektra des Sophokles und ihre Erneuerung durch Hofmannsthal," *Neue Jahrbücher für das klassische Altertum,* 23 (1920), 159-70.

Miles, David H. *Hofmannsthals Novel "Andreas": Memory and Self.* Princeton, 1972.

Moeller, Jack Raymond. "Hofmannsthal and Romanticism." Diss. Princeton University, 1955.

Mommsen, Katharina. "Treue und Untreue in Hofmannsthals Frühwerken," *Germanisch-Romanische Monatsschrift,* NS 13 (1963) 306-34.

Mühlher, Robert. *"Der Rosenkavalier—Ariadne auf Naxos,"* In *Österreichische Dichter seit Grillparzer,* Vienna, 1973, 312-54.

Müller, Paul Werner. *Hugo von Hofmannsthals Lustspieldichtung.* Diss. Basel, 1935.

Nadler, Josef. "Hofmannsthal und das Sozialproblem," *Die Neue Rundschau,* 40 (1929), 648-54.

-----. "Hugo von Hofmannsthal: Gedenkrede, gehalten in Königsberg, Oktober, 1929." *Corona,* 2 (1931), 206-17.

Naef, Karl J. *Hugo von Hofmannsthal: Wesen und Werk.* Zürich, 1938.

Nagl, Johann Willibald, Jakob Seidler, and Eduard Castle, eds. *Deutsch-Österreichische Literaturgeschichte,* IV. Vienna, 1937.

Nagler, Alois M. "Hugo von Hofmannsthal und das Theater," *Maske und Kothurn,* 5 (1959), 97-106.

Naumann, Walter. *Hofmannsthal—der jüngste deutsche Klassiker.* Darmstadt, 1967.

-----. "Drei Wege der Erlösung in Hofmannsthals Werken," *The Germanic Review,* 19 (1944), 150-55.

-----. "Die Form des Dramas bei Grillparzer und Hofmannsthal,"

Deutsche Vierteljahrsschrift, 33 (1959), 20-37.

-----. "Hofmannsthals Auffassung von seiner Sendung als Dichter," *Monatshefte,* 39 (1947), 184-87.

-----. "Hofmannsthals Verhältnis zur Tradition," *Deutsche Rundschau,* 7 (1959), 612-25.

-----. "Das Visuelle und das Plastische bei Hofmannsthal," *Monatshefte,* 37 (1945), 159-69.

Nehring, Wolfgang. *Die Tat bei Hofmannsthal: Eine Untersuchung zu Hofmannsthals großen Dramen.* Stuttgart, 1966.

Neisser, Artur. "Ariadne auf Naxos," *Bühne und Welt,* 15 (1912), 153-58.

Niebuhr, Walter. *Das Problem der Einsamkeit im Werke von Hugo von Hofmannsthal und Stefan George.* Diss. Kiel, 1949.

Nolte, Fritz. *Der Todesbegriff bei Rilke, Hofmannsthal, Mann.* Diss. Heidelberg, 1934.

Norman, F., ed. *Hofmannsthal: Studies in Commemoration.* London, 1963.

Norton, Roger C. "Hofmannsthal's 'Magische Werkstätte': Unpublished Notebooks from the Harvard Collection," *The Germanic Review,* 36 (1961), 50-64.

Obenauer, Karl Justus. "Hugo von Hofmannsthal: Eine Studie über den ästhetischen Menschen," *Preußische Jahrbücher,* 173 (1918), 19-51.

Oswald, Victor A., Jr. "Hofmannsthal's Collaboration with Molière," *The Germanic Review,* 29 (1954), 18-30.

Pabst, Valentin. *Hugo von Hofmannsthals Weg und Wandlung vom Lyriker zum Dramatiker.* Diss. Würzburg, 1952.

Pannwitz, Rudolf. "Hofmannsthals Komödien," *Blätter des deutschen Theaters,* 4 (1918), 209-12.

Perl, Walter H. "Hofmannsthal und Andrian: Spiegelung einer Freundschaft," *Die Neue Rundschau,* 73 (1962), 505-29.

Pestalozzi, Karl. *Sprachskepsis und Sprachmagie im Werk des jungen Hofmannsthal.* Zürich, 1958.

Pörnbacher, Karl. *Hofmannsthal-Strauss "Der Rosenkavalier."* Munich, 1964.

Pulver, Elsbeth. *Hofmannsthals Schriften zur Literatur.* Bern, 1956.

Razumovsky, Andreas. "Über den Text des Rosenkavalier," In *Zeugnisse—Theodor W. Adorno zum sechzigsten Geburtstag,* ed. Max Horkheimer, pp. 225-40. Frankfurt am Main, 1963.

Requadt, Paul "Hofmannsthals Lustspiel *Der Unbestechliche,*" *Wirkendes Wort,* 13 (1963), 222-29.

-----. "Sprachverleugnung und Mantelsymbolik im Werke Hofmannsthals," *Deutsche Vierteljahrsschrift,* 29 (1955), 255-83.

Reuschel, Karl. "Über Bearbeitungen der Geschichte des Bergmanns von Falun," *Studien zur Vergleichenden Literaturgeschichte,* 3 (1903), 1-28.

Rey, William H. "Dichter und Abenteurer bei Hugo von Hofmannsthal," *Euphorion,* 49 (1955), 56-69.

-----. "Die Drohung der Zeit in Hofmannsthals Frühwerk," *Euphorion,* 48 (1954), 280-310.

-----. "Eros und Ethos in Hofmannsthals Lustspielen," *Deutsche Vierteljahrsschrift,* 30 (1956), 449-73.

-----. *Weltentzweiung und Weltversöhnung in Hofmannsthals Griechischen Dramen.* Philadelphia, 1962.

Rheinländer-Schmitt, Hildegard. *Dekadenz und ihre Überwindung bei Hugo von Hofmannsthal.* Diss. Münster, 1936.

Ritter, Frederick. *Hugo von Hofmannsthal und Österreich.* Heidelberg, 1967.

Rösch, Ewald. *Die Komödien Hofmannsthals: Die Entfaltung ihrer Sinnstruktur aus dem Thema der Daseinsstufen.* Marburg, 1963.

Ryan, Judith. "Die 'Allomatische Lösung': Gespaltene Persönlichkeit und Konfiguration bei Hugo von Hofmannsthal," *Deutsche Vierteljahrsschrift,* 44 (1970), 189-207.

Rychner, Max. "Hofmannsthal und diese Zeit", *Die Neue Schweizer Rundschau,* 2 (1959), 561-66.

Sayler, Oliver M., ed. *Max Reinhardt and his Theatre.* New York, 1926.

Schaeder, Grete. *Hugo von Hofmannsthal und Goethe.* Hameln, 1947.

-----. "Hugo von Hofmannsthals Weg zur Tragödie," *Deutsche Vierteljahrsschrift,* 23 (1949), 306-50.

Scharf, Ursula. "Hofmannsthal's Libretti," *German Life and Letters,* 8 (1955), 130-36.

Schmid, Martin Erich. *Symbol und Funktion der Musik im Werk Hugo von Hofmannsthals.* Heidelberg, 1968.

Schröder, Rudolf Alexander. "In Memoriam Hugo von Hofmannsthal," *Die Neue Rundschau,* 40 (1929), 577-95.

-----. "Zeit und Gerechtigkeit: Gedanken zum Werk Hugo von Hofmannsthals zur 25. Wiederkehr seines Todestages am 15. Juli," *Merkur,* 8 (1954), 603-17.

Schrögendorfer, Konrad. *Hugo von Hofmannsthals Dramen des antiken Stoffkreises in theaterwissenschaftlicher Beurteilung.* Diss. Vienna, 1954.

Schuh, Willi., ed. *Hugo von Hofmannsthal-Richard Strauss: Der Rosenkavalier.* Frankfurt am Main, 1971.

-----. "Zu Hofmannsthals 'Ariadne'-Szenarium und -notizen." *Die Neue Rundschau,* 71 (1960), 84-90.

Schumann, Detlev W. "Gedanken zu Hofmannsthals Begriff der 'Konservativen Revolution'," *Publications of the Modern Language Association,* 54 (1939), 853-99.

Schwarz, Egon. *Hofmannsthal and Calderon.* The Hague, 1962.

-----. "Hofmannsthal and the Problem of Reality," *Wisconsin Studies in Contemporary Literature,* 8 (1967), 484-504.

Steiner, Herbert. "The Harvard Collection of Hugo von Hofmannsthal," *Harvard Library Bulletin,* 8 (1954), 54-64.

-----. "Über Hugo von Hofmannsthal," *Monatshefte,* 42 (1950), 321-24.

Stern, Ernest Julian. *My Life, My Stage.* London, 1951.

Stern, Ernst and Heinz Herald, eds. *Reinhardt und seine Bühne.* Berlin, 1920.

Stern, Martin. "Hofmannsthals erstes Lustspielfragment," *Die Neue Rundschau,* 70 (1959), 463-98.

Sulger-Gebing, Emil. *Hugo von Hofmannsthal: Eine literarische Studie.* Breslauer Beiträge zur Literaturgeschichte, 3. Leipzig, 1905.

Szondi, Peter. "Hofmannsthals 'Weißer Fächer,' " *Die Neue Rundschau,* 74 (1963), 81-87.

-----. *Satz und Gegensatz.* Frankfurt am Main, 1964.

Tarot, Rolf. *Hugo von Hofmannsthal.* Tübingen, 1970.

Thomas, P. W. "Appearance and Reality in Grillparzer and Hofmannsthal," *Germania,* 3 (1965), 17-19.

Thomése, Ika A. *Romantik und Neuromantik: Mit besonderer Berücksichtigung Hugo von Hofmannsthals.* The Hague, 1923, pp. 141-90.

Tober, Karl. *Der Begriff der Zeit im Werk Hugo von Hofmannsthals.* Germanistische Abhandlungen 3. Innsbruck, 1959.

Trappmann, Wilhelm. *Das Ich-Du Problem in seiner Existenzbedeutung im dramatischen Jugendwerk Hugo von Hofmannsthals.* Diss. Bonn, 1937.

von Trentini, Albert. "Gedenkrede auf Hofmannsthal," *Europäische Revue,* 6 (1930), 505-16.

Vanhelleputte, Michel. "Hofmannsthals Ringen um die Tragödie," *Revue des langues vivantes,* 24-25 (1958-1959), 231-68.

-----. "Le patriotisme autrichien de Hugo von Hofmannsthal et la première guerre mondiale," *Revue belge de philologie et d'histoire,* 35 (1957), 683-704.

-----. "Zur Sozialkritik im Werke Hugo von Hofmannsthals," *Revue des langues vivantes,* 22 (1956), 257-69.

Vietta, Egon. "Die Entstehung der 'Ariadne'," *Das Musikleben,* 7 (1954), 8-11.

Volke, Werner. *Hugo von Hofmannsthal in Selbstzeugnissen und Bilddokumenten.* Hamburg, 1967.

Wagener, Luise. *Hofmannsthal und das Barock.* Diss. Bonn, 1931.

Waldmann, Elisabeth. *Hugo von Hofmannsthals Ethos und Bildungswelt.* Heidelberg, 1939.

Warnke, Frank J. "The Poet as Librettist," *Opera News,* 20 (1956), 4-5, 26-29.

Wassermann, Jakob. *Hofmannsthal der Freund.* Berlin, 1930.

-----. "Hofmannsthals Texte für Musik," *Die Neue Rundschau,* 24 (1913), 263-66.

Weber, Horst. *Hugo von Hofmannsthal: Bibliographie des Schrifttums.*

Berlin, 1966.

Weber, Irmgard. *Monologische und dialogische Sprachhaltung im Werke Hugo von Hofmannsthals.* Diss. Freiburg, 1954.

Weischedel, Hanna. "Hofmannsthal-Forschung 1945-1958," *Deutsche Vierteljahrsschrift,* 33 (1959), 63-103.

Wellesz, Egon. "Die Einrichtung für Musik von Hofmannsthals 'Alkestis'," *Die Neue Rundschau,* 72 (1961), 28-35.

Wilkinson, Elizabeth M. "The Inexpressible and the Unspeakable: Some Romantic Attitudes to Art and Language," *German Life and Letters,* 16 (1963), 308-20.

Winder, Marianne. "The Psychological Significance of Hofmannsthal's 'Ariadne auf Naxos'," *German Life and Letters,* 15 (1961), 100-109.

Wittmann, Horst. "Hofmannsthals Lustspielsprache: Die Sprachkrise und ihre Überwindung in den Komödien *Der Schwierige, Der Rosenkavalier* und *Ariadne auf Naxos."* Diss. University of Massachusetts, 1969.

Wittmann, Lothar. *Sprachthematik und dramatische Form im Werke Hofmannsthals.* Stuttgart, 1966.

Wocke, Helmut. "Hofmannsthal und Molière," *Neuphilologische Zeitschrift,* 2 (1950), 127-37.

-----. "Hugo von Hofmannsthal und Italien," *Romanistisches Jahrbuch,* 4 (1951), 374-92.

Wunberg, Gotthart. *Der frühe Hofmannsthal: Schizophrenie als dichterische Struktur.* Stuttgart, 1956.

Wyss, Hugo. *Die Frau in der Dichtung Hofmannsthals.* Zürich, 1954.

Zimmermann, Helga. *Die Bühnentechnik Hugo von Hofmannsthals.* Diss. Innsbruck, 1955.

Richard Strauss

A Select Bibliography

von Asow, Erich H. Müller. *Richard Strauss Thematisches Verzeichnis.* 3 vols. Vienna, 1955-1974.

Bab, Julius. "Ariadne auf Naxos," *Die Schaubühne,* 9 (1913), 455-61.

-----. "Ariadne auf Naxos," *Die Gegenwart,* 42 (1915), 230-32.

Beck, Joachim. "Die neue 'Ariadne auf Naxos'," *Die Schaubühne,* 12 (1916), 436-38.

Bekker, Paul. *Kritische Zeitbilder.* Berlin, 1921.

Bie, Oskar. *Die moderne Musik und Richard Strauss. Die Kultur,* 11. Berlin, 1916.

Böhm, Karl. *Begegnung mit Richard Strauss.* Vienna, 1964.

Brandl, Willy. *Richard Strauss: Leben und Werk.* Wiesbaden, 1949.

Breuer, Robert. "The Strauss Legacy," *The American-German Review,* 22 (1955), 16-18, 32.

Cimbro, Attilio, "L'Arianna a Nasso," I *Pianoforte,* 6 (1926).

Del Mar, Norman. *Richard Strauss.* 3 vols. London, 1962-1972.

Eckstein-Ehrenegg, O. "Richard Strauss 'Ariadne auf Naxos' im Markgräflichen Opernhaus in Bayreuth," *Zeitschrift für Musik,* 107 (1940), 629-30.

Einstein, Alfred. "Strauss and Hofmannsthal," *Essays on Music.* New York, 1956; paperback, 1962.

Erhardt, Otto. *Richard Strauss: Leben, Wirken, Schaffen.* Freiburg im Breisgau, 1953.

Fähnrich, Hermann. "Das 'Mozart-Wagner-Element' im Schaffen von Richard Strauss," *Schweizerische Musikzeitung,* 99 (1959), 311-16.

-----. "Richard Strauss über das Verhältnis von Dichtung und Musik (Wort und Ton) in seinem Opernschaffen," *Die Musikforschung,* 14 (1961), 22-35.

Finck, Henry T. *Richard Strauss: The Man and His Works.* Boston, 1917.

Fred, Will [Wilhelm Schmidt Gentner]. "Ein neuer Weg der Bühnenkunst," *Westermanns Monatshefte,* 57 (1913), 727-38.

Garten, Hugh F. "The Strauss-Hofmannsthal Letters," *Opera,* 4 (1953), 274-77.

Gatscha, Otto. *Librettist und Komponist dargestellt an Opern Richard Strauss.* Diss. Vienna, 1947.

Grasberger, Franz, ed. *Der Strom der Töne trug mich fort: Die Welt um Richard Strauss in Briefen.* Tutzing, 1967.

----- and Franz Hadamowsky. *Richard Strauss-Ausstellung zum 100. Geburtstag.* Vienna, 1964.

Gregor, Josef. *Richard Strauss: Der Meister der Oper.* Munich, 1939.

Grunsky, K. "'Ariadne auf Naxos' von Richard Strauss," *Blätter für Haus- und Kirchenmusik,* 17 (1912), 44-45.

Gysi, Fritz. *Richard Strauss.* Potsdam, 1934.

Gruhn, Wilfried. *Die Instrumentation in den Orchesterwerken von Richard Strauss.* Diss. Mainz, 1968.

Hausswald, Günter. "Antiker Mythos bei Richard Strauss," *Musica,* 12 (1958), 323-26.

Hempel, Frieda. *Mein Leben dem Gesang: Erinnerungen.* Berlin, 1955.

Isler, Ernst. "Richard Strauss' 'Ariadne auf Naxos' im Zürcher Stadttheater," *Schweizerische Musikzeitung,* 52 (1912), 490-91, 505-07.

Istel, Edgar. "Ariadne auf Naxos," *Monthly Musical Record,* 42 (1912), 315.

-----. "German Opera since Richard Wagner," *Musical Quarterly,* 12 (1935), 73-78.

Jacobsohn, Fritz. "Ariadne auf Naxos: Die Dichtung, die Musik," *Die Schaubühne,* 9 (1913), 276-80.

Jefferson, Alan. *The Operas of Richard Strauss in Britain, 1910-1963.* London, 1963.

Joubert, M. "Hofmannsthal and his Collaboration with Strauss," *Contemporary Review,* 136 (1929), 632-37.

Kallenberg, Siegfried. *Richard Strauss: Leben und Werk.* Leipzig, 1926.

Kapp, Julius, ed. "Richard Strauss und die Berliner Oper," *Festschrift der Berliner Staatsoper zu des Meisters 70. Geburtstage.* Berlin, 1934.

Korngold, Julius. "Ariadne auf Naxos," *Neue Freie Presse* (5 October 1916), 1-4.

-----. *Deutsches Opernschaffen der Gegenwart.* Leipzig, 1921.

-----. "Der Bürger als Edelmann," *Neue Freie Presse* (3 October 1924), 2-4.

Kralik, Heinrich. *Richard Strauss: Weltbürger der Musik.* Vienna, 1963.

Krause, Ernst. *Richard Strauss: Gestalt und Werk.* Leipzig, 1956.

Kraussold, Max. *Geist und Stoff der Operndichtung.* Vienna, 1931.

Krüger, Karl-Joachim. *Hugo von Hofmannsthal und Richard Strauss.* Berlin, 1935.

Lehmann, Lotte. *Five Operas and Richard Strauss.* Trans. Ernst Pawel. New York, 1964.

Lusztig, J. C. "Ariadne auf Naxos," *Musikpädagogische Blätter,* 35 (1912), 465-66.

Mann, Alfred. "The Artistic Testament of Richard Strauss," *Musical*

Quarterly, 36 (1950), 1-8.

Mann, William. *Richard Strauss: A Critical Study of His Operas.* London, 1964.

Marek, George R. *Richard Strauss: The Life of a Non-Hero.* New York, 1967.

Marschalk, Max. "Ariadne auf Naxos," *Vossische Zeitung,* 547-548 (26 October 1912), 99 (24 February 1913), 104 (26 February 1913), 107 (28 February 1913).

-----. "Die neue Ariadne auf Naxos," *Vossische Zeitung,* 562 (2 November 1916).

Moser, Hans Joachim. *Richard Strauss: Leben und Werk.* Cracow, 1944.

Muschler, Reinhard C. *Richard Strauss.* Hildesheim, 1924.

Natan, Alex. *Richard Strauss Opern.* Basel, 1963.

Newman, Ernst. *Richard Strauss.* London, 1908.

von Pander, Oscar. *Clemens Krauss in München.* Munich, 1955.

Panofsky, Walter. *Richard Strauss: Partitur eines Lebens.* Munich, 1965.

Petzoldt, Richard. *Richard Strauss: Sein Leben in Bildern.* Leipzig, 1960.

Pfister, Kurt. *Richard Strauss: Weg, Gestalt, Denkmal.* Vienna, 1949.

Richard, August. "Ariadne auf Naxos," *Schweizerische Musikzeitung,* 52 (1912), 399-401.

Röttger, Heinz. *Das Formproblem bei Richard Strauss.* Berlin, 1937.

Rolland, Romain. *Musiciens d'aujourd'hui.* Paris, 1908.

Rosenthal, Harold. *Two Centuries of Opera at Covent Garden.* London, 1958.

Rostand, Claude. *Richard Strauss: l'ambiance, les origines, la vie, l'oeuvre, l'estétique et le style.* Paris, 1949.

Roth, Ernst, ed. *Richard Strauss' Bühnenwerke.* London, 1954.

Saminsky, Lazare. "The Downfall of Strauss," *Modern Music,* 1 (1924), 11-13.

Schäfer, Theo. *Also sprach Richard Strauss zu mir.* Dortmund, 1924.

Scherber, Ferdinand. "Die Wiedererweckung der 'Ariadne'," *Signale für die Musikalische Welt,* 74 (1916), 687-90.

Schmidt, Leopold. *Richard Strauss' 'Ariadne auf Naxos': Ein Führer durch das Werk.* Berlin, 1912.

-----. *Ariadne auf Naxos (Erlebnisse und Betrachtungen).* Berlin, 1921.

Schmitz, Eugen. "*Ariadne* von Richard Strauss," *Hochland,* 10 (1913), 727-32.

-----. "Die Neubearbeitung der Ariadne von Richard Strauss," *Hochland,* 15 (1918), 718-20.

-----. *Richard Strauss als Musikdramatiker.* Munich, 1907.

Schopenhauer, Ruth. *Die antiken Frauengestalten bei Richard Strauss.* Diss. Vienna, 1952.

Schrenk, Walter. *Richard Strauss und die neue Musik.* Berlin, 1924.

Schröter, Oscar. "Ariadne auf Naxos," *Die Musik,* 12 (1912), 226-29.
-----. "Ariadne auf Naxos, ein Momentbild," *Allgemeine Musikzeitung,* 39 (1912), 1045-47.
von Schuch, Friedrich. *Richard Strauss, Ernst von Schuch und die Dresdener Oper.* Leipzig, 1953.
Schuh, Willi. *Hugo von Hofmannsthal und Richard Strauss: Legende und Wirklichkeit.* Munich, 1964.
-----. *Ein Paar Erinnerungen an Richard Strauss.* Zürich, 1964.
-----, ed. *Richard Strauss Jahrbuch 1954.* Bonn, 1953.
-----, ed. *Richard Strauss Jahrbuch 1959-1960.* Bonn, 1960.
-----. *The Stageworks of Richard Strauss.* Zürich, 1954.
-----. "Richard Strauss," *Die Musik in Geschichte und Gegenwart,* 12 (1965), col. 1485-95.
-----. *Über Opern von Richard Strauss.* Zürich, 1947.
Schünemann, Georg. "Ariadne auf Naxos," *Westermanns Monatshefte,* 57 (1912), 638-40.
Schwers, Paul. "Ariadne in Berlin," *Allgemeine Musikzeitung,* 40 (1913), 316-17.
Seidl, Arthur. "Das 'Ariadne'-Problem," *Deutsche Musikbücherei,* 8: *Straussiana* (Regensburg, 1913), 192-227.
Smith, Patrick J. *The Tenth Music. A Historical Study of the Opera Libretto.* New York, 1970.
Sonne, O. "Das jüngste Bühnenwerk von Richard Strauss," *Leipziger Illustrierte Zeitung* (31 October 1912) 803-804.
Spanuth, August. "Ariadne auf Naxos: Uraufführung im Hoftheater in Stuttgart," *Signale für die musikalische Welt,* 70 (1912), 1437-42.
Specht, Richard. "Gespräch über 'Ariadne auf Naxos': Nach der Uraufführung," *Merkur,* 3 (1912), 793-99.
-----. *Richard Strauss und sein Werk.* Leipzig, 1921.
Starcke, Hermann. "Ariadne auf Naxos in der Dresdener Hofoper," *Allgemeine Musikzeitung,* 39 (1912), 1237-38.
Stefan, Paul. "'Ariadne auf Naxos' in Stuttgart," *Die Schaubühne,* 8 (1912), 446-50.
Steinitzer, Max. *Richard Strauss.* Berlin, 1911.
-----. *Richard Strauss in seiner Zeit.* Leipzig, 1914.
Strauss, Richard. *Betrachtungen und Erinnerungen,* ed. Willi Schuh (Zürich, 1949; 2nd ed. 1957); trans. L. J. Lawrence as *Recollections and Reflections,* London, 1953.
-----. *Briefe an die Eltern,* ed. Willi Schuh. Zürich, 1954.
-----. *Eine Welt in Briefen.* Tutzing, 1967.
----- and Joseph Gregor. *Briefwechsel,* ed. Roland Tenschert. Salzburg, 1955.
----- and Hugo von Hofmannsthal. *Briefwechsel,* ed. Willi Schuh. 3rd ed. Zürich, 1964.
----- and Hugo von Hofmannsthal. *The Correspondence between Richard Strauss and Hugo von Hofmannsthal,* ed. Franz and Alice

Strauss, trans. Hanns Hammelmann and Ewald Osers. London, 1961.

----- and Clemens Krauss. *Briefwechsel,* ed. O. K. Kende and Willi Schuh. Munich, 1963.

----- and Romain Rolland. "Correspondence," *Fragments du Journal Cahiers Romain Rolland* III, ed. G. Samazeuilh. Paris, 1951.

----- and Romain Rolland. *Correspondence, Diary, and Essays,* ed. Rollo Myers. Berkeley, 1968.

----- and Willi Schuh. *Briefwechsel.* Zürich, 1969.

----- and Franz Wüllner. *Richard Strauss und Franz Wüllner im Briefwechsel,* ed. D. Kämper. Beiträge zur Rheinischen Musikgeschichte, 51. Cologne, 1963.

----- and Stefan Zweig. *Briefwechsel,* ed. Willi Schuh. Frankfurt am Main, 1957.

Tenschert, Roland. *Dreimal sieben Variationen über das Thema Richard Strauss.* Vienna, 1944.

-----. "Die Kadenzbehandlung bei Richard Strauss," *Zeitschrift für Musikwissenschaft,* 8 (1925-1926), 161-82.

-----. "Versuch einer Typologie der Richard Strausschen Melodik," *Zeitschrift für Musikwissenschaft,* 16 (1934-1935), 274-93.

Trenner, Franz. *Richard Strauss: Dokumente seines Lebens und Schaffens.* Munich, 1954.

Ullrich, Hermann. *Fortschritt und Tradition: Zehn Jahre Musik in Wien 1945-1955.* Vienna, 1956.

Vuillermoz, Emile. "La 'Festwoche' Richard Strauss à Stuttgart," *Revue musicale (S.I.M.),* 8 (1912), 49-53.

Wachten, Edmund. "Der einheitliche Grundzug der Strausschen Formgestaltung," *Zeitschrift für Musikwissenschaft,* 16 (1934-1935), 257-74.

von Waltershausen, Hermann. *Richard Strauss, ein Versuch.* Munich, 1921.

Wellesz, Egon. *Essays on Opera.* London, 1959.

-----. "Hofmannsthal and Strauss," *Music and Letters,* 33 (1952), 239-42.

Zweig, Stefan. *The World of Yesterday.* New York, 1943.

UNIVERSITY OF NORTH CAROLINA
STUDIES IN THE GERMANIC LANGUAGES
AND LITERATURES

Initiated by RICHARD JENTE (1949-1952), established by F. E. COENEN (1952-1968)

Publication Committee

SIEGFRIED MEWS, EDITOR   JOHN G. KUNSTMANN   GEORGE S. LANE

HERBERT W. REICHERT   CHRISTOPH E. SCHWEITZER   SIDNEY R. SMITH

For other volumes in the "Studies" see following pages and p. ii

Send orders to: (U.S. and Canada)

The University of North Carolina Press, P.O. Box 2288
Chapel Hill, N.C. 27514

(All other countries) Feffer and Simons, Inc., 31 Union Square, New York, N.Y. 10003

UNIVERSITY OF NORTH CAROLINA
STUDIES IN THE GERMANIC LANGUAGES
AND LITERATURES

Initiated by RICHARD JENTE (1949-1952), *established by* F. E. COENEN (1952-1968)

Publication Committee

SIEGFRIED MEWS, EDITOR   JOHN G. KUNSTMANN   GEORGE S. LANE

HERBERT W. REICHERT   CHRISTOPH E. SCHWEITZER   SIDNEY R. SMITH

For other volumes in the "Studies" see preceding and following pages and p. ii

Order reprinted books from: AMS PRESS, Inc.,
56 East 13th Street, New York, N.Y. 10003

UNIVERSITY OF NORTH CAROLINA
STUDIES IN THE GERMANIC LANGUAGES
AND LITERATURES

Initiated by RICHARD JENTE (1949-1952), established by F. E. COENEN (1952-1968)

Publication Committee

SIEGFRIED MEWS, EDITOR   JOHN G. KUNSTMANN   GEORGE S. LANE

HERBERT W. REICHERT   CHRISTOPH E. SCHWEITZER   SIDNEY R. SMITH

For other volumes in the "Studies" see preceding pages and p. ii

Order reprinted books from: AMS PRESS, Inc.,
56 East 13th Street, New York, N.Y. 10003